THE TELEVISION GENRE BOOK

2nd Edition

Edited by
Glen Creeber

Associate Editors
Toby Miller and John Tulloch

A BFI book published by Palgrave Macmillan

FOR DANIEL AND ALEX

Second Edition published in 2008 by
PALGRAVE MACMILLAN

on behalf of the

BRITISH FILM INSTITUTE
21 Stephen Street, London W1T 1LN
www.bfi.org.uk

There's more to discover about film and television through the BFI. Our world-renowned archive, cinemas, festivals, films, publications and learning resources are here to inspire you.

Palgrave Macmillan in the UK is an imprint of Macmillan Publishers Limited, registered in England, company number 785998, of Houndmills, Basingstoke, Hampshire RG21 6XS.

Palgrave Macmillan in the US is a division of St Martin's Press LLC, 175 Fifth Avenue, New York, NY 10010.

Palgrave Macmillan is the global academic imprint of the above companies and has companies and representatives throughout the world.

Palgrave® and Macmillan® are registered trademarks in the United States, the United Kingdom, Europe and other countries.

Set by Cambrian Typesetters, Camberley, Surrey
Printed in Great Britain by Cromwell Press Ltd, Trowbridge, Wiltshire

This book is printed on paper suitable for recycling and made from fully managed and sustained forest sources. Logging, pulping and manufacturing processes are expected to conform to the environmental regulations of the country of origin.

British Library Cataloguing-in-Publication Data
A catalogue record for this book is available from the British Library

ISBN 978–1–84457–218–2 (pb)
ISBN 978–1–84457–217–5 (hb)

Contents

(Grey box case studies are indicated in brackets)

Preface (1st Edition)

Some years ago I began a television-based PhD at the University of East Anglia. Coming from a primarily literary background, I visited both the library and the university bookshop in the search of a general, accessible and up-to-date introduction to television studies. However, I was surprised to find few books that satisfied my needs. Although some important academic material had been published, I found few texts gave me the sort of clear and comprehensive outline to the subject (particularly its existing debates and criticism) that I needed or desired. When I began teaching television studies a few years later things had improved, but I found my students still complained that they lacked a solid and straightforward introduction to the subject or a clear summary of what had already been written on it. While things are clearly changing and students have a much better choice today than ever before, this book is really an attempt to write the sort of volume that I hoped to find in the bookshop or library when I first naively arrived at East Anglia.

As this suggests, *The Television Genre Book* is aimed as an introduction to the study of television, in particular to the study of genre. As part of a series of books (which will finally make up *The Television Book*) it is loosely based on Pam Cook's *The Cinema Book* (BFI). This new venture aims to reflect and celebrate a growing confidence and maturity in the field of television studies, taking the opportunity to now emulate the BFI's originally ambitious format and apply to it the small screen. Like its predecessor, the book brings together overviews of the leading areas in the subject of study by authorities in the field, placing emphasis on linking theoretical discussion to the concrete analysis of television programmes and specific critical debates (particularly through the apparatus of the 'grey boxes' that adorn the text throughout). Likewise there are recommendations for selected reading on a topic and an overall bibliography presented at the back.

As such, the book is aimed to be one of the first places of reference to which a student might turn when they begin researching a particular TV genre, debate or programme. While it has been impossible to cover every genre, every debate, every programme we might have desired (or in the detail we might have liked), the book clearly covers some of the most important, historical and recurrent areas of interest that occupy the study of television genre today. As Pam Cook put it to her 1985 introduction to *The Cinema Book*, 'This precept has informed the book's structure, which is intended to be open to many different kinds of reader.' Similarly, I hope the structure and the level of analysis that this book incorporates will provide both the newcomer and those more familiar with the subject an equal amount of interest and pleasure. Each separate contribution attempts not only to introduce the major debates of a particular genre (such as its institutional, textual and cultural context), but also provoke new areas of debate, dispute and discussion. Despite these aims, readers may be alerted to the relative absence of a longer historical context, of a broader and deeper discussion of theoretical models and methodologies, of a discussion of television as an industry and lastly as a medium facing a whole host of technological and cultural changes in a globalising and increasingly diversifying world. However, further volumes on Television History, Television Studies, Television Industries and Contemporary Issues will address these topics in more detail than we could ever provide here.

Needless to say, the generic sections we have chosen to concentrate on are always open to debate and interpretation. For example, chapters such as 'Popular Entertainment' are clearly less generic specific than say a section such as 'News' or 'Documentary' (although that is increasingly open to debate – see, for example, p. 114). However, we hope the reader will understand that genre (as many of the contributors are at pains to point out) does not always fit into neat and tidy categorisations for the discerning critic, student or viewer. 'Soap Opera', for instance, should clearly be part of the 'Drama' section, but to reflect both its institutional proliferation and historical significance in television studies, it seemed justified (and intensely practical) to grant it a section to itself. Similarly, the increasing hybridity of newer genres (such as the 'Docusoap' or 'Reality TV') means it is not always easy to decide what genres should go where and which ones should or should not be included in detail. Choices had to be made and I can only assure the reader they were taken purely on practical rather than any hierarchical considerations. A similarly practical consideration has meant that in the main the focus has been on Anglo-American genres and programmes. Honourable exceptions there are, including material on, for example, Brazilian Telenovelas (see p. 72), but television still travels much more unevenly over national boundaries than cinema, and it seemed, for our aims at least, important to retain a focus on the two dominant English-language traditions, though retaining an awareness that this is only ever part of a much larger picture. The simple aim of this book has been to help the study of television (and that means all television) continue to get the critical attention it has so long deserved.

Glen Creeber, July 2001

Preface (2nd Edition)

I was taken by surprise at the popularity of the first edition *The Television Genre Book* (2001). I thought it would only find a market in a small group of students, teachers and lecturers. Yet, it appeared to go beyond its original remit – its combination of genre sections and case studies seemed to provide an accessible and interesting way of teaching television as a whole. While it was never intended to cover the entire area of TV studies, it was satisfying to know that so many had found it useful for more than just simply issues of genre.

However, the book also received some criticism. Jason Mittell argued in *Genre and Television: From Cop Shows to Cartoons in American Culture* (2004) that rather than examining how genres work as part of the system of television production and consumption, it foregounded it primarily as a *textual* strategy. Critics such as Frances Bonner also criticised the book for its choice of television genres, arguing that it had left important areas of television programming (such as the lifestyle genre) out of its pages. Bonner's *Ordinary Television* (2003) reclaimed those texts and filled the spaces that larger accounts of TV genre had tended to marginalise. I also personally felt that the book could have covered the whole area of 'genre studies' a little more, perhaps examining its historical roots in more detail.

Added to this, the landscape of television had changed radically since the book was first published. It seems unbelievable now that the original edition did not have a section devoted to 'Reality TV', but in 2001 the genre was still yet to fully make its mark. *Big Brother* only arrived in the UK a year before the first edition was published and important books on the genre (such as Annette Hill's *Reality TV: Audiences and Popular Factual Television* (2005) and Anita Biressi and Heather Nunn's *Reality TV: Realism and Revelations* (2004)) were yet to be written. Meanwhile, genres like the sitcom were to develop and mutate in sometimes unpredictable and sensational ways. In the original section on comedy, for example, John Hartley could still confidently conclude that the sticom had enjoyed a 'stable semiotic history' (p. 65). However, such a statement was about to be radically transformed by a new form of 'mockumentary comedy' like *The Office* – what Matt Hills has termed 'comedy vérité'. I also thought that the presence and importance of animation on television had grown considerably over the intervening years and that its small acknowledgment by the book now seemed rather miserly.

The time seemed right, therefore, for a second edition. In doing so, I brought in academics like Jason Mittell, Frances Bonner, Annette Hill and Brett Mills to help with this new edition; hoping that they would fill the gaps and blind spots of the earlier book. Mittell addresses the wider implications of genre by going 'Beyond the Text' in section one, while I also add further background information to the area of 'genre theory' as a whole. Meanwhile, Bonner addresses the genre of 'Ordinary Television' while Mills tackles the generic mutations of the contemporary sitcom. Elsewhere, we now have new chapters devoted entirely to 'Reality TV' and 'Animation', reflecting not just the changes that have taken place in the television schedules themselves, but perhaps also the growing academic respectability of certain genres.

The book still does not touch upon on all the genres and programmes that I would have liked. However, I am confident that this is a substantial improvement and update from the first edition. I only hope that the changes that have been implemented have not made the book any less useful, accessible and interesting than it originally was.

Glen Creeber, March 2008

Acknowledgments (1st Edition)

My thanks must firstly go to Andrew Lockett and Ann Simmonds at the BFI for their enormous help and support during the making of this book. I would also like to thank all the contributors for their time, effort and understanding; particularly John Hartley and my associate editors John Tulloch and Toby Miller for their continued help and encouragement. Thanks also to Jamie Sexton for originally helping me to conceive the idea in the first place. On a personal note, I would also like to thank Catrin, John, Valmai, Elen and Rowen for making it such an enjoyable experience – iechyd da!

Acknowledgments (2nd Edition)

I would like to thank Rebecca Barden and Sophia Contento for their continued help at the BFI, and for helping to get this second edition off the ground. I should have thanked Brett Mills in the first edition for helping me reconceive much of the book's original structure and layout at a crucial time during its development. On a personal note, the last few years have not been an easy time for me so I would like to thank everybody who has supported me and got me back on my feet. In the words of Silvio Dante and Michael Corleone, 'Just when I thought I was out – THEY PULL ME BACK IN!'

Notes on Contributors

William Boddy is a professor in the Department of Communication Studies at Baruch College and in the Certificate Program in Film Studies at the Graduate Center, both of the City University of New York. He is the author of *New Media and Popular Imagination: Launching Radio, Television, and Digital Media in the United States* (Oxford University Press, 2004) and *Fifties Television: The Industry and Its Critics* (University of Illinois Press, 1990; paperback 1992). He is an associate editor of *Cinema Journal*, and a member of the editorial advisory boards of *Screen*, *The Velvet Light Trap* and *International Journal of Cultural Studies*.

Dr Frances Bonner is a reader in Television and Popular Culture in the English, Media Studies and Art History School at the University of Queensland. She writes on celebrity and on magazines, as well as on non-fiction television, and is the author of *Ordinary Television* (Sage, 2003). Her current research focus is on television presenters.

Dr Rod Brookes is a lecturer in the School of Journalism, Media and Cultural Studies at Cardiff University. He is author of *Representing Sport* (Arnold, 2002) and co-author (with J. Lewis, N. Mosdell and T. Threadgold) of *Shoot First and Ask Questions Later: Media Coverage of the 2003 Iraq War* (Peter Lang, 2003).

Stella Bruzzi is Professor in and Head of Department of Film and Television Studies at the University of Warwick. Her publications include *Undressing Cinema* (Routledge, 1997), *New Documentary* (Routledge, 2000), *Fashion Cultures* (Routledge, 2000), co-edited with Pamela Church Gibson, and *Bringing Up Daddy: Fatherhood and Masculinity in Postwar Hollywood* (BFI, 2005).

Dr Daniel Chandler is a lecturer in the department of Theatre, Film and Television Studies at Aberystwyth University. His primary specialism is in visual semiotics,

and his current research interests include the semiotics of advertising and gender. He has been a semiotics consultant for a number of advertising campaigns, including Jamie Oliver's Sainsbury commercials, and is the author of *Semiotics: The Basics* (Routledge, 2004).

Dr Lez Cooke is a research fellow in Television Drama in the Department of Contemporary Arts at Manchester Metropolitan University. His publications include *Troy Kennedy Martin* (Manchester University Press, 2007) and *British Television Drama: A History* (BFI, 2003).

John Corner is a professor in the School of Politics and Communication Studies at the University of Liverpool. His latest book is the edited collection *Media and the Restyling of Politics* (with Dick Pels) (Sage, 2003) and (with Peter Goddard and Kay Richardson) *Public Issue Television: World in Action 1963–98* (Manchester University Press, 2007). He is an editor of the journal *Media, Culture and Society*.

Dr Glen Creeber is a Senior Lecturer in Film and Television at Aberystwyth University. His publications include *Dennis Potter: Between Two Worlds, A Critical Reassessment* (Macmillan, 1998), *Serial Television: Big Drama on the Small Screen* (BFI, 2004), *The Singing Detective: BFI Television Classic* (BFI, 2007), and he has edited *50 Key Television Programmes* (Arnold, 2004), *Tele-Visions: An Introduction to Studying Television* (BFI, 2006) and (with Royston Martin) *Digital Culture: Understanding New Media* (Open University, 2008).

Dr K. J. Donnelly is a Reader in Film Studies in the Department of Film Studies at the University of Southampton. He is author of *Pop Music in British Cinema* (BFI, 2001), *The Spectre of Sound: Film and Television Music* (BFI, 2005), editor of *Film Music* (Edinburgh University Press, 2001) and *Music and the Moving Image: A Reader* (Edinburgh University Press, 2008).

Jon Dovey is a reader in Screen Theory at the University of Bristol. He is the editor of *Fractal Dreams: New Media in Social Context* (Lawrence & Wishart, 1996) and the author of *Freakshow: First Person Media and Factual Television* (Pluto Press, 2000).

Jane Feuer is Professor of English at the University of Pittsburgh. She is the author of *The Hollywood Musical* (University of Illinois Press, 1993), *Seeing Through the Eighties: Television and Reaganism* (BFI, 1995) and the co-author of *MTM: Quality Television* (BFI, 1984).

Dr Merris Griffiths is a lecturer in Film, Television and Media in the Department of Theatre, Film and Television Studies at Aberystwyth University. Her research interests include advertising, children and the media, media literacy, 'kid' culture, media representations of children and childhood, and gendered readerships of media texts.

Dr Jackie Harrison is a lecturer in the Department of Journalism at the University of Sheffield. She teaches and has published books and papers on television violence, European audiovisual policy, the culture of news production and the changing digital television environment. Her publications include *Terrestrial Television News in Britain: The Culture of Production* (Manchester University Press, 2000), *The Changing Face of Television* (Garnet Publishing, 2000) and *News* (Routledge Introductions to Media and Communications, 2005).

John Hartley is ARC Federation Fellow in the Faculty of Creative Industries, Queensland University of Technology, Australia. Previously he was Head of the School of Journalism, Media and Cultural Studies at the University of Wales, Cardiff. He is author of many books and articles on TV studies going back to the 1970s (*Reading Television*, with John Fiske (Routledge, 1978)), *Uses of Television* (Routledge, 1999), *The Indigenous Public Sphere: The Reporting and Reception of Aboriginal Issues in the Australian Media* (with Alan McKee, Oxford University Press, 2000) and *Communication, Cultural and Media Studies: The Key Concepts* (Routledge, 2002).

Annette Hill is Professor of Media, Communication and Media Research Institute, University of Westminster, UK. She is the author of *Reality TV* (Routledge 2004) and *Restyling Factual TV* (Routledge 2007). Her previous books include *Shocking Entertainment* (University of Luton Press, 1997), *TV Living* (with David Gauntlett) (Routledge, 1999), as well as a variety of articles on audiences and

popular culture. She is co-editor (with Robert C. Allen) of the *Television Studies Reader* (Routledge, 2003). Her next book, *Extreme Beliefs*, is about ghosts and media audiences.

Dr Matt Hills is a senior lecturer in the School of Journalism, Media and Cultural Studies at Cardiff University. His research interests focus on cult media and fan cultures, situated more generally in terms of cultural studies work on audiences. His books include *How To Do Things With Cultural Theory* (Hodder-Arnold, 2005), *The Pleasures of Horror* (Continuum, 2005) and *Fan Cultures* (Routledge, 2002).

Dr Luke Hockley is Professor of Media Analysis at the University of Bedfordshire. He is a founder executive member of the International Association for Jungian Studies (IAJS) and a Fellow of the Royal Society of Arts (FRSA). Luke has lectured in the USA, South East Asia and across Europe, including the C. G. Jung Institute in Zurich. His publications include *Cinematic Projections: The Analytical Psychology of C. G. Jung and Film Theory* (University of Luton Press, 2001) and 'Spectacle as Commodity: Special Effects in Feature Films', in Richard Wise and Jeanette Steemers (eds), *Multimedia: A Critical Introduction* (Routledge, 2000).

Dr Jason Jacobs is a reader in Cultural History at the School of English, Media Studies and Art History at the University of Queensland, Australia. He is author of *The Intimate Screen: Early British Television Drama* (Oxford University Press, 2000) and *Body Trauma TV: The New Hospital Dramas* (BFI, 2003). His research interests include television history, television aesthetics and issues of judgment and value in television studies.

Dr Catherine Johnson is Lecturer in Television History and Theory, Department of Media Arts, Royal Holloway, University of London. She has published on factual entertainment, US television drama and early British television. She is also author of *Telefantasy* (2005: BFI) and editor (with Rob Turnock) of *ITV Cultures: Independent Television over 50 Years* (Open University, 2005).

Justin Lewis is Professor of Communication and Cultural Industries at the University of Wales, Cardiff. He has written several books about media and culture. His particular interests are media influence, cultural policy and the ideological role of media in contemporary societies. His books include *Constructing Public Opinion: How Elites Do What They Like and Why We Seem to Go Along With It* (Columbia

University Press, 2001) and (with Toby Miller) *Critical Cultural Policy Studies: A Reader* (Wiley-Blackwell, 2002).

Anna McCarthy is Assistant Professor of Cinema Studies at the Tisch School of the Arts, New York University. She is the author of *Ambient Television: Visual Culture and Public Space* (Duke University Press, 2001). Her current research is on the history of advertising and corporate speech in American television.

Dr Máire Messenger-Davies is Professor of Media Studies, Director of the Centre for Media Research and project leader for the Policy strand of the Centre for Media Research at the University of Ulster. She is the author of *Television is Good for Your Kids* (Hilary Shipman, 1989) and *'Dear BBC': Children, Television Storytelling and the Public Sphere* (Cambridge University Press, 2001).

Toby Miller is Professor of Cultural Studies and Cultural Policy in the Center for Latin American and Caribbean Studies, the Program in American Studies and the Department of Cinema Studies at New York University. He is the editor of the journal *Television and New Media*, co-editor of the journal *Social Text* and is the author and editor of twenty-one books. In 2003 he became Distinguished Faculty Visitor at the Center for Ideas of Society, University of California, Riverside.

Dr Brett Mills is a lecturer in Film and Television Studies at the University of East Anglia. He is the author of *Television Sitcom* (BFI, 2005) and 'Comedy Vérité: Contemporary Sitcom Form', *Screen*, 2004.

Dr Jason Mittell is Associate Professor of American Studies and Film and Media Culture at Middlebury College, USA. His research interests include television history and criticism, media and cultural history, genre theory, narratology, animation and children's media, cultural historiography, race and gender studies, and new media studies and technological convergence. He is the author of *Genre and Television: From Cop Shows to Cartoons in American Culture* (Routledge, 2004), and is currently working on a textbook entitled *Television and American Culture* and a book on contemporary American television narrative.

Dr Rachel Moseley is a senior lecturer in the department of Film and Television Studies at the University of Warwick. She is the author of *Growing Up with Audrey Hepburn: Text, Audience, Resonance* (Manchester University Press,

2002) and *Fashioning Film Stars: Dress, Culture, Identity* (BFI, 2005).

Steve Neale is a Professor in the Department of English at the University of Exeter. He is author of *Genre* (BFI, 1980) and *Genre and Hollywood* (Routledge, 2000), co-author of *Popular Film and Television Comedy* (Routledge, 1990) and co-editor of *Contemporary Hollywood Cinema* (Routledge, 1998).

Robin Nelson is Professor and Head of Department of Contemporary Arts, Manchester Metropolitan University. He has broad research interests in the arts and media and his publications on TV drama include *Boys from the Blackstuff: The Making of a TV Drama* (Comedia, 1986), *Television Drama in Transition: Forms, Values and Cultural Change* (Macmillan, 1997) and *State of Play: Contemporary 'high-end' TV Drama* (Manchester University Press, 2007).

Dr Adrian Page is Academic Leader for the Humanities and Social Sciences modular scheme at London Metropolitan University, where he also teaches and researches in the culture industries. Prior to this he was Deputy Head of Media Arts at the University of Luton. He has researched and published on many aspects of culture and philosophy, including literary theory, new technologies, film and television drama.

Jane Shattuc is an associate professor at Emerson College in Boston. Her publications include *Television, Tabloids, Tears: Fassbinder and Popular Culture* (University of Minnesota Press, 1995), *The Talking Cure: Women and TV Talk Shows* (Routledge, 1997) and (as editor) *Hop on Pop: The Politics and Pleasures of Popular Cultures* (Duke University Press, 2003).

Thomas Tufte is a professor in the Department of Communications Studies at Roskilde Universitetscenter, Denmark. He is co-editor of the *Danish Journal of Communication* and has published work on telenovelas in Latin American, American and European journals and anthologies. Main research projects have dealt with: 'Telenovelas, culture and development in Latin America' (1989–94); 'Media uses, new technology and cultural identity in Brazil' (1996–9); 'Media uses, everyday life and identity formation amongst young ethnic minorities in Copenhagen' (1999–2001) and 'HIV/AIDS Communication in South Africa – a Critique of the Dominant Paradigm' (2001–5).

John Tulloch is a professor in the School of Social Sciences and Law at Brunel University, West London. His publications have ranged from film and television studies and theatre through literary theory to history and sociology. His books include *Watching Television Audiences: Cultural Theories and Methods* (Arnold, 2000), *Performing Culture: Stories of Expertise and the Everyday* (Sage, 1999), (with Deborah Lupton) *Television, AIDS and Risk* (Allen and Unwin, 1997) and *One Day in July: Experiencing 7/7* (Little Brown, 2006).

Graeme Turner is an ARC Federation Fellow, Professor of Cultural Studies and Director of the Centre for Critical and Cultural Studies at the University of Queensland, Brisbane, Australia. He has published widely on media and cultural studies topics. His books include (with Stuart Cunningham) *The Australian TV Book* (Allen and Unwin, 2000), (with Frances Bonner and David Marshall) *Fame Games: The Production of Celebrity in Australia* (Cambridge University Press, 2000), *Ending the Affair: The Decline of Television Current Affairs in Australia* (UNSW Press, 2005) and (with Stuart Cunningham) the second edition of *The Media and Communications in Australia* (Allen and Unwin, 2006).

Paul Wells is Professor of Animation at the Loughborough University School of Art and Design. He has published widely in the field, including *Understanding Animation* (Routledge, 1998), *Animation and America* (Rutgers University Press, 2000) and *Animation: Genre and Authorship* (Wallflower Press, 2002). He has also made a Channel 4 documentary called *Cartoons Kick Ass* and three BBC programmes on British animation, as well as an educational video on *Special Effects* for the British Film Institute. Further, he has curated a touring exhibition on animation, which first appeared at the Children's Cultural Centre in Dublin, and has selected programmes of animated films for various festivals across the world.

INTRODUCTION: WHAT IS GENRE?

Genre Theory

Put crudely, genre simply allows us to organise a good deal of material into smaller categories. For example, a process of generic categorisation is used in biology to distinguish between different types of living organisms – mammals, birds, fish and so on. This is most commonly referred to as 'taxonomy', although this term is now often applied to almost anything – animate objects, inanimate objects, places, concepts, events, properties and relationships. Most supermarkets are organised along this type of 'taxonomic scheme', that is, there is usually a section for 'Fruit and Vegetables', 'Frozen Foods', 'Dairy Products', 'Toiletries' and so on. These sections are simply designed in order to make it easier for shoppers to find the particular products they want from the array of goods on offer.

Genre works in a similar way, intended to help us easily identify the artistic 'product' we want. For example, most record shops are laid out in terms of particular musical genres: these might include 'Heavy Metal', 'Rock', 'Hip Hop', 'Jungle', 'Pop', 'Country and Western' and so on. Meanwhile, films in a video shop may be arranged in categories such as 'Romantic Comedy', 'Horror', 'Musical', 'Science Fiction' and so on. In terms of television, generic categories might help us find our way around an increasing number of channels. For example, if we are in the mood to laugh we might switch to the Comedy Channel. If we want to know what's going on in the world we might choose CNN or if we want to listen to music we might switch over to MTV. However, if you're not sure what you want to watch you might tune into a mixed genre channel like the BBC in Britain and ABC in the States, where a number of different genres fill the schedules. This, then, is essentially how genre works – it enables us to make sense of a large number of choices by separating them into smaller and easily recognisable generic categories.

However, it would wrong to suggest that the use of genre is always this simple. Not all categories are easily identifiable, genres do not always remain the same and some artistic texts are a mixture (or hybrid) of a number of different genres. These difficulties in the study of genre will be discussed below, but in order to understand how 'genre theory' or 'genre studies' grew into the discipline it is today, we need to first outline and account for its historical origins and development. This is because genre theory is not a set of fixed or intractable laws, but a system of organising the world that is always open to debate, discussion and critical interpretation.

THE ORIGINS OF GENRE

It was the ancient Greeks who first began defining different artistic categories and genres, believing that certain poetic meters or rhythms were only suited to certain types of writing or storytelling. The Greek philosopher Aristotle was one of the earliest writers to attempt to outline these different stylistic characteristics, defining such forms as 'comedy', 'tragedy', the 'epic' and the 'ballad'. He argued in *Poetics* (335BC) that the function of tragedy was to purge the audience of their everyday emotions and frustrations through a process of 'catharsis'. In terms of dramatology, 'catharsis' refers to a sudden emotional climax which results in an audience's restoration, renewal and revitalisation for living. In Shakespearean tragedy, for example, narrative disruption is caused from flaws in the hero's personality such as Hamlet's indecision or Othello's jealously. Although the hero is eventually punished (usually resulting in death), he is not evil – so the tragedy comes from the gradual demise of a good man. Genre, then, is not simply important as a way of classifying different modes of artistic expression, but explaining how these different modes of expression can actually create meaning for an audience.

The Romans carried on this tradition of genre study, adding a heightened level of complexity to the original theories set out by the Greeks. However, it was not until the publication of Northrop Frye's *Anatomy of Criticism: Four Essays* (1957) that Aristotle's original ideas concerning genre were developed for a modern audience. Frye reconceived literary criticism as a total history rather than a linear progression through time – attempting to identify and classify the universal *archetypes* of literature as a whole. As a result, in Frye's model of literature it is impossible to produce a form of work that is original or 'new', in the sense that all literature follows certain laws and conventions that are inherently generic. Consequently, much of his work was attacked by critics who saw his approach to genre as a dangerous tendency to de-historicise both literature and criticism. Nevertheless, Frye's literary insights were important in their attempt to modernise the study of genre and to further differentiate among different types of literature.

The instability of generic categorisation was increasingly acknowledged and criticised by critics after Northrop Frye, particularly those who challenged the conventions of traditional artistic criticism. For example, in 'The Law of Genre' (1990) the post-structuralist Jacques Derrida denied the assumption of generic 'essence' or a fixed identity for any given genre, arguing that generic categories were essentially subjective formations. Far from conforming neatly to taxonomic labels, he argued that most texts exhibit characteristics of more than one kind of genre and sometimes of multiple kinds or indeterminacy. However, the very notion of genre tends to set down 'laws' and 'rules' that restrict this type of textual fluidity. As soon as the word 'genre' is sounded, Derrida argued, 'a limit is drawn. And when a limit is established, norms and interdictions are not far behind: "Do", "Do not"' (Derrida, 1990, p. 224).

For some theorists this type of criticism undermined the very notion of genre as they knew it, feeling that it was a theoretical approach which had little left to say to a world in which genre categorisation had become increasingly impossible to determine. However, in an attempt to rehabilitate the study of genre some critics started to reinvent and reexamine both the practice and purpose of genre in the light of such criticism. For example, Ralph Cohen published a paper in 1986 directly in response to Derrida's thoughts, titled 'History and Genre'. In this article Cohen argued that although genre categorisation was often ambiguous it still had an important and crucial part to play in modern critical analysis. Cohen (1986, p. 204) argued that:

> genre concepts in theory and in practice arise, change, and decline for historical reasons. And since each genre is composed of texts that accrue, the grouping is a process, not a determinate category. Genres are open categories. Each member alters the genre by adding, contradicting, or changing constituents, especially those of members most closely related to it. The process by which genres are established always involves the human need for distinction and interrelation. Since the purposes of critics who establish genres vary, it is self-evident that the same texts can belong to different groupings of genres and serve different generic purposes.

CONTEMPORARY GENRE STUDY

Discussions of this sort have led many genre critics to create a more complex way of defining and applying genre today. As genre studies gradually moved into film, television and media studies, so critics attempted to find methodological rules and procedures that better reflected and accounted for their own particular medium. Jane Feuer, for example, argued that the study of television genre should take place on a number of different critical levels (1992, p. 145):

> The Aesthetic Approach 'includes all attempts to define genre in terms of a system of conventions that permits artistic expression, especially involving individual authorship. The aesthetic approach also includes attempts to assess whether an individual work fulfills or transcends its genre.'

> The Ritual Approach 'sees genre as an exchange between industry and audience, an exchange through which culture speaks for itself'. This involves conceiving 'television as a "cultural form" that involves the negotiation of shared beliefs and values and helps to maintain and rejuvenate the social order as well as assisting it in adapting to change'.

> The Ideological Approach 'views genre as an instrument of control. At the industrial level, genres assure the advertisers of an audience for their messages. At the textual level, genres are ideological insofar as they serve to reproduce the dominant ideology of the capitalist system. The genre positions the interpretive community in such a way as to naturalize the dominant ideologies expressed in the text.'

This attempt to offer a more complex form of genre interpretation has recently been continued by critics like Jason Mittell (2004), whose work on television aims to take the study of genre beyond the limits of the text. For Mittell, genre analysis is still useful and can be used to examine a number of 'extra-textual' areas such as industry, audiences and history (see below). Common to accounts such as these is the notion that genre is more than simply a form of classification, that it is what Steve Neale refers to as a 'multi-dimensional phenomenon'. By this, Neale means that it 'encompasses systems of expectations, categories, labels and names, discourses, texts and groups or corpuses of texts, and the conventions that govern them all' (2000, p. 2).

It is not essential to understand all these historical debates and critical traditions in detail in order to use and employ genre study. However, it is always important to keep in mind that genre theory is not an exact science; that it is always a changing and developing field of study with its own historical debates, traditions and schools of thought. As such, it is wise to keep abreast of current genre theories and to always keep in mind that, however clear and precise your own application of genre might be, it is always open to criticism and reassessment. Genre studies is not a precise taxonomy, it is simply a theoretical tool which will hopefully help you to unravel the structure, meaning and context of a particular category. However, like any other methodological tool it should be used carefully, self-critically and self-consciously if its insights are to remain relevant for future interpretations.

Glen Creeber

Studying Genre

'Genre' is a French word meaning 'type' or 'kind'. As such, it has played an important role in the study of literature, theatre, film, television and other art and media forms. It has long been recognised that output in each of these fields can be grouped into categories, and that each category or class is marked by a particular set of conventions, features and norms. However, among those who have studied genre in these and other fields, debates and disagreements of various kinds have arisen. Some are particular to individual fields (those concerning television will be discussed in more detail in the section on 'Genre and Television' below), but others are more general in nature or import. They concern the scope of genre as a concept and as a phenomenon, and they concern the role and the purpose of genre study.

Most theorists of genre now argue that generic norms and conventions are recognised and shared not only by theorists themselves, but also by audiences, readers and viewers. The classification of texts is not just the province of academic specialists, it is a fundamental aspect of the way texts of all kinds are understood. Thus if a character walking down the street on screen suddenly bursts into song, audiences accustomed to the genre are likely to classify the film they are watching as a musical, to understand that this is the kind of thing that happens in this kind of film, and to anticipate that other instances of singing – perhaps accompanied by dancing – are likely to occur during the rest of the film. In many cases, of course, it is likely that audiences will have some idea in advance of the kind of film (or play or programme) they are going to watch. They will have made an active choice either to watch or, if their preferences dictate, to avoid it. They will have done so on the basis of information supplied by advertising, by reviews and previews, perhaps by a title (such as *Singin' in the Rain*) or by the presence of particular performers. They are therefore likely to bring with them a set of expectations, and to anticipate that these expectations will be met in one way or another.

Many theorists have recognised these aspects of genre, and have devised a number of terms to mark them. Drawing on the work of Todorov (1977, pp. 42–52, 80–8; 1981, pp. 118–19), Neale has written about forms of 'generic verisimilitude', the ways in which otherwise unlikely occurrences can properly and predictably occur in genres such as the musical (1980, pp. 36–41; 1990, pp. 46–8; 2000, pp. 31–9). Jauss (1982) has talked about the extent to which genres entail 'horizons of expectation'. Altman (1996, p. 280) has written about the 'generic audience' as a means of identifying those sectors of any population 'sufficiently familiar with the genre to participate in a fully genre-based viewing', as well as about 'generic frustration' as 'the emotion generated by ... a failure to respect generic norms' – often the product of what he calls 'generic tension'. Roberts (1990, pp. 71–86) has stressed the extent to which audiences and readerships possess different degrees of generic knowledge and exhibit different degrees of generic preference, varying from 'exclusivists' and 'fans' to 'allergics', and Frith (1996, pp. 47–95) has discussed the role of groups of this kind within the field of popular music. Drawing on the work of Lukow and Ricci (1984), Neale (1990, pp. 48–52; 2000, pp. 39–43) has stressed the ways in which the 'inter-textual relay' – the systems and forms of publicity, marketing and reviewing that each media institution possesses – plays a key role not only in generating expectations, but also in providing labels and names for its genres and thus a basis for grouping films, television programmes, or other works and texts together.

This last point is a point of disagreement. Altman (1984; 1987, pp. 5–15) has argued that institutions and their terms only provide a starting point for constructing generic 'corpuses' or groupings. For him, it is the job of the 'genre critic' to study such corpuses, to identify and to define their principal features, and to use these definitions as a means of deciding which works properly belong to each corpus and which do not. Only once this is done is it possible to construct the histories of genres and to theorise about the social and cultural roles these genres perform. For Altman (1996, pp. 283–5), genre history then becomes a matter of locating the 'semantic' and 'syntactic' components of a genre (broadly speaking, those items of setting, character and action that repeatedly mark them and the structures into which they are organised) and tracing the patterns of change and interaction among and between them. He divides sociocultural theories, meanwhile, into two basic kinds: 'ritual theories', which stress the extent to which the popularity of genres is an index of audience allegiance to the values they encode; and 'ideological theories', which stress the extent to which these values are imposed by the industries that produce them in the first place (1987, p. 94; 1996, p. 285. For examples of the former, see Cawelti, 1971, 1976; Schatz, 1981; Wright, 1975. For examples of the latter, see Hess Wright, 1986; Neale, 1980, 1990 pp. 58–65, 2000 pp. 214–29). These approaches are, however, too schematic. Altman argues that ritual and ideological theories alike tend to underplay the heterogeneity of audiences and their responses to genres themselves. Echoing Kapsis (1991), he argues that theory and history should take much more account of local institutional and sociocultural conditions.

These disagreements hinge on the role of the critic and theorist and on the ways in which genre itself is defined. As Feuer (1992, p. 139) has pointed out, often theorists have sought to define what she calls 'ideal types' – to specify what a genre should be rather than what it is – and have often tended to use these types as an evaluative tool (the same might be said, incidentally, of fans – see Jancovich, 2001). For several centuries, it was the role of academies and other cultural institutions precisely to specify the generic norms and ideal types to which artists and writers were meant to adhere or aspire. Feuer also points out that what counts as a genre can vary in kind from one aesthetic field to another: 'literary categories are very broad ones. Such literary types as drama and lyric, tragedy, and comedy span numerous diverse works and numerous cultures and centuries. Film and television, however, are culturally specific and temporally limited.' In some cases, literary theorists have augmented these differences by constructing 'theoretical genres', categories modelled on the possible properties of literary modes (p. 140. For an example, see Todorov, 1975).

These differences have been noted by Ryall (1975/6, p. 27), by Williams (1984, p. 121) and by others. They reflect some of the historical and institutional differences between the fields in question. However, they also reflect a tendency to conceive of genres and fields as single, self-contained entities, and a corresponding tendency to limit the scope of the concept of genre itself. In so far as they do that, they reflect the history of the concept and of the uses to which it has often been put.

In English-speaking countries, the term 'genre' came to be applied to literary works during the nineteenth century, at a point in history at which art of all kinds began to be industrialised, mass-produced for a popular public (Cohen, 1986, p. 120). Genres came to be identified with

impersonal, formulaic, commercial forms and distinguished from individualised art. Ironically, this represented a reversal of previous characterisations, which saw 'high art' as rule-bound and ordered (as evident in genres like the sonnet and tragedy) and 'low art' as unconstrained by the rules of decorum (Threadgold, 1989, pp. 121–2). Nevertheless, this characterisation, and the distinction that underlies it, has continued to prevail, not only among those who sought to attack mass culture, but also among those who sought to defend it. It has given rise, for example, to the concept of the 'genre film', 'genre fiction' and the 'genre text', entities that differ from non-genre texts in so far as they are commercially formulaic, marked by norms and conventions, and presumed to cater to consumer demand and audience expectation (Neale, 2000, pp. 25–8).

Thus segregated, the genres recognised within each area of cultural production have been subject to further segregation, not only from one another but from other areas too. The degree of hybridity and overlap among and between genres and areas has all too often been underplayed. ('Comedy drama' in all its varieties has rarely if ever been discussed in studies of film, theatre, radio and television. 'News' is a genre that clearly plays a part in newspapers and magazines, in radio and television, and, though far less frequently now than it once did, in the cinema too.) Underplayed, too, has been the degree to which texts of all kinds necessarily 'participate' in genre (Derrida, 1990), and the extent to which they are likely to participate in more than one genre at once.

These last points emerge from the study of 'speech-acts' and other forms of communication in linguistics and philosophy (Blakemore, 1992; Davis, 1991; Pratt, 1977, 1981). The position here is that all instances of communication are framed in the light of particular norms and encounter, in context, a specific array of expectations, cued in various ways by various means. There is thus a generic aspect to all instances and forms of communication. Even instances designed to flaunt norms and expectations find themselves placed alongside others that do so as well (Freadman, 1988). In addition, more than one set of norms can be involved. Neale, for example, argues that 'both *Star Wars* (Lucas, 1977) and *Body Heat* (Kasdan, 1981) participate in the genre "film", "fiction film", "Hollywood film" and "narrative feature film". The former also participates in the genre "science-fiction", and the latter in the genre "thriller"' (2000, p. 25; see also Altman, 1987, p. 123).

As a result, the category 'genre' expands beyond the confines established in traditional areas of study both within and across particular fields of cultural production. Quite apart from generic hybrids, instances in which genres occur in or cross over from one medium or art form to another (comedy, melodrama, science fiction, documentary and news, for example), it should be recognised that categories such as 'narrative' and 'fiction' – even 'film' and 'television' – are generic in nature, that there is a generic aspect to all instances of cultural production, and that these instances are usually multiple, not single, in kind.

These points serve to underline the multidimensional nature of genre itself: its numerous aspects, the numerous meanings it can have, and the numerous analytical uses to which it can be put. Genre can mean 'category' or 'class', generic can mean 'constructed or marked for commercial consumption'; genre can mean a 'corpus' or 'grouping', generic can mean 'conventionally comprehensible'; genre can mean 'formulaic', generic can mean 'those aspects of communication that entail expectation'; and so on. When thinking about genre and television, it is useful to bear all these dimensions in mind.

Steve Neale

Genre and Television

The study of genre and television has been conditioned not just by the formats and forms of television itself but also by the history of genre as a concept, the uses to which it has been put, and the other art and media forms to which it has been applied. The definitions and issues that have arisen as a consequence have also been heavily influenced by the fact that television has adopted and adapted formats and forms from a number of different sources since its inception. Radio, film, written fiction, theatre, journalism, music and other art and media forms have all played an important part in television and its history. The ways in which genre has figured in these forms, and in the theories and debates that have surrounded them, has had an important effect on theories and debates about genre and television itself. Several examples will be noted in the sections on individual genres in this book. The focus here will be on general theories and conceptions, and the ways in which they relate to some of the issues raised in this chapter.

A key issue here is that of definition. What counts as a genre? What counts as a genre in television? Lacey (2000, p. 133) argues that the 'repertoire of elements' that serve to identify genres consists of character types, setting, iconography, narrative and style. This definition derives from, and seeks to encompass, popular fiction and films as well as television. It is thus well suited to the study of Westerns, cop, detective and crime forms, melodrama, adventure and

science fiction, all of which can be found, though in some cases only intermittently or cyclically, in all three spheres of cultural production. However, in particular when it comes to more medium-specific genres with a less clear-cut narrative or fictional base, ambiguities can arise. Lacey looks at game shows (p. 206), and argues that they can be defined in terms of the repertoire mentioned above: there is a standard setting (the television studio), a standard set of characters (the studio audience, 'ordinary people', an 'avuncular host'), a narrative ('the questions or tasks [that] must be overcome to win the prizes'), an iconography ('a high-tech, glitzy set') and a style ('basic "live" television'). However, both narrative and style here are either weakly defined or weakly specific. Is the overcoming of tasks a sufficient definition of narrative? Is 'basic "live" television' sufficiently marked as a style to constitute a particular generic ingredient? (See 'The Quiz Show' below.)

There are several even more ambiguous cases than this. Style is a strongly marked feature of advertisements and music videos, both of them staple ingredients of modern television. Yet styles vary from advert to advert, video to video. In addition, some adverts and videos are narrative in form and others are not, and most adverts and videos are presented in segments, blocks and programme contexts that lack any kind of narrative dimension. Like news programmes, variety shows, talk shows and most forms of religious programming, these contexts (popular music shows, teen magazine programmes, advertising segments and so on) possess a structure, a time frame and a set of basic ingredients. Some or all of them may involve the presentation of mini-narratives, but they are not themselves narrative in form (see 'Music on Television' and 'Advertising').

Does that mean, then, that they should not be considered as genres? For Lacey, for Selby and Cowdery (1995) and for Feuer (who refers only to soap operas, crime shows and sitcoms in her 1992 essay) the answer might well be 'yes'. These writers are heavily influenced by film and literary theory, and therefore tend to focus on genres that have their parallels or origins in the cinema, on stage or in popular fiction. They thus tend to stress the importance of narrative forms and conventions. For others, however, the answer is 'no'. News programmes, talk shows, religious programmes and variety shows are all treated as genres in Rose (1985a). Although he acknowledges the lure and importance of narrative, Butler (1994b) not only stresses the existence of 'non-narrative genres', but also discusses news programmes, sports programmes, 'non-narrative commercials', music television and, indeed, game shows as specific examples. Like Lacey and Selby and Cowdery, Butler tends to distinguish between genres and other categories ('modes', 'formats', 'forms' and the like), and thus to underplay the extent to which multiple generic participation is as much a feature of television as it is of other media. (Just as *Friends* (NBC, 1994–2004) could be said to participate in the genres 'television programme', 'television series', 'fictional narrative', 'comedy', 'situation comedy' and so on, so most breakfast shows could be said to participate in the genres 'television programme', 'television magazine programme', 'actuality' and, depending on the nature of the programme, 'news' and/or 'topical variety' and perhaps even 'daytime' or 'morning' TV.) However, his position is otherwise consonant with some of the broader conceptions of genre outlined in this chapter.

The same is true of those who recognise or stress hybridity and overlap. Hoffer, Musburger and Nelson (1985), for instance, underline the hybrid nature of docudrama, Norden (1985, p. 34) the extent to which 'the detective genre overlaps considerably with … cop shows, spy shows, lawyer shows, and even newspaper shows' and Edgerton (1985) the extent to which, as well as proliferating its own generic categories and types (telefeatures, docudramas and mini-series; biopics, family sagas, social problem dramas and so on), the telefilm can be seen as combining elements of the Hollywood feature film, anthology drama and television drama in general (see also Rose, 1985b). In addition, and as a separate point, several commentators have noted the influence of soap opera and/or sitcom not only on medical dramas, cop shows and Westerns, but on game shows and talk shows as well (Alley, 1985, p. 82; Robards, 1985, pp. 20, 22; Barson, 1985, pp. 64–5; Goedkoop, 1985, pp. 8–9; Rose, 1985c, pp. 80–1). The recent advent of the 'docusoap' clearly confirms the pertinence of points such as these (see 'Docusoaps').

Meanwhile, the institutional aspects of genre and television – the relationship between genres and scheduling regimes, modes of production, the varying demands of advertisers and audiences, and developments in adjacent institutions of entertainment and in the media field as a whole – have been noted by most of those who have written on individual genres or on television and genre in general. The role of television's intertextual relay in the categorisation of programmes and in the generation of expectations has been discussed by Tolson (1996, pp. 97–105), who underlines the historicity of categories, genres and time slots. He also underlines the extent to which, for the *Radio Times* and the BBC at least, they have served as a means by which to cultivate a 'socially responsible, family-oriented, discriminating' viewership. As

such he raises issues to do with the sociocultural roles performed both by television genres and by television institutions in general.

These issues are complex. They have been rendered even more complex by changes in the distribution and consumption of television programmes during the course of the last two decades. As Feuer points out (1992, p. 157), the advent of remote control and multichannel cable and satellite TV has helped generate a tendency to 'zap' from one channel to another. Along with the advent of videorecording, these developments have served to fragment and to customise the consumption of programmes and genres alike, making it difficult (especially at a time when 'classic' television is increasingly being recycled) to align ritual or ideological readings of programmes and genres with contemporary audiences and viewing populations. At the same time, the proliferation of generic channels like Comedy Central, the Sci-Fi Channel, MTV, CNN News and TCM alongside viewing practices such as zapping – which, as Feuer points out (1992, p. 158), entails the rapid deployment of genre-recognition skills – suggests that genre, in each of its facets and dimensions, remains central to television, its organisations, and its viewers and consumers.

Steve Neale

The Uses and Limitations of Genre

As it has been used within film and literary studies, genre is a means of constructing groups of texts and then discriminating between them. As Steve Neale points out in the first section of this book, for a critic such as Rick Altman this is a preliminary to the construction of a history of the genre concerned, itself a preliminary to understanding its social function (Altman, 1999). For others, particularly in literary study, it is an end in itself: the construction of a defensible definition of the genre (see Todorov, 1975).

Literary genres are routinely traced back to classical models (see Frye, 1957), so that it is deemed possible to determine if a contemporary play is properly a 'tragedy', for instance, by referring back to Aristotle's definition. In such a disciplinary context, generic structures are timeless and universal, carrying with them a cachet of authenticity and purity that is not easily replicated in the study of television. As popular cultural forms, television and film genres are much more historically, culturally and temporally contingent (see Feuer, 1992). Products, for the most part, of the commercial media, many television genres are also subject to market pressures that influence the shape of their texts.

Given such differences, how is the concept of genre used in relation to television? We can approach this question through thinking about the uses of genre for audiences, for academic researchers and critics, and for the television industry.

As is the case with film, genre operates as an important means of communicating information about the television text to prospective audiences. Through its inscription in publicity, in the listings in the TV guide, in the repertoires of cultural knowledge around individual personalities and other intertextual experiences, genre helps to frame audience expectations. For the television viewer, genre plays a major role in how television texts are classified, selected and understood.

For those who study television, genre is a means of managing TV's notorious extensiveness as a cultural form by breaking it up into more discrete or comprehensible segments. The diversity and variety of television programming, as well as television's modes of consumption, makes it very difficult to describe what 'television' is. From the beginning, television studies have approached the medium through the analysis of specific generic forms (see Newcomb, 1974): discussing news or soap opera rather than the whole of television. Researchers have found that to understand the characteristics, conventions and pleasures of a particular television genre is also to understand a great deal about television as a cultural form.

For those producing television, genre participates in the definition of a project by mapping its relation to other, similar, texts. Once we move from production to programming and transmission, genre becomes an even more important descriptor of the project. On pay or cable TV, whole channels are named after the genre to which their programming belongs. The development of pay TV, in fact, has been structured around niche-marketing to audience genre preferences for sports, music video, lifestyle programming, documentary and so on.

The component that is often left out of the conventional media industry/text/audience triangle is the programmer or scheduler: the person who places the programme within the channel or network schedule. There has been very little academic attention paid to the work of the programmer, but it would seem logical to assume that their practices – and thus TV schedules – are influenced by their understanding of genre. One would imagine that an understanding of the pattern of differences and similarities that help define the individual programme must be built into the strategic structuring of a schedule that will match the competition and maximise audience capture. These are the strategies, for instance, that have networks programming *Friends* against *Seinfeld* (NBC, 1989–98) or *ER* (NBC, 1994–) against *Chicago Hope* (CBS, 1994–2000) or deciding to produce the tabloid news programme like *A Current Affair* (Fox, 1986–96) rather than the more serious *Lateline* (ABC, 1990–). However, it has to be said that there is not much evidence that the term 'genre' or any equivalent abstraction is actually used in this industrial process. In one of the most successful handbooks on programming currently in use in the USA (Vane and Gross, 1994), the word 'genre' does not appear at all and the commercial practices described are conceptualised almost entirely on a case-by-case basis. This suggests that, at the industry level at least, there may be practical limitations to the usefulness of the notion of genre.

Graeme Turner

ER: an example of hybridised genre?

Genre, Hybridity and Mutation

As has already been suggested in this book, there are many that would argue that there are limitations to the usefulness of genre theory in general, let alone in relation to television. Debates within film theory, in particular, have been vigorous and continuing. A familiar complaint is that genre criticism is circular: the critic constructs their own, perhaps quite idiosyncratic, definition of the genre in question which then licenses them to dismiss texts that fail to conform to this definition. A further complaint is that genre criticism is prescriptive. Although some accounts are content to map changes in genres over time, more characteristic is the insistence on maintaining an ideal version of the genre and criticising any departures from this ideal (Tudor, 1976).

With television, such problems are multiplied. It is pointless to insist on generic purity in relation to television programmes (Feuer, 1992). Television genres and programming formats are notoriously hybridised (Allen, 1989) and becoming more so. John Ellis, in the first edition of *Visible Fictions* (1982), confidently outlined the difference between the series and the serial. One of the key differences, it seemed then, was the series' use of self-contained episodes with relatively autonomous plotlines as against the serial's use of continuing storylines with characters who learned from episode to episode. Today, there are elements of the serial in many of what the industry would regard as series: US sitcoms such as *Friends*, hospital dramas such as *ER* and cop shows such as *NYPD Blue* (NBC, 1993–2005) (see 'The Mini-Series', p. 46). In the UK, the self-contained, narratively low-key, realist format of the police series *The Bill* (ITV, 1983–) has given way to the continuing storylines and the focus on characters' private lives that is typical of soap opera.

The fact that such examples have mutated over time raises another important characteristic of television genres. Unlike the audiences for films or the readers of novels, the audiences for continuing television programmes respond to the texts they consume directly through ratings figures, phone calls to the network, talk radio and so on. Much television programming is produced either live or in relatively close proximity to its screening date. This is obvious in the case of news or current affairs, but it also affects comedy and drama series as well. Television producers change aspects of their programmes in response to audience feedback: characters can

be killed off or foregrounded; presenters can be siphoned out of prime time into late night or weekends, or off-air altogether.

In some cases, the cumulative effect of repeated tweaking of the format and content amounts to a change in genre. The introduction of soap opera-like continuing domestic storylines has been a constant feature of Australian television drama, for instance, as series gradually mutate into serials. Often this shift is accompanied by a move downmarket, both in storylines and in production values.

Changes in technology have reinforced the direct nature of the relationship between viewers and programming. The introduction of alternatives to old-fashioned ratings surveys (replacing the ratings book with the people meter, for instance) has responded to networks' interest in detailed audience information by providing more finely grained, and more readily available, viewing figures (Ang, 1991, pp. 78–84). The increasing use of programme-based websites and email addresses has also provided another means of recording audience interest in programmes or in particular aspects or segments of programmes. This may be reflected in the increased number of magazine-styled formats now found across the television schedule. In addition to the ratings information on such shows, which can record the viewers' choices every fifteen minutes, the success of specific segments can be deduced from such things as requests for recipes, building instructions or 'fact sheets'. In a cautious industry with few opportunities to take commercial decisions on the basis of hard evidence, the effect of these developments is significantly to influence content, format and, ultimately, genre.

Graeme Turner

Genre, Format and 'Live' Television

Television genres are not constructed in relation to an Aristotelian model; individual programmes may evolve out of an originating premise that can itself be revised or shelved without guilt or hesitation. Contemporary arguments over the changes in news values claimed to mark the decline in television news and current affairs reflect a shift from what was predominantly an information genre to one that is predominantly aimed at providing entertainment. Williams and Carpini (2000) argue that the Bill Clinton–Monica Lewinsky story was in fact kept alive by

Friends: transcending traditional generic categories

the entertainment rather than the news media – for its entertainment rather than its news value. From Russian television, recently, it has been reported that weather girls are performing a striptease while presenting the latest weather reports – certainly a shift in genre orientation (see 'The Infotainment Debate').

Even the metaphor of evolution is perhaps too systemic to describe the promiscuous hybridity that informs the generation of programme formats. Consider the example of television makeover shows, a genre that has developed in recent years. Building on audience interest in specific segments within lifestyle, DIY home-decorating or other infotainment shows (as well as home-decorating and fashion magazines in print), the makeover show such as the UK *Ground Force* (BBC, 1997–2005) or *Changing Rooms* (BBC, 1996–2004) has a richer generic origin than this. The characteristics of makeover programmes come from at least the following television genres: game shows, soap opera, reality TV or 'fly-on-the-wall' documentary, confessional talk shows, daytime product-based talk shows and gardening advice programmes (see 'Reality TV').

It is important to recognise here the importance of a related, in some ways competing, term – 'format'. Unlike genre, format is widely used within the industry and among consumers as a way of describing the kind of programme they are watching. Formats can be original and thus copyright, franchised under licence, and traded as a commercial property. Genres, by definition, are not original. Format is a production category with relatively rigid boundaries that are difficult to transgress without coming up with a new format. Genre is the product of a text- and audience-based negotiation activated by the viewer's

expectations. Genre is the larger, more inclusive category and can be used to describe programmes that use a number of related formats, such as the game show.

Finally, it has to be acknowledged that some television formats actively challenge the idea of genre. The 'liveness' of television, its investment in immediacy and provisionality, is in direct conflict with the regulated production imperatives implied by genre and format. Further, the cultural richness of the television message, its capacity to carry an excess of meaning for its viewing audience (Hartley, 1992a, pp. 36–8), means that the television message is always difficult to control. A contradiction deeply embedded in television's function and appeal, television's probing of the boundaries between the 'produced' and the 'real' is built into television formats that include the potential for their own disruption. The most radical examples of this would include the Jerry Springer style of talk show, or the antics represented as disruptive in *World Championship Wrestling* (1988–2001). However, it is more extensive than this. What Adrian Martin has called 'stretch-TV' (see Turner, 1989) can range from the self-reflexive or deconstructive tactics used by the host or presenter, such as those used by David Letterman, Ruby Wax or Graham Norton, to the deliberately unstructured format for the UK comedy series *Baddiel and Skinner Unplanned* (ITV, 2000–5). In such cases, the format/genre includes the attempt to create 'liveness' that is disruptive and immediate. There are even programmes that simulate this potential: *Funniest Home Videos* (ABC, 1989–), or blooper and out-take shows. Although this may indicate the limits of the uses to which genre may be put, it is important to recognise that it would be very difficult to produce the above description without recourse to the notion of genre itself.

Graeme Turner

Genre Study – Beyond the Text

Television genres have traditionally been seen as a facet of programming – to understand a police drama, we must analyse the shows most representative of and important to the history of the cop show. As other entries in this volume suggest, genre criticism has often examined the social function of specific genres, either as vehicles for conveying ideological messages to audiences, or as a ritual practice for viewers to tune in for affirmation or reconciliation of issues in their lives. Other critics have approached genres more

Lost (ABC, 2004–)

When *Lost* (ABC, 2004–) debuted on ABC in September of 2004, it offered a fairly rare situation for commercial television: it was not easily placed within any particular genre. Certainly the show was a drama, but did not immediately seem to fit with more specific dramatic genres like soap opera, crime drama, or science fiction. Yet, it would be misleading to suggest that genre is unimportant to our understanding of *Lost* – throughout its creation, promotion and reception, genre categories have played key roles in situating this innovative and unique programme. By tracing out the role of genre for *Lost*, we can both gain a better understanding of the show's cultural importance and use the programme as a case study to illuminate the varying approaches to genre explored in this book.

Nearly every television programme is explicit in its genre identity, clearly branded by its channel, promotional campaign, narrative form and iconography. At first, *Lost* appeared to be a disaster programme, a genre seemingly unsuited for an ongoing storyline, with narrative focus on the castaways' struggles to escape from and survive in an isolated world. The pilot episode's opening segments present the disaster of a plane crash in some of the most harrowing and intense scenes ever dramatised for commercial television. But if the disaster was the narrative's primary thrust, it would probably have been quite a disappointing show, as little could match the intensity and dramatic stakes of the show's opening moments. But within the programme's first two hours, it becomes clear that the island is not what it first seems, with a monster roaming the jungle, a sixteen-year-old distress signal from previous castaways and a polar bear oddly living in the South Pacific – not to mention dozens of other mystical and 'science-fiction' developments that have since been revealed. The show's genre remained uncertain even after an entire season – is it a supernatural thriller, a scientific mystery, a wilderness soap opera, or a religious fantasy (or all of the above)?

The text of *Lost* is a genre mixture, combining elements from a range of other genres and previous programmes. But unlike previously celebrated genre mixtures like *Twin Peaks* (ABC, 1990–1) or *Buffy the Vampire Slayer* (WB, 1997–2001, UPN, 2001–3), *Lost* refuses to highlight its own genre references and antecedents. Instead, it forces viewers to speculate on relevant generic frameworks, and then confounds our expectations through twists and reversals. When the castaways discover a research station on the island, the show does not fully convert to the conventions of science fiction to explain this unusual presence, but rather leaves the origins and function of the station ambiguous as to complicate any simple conventions of the genre that viewers might assume could explain the mysteries. The show is plotted as an elaborate mystery, but unlike traditional murder or crime mysteries, part of *Lost*'s narrative design is determining what unknown enigmas lurk beneath the surface, not just discovering the answers to clearly posed questions.

While *Lost*'s narrative and storyworld connect to a number of television genres, it is important to remember that genres are not ultimately limited to the texts of programmes themselves. Genre categories are defined and utilised through the practices of critics, producers, networks and fans, as how a genre is discussed helps shape the meanings and assumptions that are tied to a text. *Lost* originated from an experiment across genre categories – ABC executive Lloyd Braun had developed an idea for a fictional programme building off the premise of the hit reality show *Survivor* (Planet 24, 1997–), hoping to combine the dramatic intrigue of life on a desert island with the production control and storytelling polish available to a fictional show. Obviously, the resulting programme bears little resemblance to *Survivor*, as *Lost* is far from realistic in design; however, the origins of the programme tapped into both the popularity of reality television and the sense of dramatic intrigue achieved by *Survivor*, but linked the show to the prestige, production values and sense of creative innovation enabled by fictional programming.

Critics and fans similarly approached the new show by trying to fit it into the precedents of previously aired programming. Many critics noted the parallel to *Survivor*'s island milieu, as well as the shared physical attractiveness of most reality show contestants and *Lost*'s cast. Critics also tried to link the show to previous island tales, from William Golding's dystopic *Lord of the Flies* (1954) to the ridiculous *Gilligan's Island* (CBS, 1964–7); more often than not, such references serve more to highlight how unique *Lost* is than to draw significant continuities. Fans and some critics took to more pertinent references as well, connecting the show to previous examples of innovative and complex narrative worlds, grounding the show in a tradition of groundbreaking television like *The Prisoner* (ITV, 1967–8), *Twin Peaks* and *The X-Files* (Fox, 1993–2002). While narrative complexity is not itself a genre, *Lost*'s viewers connected threads from these ancestors in the genres of conspiracy-laden espionage, science fiction and supernatural horror, all of which have proven relevant to the island's evolving storyworld and assumed viewer expectations.

As the show peaked in popularity in its second season, genre categories proved relevant for a backlash against the show as well. With plotlines becoming more convoluted and

Lost: confounding our generic expectations

requiring a collaborate online fanbase using wikis and discussion forums to decode each episode, some *Lost* fans lobbied to have the show focus more on revealing answers and simplifying the mythology, playing up relationships and action sequences to fall more squarely into traditional genre categories. But at the beginning of the third season, as the show embraced more melodramatic relationship plotlines, other fans decried this shift as violating what they saw as the show's core genre allegiances to science-fiction conspiracies and mysteries. Such divergent fan reactions highlight the danger of genre mixing – just as including a range of genre conventions and norms invites a variety of viewing pleasures, fans can overly focus on the particular genres that they feel define the show, rejecting the other aspects that fall outside their pleasurable horizons. For every fan that is drawn to the show's

romantic elements, others are turned off, necessitating a complex balancing act both for producers and fans themselves.

Ultimately *Lost* is probably one of the least 'generic' shows appearing on commercial television. Yet genre is so crucial to the television industry, audience, creators and critics that it is nearly impossible to imagine a programme without one or more genres, and thus discussions of genre matter quite centrally for the cultural circulation of *Lost*. We all approach new shows with a horizon of expectations that is formed in large part from genre categories. Even a show like *Lost* that refuses simple categorisation exists in a television context where genres are everywhere, serving as the primary framework to create and understand new programming.

Jason Mittell

formally, attempting to define the core features constituting a particular genre and illustrate the common threads linking a number of different programmes. These modes of genre criticism all focus on studying the meanings and forms of programming as the avenue for understanding a genre, an approach we might consider textual criticism.

However, as the study of television genres has grown within media studies, critics have expanded their methods

beyond textual criticism. A number of scholars have explored how genres work as part of the system of television production and consumption, exploring how the practices of audiences and institutions are involved in the process of creating and constituting genres (for instance, Allen, 1985; Kackman, 2005). One paradigm emerging in recent years suggests a different orientation towards the cultural role of genres that foregrounds the practices of the television industry and audience. Rather than regarding genres as properties of television programmes to be analysed, defined, or interpreted, genres can be viewed as cultural categories that circulate around and through television programming. This approach, influenced by a broader paradigm of post-structuralist theory, suggests a different orientation for understanding the cultural importance and function of genres, leading to a distinctive avenue for researching the history of television genres through discursive analysis (Mittell, 2004).

According to this approach, genres are not lodged in the texts or programmes categorised by particular genres; instead, genres are forged by the cultural processes of categorisation itself. Genres are conceptual categories used to link together a number of television programmes, but they also articulate a range of cultural assumptions that become linked to the category beyond the programming itself. These categories are forged by a wide range of cultural practices that add to the discourses of television genres, from critical commentaries to network promos, fan websites to governmental regulations. Mittell (2004) identifies three particular discursive practices that are commonly used to constitute television genres: definition (for instance, 'this show is a sports programme because it features athletic competition'), interpretation ('sports programming celebrates national identity') and evaluation ('sports are more legitimate than reality TV'). Through these discursive practices the category of a sports programme is made culturally coherent and accumulates meanings and associations that link it to particular social norms and values, aspects of the genre that would not be discernable just by analysing the programmes themselves.

For another instance, instead of examining the evolving meanings of police shows by analysing the programmes falling under this genre, we might examine how the television industry, critics and viewers have made sense of the category of 'police drama' throughout different historical and social contexts. We might consider whether police dramas are understood as critical or supportive of dominant social norms, whether they are seen as tied to real-life cases or functioning as escapist fantasies, or how the genre is regarded as a valued cultural form or dismissed as trashy and violent – all meanings of the police drama that have been relevant within different historical moments and contexts. Researching a genre as a cultural category requires critics to analyse the broad array of ways institutions and people talk about and use genre categories, and chart the shifts in discourses surrounding a particular genre category through different historical contexts, a technique Mittell (2004) terms 'generic genealogy'. This approach to studying

television genres as cultural categories also takes a 'bottom-up' approach to the formation of a given genre's corpus – rather than a critic attempting to clearly define the limits or parameters of a genre, we can look to the cultural circulation of definitions to understand how a given text is categorised or how there might be competing definitions of the genre which suggest varying cultural assumptions and values. As Mittell (2004, p. 14) puts it:

> Our goal in analyzing generic discourses is not to arrive at a genre's 'proper' definition, interpretation or evaluation, but to explore the material ways in which genres are culturally operative. By shifting focus away from projects that attempt to provide the definitive definition or most nuanced interpretation of a genre, we can look towards ways in which genre definitions, interpretations and evaluations are part of the larger cultural operations of genre. Instead of asking questions such as 'What do police dramas mean?' or 'How do we define quiz shows?' we might look to widespread cultural practices of genre interpretation and definition leading to questions such as 'What do talk shows mean for a specific community?' or 'How is the definition of animation articulated by socially-situated groups?'

Such an approach also demands cultural specificity, recognising that a genre might have various categorical boundaries and meanings in different cultures. A good example of such differences is the status of the television cartoon across cultures. In the USA, the television cartoon genre has been constituted via industrial practices like scheduling on Saturday mornings in the 1960s, and channel branding through the creation of Cartoon Network in the 1990s. As a set of assumed meanings and values, the cartoon genre changed from a mass-audience component of theatrical film bills in the 1940s, to a low-value, highly commercialised kids-only genre in the 1960s, to a hip, nostalgic facet of Americana in the 1990s, even when the actual cartoons themselves were unchanged, as with Bugs Bunny shorts produced for cinema in the 1940s (Mittell, 2004). However in Japan, television animation is regarded as a mainstream form for all ages, with a legitimate role as a site of social commentary and artistic innovation. These genre categories have been further transformed with the rise of Japanese animation imports onto US television in recent years, making anime a generic category itself in America, with its own distinct cultural assumptions and values (Leonard, 2005) (see 'Animation').

This approach to studying genres as cultural categories has been extended to a number of genres and contexts, including transnational reality television (Hill, 2007, 2004), British quiz shows (Holmes, 2007) and Dutch police dramas

(Hermes, 2005). Studying genres as cultural categories offers a different perspective to more common textual genre criticism, as it can suggest ways that genres transform and shape cultural practices beyond the site of the television programme; when textual and discursive analysis work together, we can get a better sense of how genres operate both around and within television programming. As television genre studies moves forward, critics might look to a wide range of sites and modes of genre practice to understand how the categories of television programming both shape and are shaped by their cultural contexts.

Jason Mittell

RECOMMENDED READING

Feuer, Jane (1992), 'Genre and Television', in R. Allen (ed.), *Channels of Discourse, Reassembled: Television and Contemporary Criticism*, London and New York: Routledge.

Frow, John (2006), *Genre*, London and New York: Routledge.

Lacey, Nick (2000), *Narrative and Genre*, London and New York: Palgrave Macmillan.

Mittell, Jason (2004), *Genre and Television: From Cop Shows to Cartoons in American Culture*, London and New York: Routledge.

DRAMA

Studying Television Drama

Television drama studies has mixed origins and is yet to emerge as a domain in its own right to complement film studies. Nevertheless, as courses in media, cultural and communication studies have proliferated alongside those in performing arts and screen studies, interest in the analysis of TV drama has extended considerably. One reason why the study of drama on television has lagged behind film (in spite of television's relative predominance in our everyday lives) is that television programmes are short-lived. In addition, the 'box' is so commonplace as to pass almost unnoticed, at times even unwatched, despite being switched on. In the academic world, the content of television was for some time considered unworthy as an object of study. Whereas films might be viewed several times and have had some pretensions to art, TV dramas were dismissed as ephemeral diversions. Until the relatively recent arrival of videos recirculating TV favourites and repeats of past programmes on such channels as UK Gold, old TV programmes were consigned either to memory or oblivion.

In turn, academic writing about specific television programmes is limited by the time it takes to publish an article or book, by when (or so publishers think) the programmes themselves will be of little interest. Notwithstanding these hindrances, a considerable body of literature relating to drama on television has emerged and several teacher-researchers have made significant contributions to a changing field, two of whom (Brandt and Tulloch) are featured here in more detail (see box) since key shifts in the approach to TV drama studies are reflected in their work.

Bearing still the traces of its theatre origins, early TV drama typically took the form of the single play (see below). Even though the studio-based production and live distribution of these plays was an extremely complex multi-camera procedure, credit for the outcome was given to the playwright, as in theatre. Accordingly, early academic study tended to be literary and writer-centred (see Brandt, 1981). Subsequently, more theoretical debate about TV drama forms and functions reflected the 1970s dominance of 'screen theory' (see Tulloch, 1990, p. 11) in film studies.

Drawing on Althusser, there was a tendency to privilege textual form and its alleged capacity to position viewers. In the famous *Days of Hope* debate (see Bennett et al., 1981), the 'classic realist text' through its very form was alleged to fix subjectivity by drawing all viewers to a singular viewpoint consistent with that of the 'dominant ideology'. All potential contradiction between differing views was apparently resolved by a controlling 'meta-discourse', rendering viewers 'passive' subjects in ideology. The consequence of such a view was the advocacy of a formal experimentation more suited perhaps to avant-garde cinema than to television, but the non-naturalist work of Dennis Potter (see the box in the section headed 'The Single Play' and the section 'The Mini-Series') might serve as a TV drama example.

A consonance may be noted between the formalist 'screen theory' view and that of Brandt, which tends to privilege the author-playwright as a guarantor of fixed meanings. To Brandt, the audience benefits by an author's insights into the human condition inscribed in the text and available to the discerning reader. It is perhaps ironic that, though different in their political affiliations, both 'screen theory' (coming from a Marxian left) and Brandt (coming from a centrist liberal tradition) invite academic interpretations of the scriptures to be passed down where a stable significance is allegedly fixed and transparent.

Partly in reaction to the textual determinism of 'screen theory' and partly in an attempt to rescue members of the mass audience from their construction as 'cultural dupes', cultural studies approaches turned their attentions to the audience. Conceiving the audience not as the homogeneous mass of earlier paradigms, ethnographers set about finding out how subgroups, or even individual members, of the audience, actually read the texts transmitted into their living rooms. Ang and Morley, in particular, established in their audience studies that a range of readings and pleasures is taken by different people engaging with texts from different positions in different ways (see 'Soap Operas and their Audiences'). In *Television Culture* (1987b), an influential television studies primer, Fiske celebrates 'producerly texts' (p. 239), constructed in readings resistant to normative ideology or simply through the popular pleasures of subordinate groups. Where high-gloss, fast-moving, machine-made series and serials had been dismissed as inferior by commentators like Brandt, Fiske talked up what people did with them by way of evading social control (see 'The Populist Debate').

Taken to its logical extension in the reception theory of Stanley Fish, there may be as many readings as there are readers. Indeed, Schroder (Skovmand and Schroder, 1992, p. 207) claims that: '[t]he text itself has no existence, no life, and therefore no quality until it is deciphered by an individual and triggers the meaning potential carried by this individual'. Thus, in the span of a decade between the late 1970s and late 1980s, the preferred model had been inverted from one of a stable text fixing the subjectivity of *passive* spectators to one of *active* readers negotiating their own meanings and pleasures in play with a slippery text. The influence of postmodern accounts of the unstable signifier and dialogic negotiations of meanings and pleasures between texts and readers are patently influential in this shift (see 'Postmodern Drama').

An excessive emphasis on readers' freedom to play with texts began in time to be balanced by a sense of 'bounded knowledgeability' (see Tulloch, 1990, p. 13) and a renewed acceptance that the form of texts imposes some constraints. Nelson (1997a) sustains a view, traceable back to aspects of Brandt, that the compositional principles of texts matter and tend to dispose some readings rather than others. His analysis of *Casualty* (BBC, 1986–) shows, however, how television's dominant 'flexi-narrative' has emerged as a relatively open dramatic form (see 'Hospital Drama'). Absorbing the insights of cultural studies approaches and postmodern theory, Nelson avoids a simple reassertion of Brandt's textual hierarchy. With Tulloch, he acknowledges that the writer is but one of many contributors to a complex industrial process that shapes the text. Indeed, in his account of the making of *Heartbeat* (ITV, 1992–), he demonstrates how the focus group of

Heartbeat: market research can allow reception to influence 'authorship'

modern market research may be used in a feedback loop to allow reception to influence 'authorship'.

Thus in television drama studies today, attention may usefully be paid to the production context (particularly the impact of new technologies), to the compositional principles of the text itself and to readers' active engagements with the text to produce various meanings and pleasures. The kinds of drama that form the object of study now range from the rare single play (see below) through to the most popular series/serial hybrid. Given the range of possibilities, it is necessary above all for scholars in the field to be self-reflexive about their approaches (see McCabe and Akass, 2007).

Robin Nelson

RECOMMENDED READING

Brandt, George (ed.) (1981) *British Television Drama*, Cambridge: Cambridge University Press.

Nelson, Robin (1997a), *Television Drama in Transition: Forms, Values and Cultural Change*, London: Macmillan.

Tulloch, John (1990), *Television Drama: Agency, Audience and Myth*, London and New York: Routledge.

The Single Play

The single play (or 'teleplay') has been through many mutations since it first became a staple ingredient of early television. From its origins in live, studio-bound drama, through to its increasing use of outside location, videotape, editing and film, it produced some of the landmark productions of television history. In its heyday in the 1950s and 1960s it was one of the most highly acclaimed and frequently controversial of genres, making a name for itself as a natural site for 'agitational' television (see Macmurraugh-Kavanagh, 1997, pp. 367–81) and the dramatic airing of topical issues (see box). Its early origins in the theatre and radio helped to establish this cultural reputation, with some critics conceiving it as almost 'literary' in its artistic themes and aspirations. It has subsequently tended to be conceived in high cultural regard, marketed and received differently from the likes of soap opera (see p. 60) or the drama series or mini-series (see p. 46), with a writer of a single play often perceived as its sole 'author' (for a discussion of this, see Creeber, 1998, pp. 19–24). This may partly explain why it has become a natural symbol for social commentators who wish to criticise the apparent 'dumbing-down' of contemporary television, presenting it (somewhat nostalgically) as representative of a 'golden age' when television was, in their view, still interested in challenging its audience's views and expectations.

George Brandt, *British Television Drama* (1981) and John Tulloch, *Television Drama: Agency, Audience and Myth* (1990)

George W. Brandt helped to establish drama on television as an object worthy of study. The introduction to his first edited book of essays concludes with the assertion that: 'television drama matters. It is an important aspect of the culture of today. It merits critical attention' (1981, p. 35). To draw this attention, however, Brandt located TV drama in a discourse of 'quality' in a literary–theatrical tradition with a strong canonical sense of individual writers. Conscious of 'some bias in the book towards the single play', he claims, 'it is more a matter of convenience than dogma'. But his emphasis on 'the quality of the writing' (p. 30) leaves the impression (as subsequent commentators have read him) that quality resides in 'the "cultural high ground" of the single play' (Buckingham, 1987, p. 29). By Brandt's second review of British television (1993), not only was that discourse of 'quality' scarcely sustainable but the authored single play form had itself almost disappeared (see below). To Brandt (1993, p. 17), TV drama's 'brightest moments of glory in the eighties may prove to have been the golden glow of a setting sun'.

Tulloch does not share Brandt's pessimism. Locating himself in the cultural studies tradition emergent in the decade between Brandt's two essay collections, Tulloch sees not so much the rich complexity of the authored text as the complexity of the process of producing meanings and pleasures in culture. For him, it is a matter of what people do with texts at least as much as a matter of what texts do to people. Tulloch examines the functioning in culture of popular genres in series/serial formats writing extensively, for example, about science fiction (see below). Furthermore, he was among the first to see the need for an account of 'the audience and the notion of differential readings' (Tulloch and Alvarado, 1983, p. 9). His later work explicitly examines the range of meanings and pleasures produced by viewers in engagements with a wide range of texts, though he is critically reflexive about audience study (see Tulloch and Jenkins, 1995, and 'Soap Operas and their Audiences').

Despite their differences, however, there are correspondences between the contributions of Brandt and Tulloch. Brandt's (1981) introduction offers a useful summary of changes in television culture from its early days to the 1970s. The impact of institutional changes in Britain (the introduction of ITV and BBC2) are noted along with technological developments (colour, videotape, lightweight 16mm film cameras). In parallel, Tulloch's earlier work on *Doctor Who* (BBC, 1963–) takes an 'extensive approach' conducting 'an investigation in terms of the industrial, institutional, narrative, generic, professional and other practices' (Tulloch and Alvarado, 1983, p. 2) shaping the series' twenty-year development. Both address the seminal debate about television naturalism, and Tulloch to some extent echoes Brandt in his (1981) concern with 'authored' and 'serious' drama. The naturalism debate (see Bennett et al., 1981, pp. 302–53) questioned whether 'progressive' drama could be mobilised in the allegedly compromised form of television naturalism. To a considerable extent the debate was overtaken by new approaches to understanding how television functions culturally in the cultural studies approach of people like Tulloch.

For Tulloch's overall approach to the study of TV drama ultimately differs from Brandt's methodologically and ideologically. Brandt (as Tulloch himself points out) celebrates the authored single play as the form affording ventilation of public issues through creativity in a liberal tradition of the distinctive individual voice in opposition to 'the popular historical series as carrier of national myth' (Tulloch, 1990, p. 3). Tulloch, in contrast, recognises that myth-circulation through popular television creates sites of struggle for meanings.

Tulloch's position is a thought-through and self-reflexive mix of practical consciousness with postmodern relativism. As a liberal-left academic, he allies himself with the audience ethnographers who celebrate resistant pleasures and readings, but he also finds 'analytic mutuality' with the agency of the avowedly left-wing writers, directors and producers (e.g. Griffiths, Loach and Garnett) who form a substantial part of his study. Thus he avoids capitulation to utter relativism. A key point, following Giddens, is that agency in the sense of active reproduction must be acknowledged in a range of production and reception spaces. Nor is this simply a matter of discursive practice. Citing Giddens, Tulloch explains that: '[w]hat agents know about what they do, and why they do it – their knowledgeability *as* agents – is largely carried out in practical consciousness' (Giddens, 1979, p. 250, cited in Tulloch, 1990, p. 11).

It is possible, then, for Tulloch to see potential in those 'machine-made' serials and series with high gloss so worrying to Brandt, since it is what people do with those texts that ultimately matters. At the same time he can hold reservations about Fiske's wilder celebrations of allegedly resistant pleasures through 'producerly texts' (1987b, p. 239) because he recognises that the structuring principles of TV dramas may dispose some readings rather than others. Agency is thus afforded to writers and producers. In Tulloch's account, some writers – as familiar as their audiences with genre and form –

can mobilise a radical 'text' in their subtle reworking of conventions. He follows Janet Wolff in retrieving the author from the brink of death, but it is an author 'now understood as constituted in language, ideology and social relations … the author being the first person to fix meanings, which will of course subsequently be subject to redefinition and fixing by all future readers' (Wolff, 1981, p.136, cited in Tulloch, 1990, p. 17).

In this light it becomes important to research the institutional constraints on writers' and producers' agency, and Tulloch's book demonstrates the value of extending an ethnographic approach beyond audience to 'all those institutional, industrial, educational and leisure spaces where pleasures and meanings contest in the construction of TV drama "texts"' (1990, pp. 20–1).

Tulloch readily acknowledges his debts to colleagues' development of parallel cultural studies approaches in other disciplines (e.g. Janice Radway in literature). His work serves here to mark a distinct shift from Brandt's more hierarchical and canonical approach and to show how self-reflection is important in an academic context where a range of possible approaches may make insightful contributions to understanding.

Robin Nelson

Critics have tended to assume that, because many early single plays were adapted from classical theatre and were broadcast live (early recording technology was both primitive and expensive), the *style* itself of those early transmissions was also inherently *theatrical*. According to Gardner and Wyver (1983, p. 115), early single plays were 'tediously broadcast from the theatre, or reconstructed in the studio, even down to intervals, prosceniums and curtains'. However, Jacobs (1998, p. 58; 2000) has recently argued that the early single play was already evolving a televisual style and aesthetic of its own, developing '*multi-camera studio drama*' that broke down the theatrical dynamics of the stage play. As writers began to produce original dramas for the small screen, so this style gradually became inherently televisual in its own right. 'The structure of these plays related to circumstances under which they were produced. Such problems as costume changes and ageing were unwelcome. This encouraged plays of a tight structure, attacking a story close to its climax – very different from the loose, multiscene structure of films' (Barnouw, 1975, p. 160).

Certainly by the 1950s the single television play was beginning to distinguish itself radically from classical theatre, in terms of both content and style. In America, writers like Paddy Chayefsky (1923–1981) began producing original single dramas for television that attracted both large audiences and huge critical acclaim. Chayefsky signed on for the Philco–Goodyear anthology series on NBC in 1952 where he wrote many of his most famous single plays, including *Holiday Song* (1953), *The Mother* (1954), *Bachelor's Party* (1955), *A Catered Affair* (1955) and *Marty* (1953).

Chayefsky's characters were usually from the lower middle class, the dialogue they spoke and the problems they encountered always reflecting everyday, personal dilemmas. It was this deceptively ordinary world that seemed so uniquely suited to the domestic dynamics and interior style of television drama at the time. 'The technical requirements of live broadcast were a good fit with Chayefsky's dramatic gestalt: cramped living rooms, small working-class bars, neighbourhood mom-and-pop stores. Car chases, big crowds, and location shots were strictly out of the question' (Marc and Thompson, 1992, p. 122). The most well known of his single plays is undoubtedly *Marty* (starring a young Rod Steiger), which is still remembered today for its moving portrayal of a lonely middle-aged man, living in quiet desperation with his domineering mother. Transmitted live, much of it in close-up, its understated method acting and long claustrophobic scenes helped to give shape to what Chayefsky famously termed 'the marvellous world of the ordinary' (cited by Brandt, 1981, p. 15. See also Hey, 1983, pp. 124–33).

Despite strong editorial interference and heavy censorship from their sponsors (see Boddy, 1992, pp. 187–213), successful American single plays like Rod Serling's *Requiem for a Heavyweight* (CBS, 1956), Gore Vidal's *Visit to a Small Planet* (NBC, 1955) and Reginald Rose's *Thunder on Sycamore Street* (CBS, 1954) continued to develop this new aesthetic, proving that the limitations of the live studio could still produce exciting and innovative drama. Although generally less celebrated than Chayefsky, Reginald Rose was no less significant in terms of his ability to utilise the specific power and dynamics of the small screen. In particular, his claustrophobic and powerful *Twelve Angry Men* (directed by Franklin Schaffner, CBS, 1954) was justifiably celebrated for the way in which it found large-scale drama in an extremely limited setting (the twelve jury members of a homicide case). Like *Marty*, it was later adapted for the big screen, the director Sidney Lumet turning it into a successful Hollywood movie (1955) starring Henry Fonda.

Marty: 'the marvelous world of the ordinary'

This style of single play soon caught on in the UK, particularly with the introduction of the new commercial channel in 1955. One of the significant figures of this time was Sydney Newman (1917–1997), a successful Canadian television producer brought to Britain to work for ABC (see box). Although British single plays like Ted Willis's *Woman in a Dressing Gown* (ITV, 1956) were already tackling lower-class themes, Newman's influence was unmistakable. Under the title Armchair Theatre, he helped put together a startling collection of new and original single plays during the period 1958–63. Although classical playwrights such as Ibsen were favourites of the series, original plays (Alun Owen's *No Trams to Lime Street* (ITV, 1959), Clive Exton's *Where I Live* (ITV, 1960) and Harold Pinter's *A Night Out* (ITV, 1960), for example) gradually placed working-class and regional accents to the forefront of the action. Despite the limitations of live drama, directors and set designers also became increasingly experimental in their attempts to produce a new form of 'realism', and cameras became more fluid as directors tried to create three-dimensional space, incorporating long tracking shots that

would weave in and out of intricate sets. Newman would later continue and develop this tradition at the BBC, under the title The Wednesday Play (see box).

By the 1970s the harsh economic realities of television put the future of the single play increasingly under threat. In the USA, prime-time advertising rates became progressively expensive, making full sponsorship of an anthology series a rarity. Whereas a 'themed' series like *The Twilight Zone* (CBS, 1959–64 – see 'Science Fiction', p. 36) proved popular, the individual single play gradually became less desirable. As the networks rejected the genre, so writers like Chayefsky were forced to leave for Hollywood. Ironically, his most famous movie was *Network* (1976), a vicious satire on American television, directed by one of his earlier television collaborators, Sidney Lumet.

Although the single play survived longer in the UK (see box), the move towards long-form drama was inevitable, quickened by the relatively high costs of the genre in comparison with the series or serial. The eclectic style and content of each individual play also made it difficult to schedule, whereas the reassuring predictability of the

The Wednesday Play and Play for Today

Hoping to emulate the success of ITV's Armchair Theatre, the BBC 'poached' Sydney Newman in 1962 and appointed him Head of Drama. The Wednesday Play (1964–84) followed two years later with some plays left over from Peter Luke's Festival series. However, it is generally seen to have got properly under way on 6 January 1965 with *A Tap on the Shoulder*, written by James O'Connor. Although responsible for adapting many European classics, the series is now primarily remembered for broadcasting original, contemporary and often 'politicised' drama, reportedly provoking national discussion on a scale never witnessed before or since. Frequently dealing with controversial issues such as homelessness or the legalisation of homosexuality, the series ingeniously gave the BBC both cultural credibility and exciting drama, although the relationship between practitioners and institution was seldom an easy one (see Macmurraugh-Kavanagh, 1997, pp. 367–81). The series certainly signalled an important shift in television drama generally, with its reputation for 'social realism' aided by the introduction of new recording techniques, easier editing facilities and newer lightweight cameras. As the producer Tony Garnett remembers, 'The whole logic of the scripts we were getting was forcing us to use film and to shoot outside the studios on location' (cited by Hudson, 1972, p. 20).

Among some of the series' most well-known plays were Dennis Potter's *Vote, Vote, Vote for Nigel Barton* and its companion piece, *Stand Up, Nigel Barton* (director Gareth Davies, 1965), David Mercer's *And Did Those Feet?* (director Don Taylor, 1965) and Jeremy Sandford's groundbreaking *Cathy Come Home* (director Ken Loach, 1966 – see 'Drama–Documentary', p. 42). Although generally less celebrated than *Cathy*, Nell Dunn's *Up the Junction* (1965) was both controversial and innovative in terms of its own radical style and subject matter. Also directed by Ken Loach, this single play dealt with the harsh realities of working-class life in and around London's Clapham Junction. Constructed around a number of loosely connecting storylines (adapted by Dunn from her own book of short stories), Loach's 'documentary' style of film-making gave a harsh realism to the drama's graphic depiction of unwanted pregnancy and back-street abortion. Utilising the new improvements in technology, *Up the Junction* was one of a number of dramas that helped produce a new aesthetic for television. Mixing elements of montage, voice-over and location filming, it built on and helped to establish the medium's 'unique capabilities for the representation of the social real' (Caughie, 2000, p.122).

The series was renamed Play for Today in 1970. Single plays such as Mike Leigh's suburban tragi-comedy, *Abigail's Party* (devised by Mike Leigh, 1977), Jim Allen's politically committed *The Rank and File* (director, Ken Loach, 1971) and Jack Rosenthal's *Bar Mitzvah Boy* (director, Michael Tuchner, 1976) seemed to continue the radical remit of the earlier series. Employing many of the same writers, directors and producers as before, the writer Dennis Potter is perhaps the consummate example of a creative force whose talent was nurtured and sustained by the series as a whole (see also 'The Mini-Series', p. 46). Frequently provocative, Potter's *Blue Remembered Hills* (director, Brian Bibson, 1979) was an award-winning ensemble piece that consisted entirely of adult actors dressed as children. However, the series' uneasy relationship with the BBC continued and both Potter's *Brimstone and Treacle* (director, Barry Davis, 1976) and Roy Minton's *Scum* (director, Alan Clarke, 1979) were banned by an institution that had become increasingly paranoid (see Hollingsworth and Norton-Taylor, 1988, p. 116). Both plays were later transferred to the big screen before finally being transmitted a decade later on television. The series finally came to the end of its long and celebrated run in 1984.

Glen Creeber

drama series could quickly build up a large and loyal audience that tuned in week after week (see 'The Mini-Series', p. 46). The single play was also seen as too 'idiosyncratic' and 'parochial' to attract foreign buyers or co-production money (see Gardner and Wyver, 1983, p. 118).

Such economic concerns became even more pressing with the arrival of satellite and cable in the 1980s. In the USA, the 'made-for-TV movie' became increasingly popular, while in the UK Channel 4 Films ingeniously pioneered the way for commissioned drama to be made with both the big screen and the small screen in mind (a TV broadcast coming only after its cinematic release). Developments in technology and the success of films like *Angel* (Jordan, 1982) and *My Beautiful Laundrette* (Frears, 1985) meant that single television drama had now become virtually indistinguishable from its big-screen rival.

More recently, critics have argued that the soap opera (see p. 60) is now helping to keep 'quality drama' alive, with some episodes of *EastEnders* (BBC, 1985–) worthy of being called single plays in their own right (see Tulloch, 1990, p. 3). However, other critics have complained that there are now virtually no opportunities left for new writers to experiment and take chances with the medium as there were in the 1950s and 1960s. The single television 'play' is now almost a rarity, apparently confined to that period of television history that was continually breaking new ground as its drama strove to define an aesthetic, style and content of its own. Ironically, that process would finally reject the very genre that gradually enabled it to come of age.

Glen Creeber

RECOMMENDED READING

Gardner, Carl and Wyver, John (1983), 'The Single Play: From Reithian Reverence to Cost-accounting and Censorship', *Screen*, vol. 24, no. 4–5.

Hey, Kenneth (1983), '*Marty*: Aesthetics vs Medium in Early TV Drama', in Leslie Fishbein (ed.), *American History/American Television: Interpreting the Video Past*, New York: Frederick Ungar.

Shubik, Irene (1975), *Play for Today: The Evolution of Television Drama*, London: Davis-Poynter.

The Western

In many ways, the conventions of the Western genre would seem to make it uniquely suited to the demands of episodic television, balancing the need for narrative novelty within the production and promotional constraints of recurring characters and situations. The TV Western's nomadic hero, whether the hired gunslinger of *Have Gun, Will Travel* (CBS, 1957–63), the trail boss of *Wagon Train* (NBC, 1957–62; ABC, 1962–5), or the professional gambler of *Maverick* (ABC, 1957–63), allowed for a variety of plot situations, guest stars and incomplete resolutions, to the degree that many TV Westerns became near-anthology programmes in disguise. The Western genre on television also seemed robust enough to spawn several generic hybrids, including the domestic Western of *Bonanza* (NBC, 1959–73), comedies like *F Troop* (ABC, 1965–7) and even a nineteenth-century espionage Western, *The Wild, Wild West* (CBS, 1965–9).

The lone protagonist of the TV Western links the genre most directly to that of television's private eye, so much so that *Maverick* creator Roy Huggins recycled several storylines from his Western series into his subsequent private-detective shows *77 Sunset Strip* (ABC, 1958–64) and *The Rockford Files* (NBC, 1974–80) (see 'The Action Series', p. 24, and 'The Crime Series', p. 29). Over its history, the TV Western has been represented by everything from low-budget juvenile programmes in fringe time, a range of thirty- and sixty-minute prime-time action-adventures, to

the first ninety-minute series, *The Virginian* (NBC, 1962–70) and a number of made-for-TV movies and mini-series (see p. 46). Whereas the genre on television depended less upon the dramatic treatment of the Western landscape typical of Western feature films, due to the near-prohibitive expense of extensive location shooting and the medium's proclivity for close-ups, the TV Western has drawn upon the Western feature for its iconography, historical settings and characterisations.

At the same time, the case of the Western genre on television contradicts the conventional notion that prime-time programme genres are historically relatively stable in popularity and form. Even compared with the uneven fortunes of the Western at the theatrical box office over the past four decades, the Western genre seems to have enjoyed a remarkably circumscribed life span on US television network prime time, roughly encompassing the decade between the launch of the so-called 'adult Western' in 1955 and the mid-1960s, when only a pair of long-running Western series lingered in the list of the top twenty prime-time shows. Indeed, the spectacular rise of the TV Western in the late 1950s, a time of traumatic change throughout the television industry, briefly transformed the genre into the subject of intense and sometimes hyperbolic critical scrutiny. Perhaps inevitably, the TV Western became the lens through which larger changes in American television were debated within and outside the industry. More than any other genre, the Western was the vehicle for the integration of the Hollywood studios and network television in the second half of the 1950s, and the early years of the genre feature the work of both veteran directors (including Budd Boetticher, Lewis Milestone, Sam Fuller and Tay Garnett) and an emerging generation of directors, including Sam Peckinpah and Robert Altman.

Although at the height of the genre's popularity, between 1957 and 1959, nearly one-third of network prime time consisted of Westerns, the decline of the TV Western only a few years later was precipitous and nearly permanent. Since the 1960s, the Western genre has been barely represented in the hundreds of TV movies, mini-series and episodic series aired in network prime time, and many of the most popular TV Westerns of the past are almost unknown in the domestic and international syndication markets. For a genre that once dominated both network programme schedules and general critical debates over commercial television, the TV Western had all but disappeared in popular memory until very recently (see grey box). More than for any other genre, the case of the television Western invites a consideration of the specific historical circumstances associated with both its sudden

Bonanza: the family- and domestic-centred Western

flourishing and its virtual disappearance by the end of the century.

Like many other television genres, the TV Western has roots in earlier media, including popular fiction, Hollywood film-making and network radio. Indeed, some of the earliest television successes, including the immensely popular *Hopalong Cassidy* (NBC, 1949–51, syndicated 1952–4), involved the repackaging for television of Western shorts and B-films from Hollywood's Poverty Row studios of the 1930s and 1940s. The remarkable success of *Davy Crockett* (an occasional episodic series within ABC's 1954 anthology show *Disneyland*) not only inspired a flood of new prime-time Westerns, but also marked the entrance of the Hollywood studios into the network television market. The following season saw the launch of four so-called 'adult Westerns' on television, which the networks took pains to distinguish from previous Westerns; *Gunsmoke*

(CBS, 1955–75), for example, used actor John Wayne to introduce its first episode in order to distinguish the programme from its juvenile precursors.

Besides the long-running *Gunsmoke*, the other major TV Western introduced in the 1955/56 season was *Cheyenne* (1955–63), produced by Roy Huggins at Warner Bros. for ABC, the producer, studio and network most associated with the early success of the genre. Within two years Huggins helped launch *Colt 45* (ABC, 1957–60) and *Maverick*, and the popularity of the new Warner Bros. Western and crime dramas brought ABC into genuine prime-time competition with the larger two networks for the first time in its history. By the end of the 1958/59 season ABC had four of television's top ten programmes, and ABC devoted 30 per cent of its autumn 1959 prime-time schedule to Warner Bros.-produced programmes. The two larger networks soon followed ABC's move to the prime-time

Western, and there were fifteen new Western series in the 1957/58 season alone; the growing number of Westerns also reflected the collapse of the popular quiz show programmes at NBC and CBS following the revelations of widespread fraud in 1958 (see 'The Quiz Show', p. 162). The following season there were twenty-four Western series in prime time, and in 1959/60 the genre reached a peak with twenty-eight Western programmes. Whereas in the 1959/60 season both ABC and NBC offered eleven different Westerns in prime time, over the next two seasons NBC actually aired more Westerns than did ABC. Thus, although ABC and Warner Bros. remained associated with the early

success of the genre, the TV Western quickly became an important part of the prime-time schedules of all three networks.

If the rise of the prime-time Western in the late 1950s was precipitous, the decline of the genre only a few years later was nearly as abrupt. By 1962 Warner Bros. Television was laying off 25 per cent of its staff; between the 1961/62 and 1963/64 seasons, the number of Westerns in TV's top ten programmes declined from four to three to one. As the studio and network most committed to the genre, Warner Bros. and ABC suffered the most, as other production companies and networks shifted to a new generation of rural

Alias Smith and Jones

As one of the few TV Western series introduced on US prime-time television since the mid-1960s to survive more than a single season, *Alias Smith and Jones* (ABC, 1971–3) occupies an unusual place in the history of the genre. Dismissed by many critics at the time as derivative of the 1969 Hollywood hit *Butch Cassidy and the Sundance Kid* (Hill, 1969), the series in fact owes more to television's *Maverick*, produced by *Alias Smith and Jones*'s executive producer Roy Huggins. Huggins, under the pseudonym John Thomas James, received exclusive or joint writer or story credit on forty-five of the fifty episodes of *Alias Smith and Jones*, and the series represents the last of many TV Westerns on which Huggins worked, beginning with the opening season of *Cheyenne*, one of the first so-called 'adult Westerns'.

Alias Smith and Jones continued the anti-heroic tone of Huggins's *Maverick*, for which he served as producer and frequent writer in its first two seasons. Glen A. Larson, the creator and producer of *Alias Smith and Jones*, had worked with Huggins as writer and producer on *The Virginian* and *Run for Your Life* (NBC, 1965–8); Larson went on to create and produce several successful, if undistinguished, series, including *The Six Million Dollar Man* (ABC, 1974–8), *The Fall Guy* (ABC, 1981–8) and *Knight Rider* (NBC, 1982–6).

The self-conscious and ironic tone of *Alias Smith and Jones* was established in the opening narration of the ninety-minute pilot: 'Into the West came many men. Some were good men and some were bad men. Some were good men with some bad in them, and some were bad men with some good in them. This is the story of two pretty good bad men.' The series went on to recount the adventures of Hannibal Hayes (Pete Duel/Roger Davis) and Kid Curry (Ben Murphy), leaders of a gang of train and bank robbers who, faced with increasingly

sophisticated safes and determined posses, decide to take up a Western Governor's general offer of amnesty. However, the Governor's amnesty offer is secret, and contingent upon the pair staying out of trouble for one year, so the two outlaws take on the aliases of Smith and Jones and attempt to dodge assorted bounty hunters, former gang members and lawmen who seek to arrest them for past crimes or entice them into new ones. The heroes' uncertain legal situation and their ambivalence about repudiating their criminal pasts suggest their links to a line of nomadic anti-heroes of 1960s' television, from *Route 66* (CBS, 1960–4) to *The Fugitive* (ABC, 1963–7), and the picaresque possibilities of the Western allowed the programme to challenge occasionally the genre's traditional masculine hero.

Alias Smith and Jones was launched at a time of unusual volatility in network prime-time schedules and had the misfortune of being scheduled against two emerging hits on rival networks, the number two-rated *Flip Wilson Show* (NBC, 1970–4) in *Alias Smith and Jones*'s first season and the number one-rated *All in the Family* (CBS, 1971–9) in the Western's second season. Even for the third-ranked ABC, the ratings for *Alias Smith and Jones* were disappointing, declining from thirty-eighth among all network prime-time shows in the first season to sixty-fifth of sixty-five network shows in the second season. Some critics argued that the show was hurt by the loss of co-star Pete Duel, who committed suicide after only sixteen completed episodes; Duel was quickly replaced by Roger Davis, who had been the narrator on earlier episodes. Duel's death has contributed to the subsequent semi-cult status of *Alias Smith and Jones*; despite its relatively brief run, the series has enjoyed intermittent revivals in both domestic and international syndication and has generated a number of fan groups, Internet sites and works of slash fiction and viewing pleasure.

William Boddy

Deadwood

The recent success of *Deadwood* (HBO, 2004–6) proved that the Western genre could still captivate and excite television audiences in the twenty-first century. Set in the 1870s in the real settlement of Deadwood in the state of South Dakota, the series centred on the growth of the community from a makeshift camp (popular with those prospecting for gold in the nearby Black Hills) to a vibrant and complex town. This real historical setting means that the show possessed all the iconic ingredients that one would expect to find in the classic Western, immediately suggested by its enigmatic opening credits that are 'culled from almost two hundred years of Western tradition' (Klein, 2006, p. 140). The inclusion of a number of historical figures from the period, such as Wild Bill Hickok (Keith Carradine), Sol Star (John Hawkes), Calamity Jane (Robin Weigert) and Al Swearengen (Ian McShane), only adds further intertextual levels to a series that is acutely (self) aware of its own generic tradition. Yet, the fact that few of these figures live up to their public mythology (Hickock is a drunken gambler, Calamity Jane is a foul-mouthed boozer and brawler) only seems to add to the realism of a drama that appeared intent on vividly deconstructing the very genre it helped to reinvent.

Deadwood was created by David Milch who began his career writing for *Hill Street Blues* (NBC, 1981–7) and later went onto create *NYPD Blue* (ABC, 1993–2005) with Steven Bochco (see 'Crime Series'). However, Milch never directed a single episode of *Deadwood* and wrote only five episodes (two of which he actually co-wrote). Yet, as Joshua Wolk points out, Milch's influence is not limited to the script, with actors having to listen to 'long preparatory lectures about context and subtext, dappled with historical metaphors to explain the many levels he's aiming for' (cited by Lavery, 2006, p. 3). This complex portrayal of American's Wild West may well lie at the heart of the show's success, its unwillingness to compromise on its portrayal of profanity, violence, misogyny, racism and sexuality, creating a gritty realism that harked back to the darker tones of Sergio Leone's big-screen spaghetti Westerns rather than its more sanitised TV incarnations.

Deadwood is primarily a town of anti-heroes, where murdered bodies are routinely fed to Mr Woo's (Keone Young) pigs, where a young brother and sister are tortured and killed for thieving and where a man is found in a compromising position with a horse. All this is presided over by the aptly named Al Swearengen, owner of the Gem saloon, who provides the sex, drugs and gambling that fuels the town's lawlessness and lines his own pockets. According to Jason Jacobs, Al offers the viewer an 'insight is into the darkness of men's appetites

Deadwood: a TV Western for the twenty-first century

rather than their aspiration for joy; into the primitive, sometimes brutal, urges of men rather than their hopes for a better life' (Jacobs, 2006, p. 13). When he learns that his favourite whore Trixie (Paula Malcomson) has offered her services elsewhere without profit he viciously beats her to a senseless pulp. Such a reaction is ambiguous: is his violence towards her a consequence of her rejection of him or simply his refusal to accept her independence? Whatever way you read it, his misogyny is unmistakable (see Akass, 2006, p. 23). 'The only time you're supposed to open your yap', he tells another whore, 'is so I can put my fuckin' prick in it' (cited in Akass, 2006).

Yet, despite its dark matter and sepia-toned *mise en scène*, *Deadwood* surprisingly appears to comply with the classical Western structure as defined by Will Wright in *Sixguns and Society* (1975). According to Wright, the traditional Western is 'the story of the lone stranger who rides into a troubled town and cleans it up, winning the respect of the townsfolk and the love of the schoolmarm' (p. 32). As David Drysdale puts it, by 'the end of the first season, Bullock [Timothy Olyphant] has not yet rid the town of the undesirable elements, but he does accept the position of being "the fuckin' sheriff" ('Sold Under Sin,' 1.12), suggesting that he will indeed bring order to the camp' (Drysdale, 2006, p. 138).

As Deadwood grows from a lawless shambles into a fully operative town, so the series continues to explore the Western genre's central concern; namely the enduring struggle between civilisation and savagery. As rugged individualism is gradually replaced by a form of corporate capitalism, so the narrative is able to examine aspects of power, politics, corruption, law, order and the role of business and the media in America's past. Perhaps it took George Bush's frontier-like reaction to 9/11 to remind us all of the moral ambiguity at the heart of the American Dream – *Deadwood* perhaps offering us an insight into the historical roots of America's present nightmare.

Glen Creeber

sitcoms, so-called 'magic sitcoms', spy dramas and variety shows. The nature of the surviving TV Westerns in 1960s' prime time began to change as well, moving away from the unattached nomadic hero towards the increasingly family- and domestic-centred narratives of *Gunsmoke* and *Bonanza*. As well as the inevitable effects of a surfeit of nearly indistinguishable Western series at the beginning of the decade, other circumstances worked to diminish the appeal of the genre for networks and advertisers, if not necessarily for audiences.

One contributor to the TV Western's decline in the early 1960s was the initiation of a nearly continuous decade-long string of Congressional hearings and government reports about the harmful effects of TV violence. The first rounds of hearings, led by Senator Thomas Dodd between 1960 and 1963, brought several prominent TV Western actors, writers and producers (as well as network and other industry officials) before the Subcommittee on Juvenile Delinquency to respond to screenings of committee-assembled violent excerpts of popular Western programmes. Although inconclusive in terms of legislation, the extended series of Congressional hearings on television violence encouraged networks and sponsors to seek out less potentially controversial programme fare. By the time the second round of Congressional anti-violence probes rolled out in the late-1960s, the television Western, like the Hollywood Western, seemed nearly irrelevant to American culture. With the exception of *Alias Smith and Jones* (ABC, 1971–3 – see box, p. 22), no prime-time Western launched since the mid-1960s managed to survive more than a single season and, despite the occasional TV movie, mini-series and quickly cancelled episodic series, the TV Western has virtually disappeared from network prime time until its recent reemergence with the arrival of HBO's *Deadwood* (2004–6) (see box).

William Boddy

RECOMMENDED READING

Anderson, Christopher (1994), *Hollywood TV: The Studio System in the Fifties*, Austin: University of Texas Press.

Barson, Michale (1985), 'The TV Western', in B. G. Rose (ed.), *TV Genres*, Westport: Greenwood.

MacDonald, Fred J. (1987), *Who Shot the Sheriff? The Rise and Fall of the Television Western*, New York: Praeger.

The Action Series

Several genres within US and UK TV drama focus on action rather than character, in keeping with the history of the medium and its social intertexts. There are some obvious examples: police programmes that feature violence rather than detection (*The Sweeney*, ITV, 1975–8 – see 'The Crime Series'), war shows that stress fighting over politics (*Combat!*, ABC, 1962–7) and action-packed historical (*The Adventures of Robin Hood*, ITV, 1955–9) and science-fiction (*Xena: Warrior Princess*, Universal, 1995–2001) epics. Then there are espionage series (*Mission: Impossible*, CBS, 1966–73, 1988–9), off-beat buddy shows (*The A-Team*, NBC, 1983–7), cyborg/superhuman series (*Lois and Clark*, ABC, 1993–7), Westerns (*Gunsmoke*, CBS, 1955–75 – see 'The Western') and spoofs (*Get Smart*, NBC, 1965–70, 1993).

We can identify these genres with particular historical moments and ideological preoccupations. For example, *The Sweeney* combines British social realism with US-style violence in a bitter account of working-class strife (see 'The Crime Series'). *Combat!* represents the Second World War celebration of returning heroes. *Robin Hood* stands for the 1950s investment by British commercial producers in swordplay and costume history as a potential export commodity via fantasy reconstructions that embody a heroic age where the ruling class can romantically represent peasant interests. *Xena* is a millennial celebration of girl power with a lesbian subtext. *Mission: Impossible* rises and falls with the high moment of covert action by US spy agencies, before Watergate de-glamorises breaking the law in the name of security. *The A-Team* calls to mind the privatisation and machismo of the Reagan presidency. *Lois and Clark* is the fleeting hope that the Clintons-as-power-couple might revive the rule of truth, justice and the remainder. *Gunsmoke*'s longevity straddles the birth and death of the TV Western, its ubiquity undermined by network desires for youthful audiences (see 'The Western'). And *Get Smart* embodies both the 1960s' popularity of stylish espionage, as per James Bond, and TV's proclivity to parody its own genres.

Despite this polysemous quality, the action-adventure category is largely over as far as broadcast TV is concerned. The genre once took up perhaps a fifth of North American prime time on the main networks, but by the mid-1990s action series occupied only about 1 per cent of the schedule. Infotainment grew from virtually nowhere in 1990 to earn US $1 billion *per annum* by 1994. An hour of reality television at that time cost US $700,000, as opposed to US $1.3–2 million for action and US $1 million for studio-based drama (see 'Reality TV'). Infotainment is excellent prime-time cost-cutting. Cheap or rerun action series survive on cable networks and satellite services dedicated to particular genres or periods of television.

The Man from UNCLE and *The Avengers*

For many people, *The Man from UNCLE* (NBC, 1964–8) represents the nadir of the TV spy genre, full of improbable plots, cheap sets, cliché gadgets taken from Bond-like prototypes (pens that were two-way radios, pistols that became machine guns, a Piranha sports coupé with rockets and machine guns), and amateur-hour performances below camp. In short, US television discovered how to make Bond blandly suitable to the Cold War. But from another perspective, UNCLE ushered in a productive era of programmes prepared to poke fun at the the military–industrial complex. They were very different from their stiffly right-wing predecessors.

After a shaky start, the series was a huge ratings success in 1965 and 1966, at times receiving 10,000 fan letters a week. It was sold in sixty countries, and merchandising included twenty-three books, countless toys, comics, bubblegum cards, a lunch box, of which I was very proud, and three records, plus the spin-off *Girl from UNCLE* (NBC, 1966–7) and eight movies, mostly designed for release outside the USA and made from newly filmed 'adult' material and TV episodes. Today there are many ezines, feminist slash literature, fan conventions and Internet discussion groups.

It was an American form of pop, dedicated to requiring us all to be up with the times, to get onside with new technology. The fact that the principal enemy, THRUSH, was a multinational corporation, is also significant. One of the show's creators, Sam Rolfe, referred to *UNCLE* as an 'international organisation that had no cold war philosophical differences to contend with'. To underscore the point, 'The Jingle Bells Affair' episode featured a Soviet politician shopping in New York and speaking on peace at the UN.

Even hipper, *The Avengers* ran on British TV (ITV) from 1961 to 1969 and was exported to scores of other nations. It was the first (and still the only) UK show that aired during prime-time sweeps on the US networks. A hybrid of espionage and thriller, the programme was notable for its lead characters. John Steed (Patrick MacNee) was a dandyish gentleman who embodied both a foppish style harking back to the Regency and modish 1960s' chic. The successive women leads, Catherine Gale (Honor Blackman) and Emma Peel (Diana Rigg), personified modernity tout court: hip, leggy, sexy, brilliant, physically competent women who took nonsense from no man and were Steed's superiors intellectually and his equal in combat. Gale and Peel were single women who flirted with Steed, but could live without him. Each drew appreciative female audiences as a consequence. Perhaps women viewers witnessing uninhibited female stars who dressed for success through power saw the flip side to the uncompromising but sexy figures that leapt out to male fans.

Along with issues of gender, the once and doomed empire is ever-present in *The Avengers*. What looked like escapist spy television was also an allegory that resonated with progressive political practice and viewing protocols. The series materialised a transcendent new world, after patriarchy (or at least on the way there, via a utopian alternative universe) and after empire (an unfurling narrative – TV series 1961–9, independence of Britain's 'possessions' 1957 onwards). As well as being figures of high modernity, reacting against and with the constraints of femininity even as they played with them, Mrs Gale and Mrs Peel were also representatives of a ruling-class white background from the former empire, with 'winds of change' blowing through their political and domestic lives. Steed sat on the cross-benches of tradition and modernity, a playboy who destabilised conventional masculinity and simultaneously signified a disappearing genteel world and a new, brash one.

The programme garnered ratings and acclaim as both a harbinger of feminism and a sign that action television could be stylish and knowing as well as popular. It continues to fascinate. In the 1990s, Diana Rigg was still getting letters from

The Man from UNCLE: a spy drama for the small screen

The Avengers: stylish, knowing and popular

women for whom Mrs Peel had been an icon, and in 2000 the programme could be seen on the US Mystery cable channel, Radio Canada, Foxtel cable in Australia and TF1 in France, as *Agenti Speciali* on Italy's satellite Channel Jimmy and as *Los Vengadores* in Argentina on Uniseries. The Web is sticky with related sites.

Toby Miller

I focus here on perhaps the high point of the genre – the 1960s – and its most memorable subcategories – espionage and detection. The late 1950s and early 1960s on US network TV had been characterised by male action adventure (*77 Sunset Strip* (ABC, 1958–64), *Hawaiian Eye* (ABC, 1959–63), *Bourbon Street Beat* (ABC, 1959–60), *Peter Gunn* (NBC/NBC, 1958–61), *Burke's Law* (ABC, 1963–6), *Checkmate* (CBA, 1960), *Michael Shayne* (1960–1), *Route 66* (CBS, 1960–4), *Follow the Sun* (ABC, 1961–2) and *Adventures in Paradise* (ABC, 1959–62)), frequently in dyadic form.

The mid-1960s on American TV were, however, rather like the mid-1990s: full of situation comedy, which was

24

24 (Fox, 2001–) is a contemporary action series centred around Jack Bauer (Kiefer Sutherland), a government agent who works for the fictional Los Angeles branch of the US government's Counter Terrorist Unit (CTU). His job entails a constant fight against international terrorism, sometimes risking his life and the lives of others for the 'greater good' of the USA. In this sense, *24* is clearly reminiscent of earlier action series, our hero struggling to save us all from imminent annihilation at the hands of evildoers.

However, *24* was distinctly different in form and style to the action series of the past. Created by Robert Cochran and Joel Surnow, it has been praised by critics like Mark Lawson for changing 'the rules of television by making format central to a drama' (cited by Jermyn, 2007, p. 49). First, as Jack reminds us at the start of each episode, 'Events occur in real time'. This means that each minute of airtime (including commercial breaks) corresponds to a minute in the lives of its characters. This real-time nature of the show is emphasised by an on-screen digital clock that intermittently appears on screen, with a harsh and distinctive ticking noise accompanying each second as the digits dramatically count down.

This technique not only adds to the realism of the drama (perhaps aping the sort of verisimilitude we have come to expect from 'Reality TV') but also alerts viewers to exactly how much time Jack has left to achieve a crucial task; thereby heightening the show's ongoing levels of suspense. As Rod Brookes puts it, when 'a Serbian terrorist warns Jack that he must deliver a cellphone for Senator Palmer to answer at 10.45 exactly or his daughter will be killed, this phone call will happen 45 minutes in the episode' (2004b, p. 1). Second, the drama's innovative use of split-screen allows the viewer to watch various parts of the action simultaneously. This not only helps its makers to avoid the boring parts of the narrative (for example, Jack simply driving), but also allows the viewer to keep up with the complex subplots and narrative twists and turns that are an inevitable part of each episode.

It is this distinctive style that has won *24* so much of its praise. In particular, critics argue that it reflects John Caldwell's description of the 'videographic' tendency of contemporary TV that began in the 1980s; resembling the look of twenty-four-hour cable news channels such as CNN with its busier, visually complex, graphic-crunching style of 'televisuality' (see Daniel Herbert, 2007, p. 93 – see also 'News'). Such stylistic devices have also been linked to the programme's attempt to reflect a new media age (perhaps also enhanced by its obsession with state-of-the-art technology), the very style

24: stylistically innovative but ideologically conservative?

of the drama mimicking computer screens, websites, digital TV and video games with their multilayered, multitasking 'windows' aesthetic. While some critics argue that such stylistic flourishes are simply the inevitable 'dumbing down' of TV drama for a generation of MTV kids with a 'three-minute attention span', critics like Deborah Jermyn argue that it actually forces the viewer to become more active in their viewing practices. For Jermyn, it 'invites the viewer to embrace the act of editing for themselves, mobilizing them to actively engage with the screen and its drama by demanding they move between planes of action simultaneously' (2007, p. 51).

Few would argue that *24* is stylistically innovative, but ideologically it seems that little really changes in the universe of action TV. Although the first season was made just before the bombing of the twin towers, the vision of America it represents has clearly been informed by a post-9/11 world. Indeed, critics have accused it of simply being a vehicle of propaganda for the Fox Broadcasting Company's parent company News Corp. Its frequent depictions of torture as an effective and necessary interrogation tactic particularly have prompted considerable criticism from human rights activists, military officials and experts in questioning and interrogation. Accusations of racism have also dogged the show, particularly the opening episodes of the fourth series that showed a Turkish Muslim family involved in a terrorist plot against America. After a series of complaints, Fox was forced to counter charges of 'Islamophobia' by screening adverts during commercial breaks showing 'positive' images of Muslims.

The show also faired badly with feminist critics who accused it of simply perpetuating the old stereotypes of the past that relied upon the active male and the passive female binary oppositions. As Janet McCabe puts it, *24* 'looks like a standard action thriller where characters and plot are sustained by suspense', producing a genre where 'convention dictates that women should await male assistance or face the consequences for defiantly going it alone' (2007, p. 150). As this suggests, Jack Bauer's view of gender (perhaps like his view of the world) shares a great deal with past Cold War action heroes like James Bond (with whom he shares the same initials). However, in terms of form, structure and style, *24* is clearly a product of twenty-first-century television. Indeed, as Chamberlain and Ruston argue, 'the show's narrative tension is driven more by its structure than through the complexity of its characters or plot' (2007, p. 19).

Glen Creeber

cheap to produce and, when the networks or production houses colluded, a neat way of roadblocking viewers who might switch channels. Thirty years ago, life was stable for NBC, ABC and CBS. But matters changed suddenly with the 1965/66 TV spy craze, when eight espionage programmes appeared, spread across each network. Some were hastily madeover cop shows (see 'The Crime Series'). The networks had wrested control of programme production from sponsors in the wake of the 1950s' quiz-show scandals (see 'The Quiz Show'). This made it possible to diversify commercial sources, which made programming less susceptible to such 'active audiences' as the hysterical anti-Soviet lobby group, Aware Inc.

The stylish commodity/sex motifs of the 1960s meant that although spy-theme storylines often clearly bifurcated good from evil, which recreated the structural opposition of West and East, this narrative tendency was moderated by their visual style. Once an accomplice to straight, unstylish, empiricist but ideological policing in the 1950s, the 1960s focused on a hip, modern look that privileged individuation and commodity fun over group identity and uniformity. Storylines allegorised, cars and clothes diverted and satire displaced didactic ideology. Ironically, a very peaceful era in American imperialism, the mid- to late 1950s, had produced a stuffy and stiff action genre, whereas the hyperviolent Vietnam years saw series that were self-consciously quirky.

What of the detective programme? Classically, detection has meant the identification and defeat of wrongdoers, by applying reason to explain events that are irregular and socially undesirable. Both villains and detectives lose their individual identities through cloaks of substitution, commodity changes of costume, task, face, voice and history that free them from the traces of origin. Identity is assumed and discarded, in keeping with the self-actualising, transcendent subject of urban modernity who can move with ease across time and space. The villain and the detective depend on each other through an overarching third term: the law and its embodiment in the state, which one must elude and the other convince that justice be meted out. This nexus of violence and vacuousness leads critics of the crime genre to blame it for modelling anti-social conduct, heroising the capitalist state, or delighting in base consumerism (see 'The Crime Series').

Most detective shows on TV connect their officers of the law to the quotidian, ever-vigilant and ready to deal with infringements of order. Typically working in couples, they may not be equals, but the police need togetherness to survive rather than utility-maximising individualism. This affective bond allows protagonists to maintain a sense of self as they are sent into situations that frequently bear no relationship to their own existence. When the police move onto a case, they often become involved in its detail and its people: informers, criminals, business proprietors or the ruling class. The narrative generally involves the following: the law is violated; the state finds out about it; the heroes try to find out why and how this happened and who was responsible; they encounter informants (some useful, others dangerous) and have initial struggles with the enemy; the villain is revealed and defeated in a fight sequence; and a coda restores equilibrium.

In both subgenres, heroes are forced to deal with elemental fears, most notably a personal, professional and frequently physical claustrophobia. Because open space is central to much action TV, when protagonists are restricted the spaces they occupy illustrate the impossibility of ever truly relaxing as a spy or police officer: inevitably, they will find themselves somewhere that emblematises the gruesome interiority and tension of their profession. Other typical ingredients include sexual conflict and spectacle, following a particular formula: attractive travellers, often in disguise but with ultimately stereotyped national characteristics, meet and pass information. Despite the openness of their good looks, their secret identities bespeak an untrustworthy world where threats are not just personal. They pose risks to the very fabric of society, so misrecognition, an effect of deception, is endemic, and the very act of travel shows that the apparently eternal verities and loyalties of blood and soil may be compromised. The great ability of the protagonists is to see through the fictions of others and uncover the truth.

For conservatives, the success of 1960s' action series showed that citizens approved of their governments acting covertly or brutally in the interest of state security. For other watchers, the appeal lay in the romance of citizenship: within the norms of governance, viewers test and enjoy to the limit cases presented by life outside, in the comparative anarchy of international relations or crime, where loyalty and patriotism (even the mundanity of public employment) are suddenly reforged as a play with death and doom. They are equally associated with the fate of the individual 'under' technologisation and bureaucratisation, an existential dilemma that is not about an abstract absurdity, but material relations that are part of the everyday (as per overt commercial surveillance). This reliance on the banal as both an underpinning and an 'other' for action series sums up the quaint dependencies of a genre often associated with rugged individualism.

Toby Miller

Author's note: My thanks to Marie Leger for her comments.

RECOMMENDED READING

D'Acci, Julie (1994), *Defining Women: Television and the Case of Cagney and Lacey*, Chapel Hill: University of North Carolina Press.

Miller, Jeffrey S. (2000), *Something Completely Different: British Television and American Culture*, Minneapolis: University of Minnesota Press.

Miller, Toby (1997), *The Avengers*, London: BFI; Bloomington: Indiana University Press.

The Crime Series

For more than five decades the crime series has been one of the most popular genres on television, with some series proving so successful that they have retained a presence in the schedules for ten years or more. In recent years, as the television companies compete for a diminishing share of the audience, there has been a proliferation of police, detective and crime drama (see 'The Action Series'), with endless variations and reworkings of a basic formula in which society is protected and the status quo maintained by the forces of law and order.

In the mid-1950s the tradition was established in Britain by the parochial and reassuring *Dixon of Dock Green* (BBC, 1955–76). George Dixon (Jack Warner) was an ordinary 'bobby on the beat', working close to the people and on their behalf against the occasional anti-social

---

Hill Street Blues

The appearance of *Hill Street Blues* (NBC, 1981–9) on NBC in 1981 was a landmark in the history of American television, breaking all the rules of series drama. It used a large ensemble cast of thirteen to fourteen central characters, overlapping dialogue, multiple narrative strands with a lack of resolution to many of the storylines, documentary-style camerawork, a multi-ethnic cast and strong female characters, and took a liberal attitude towards policing and social issues.

The series was a product of MTM, an independent company, and was screened on one of the main US networks, NBC. However, it was not an immediate success. In fact, the ratings were poor for the first series, but it received favourable reviews, and it gradually attracted a loyal and dedicated audience. Inspired by the vérité style of *The Police Tapes*, a documentary series shown on the US Public Broadcasting System in 1976, *Hill Street* replicated the hand-held, observational style of that series in its morning roll call (see 'Observational ('Fly-on-the-Wall') Documentary'), and ended with the now famous warning: 'And hey, let's be careful out there.'

This traditional opening to each episode established a

realistic and authentic ambience from the outset. The complex narrative structure – moving from one character, or pair of characters, to another, and from one storyline to another as the episode developed, with dialogue often overlapping as a consequence of the ensemble interplay and the interweaving of storylines – was all part of the objective of establishing a new realism in drama as a whole (see Nelson, 1997a, pp. 30–9). The series was as far removed from *Kojak* and *Starsky and Hutch* as those series were from *Highway Patrol*.

It was a mark of the radicalism of *Hill Street Blues* that writer/producer Steve Bochco fought numerous battles with NBC's Broadcast Standards Department over what was permissible in the series. From the outset he and co-creator Michael Kozoll set out to break all the rules of the TV cop show, and they fought battles all along the way to get the series on the screen in the form and style that they wanted. The 'difference' of *Hill Street* was immediately apparent and its bold and innovative approach paved the way for *NYPD Blue* (ABC, 1993–2005), *Homicide: Life on the Streets* (NBC, 1993–9) and numerous subsequent series, within and outside of the police genre (see Jenkins, 1984; Kerr, 1984; Thompson, 1996).

Lez Cooke

CSI: Crime Scene Investigation

Originally inspired by a true-crime TV documentary called *The New Detectives: Case Studies in Forensic Science* (Discovery, 1996), *CSI: Crime Scene Investigation* (CBS, 2000–) is an American drama series that follows a team of Las Vegas forensic scientists as they unravel the circumstances behind mysterious and unusual crimes. So popular has it proven to be that two spin-off shows have also been created in its wake, *CSI: Miami* (CBS, 2002–) and *CSI: NY* (CBS, 2004–).

CSI's narrative structure tends to follow the traditional lines of investigation found in the conventional detective story. This means that the crimes are usually perpetuated at the beginning of an episode, with the detectives (led by Gil Grissom (William Petersen) and Catherine Willows (Marg Helgenberger)) quickly arriving on the scene. The narrative then develops with the detectives (most commonly investigating two separate crimes simultaneously) carrying out forensic investigations, while also interviewing a number of prime suspects. Finally they discover and reveal 'whodunnit' at the conclusion of the show.

Although its narrative structure may be predictable, the most distinctive element of *CSI* is arguably its pronounced and distinctive visual style. Perhaps the presence of Hollywood producer Jerry Bruckheimer (*Top Gun* (Scott, 1986), *Armageddon* (Bay, 1998), *Enemy of the State* (Marconi, 1998), *Black Hawk Down* (Scott, 2001)), meant that it could immediately demand the expense of high production values, the show

CSI: an example of a '*CSI* shot'

being shot on 35mm from its very first run. As Karen Lury points out, the use of 35mm ensured that its 'visual image provides a relatively rich, textured and "deep" look, as opposed to other television programmes, such as studio-bound, video-taped sitcoms or magazine shows characterized by images that are flatter and less textured' (2005, p. 46). This can be seen in all three shows from the *CSI* franchise, which clearly constructs a distinct 'personality' of their own by being implicitly associated with one particular visual style. According to Michael Allen, this is 'figured in terms of their overall colour scheme – Las Vegas' neon glare, Miami's oranges and whites, New York's muted greys and blues' (2007, p. 66).

The programme is, however, most often associated with its range of post-production digital video effects that include CGI sequences (now known as '*CSI* shots') where an accelerated zoom recreates the entry of weapons (such as bullets, knives etc.) into the human body. So while most detective series talk about how a crime was committed, *CSI* actually shows exactly what happened to a victim. Indeed, it is frequently *how* the detectives discover their evidence (from bodies, body parts, clothing, hair, dust, bullets, insects, blood, fingerprints, footprints, DNA samples and so on) that really provides the real 'hook' of the show, celebrating the ability of technology to unravel even the minutest of detail to discover the whole truth. In this way, Sue Turnbull argues that the show becomes profoundly 'televisual' (see Caldwell, 1995), 'the screen becoming more like that of a computer which, with the click of a mouse, opens up its graphic interface to reveal proliferating fields of information' (2007, p. 30).

It is for this reason that *CSI* has sometimes been described as aesthetically and visually cutting-edge but ideologically conservative. While it may look like state-of-the-art television (see Janine Hiddlestone, 2006), its strict narrative structure and the uncanny ability of its detectives to almost always uncover the whole truth has more in common with the perfect crime detection of Sherlock Holmes than the imperfect police officers of *Hill Street Blues* (see box). As Andrew Anthony puts it, '*CSI*'s international success may come down to the fact that in place of postmodern doubt it offers postmortem certainty' (2007, p. 34).

Glen Creeber

elements that dared to disturb the comfortable consensus of postwar Britain. He first began life as a character in the 1949 Ealing Studios film *The Blue Lamp* (Dearden, 1950), where he was shot and killed by Dirk Bogarde's ruthless juvenile delinquent. Seeking a replacement for *Fabian of Scotland Yard* (BBC, 1954–6), the BBC persuaded Ted

Willis (Dixon's creator) to resurrect the character for a new police series. Jack Warner returned to play the part of Dixon for the remainder of his career, until the series finally came to an end in 1976 (by which time Warner was eighty years old and Dixon had retired from the force).

In the early days the series was transmitted live from the BBC studios and featured little in the way of action, crimes usually being resolved with barely more than a minor tussle. Each episode dealt with one main story, introduced by George in a trademark address to camera at the beginning, which was matched by a similar coda at the end. This provided George with the opportunity to point out the moral of the story and, in so doing, deliver the ideological message: that the police were working for the common good of society at large.

When it was first introduced *Dixon of Dock Green* was lauded for its realism, largely because it focused on an ordinary, working-class policeman on the beat, rather than the more idealised detectives of other crime dramas. It had been preceded by *Fabian of Scotland Yard*, the first British drama series to be shot on film, which enabled it to achieve a faster narrative pace than the studio-bound *Dixon*, adding a surface realism that the latter lacked. But *Fabian* – like the subsequent *No Hiding Place* (Associated Rediffusion, 1959–67) and *Gideon's Way* (ATV, 1965–6) – focused on Scotland Yard detectives (rather than ordinary policemen) who used their analytical skills to solve the crime, as opposed to the more intuitive and common-sense attitudes of Dixon.

These two approaches to the police series – the ordinary uniformed policeman on the one hand, the skilled plain-clothes police detective on the other – set a pattern for the genre that has prevailed throughout its history. However, in 1962 the 'gritty' *Z Cars* (BBC, 1962–78) burst on to British television screens, exploding the cosy myth of its predecessors. In devising the series, writer Troy Kennedy Martin and director John McGrath were influenced by the pioneering American police series *Highway Patrol* (ITV, 1955–9), wishing to combine the faster narrative pace of that series with the social realism popular in Britain at the time (see Laing, 1991).

The setting for *Z Cars* was the fictional Newtown (based on Kirkby, Liverpool), and the 'documentary' impulse behind the series was used to explore changes in British society at the beginning of the 1960s. Rather than being named after an individual, it took its title from the new police cars that were being introduced into British policing, as Britain moved away from the older tradition of the policeman on the beat (a part of the community) towards a more depersonalised form of policing.

Concern to get the details of modern policing methods right (and to accurately reproduce the local dialect) was part of the documentary attention to detail of the series. This documentary research, as well as the decision to show violence as a routine fact of life, contributed to its reputation for being more 'realistic' than other police

Z Cars moved away from the individual policeman

dramas. However, the intention of Kennedy Martin and McGrath was not to focus exclusively on the police. Instead, they wanted to use the police as a means to explore the lives of ordinary people living in the north west of England.

Originally transmitted live, early episodes of *Z Cars* used an unusually large number of filmed inserts in order to give the drama a presence in the real world, thus increasing its documentary veracity. In this respect it marked a departure from previous series and helped to pave the way for the breakthrough into filmed drama that Tony Garnett was to achieve on The Wednesday Play (see 'The Single Play') in the mid-1960s. The narrative pace of some of the early episodes was very fast, and Kennedy Martin, in particular, specialised in interweaving a number of different stories in each episode, thereby increasing the complexity of the narrative structure and maximising audience interest and involvement with a range of different characters and stories. To a large extent episodes were character-driven, rather than plot-driven, all part of the original objective of using the police series to explore the reality of people's lives. Originally conceived as a thirteen-part series, *Z Cars* proved an immediate success, with audiences increasing from 9 million to 14 million within eight weeks (Hurd, 1981; Laing, 1991).

In the 1970s the emphasis in police series shifted once again to individual policemen, this time rather more colourful (literally, as the series were now filmed in colour) and aggressive than the likes of Dixon and Fabian. In America, *Kojak* (CBS, 1973–8) and *Starsky and Hutch* (ABC, 1975–9) championed the police detective as fashionable and charismatic heroes, while in Britain a new, more ruthless breed of police detective was introduced in *The*

The Sopranos

The Sopranos (HBO, 1999–2007) is an American television crime series created by David Chase, spanning six seasons and eighty-six episodes in total. Set and produced in New Jersey, the series revolves around mobster Tony Soprano (James Gandolfini) and the difficulties he faces in balancing the needs of both his families, that is, his real family at home and his mafia family at work. This, then, is not a detective drama, but a drama that tends to encourage audiences to see the world through the eyes of its *criminals*; Tony visiting a psychiatrist because of recurring panic attacks caused by stress offers an illustration of this. Although it received some disapproval (most notably from those who denounced it for its stereotypical depiction of American-Italians), critics have almost unanimously praised it, particularly for its sophisticated reinvention of the gangster genre as a whole (see, for example, Robin Nelson, 2007a, pp. 27–35).

Although the gangster genre is a narrative form more at home on the big screen than the small, *The Sopranos* was clearly and self-consciously aware of its own generic heritage. As David Lavery points out, its 'mobsters are all fans of the gangster film genre – Silvio [Van Zandtt] quotes Michael Corleone (Al Pacino) from *The Godfather* films, Christopher [Michael Imperioli] tries his hand at writing an (illiterate) gangster film screenplay' and 'Tony cries while viewing *Public Enemy* (Wellman, 1931)' (2004, p. 190). Even in areas of casting this implicit intertextuality is apparent, many of its actors originally appearing in films such as *Mean Streets* (Scorsese, 1973), *The Godfather Part II* (Coppola, 1975) and *Goodfellas* (Scorsese, 1990).

Critics are divided about what such intense generic self-reflexivity means exactly, but it certainly enables the gangster genre to reinvent itself for a contemporary age through a process of implicit deconstruction. In particular, the mobsters in *The Sopranos* appear to be struggling to resist their 'downsizing' into TV characters, Tony particularly longing to return to the grandiose splendour and 'decency' of the original *Godfather* film (see Donatelli and Alward, 2002, p. 65). According to Glen Creeber, this intextual awareness also allows the programme-makers to critique more contemporary

The Sopranos: reinventing the gangster genre

(some might say 'amoral') forms of the gangster genre, particularly the kind of 'new brutalism' typified by the likes of Quentin Tarantino (see Creeber, 2004b, pp. 100–12, 2002).

Whatever the exact nuances of its self-conscious generic playfulness, it is clear that *The Sopranos* tackles a number of contemporary issues that earlier forms of crime genre would have found difficult (if not impossible) to address. The role of women in the genre is particularly explored in the light of recent feminist advances – Tony's mother Livia (Nancy Marchand), his wife Carmella (Edie Falco), his daughter Meadow (Jamie-Lynn Sigler) and his female psychiatrist Dr Jennifer Melfi (Lorraine Bracco) are all strong female characters who seem a long way away from the one-dimensional vamps, girlfriends and idealised mothers that typified the genre in the past. Not surprisingly, masculinity is also under intense scrutiny in such a show, Tony's neurotic vulnerability an example of a type of behaviour that would not have been tolerated by his world (or his genre) in the past.

Seen in this light, *The Sopranos* is not just a contemporary reinvention of the crime series, but an exploration into the very means by which traditional notions of gendered identities are being reconsidered and reconstructed within a contemporary context. Although Tony may feel the best is over, for many the gangster genre only really came of age with this contemporary adaptation for television.

Glen Creeber

Sweeney. What all of these 1970s' police detectives had in common was a self-righteous belief in the validity of their own methods, even if those methods involved a degree of violence and a bending of the rules. In a decade in which the social consensus of the postwar years was breaking down, the old, gentlemanly codes exercised by Dixon and

Fabian no longer applied. Now the ends justified the (often illegal) means. In an increasingly lawless society extreme tactics were sometimes needed by these fictional policemen in the performance of their 'duty'. In the 'law and order' decade of the 1970s, television police series became an arena where the ideological and coercive work of the police was foregrounded as never before (Clarke, 1986, 1992; Donald, 1985; Hurd, 1981).

In Britain this tendency was controversially highlighted in a four-part drama series *Law and Order* (BBC, 1978), which foregrounded issues of police and judicial corruption in a naturalistic, vérité style (see 'Observational ('Fly-on-the-Wall') Documentary'). The documentary approach of the series offered a verisimilistic counterpart to the action sequences and stylised violence of *The Sweeney* and *Starsky and Hutch* and in doing so introduced a new realism into British police drama at the end of the 1970s.

Similarly, the groundbreaking American police series *Hill Street Blues* sought to be more realistic in the early 1980s. A significant element of *Hill Street* was the more prominent role the series gave to women and ethnic minorities. Admittedly the men in its large ensemble cast still outnumbered the women, but at least the female cast had gained a significant presence as never before (see box). The 1980s, in fact, saw a significant reaction against the machismo of series like *The Sweeney* and *Starsky and Hutch*, with *The Gentle Touch* (LWT, 1980–4) and *Juliet Bravo* (BBC, 1980–5) in Britain, and *Cagney and Lacey*

Cagney and Lacey: a reaction against the male hegemony of the police series

(CBS, 1982–8) in America, emerging to challenge the masculine hegemony of the past (see D'Acci, 1987).

The 1990s also saw a significant development in the portrayal of policewomen with the appearance of Detective Chief Inspector (later Superintendent) Jane Tennison (Helen Mirren) in *Prime Suspect* (Granada, 1991–2006) (see Eaton, 1995; Brunsdon, 1998; Creeber, 2001b). More a crime drama than a police series, *Prime Suspect*, along with *Cracker* (Granada, 1993–), *NYPD Blue* and *Homicide: Life on the Streets* was part of a diversification of the police series in the 1990s as the genre reinvented itself in a more hybrid form (police/detective/crime drama) in an attempt to maximise and retain audiences in an increasingly competitive television market (Brunsdon, 1998; Eaton, 1995).

Although traditional, romantic, individualistic and typically English police detectives such as Morse, Dalgleish, Frost and Wexford remain popular on television, they appear to be a dying breed, being replaced by younger, trendier, female and ethnic counterparts (see Pines, 1995; Sparks, 1993; Thomas, 1997). Yet the ensemble-based, uniformed police series shows no signs of disappearing, with Britain's long-running *The Bill* (ITV, 1983–, see p. 8) still going strong, and new series, such as *City Central* (BBC, 1998–) and *Brooklyn South* (CBS, 1997) bearing witness to the perennial popular appeal of the genre.

Moreover, while *NYPD Blue* and *Homicide* have followed in *Hill Street Blues*' footsteps, being both experimental in style and progressive in content, two British series, *Between the Lines* (BBC, 1992–4) and *The Cops* (BBC, 1998), have shown that American television does not have a monopoly on the production of innovative, socially conscious police drama. The vérité style of *The Cops*, in particular, with its depiction of the police as 'ordinary human beings', with their own problems and flaws, demonstrates that the potential for using the police series to ask questions about the role of the police in contemporary society still survives (Eaton, 1995; MacMurraugh-Kavanagh, 2000; Nelson, 1997a; Wayne, 1998). What's more, new police shows such as *Life on Mars* (BBC, 2006–7) have become increasingly self-reflexive. By having DCI Sam Tyler (John Simm) of the Greater Manchester Police time-travel back to the year 1973, he is forced to face up to the differences between his own modern approach to policing and the more traditional methods of his historically located colleagues. Not only does a clash of cultures ensue, but also an inevitable clash of genres.

Lez Cooke

RECOMMENDED READING

Brunsdon, Charlotte (1998), 'Structure of Anxiety: Recent British Television Crime Fiction', *Screen*, vol. 39, no. 3.

Clarke, Alan (1992), '"You're Nicked!": Television Police Series and the Fictional Representation of Law and Order', in Dominic Strinati and Stephen Wagg (eds), *Come On Down? Popular Media Culture in Post-War Britain*, London: Routledge.

Jenkins, Steve (1984), '*Hill Street Blues*', in Jane Feuer, Paul Kerr and Tise Vahimagi (eds), *MTM – 'Quality Television'*, London: BFI.

Hospital Drama

In the mid-1990s a common observation made by critics and commentators was that the proliferation of television medical dramas had reached epidemic proportions. As one critic put it, 'At the moment there are so many medical series and serials being aired that if you watch a cleverly planned selection, you will soon be able to conduct your own operations' (Moir, 1996). Hospital dramas such as *ER* (NBC, 1994–), *Casualty* (BBC, 1986–) and *Chicago Hope* (CBS, 1994–2000) were at the forefront of this explosion of television's interest in medicine – which included documentaries, docusoaps, science fiction and daytime magazine programmes. Such dramas were also part of a wider growth in the depiction of professional working life on television (*NYPD Blue*, *The Bill*, *London's Burning* (ITV, 1986–2002), *This Life* (BBC, 1996–7)). The advantage of the hospital setting is that it is a ready-made receptacle for a variety of dramatic situations: as the creator of *Cardiac Arrest* (BBC, 1994–6) commented, 'anything can walk through the door – although they don't often walk' (*Radio Times*, 15–21 April 1995).

The 1950s saw the emergence of the first instances of what was to become the staple hospital drama formula, exemplified in shows such as *Medic* (NBC, 1954–5) and *Emergency – Ward 10* (BBC, 1957–67). These shows were based around an anthology format with self-contained weekly episodes and regular central characters; they were respectful of the growing power and authority of the medical institutions and took care to show that, whatever the outcome in individual cases, medical progress was inexorable. The shows were paternal in the sense that they sought to augment public trust in the medical profession, largely through the 'stamp of quality' provided by medical authorities such as the American Medical Association and

British Medical Association, which supplied medical advisers who would check scripts for 'medical accuracy', and who had a vested interest in making sure that their profession was represented positively.

It was important for these authorities that the shows did not encourage anxiety and hypochondria, but instead reassured the public. Reassurance was personified in the figure of the infallible, capable doctor – Kildare, Welby, Finlay. In the early shows the focus was on the individual doctor's central role in healing people; typically, the doctors were white males and the centre of authority in the hospital. Early hospital dramas aimed for realism and accuracy in their depiction of medical procedure (within the constraints of censorship and taste), balancing this against the gravitational pull of melodrama (understood by the industry as mere 'soap opera').

By the 1960s the hospital doctor was seen as working as part of a team, usually shown through a paternal relationship between the young doctor and more experienced teacher. The touchstone in the development of such hospital dramas was *Dr Kildare* (NBC, 1961–6), which presented the memorable 'father–son' relationship between Kildare (Richard Chamberlain) and his mentor and superior, Dr Gillespie (Raymond Massey). Set in a teaching hospital, it established the senior-to-junior doctor relationship as a nurturing one, where wisdom and knowledge were passed down without conflict. This was an important aspect of the genre: the education of a young, idealistic doctor was both instructional for the viewer and a way of showing how the eternal values of medical care and wisdom were reproduced in action. The show also situated Kildare not as an aloof member of a medical priesthood, but as a modern professional – committed, sincere, caring. Kildare also consolidated what was to become a pattern of later shows: patients (and their illnesses) were vehicles for the exploration of particular issues and topics.

By the late 1960s the figure of the individual doctor as infallible and godlike was becoming untenable. Although shows such as *Marcus Welby, MD* (ABC, 1967–75) restated many of the concerns of Kildare, it was possible to see changes in hospital drama that reflected a wider loss of confidence in medical institutions, medical science and doctors. This was also the period of an increasingly visible counter-culture populated by young people who defined themselves in conflict with the old establishment and its personifications. Television networks also needed to harvest the unpredictable youth demographic. *Medical Center* (CBS, 1971) can be seen as a response to these wider societal changes: it modifies the paternal teaching relationship to one of 'mutual respect' between senior and junior

ER

The creator of *ER* (NBC, 1994–), Michael Crichton – himself trained as a doctor at Massachussetts General Hospital – waited twenty years for his idea for the show to be taken seriously. *ER* (standing for Emergency Room) is the most successful and expensive hospital drama to date, at the time of writing in its fourteenth season. It won eight Emmys in its first year (matched only by *Hill Street Blues*) and its directors have included Quentin Tarantino. Despite the occasional (nostalgic) gesture towards the utopian view of medicine, it is unremittingly despairing. As two critics noted approvingly, 'The programme is as much about disillusionment as miracle surgery. It often ends on a downbeat, reflective note about personal and medical failures as well as the larger failures of American society … [the medical staff are rendered] gratifyingly as flawed human beings' (Cassidy and Taylor, 1997).

ER is an ensemble hospital drama, usually weaving three or four plot strands per episode, each continuing the development of the characters. It inherits many of the concerns and iconography of earlier instances of the genre – Mark Greene

(Anthony Edwards) inhabits the 'Hawkeye' role as the ban-jaxed humanist in a war zone; John Carter (Noah Wyle) is an idealistic Kildare to Peter Benton's (Eriq LaSalle) less than avuncular Gillespie; Doug Ross (George Clooney) plays the handsome but rebellious paediatrician bucking authority for the sake of his infant patients.

However, what makes *ER* stand out is the way in which complex character development is paced with the same urgency as the medical treatment itself. As one critic has put it, 'it's channel surfing without pressing the button, as scenarios and stories' progress 'through the *ER* room … at dizzying speed' (Lewis and Stempel, 1999, p. 120). The stylish pace and fluidity of *ER*'s camerawork is clearly intended to be expressive of the contemporary world as well as the emergency room – a world that is risky, uncertain and dangerous. Some have described its frenetic pace as excessive (perhaps a recognition of the way in which the show has modernised the melodramatic tendency of the genre), not in opposition to realism, but as an acknowledgment of a medicalised public sphere that is increasingly concerned with the dramatic potency of the traumatised human body.

Jason Jacobs

---

doctor. This show, like other hospital dramas of the 1970s, included frequent explicitness in the discussion of medical and social 'problems': abortion, homosexuality, rape, drug addiction, artificial insemination, venereal disease. Nonetheless, illness and injury continued to be catalysts for the exploration of human relationships, emotions, desires and morals.

Another generic change was from the single-doctor star (supported by older parental figures such as Dr Gillespie) to ward-based ensemble dramas. It was as if the impact of particular medical crises and their moral ramifications could no longer be credibly healed by one infallible figure.

M*A*S*H (CBS, 1972–83), one of the most successful television shows of all time and marketed as a sitcom, depicts the abandonment of the consensus-based depictions of medical care. Here, for the first time, we see doctors with no control over their environment, in a war zone healing patients so that they could go back to war and kill or be killed. *M*A*S*H* revitalised the form, by mixing black comedy with the humanist despair of Hawkeye (Alan Alda) so that the comedy had an ironic and desperate edge, exemplified in the title song, 'Suicide is Painless'. The doctors were no longer fighting against abstract forces of disease or the contingency of accidental injuries: their environment (including the regularly wounded patients)

were part of the problem, and contributed to their (comic, absurd) despair.

This focus on medical staff facing the negative impact of a hostile environment was continued in the UK with Paula Milne's gritty *Angels* (BBC, 1975–83), which followed the chaotic lives of student nurses, and G. K. Newman's *The Nation's Health* (C4, 1984), which sought to expose a corrupt and failing National Health Service.

These downbeat generic concerns were the focus in the two key hospital dramas of the 1980s: *St Elsewhere* (NBC, 1982–7) and *Casualty*. *St Elsewhere* was set in an under-funded Boston teaching hospital, St Eligius, and was heavily influenced by the visual and narrative style of *Hill Street Blues* (see box). The medical staff were less potent than ever, neither heroic nor cool under pressure, and they were also the primary focus: the patients were rapidly becoming background devices for the development of the central characters where we see a mainstreaming of 'existential issues' (yuppie angst) such as the spiritual burden of doing a high-pressure job: doctors were not only more fragile, but more introspective about their failing potency.

The BBC's *Casualty* is an ensemble hospital drama that began with a campaigning tone in relation to the UK welfare cuts of the 1980s; however, from the beginning it also maintained an overtly moralistic tone in relation to its patients. Inheriting the sense of the emergency ward of the hospital as a war zone, the creators of *Casualty* (originally called 'The Front Line') wanted the staff in the ward to wear military-style fatigues: the battle was with 'immoral' patients and a pernicious cost-cutting bureaucracy.

Both series showcased their sensitivity in relation to controversial issues (AIDS, homosexuality, organ donation, euthanasia) and both were dress rehearsals for the speedier dramas of the mid-1990s. They also exemplify the different styles of UK and US television: *St Elsewhere* relied on a cinematic house style that emphasised chaos and complexity, underwritten by solid acting and writing. *Casualty*'s writing was weaker, and it exemplified British cinema and television's obsession with montage as a preferred dramatic technique, using teasing vignettes of potential casualties and cross-cutting between them and the casualty ward into which they would soon (perhaps) be delivered. Both flaunted a visceral explicitness in the depiction of injury and in relation to controversial issues. At the same time the medical staff were also rendered as fragile workers caught between a rigid bureaucracy and the contingent violence of everyday life.

The 1990s represented an unprecedented intensification of the medicalisation of everyday life: regular health scares, the theorisation of the 'risk society', the state promotion of 'healthy living' as a moral as much as a medical imperative all contributed to a popular engagement with the fictional depiction of hospital life. At the same time, with the collapse of the old distinctions between Left and Right, and the narrowing of politics to a managerial role, any sense of social change became collapsed on to the body itself: 'The intense social concern about health is closely related to the cult of the body [fitness fads, body-building, dieting, piercing, plastic surgery]: once you give up on any prospect of achieving progress in society, your horizons are reduced to securing your own physical survival' (Fitzpatrick, 2000, p.160). The sense of humanist despair and impotence in the face of illness, disease and injury hinted at in *M*A*S*H* became normalised as an everyday feature of the genre. As Susan Sontag argues, 'A permanent modern scenario: apocalypse looms ... and it doesn't occur. And it still looms ... Apocalypse is now a long-running serial: not "Apocalypse Now" but "Apocalypse From Now On"' (Sontag, 1991, p.173).

Medical dramas of the mid-1990s engaged and developed this new apocalyptic ideology of health, as well as inheriting many of the generic concerns and interests of previous instances, setting them to a faster beat. In 1990s' hospital dramas there is a rapid alternation between scenes of action – emergency medical treatment – and those of reflection and introspection. The 'action mode' foregrounds the radical contingency of accidents and the 'sudden turn for the worse' that can befall patients. This is typically rendered in a fluid, restless visual style, complemented by medical technobabble that overlays the confusing immediacy of injury and treatment. These scenes alternate with moments of reflection, where characters assess the consequences of a medical procedure, for the patients and, more importantly, for themselves.

Cardiac Arrest represents a shift of attention in the genre from a concern with the patient and nation as victims of welfare cuts, to a concern with junior doctors as victims of a pernicious healthcare system who also suffer the weight of their depoliticised 'grunge' generation. The main characters, in their early to mid-twenties, are confronted by monstrous senior doctors (who represent a corrupt macho medical profession), sleep deprivation, debt and the tyranny of their bleepers. They are also faced with hospital managers interfering with their medical judgment, fuelled by the ideology and management-speak of the business sector from which they were recruited. In *Cardiac Arrest* the medical/moral education exemplified in the interaction of Gillespie and Kildare is banished to the realms of naive utopianism.

Jason Jacobs

RECOMMENDED READING

Jacobs, Jason (2003), *Body Trauma: The New Hospital Dramas*, London: BFI.

Karpf, Anne (1988), *Doctoring the Media*, London: Routledge.

Turow, Joseph (1989), *Playing Doctor: Television, Storytelling and Medical Power*, Oxford: Oxford University Press.

Science Fiction

Like much television drama, the earliest science-fiction (SF) television was based on novels or stage plays. Despite these origins, science-fiction television is not generally regarded as a high-culture form; instead, it has tended to be seen as popular entertainment, perhaps because of its association with aliens and special effects (see Baxter, 1970). The studio-bound setting of early television, and shooting on film for location work, imposed their own restrictions, and special effects work was time-consuming and expensive. However, the advent of location video in the 1970s and 1980s, gave programme-makers more flexibility, with forests and disused quarries becoming favourite stand-ins for alien landscapes (this was particularly the case at the BBC).

More significantly, the arrival of relatively affordable digital technology in the 1990s gave rise to higher production values and the opportunity for more elegant special effects. Underneath its unusual and often slightly flashy *mise en scène*, science-fiction television has a track record of addressing moral, ethical, political and philosophical themes – what Sobchack refers to as the 'intellectual development of an abstract premise' (1987, p. 25). In this respect, science fiction on television is, at best, notably different from many, although not all, of its special effects-driven counterparts in the cinema (see Hockley, 2000). For example, *Doctor Who* had an explicitly educational mission; *Star Trek* (NBC, 1966–9) tackled, on a weekly basis, problems of good and evil, the unreliable nature of technology and the potentially disastrous consequences of careless time travel (see box, and Hanely, 1997); and

Star Trek

In many ways *Star Trek*, in all its incarnations, is what people think of as science-fiction television. The first episode was transmitted in the USA on 8 September 1966 and had a run of three seasons with a total of seventy-nine fifty-minute episodes. It came to the UK some three years later, by which point the series had been axed in America. The NBC network had put considerable pressure on the creator of the series, Gene Roddenberry, to downplay some of its more unconventional aspects. But it was the multiracial (and indeed multispecies) crew and the exploration of themes such as racism, colonialism and human psychology that won the support of fans (see Jenkins, 1992b; Tulloch and Jenkins, 1995; Hills, 2004).

Although Captain James T. Kirk (William Shatner) was a full-blooded American, some critics argue that the series broke new ground in being explicitly multicultural with the female African-American Lt Uhura (Nichelle Nichols), the Japanese Mr Sulu (George Takei), the Russian Mr Chekov (Walter Koenig), the Scottish Montgomery 'Scotty' Scott (James Doohan) and the alien (or Vulcan) Mr Spock (Leonard Nimoy) on the bridge of the Starship *Enterprise*. However, as one might expect, its view of race is far from unproblematic (see, for instance, Barrett and Barrett, 2001). Indeed, some commentators have suggested that the alien species encountered in the series also represent racial caricatures – versions, for instance, of the Soviets (Klingons), Arabs (Cardassians) and Chinese (Romulans) (see Bernardi, 1998; Worland, 1998).

Largely as a result of fan pressure, a new series, *Star Trek: The Next Generation*, was commissioned in the USA in 1987 (UK, 1990). This was followed by two related series, *Star Trek: Deep Space Nine* (1993) and *Star Trek: Voyager* (1995). This amounts to 522 episodes and it is still growing. Typically, *Star Trek* is characterised as optimistic and progressive in its tone. As Kavanagh (1990, p. 74) puts it, 'Spock and Kirk are the most familiar recent mass-cultural version of [a] humanist ideological couple reconstructed in signifying practice'. But this also masks a reactionary strand to the series. For example,

the Federation's apparent willingness to make treaties with 'fascistic' regimes suggests a degree of conservatism, not unlike J. F. Kennedy's liberal domestic reforms, which contrasted with his essentially conservative foreign policy (Gregory, 2000). The colonial overtones of the imperative to 'seek out new life and new civilisations' that open every episode of *Star Trek* and *The Next Generation* cannot help but evoke some uneasy references to our history as colonisers and conquerors.

The Next Generation appears to perpetuate the omnipresence of the Federation (to which all 'right-thinking' planets belong), and reflects a particular hostility towards species that work and live as a collective, such as the Borgs. The Borgs were introduced as a genderless cyborg (part machine, part flesh) but have subsequently acquired a gender, and even a Borg Queen to lead them. They were originally intended as an evil vision of technological progress (the fear of being assimilated into the Collective), and the series thus self-consciously plays with notions of the ideal subject, subjectivity and gender (see Harrison et al., 1996; Harraway, 1995).

Originally, *Star Trek* was less than progressive in the revealing costumes it provided for female crew members: 'Uhura was little more than an intergalactic receptionist and no less than seventeen women died for the love of Kirk' (Lewis and Stempel, 1999, p. 324). The predominant sexual orientation remains heterosexual and the female crew members still have to be as attractive as they are effective. The first series to have a female captain was *Voyager*; however, even Captain Janeway (Kate Mulgrew) has been the subject of nude bathing scenes (see Penley, 1997; and Roberts, 1999).

Suggesting a postmodern self-reflexivity (see 'Postmodern Drama'), *The Next Generation* has a number of episodes that are parodies of other genres: 'The Big Goodbye' (film noir), 'Elementary Dear Data' (detective), 'A Fistful of Datas' (Western), 'Qpid' (Robin Hood) and 'Disaster' (disaster movie) (see Gregory, 2000). There is now an animated series, seven feature films and numerous novels; as such, it seems that *Star Trek*'s universe is inherently intertextual and forever expanding (see Epstein, 1996).

Luke Hockley

Star Trek produced an inherently intertextual universe

The X-Files

Moving away from the space operas of the *Star Trek* (see box) franchise, *The X-Files* (Fox, 1993–2002) situates its paranormal detective narratives within the contemporary reality of modern-day America. The series follows the investigations of two young FBI agents, Fox Mulder (David Duchovny) and Dana Scully (Gillian Anderson), into inexplicable cases of supernatural phenomena rejected by the bureau mainstream. Each episode depicts a different case, allowing the series to skirt between a number of interrelated genres: horror, detective, science fiction, thriller and comedy. The series integrates these self-contained narratives into a convoluted ongoing plot concerning a government conspiracy to conceal the presence of aliens from the general public, enabling it to combine an appeal to the loyal and the casual viewer.

The X-Files was produced by the then nascent Fox network, which was attempting to monopolise on the threat posed by cable and satellite to the three major networks that had dominated American television production from the late 1950s. At this point, Fox wanted to build on its reputation for comedies and teenage dramas by moving into drama production that would extend its demographic range into the eighteen to forty-nine age group (see 'The Teen Series'). Manipulating the generic fluidity of science-fiction television, the series attempted to integrate the basic structure of the detective genre (which was particularly successful in the early 1990s) with elements of horror and science fiction that were relatively absent from the network schedules at that time. The series became hugely successful both in America and internationally, spawning extensive marketing, a vociferous fan network and a spin-off film (*The X-Files: Fight the Future* (Bowman, 1998)), securing Fox's position as the fourth major network in American television broadcasting and reinvigorating the science-fiction genre during the 1990s.

The X-Files depicts an uncertain world in which the inability of its protagonists to prove the existence of the paranormal undermines the stability of truth and reality. This is complemented by a cinematic style, which takes advantage of the developments in film stock and digital technology to create a mysterious and foreboding visual landscape where nothing is quite what it seems. Academic attempts to address the signifi-

The X-Files: searching for meaning in an uncertain world

cance of what has since been called a 'popular culture phenomenon' (McLean, 1998, p. 4) have primarily focused on analysing the series' relevance to contemporary culture. *The X-Files'* conspiracy narratives of paranormal investigations have been associated with pre-millennial tension and the surge of interest and belief in alien abduction (Lavery, Hague and Cartwright, 1996; Dean, 1997). Postmodern theorists have argued that its treatment of history and multiplication of the truth exemplifies the ontological and epistemological crises in contemporary society (Kellner, 1999), whereas others argue for a modernist reading of the series, claiming that it maintains at its heart a belief that 'the truth is out there', to borrow from the series' oft-quoted catchphrase (McLean, 1998). These studies tend to concentrate on *The X-Files'* narrative and thematic treatment of contemporary anxiety, arguing that its success lies in its dark and unresolved storylines, which engage with a pervasive malaise in late-twentieth-century America.

Catherine Johnson

Babylon 5 (TNT, 1993–8) has more recently explored the intricate world of political intrigue.

Science-fiction television has tended to be an under-analysed and under-theorised area of academic study. Perhaps one of the reasons for this is that it eludes neat

classification (see Sobchack, 1987, for a good survey of attempts to define the science-fiction genre film). Significantly, what science-fiction television does, like its counterpart in the cinema, is to reflect contemporary social and political concerns. The genre developed dramatically

Doctor Who

Though often thought of as a science-fiction TV series by virtue of the fact that it features a time-travelling alien known only as the 'Doctor', *Doctor Who* (BBC, 1963–89; BBC/Fox, 1996; BBC Wales 2005–) is far broader and wider in its generic scope. It certainly doesn't correspond with notions of 'hard' science fiction, by which is typically meant drama extrapolating from known scientific laws (Wright, 1999). And it is also rather different from US 'space opera' of the likes of *Star Trek* (Tulloch and Jenkins, 1995), tending to carry an emphasis on the connotative 'Englishness' and eccentricity of the time-travelling Doctor. In its 'classic' version, *Doctor Who* has been described by scholars as a kind of 'Romantic gothic' science fiction (Tulloch and Alvarado, 1983, p. 134), focusing on doublings of identity (the Time Lord character, the Doctor, versus other evil Time Lords) and on transforming the earthly and familiar into something monstrous or unearthly, such as a police box which can travel through space and time, or plastic shop-window dummies animated by an alien consciousness (Newman, 2005).

The latest incarnation of the programme uses these same devices, frequently coming over as 'body-horror for tea-time television' (Miles and Wood, 2004, p. 17) just as 1970's *Doctor Who* did at the time of its peak popularity (Chapman, 2006). But what's been dubbed 'New Who' adds to the generic mix of *Doctor Who* by hybridising the show's science-fictional elements such as time travel with the generic verisimilitude of soap opera or more general 'TV drama': for example, the Doctor's young companions Rose (Billie Piper), Donna (Catherine Tate) and Martha (Freema Agyeman) are now shown to have home and family lives which they only partly leave behind to travel with the Doctor. And the 2005 show is also notably 'authored' TV, with long-term *Doctor Who* fan, Russell T. Davies (*Queer as Folk* (C4, 1990–2000)) bringing his auteurist style to the proceedings as executive producer and lead writer, most notably in bittersweet episodes such as series two's 'Love & Monsters' and the series three hymn to human faith, 'Gridlock', as well as in story arcs concerning the theme of unrequited love.

Contemporary *Doctor Who* could perhaps best be thought of as 'science fantasy-adventure with a heart' – or even two hearts – which has successfully appealed to male and female audiences through its adventure/soap hybridisations, along with adult and child viewers via its combination of political satire with scary monsters. The generic label 'telefantasy' (Johnson, 2005) is a useful term to cover the programme's mixture of real-world and fantastic elements, such as the Doctor's ability to regenerate (and hence be played by different actors, e.g. Christopher Eccleston and David Tennant), and the show's cultural icons of monstrosity, the Daleks. Doctor Who's finely tuned generic hybridity – soap/satire/science fiction/horror/adventure – has enabled it to function as Saturday-night 'family television' in the UK, despite twenty-first-century TV industry wisdom that the fragmented TV audience could no longer be united around a single drama. Indebted to the narrative structures and aesthetics of US 'cult' and 'quality' TV, BBC Wales' *Doctor Who* has nevertheless condensed these influences into quality popular Welsh television.

Matt Hills

after the bombing of Hiroshima and during the Cold War period, giving rise to a mix of technological utopias and dystopias. For example, *V* (NBC, 1984–5) and *Star Trek* (particularly in its depiction of the Klingons) suggest the continual fear of 'the Other', a fear that continues in *Star Trek: The Next Generation* (Syndicated, 1987–94) and *Star Trek: Voyager* (UPN, 1995–2001) as a fear of assimilation into the 'Borg' collective (see Gregory, 2000, and the '*Star Trek*' box).

British science-fiction television started life with two BBC one-off plays. The first was adapted from Karel Capek's philosophical drama about robots, *RUR* (1937). The second was H. G. Wells's *The Time Machine* (1949). These introduced what were to become two key themes in science-fiction television, time travel and technologically produced human simulacra, and prepared the way for the first British science-fiction television serial, *Stranger from Space* (BBC, 1951). Made for children, this was broadcast fortnightly and, showing that interactive television is nothing new, viewers were asked to write in with suggestions about how the story might develop. In 1953, the BBC returned to adult science fiction and transmitted the first of its three serials featuring the rocket scientist Quatermass (the fourth *Quatermass* serial in 1979 was produced by Euston Films, a subsidiary of Thames Television). The next attempt to produce a science-fiction series for adults in the UK came with *A for Andromeda* (BBC, 1961) and its sequel *The Andromeda Breakthrough* (BBC, 1962). It is a testament to the strength of these narratives (which explore cloning, environmental and Cold War issues) that they remain of interest today. However, as Joy Leman points out (1991, p. 123), they can never quite escape the historical moment in which they were made:

Whilst science fiction would seem to take us outside of [the] structuring elements of class and gender by a discourse of fantasy and futurism, the metaphorical transformations always speak about the historical time in which the production took place. The science fiction serials of the 1950s and 60s offered innovative possibilities both in form and content, but were finally limited to the dominant constructions of class and gender of their time.

1963 saw the start of the BBC's *Doctor Who* series, which became a British science-fiction classic and the longest-running television science-fiction series. It was created by Sydney Newman (see 'The Single Play'), who had come from ABC Television, where he had produced the sci-fi series *Target Luna* (1960) and its sequel *Pathfinders* (1960). The central character, referred to just as the 'Doctor', is a Time Lord who uses the TARDIS to travel through time and space; in a typically quirky British move this vehicle was disguised as a police telephone box. There have been eight television Doctors, and each has been played by a different actor (the Doctor can conveniently 'regenerate' his body up to thirteen times) (see grey box).

Each of the Doctors has also had a different 'Assistant', normally female. These ploys, along with the TARDIS, ensured a variety of locations and actors (see Tulloch and Alvarado, 1990a). Aliens, such as the Daleks and the Cybermen, were less psychological or political than their *Star Trek* counterparts and tended to pose a direct physical threat to the Doctor or his Assistant, or indeed to Earth itself. However, like *Star Trek* it has dedicated fans that have exerted considerable pressure on the BBC to ensure the longevity of 'their' series (see Tulloch and Jenkins, 1995; for a more subversive use by fans of *Star Trek*, see Penley, 1997). Part of its attraction was clearly its unique ability to transcend a number of generic categories. According to Tulloch and Alvarado (1990a, p. 311):

Doctor Who challenged assumptions around the 'popular/serious' debate

As a popular series, *Doctor Who* is inescapably wedded to ratings and stardom. And yet the 'popular/serious' opposition is clouded by two considerations: the origins of the programme as 'education' as well as 'entertaining' and 'adult' as well as 'children's' drama, so that a considerable 'serious' audience has been built up over the years; and more importantly, by the fact that SF as a genre challenges the 'popular/serious' interface of the culture industries.

The 1960s also saw ITV commission a clutch of children's science-fiction puppet shows. They were created by Gerry and Sylvia Anderson and developed the techniques established in their previous series *Supercar* (1961) and *Fireball XL5* (1962). *Stingray* (ITV, 1964), *Thunderbirds* (ITV, 1965), *Captain Scarlet and the Mysterons* (ITV, 1967) and *Joe 90* (ITV, 1968) all acquired a cult following. The quirky puppetry, which Anderson dubbed 'supermarionation', the special effects that were overseen by Derek Meddings and the visual novelty of the programmes ensured the popularity of the series. However, in America, science fiction was taking a rather different route, with higher production values and narratives that were explicitly moral in their message – none more so than *The Twilight Zone* (CBS, 1959–64), which explored a mixture of science fiction, fantasy and psychological themes, including psychic premonitions, alien invasions, abductions and time travel. Some of the cast of *Star Trek*, including William Shatner (Captain Kirk) and Leonard Nimoy (Mr Spock), made guest appearances on the show. As Jeffrey Scounce (1997, p. 1454) points out, science-fiction narratives were usually employed by the series simply in an attempt to create morally informed storylines.

The Twilight Zone was an anthology series that, while not exclusively based in science fiction, frequently turned to the genre to frame allegorical tales of the human condition and America's national character. Some of the most memorable episodes of the series used science fiction to defamiliarise and question the conformist values of postwar suburbia as well as the rising paranoia of Cold War confrontation.

In 1978 Terry Nation (inventor of the Daleks in *Doctor Who*) created the BBC's *Blake's 7* (BBC, 1978–81). Strong characters, but typically bad props and sets (the use of quarries and forests as locations continued) gave the series a familiar feel that endeared it to many viewers. One of the more innovative programmes produced by the BBC was the unlikely *Hitch-Hiker's Guide to the Galaxy* (BBC, 1981). The series, which started on the BBC's Radio 4, developed a dedicated following, with its mixture of comedy, philosophical musing and aurally rich backgrounds. Given the budget of the television version, it is perhaps not surprising that the appearance of a two-headed Zaphod Beeblebrox (Mark Wing-Davey) and Marvin (David Learner), a paranoid android, were not entirely successful in their costumes or make-up. However, the quality of the writing, by Douglas Adams (an earlier writer for *Doctor Who*), and the computer graphics for the book ensured that the series was consistently funny and visually appealing. In part, the series prepared the way for the science-fiction parody *Red Dwarf* (BBC, 1989–99), which became BBC2's longest-running comedy.

The 1990s saw the start of a vast number of new science-fiction series. Some were unsuccessful, like Gerry Anderson's blend of live action and puppetry in *Space Precinct* (Sky, 1994–5). Others, such as the children's *Mighty Morphin Power Rangers* (Fox, 1993–6) with its bizarre blend of martial arts and monsters, have been a success with viewers (if not critics). Derived from the film of the same title, *Stargate SG-1* (Showtime, 1997–2007) has emphasised special effects over narrative interest, while *Babylon 5* has introduced new levels of sophistication to special effects with its digitally generated spaceships against which it sets its own political narratives. Finally, just to show that there is nothing new in the cosmos, *Doctor Who* was finally relaunched to considerable acclaim in 2005 (see grey box).

Luke Hockley

RECOMMENDED READING

Fulton, Roger and Betancourt, John (2000) *Encyclopedia of TV Science Fiction*, London: Boxtree.

Harrison, Taylor, Projansky, Sarah, Ono, Kent and Helford, Elyce (eds) (1996), *Enterprise Zones: Critical Positions on 'Star Trek'*, Oxford: Westview Press.

Lavery, David, Hague, Angela and Cartwright, Marla, (eds) (1996), *Deny All Knowledge: Reading* 'The X-Files', London: Faber and Faber.

Drama–Documentary

'Drama–documentary' is the label most often used in Britain and parts of Europe to indicate the combination of dramatic and documentary elements in a programme. In the USA, the term 'docudrama' has been the preferred term. Rather than a distinct subgenre of programme, it is best to see the classification as pointing to a very wide range of different mixtures.

Drama–documentary has been a controversial area of work, one around which a good deal of analysis and

Cathy Come Home

Cathy Come Home (written by Jeremy Sandford, directed by Ken Loach, produced by Tony Garnett) was screened by BBC1 on 16 November 1966 within the regular Wednesday Play slot (see 'The Single Play'). It is a 'drama–documentary' concerning homelessness and its effect upon families (Corner, 1996, pp. 90–108, gives it a full critical appraisal). The programme has become a British TV 'classic', regularly referred to by critics and researchers. Part of the status accorded to *Cathy* is undoubtedly owing to its particular qualities of scripting, direction and acting, but part follows from the way in which it has been seen to focus and exemplify questions about the mixing of dramatic with documentary material and, more generally, about the public power of television.

Cathy is organised as a narrative about a young woman who marries, has children and who then, following an accident to her husband that results in his loss of job and family poverty, suffers various states of homelessness in poor or temporary accommodation until her children are taken into care by the social services. The programme adopts an episodic structure, depicting the stages in the decline of Cathy and her family across a number of years. It is held together by the commentary of Cathy herself, a commentary that is given in a self-reflective past tense and that not only introduces and ends the programme but is heard regularly throughout it, providing a bridge between episodes and a source of additional explanation to that obtained by watching events unfold. Cathy both tells us more about what is happening and keeps us closer to it by her subjectively involved recounting.

The 'documentary' element of *Cathy* is partly a matter of depictive style and partly a matter of the amount of time the script gives to portraying aspects of the general problem of homelessness in addition to advancing its storyline.

Stylistically, the programme has a number of scenes that are shot in the documentary mode of action-led camera, with events appearing to develop spontaneously and to be caught by the filming. The resulting effect is one of high immediacy values, providing the viewer with a strong sense of 'witness'. A documentarist element is more directly present in the use of commentary and brief 'viewpoint' voice-over at several points in the film, offering statistics on the housing situation and allowing various perspectives on it to be heard in a manner that follows conventional documentary practice.

Most of the newspaper critics recognised the impact and quality of the programme. Public discussion of it tended to circulate around two issues: the possibility of the audience being deceived into according to it a greater truth than was warranted by its fictional status, and the way in which the account was a 'biased' one, depicting officials as uncaring and often hostile in a manner that would have been unacceptable in a conventional documentary.

It is hard to imagine any viewer believing that *Cathy* was actuality footage, so extensively is it conceived of in terms of narrative fiction. However, doubt clearly existed in some viewers' minds as to whether it was a story based directly on a real incident, or whether (as was actually the case) Cathy's tale was a construction developed from a range of researched instances. The legitimacy of combining dramatic licence with the documentary requirement to be 'impartial' was queried by several commentators, not for the first time nor the last (Goodwin, Kerr and Macdonald (1983) offer several useful extracts from the contemporary debate).

Against these complaints, other critics defended the programme-makers' right to use emotional tactics in order to engage the viewer with public issues, and pointed to the way in which the programme's view of officialdom was essentially the view of Cathy herself – in their eyes, a perfectly proper use of character viewpoint from which audience members could measure their own distance.

John Corner

---

debate has developed (Paget (1998) is an essential critical commentary). Quite apart from whatever specific issue it raises in relation to chosen topics and themes, it presents us with some central questions about the nature of audiovisual representation. Some academic critics have found it problematic to separate in the first place the two 'sides' that drama–documentary brings together. They have seen 'documentary' to be a narrative form relying extensively on different kinds of artifice. Conversely, they have also seen much 'drama' to be grounded in real circumstances, carrying a commitment to the exploration of real problems. By contrast, many commentators in the press and many public figures have regarded any kind of fusion of the two modes as an unacceptable blurring of boundaries, likely to misinform and mislead the public.

It makes some sense, certainly within the British and European tradition of practice, to draw a rough division between two kinds of work. There is that work that has developed as a documentary project, with degrees of dramatisation (through scripting and acting) added to give it stronger projection. Then, there is work that has developed very much in the conventional manner of a play (a script emerging largely from individual creative work, which is then cast and shot) but that has employed some of the looks and sounds of documentary material to deliver a more 'realist' impact. Within British television, the first kind of project has often been called 'dramatised documentary' whereas the second has been referred to as 'documentary drama'.

Examples of the 'dramatising' of documentary projects can be found in the pioneer television of the 1950s. The main reason for dramatisation here was the inaccessibility of so many different areas of social life to the cumbersome technology of television at that stage of its development. Thus dramatisation was to a degree a necessity for a good range of documentary engagement, although the added popularity of presenting character and action in this way was not lost on producers. Early examples of the 'documentarisation' of drama also exist: for instance, a number of British films made in the Second World War set their fictional occurences within a very firm context of documentary-style footage. Corner (1996, pp. 35–8) gives a brief account of this earlier filmic and televisual history, with examples.

There is no doubt that it becomes quite difficult to place some works into the right category, whereas others are more easily seen as belonging to the one or the other. A good general principle is to separate off questions of *reference* from questions of *depiction*, even if this is sometimes hard to do. Questions of reference concern how a particular programme relates itself to the real world, with what degree of specificity as to people, places, times, events and actions. There is a spectrum here, running all the way from the loose 'based on a real incident' model through to the tightly researched reconstruction of, say, a trial (where transcripts are available upon which to ground the dialogue). Knowing just what the relations of reference are in any given 'drama–documentary' sometimes poses a problem, particularly since these relations often shift from scene to scene. Strong referential claims clearly raise questions about the scale and strength of the evidence that supports them and therefore about the quality of the research lying behind the depiction. In general, and not surprisingly, programmes constructed from a documentary base have a more specific, reconstructive character than those emerging directly from playscripts.

Questions of depiction concern the extent to which the audiovisual depiction follows the 'rules' either of dramatic or documentary representation. For instance, is voice-over commentary used? Do certain scenes appear to be straight actuality footage? In what ways are we asked to relate to the characters as real people appearing before the camera rather than as acted roles? It is worth noting here that, whereas 'dramatised documentary' might include conventional documentary material alongside the dramatised sequences, it is likely that, with the exception of brief scenes from archive footage, most of a documentary–drama will be the product of full directorial management of scripted action and speech.

The biggest single issue in public discussion of drama–documentary (of both kinds outlined above) is that of possible confusion among the audience. In fact, a confusion about the fundamental status of what is being watched (is it really happening or is being acted out?) is far less likely than a confusion about how what is dramatically depicted relates to what did actually happen or, more loosely, what might well have happened. It is the way in which drama–documentary stimulates and sometimes shocks the social and historical imagination of the audience that has been at the core of concern. Where the topic is itself already a sensitive one (raising questions, for instance, of national history, social inequality or injustice or misuse of official or corporate power), then a 'dramatisation' will often serve to cause a controversy to flare up.

In Britain during the 1960s and 1970s, a number of writers, directors and producers used the 'documentary drama' format precisely to generate this kind of debate around questions that had, in their view, been neglected and that had escaped the scrutiny of orthodox documentary programmes because of the timidity of programme-makers, the elusiveness of the material or its historical non-availability. Such an approach fitted well with the contemporary form of the 'realist' play, taking a theme from ordinary life and giving it a provocative realisation in which story and background were both given weight. Indeed, classic forms of the 'documentary drama' blur into the forms of television realist drama (this is certainly the case with *Cathy Come Home* (BBC, 1996)) (see the box headed 'The Wednesday Play' and the box in this section). On the whole, the strand of 'dramatised documentary' offers less fluent, less fully rendered and less aesthetically satisfying depictions, partly because it is still interested in carrying out a job of reporting and analysis alongside, and underneath, its more dramatic business.

It is interesting that dramatic reconstruction has found its way into a variety of documentary formats in recent years, including the newer 'reality TV' shows (this application is usefully explored by Kilborn and Izod, 1997). Rarely, however, is it used as the only mode of depiction within the programme. So the 'dramatised documentary' continues, if mostly in part- rather than whole-programme usage. What

The Day After

The Day After (ABC, 1983, written by Edward Hume, directed by Nicholas Meyer, produced by Robert Papazian), a drama–documentary about nuclear war and its aftermath, was screened across the USA in November 1983 and on the British ITV network some three weeks later. It gained huge ratings in America, being watched by an estimated half of the adult population. The British audience was a moderately sized one, with the film receiving a cool reception from many newspaper critics, who saw it as lacking the aesthetic discipline that the subject required.

The theme of the disastrous consequences of nuclear war had been treated in Britain almost twenty years earlier in Peter Watkin's classic *The War Game* (BBC, 1965), a film that was banned from broadcast transmission at the time (ostensibly because of its frightening nature, although it is now clear that its implications for government defence policy were seen to be unacceptable).

The Day After incorporates key features from both the American soap opera and the Hollywood disaster movie, as well as containing other generic elements. By shadowing familiar generic forms it gains increased emotional power and popular accessibility. However, such a generic project shifts it away from a 'social realist' plausibility of character, action and setting that many British audiences and critics are more used to in the handling of a major public issue on screen.

The narrative of the film involves a lengthy period of build-up, as a superpower confrontation in Europe becomes increasingly dangerous. A nuclear strike on the town of Lawrence, Kansas, is chosen as the focus for the story, and a 'community' of people working on the site of the University of Kansas provides an inner grouping of victims/survivors. To these are added others, including a group of serviceman on duty at a nearby missile silo. There is a clear 'lead' role, a medical academic, played by a well-known actor, Jason Robards. His experience and feelings provide a centre for the account, one to which it regularly returns.

In her excellent discussion of the film, Susan Boyd-Bowman notes how American drama–documentary 'privileges the dramatic fiction over the factual documentation' (1984, p. 85). This is certainly true, despite sequences of documentary-style footage, including library film of bombers and missiles. She also makes the cogent case that the interweaving of generic discourses finally becomes unsatisfactory across the different components of soap opera (see p. 47), melodrama,

The Day After combined melodrama and social exploration

science fiction (see p. 26), horror, disaster movie, documentary (see p. 124) and 'art television' (the latter strand manifest in the elegant and self-consciously symbolic styling frequently employed).

It is possible to argue, nevertheless, that this pulling together of different modes, although it might look messy to critics, was a key factor in making the film continuously watchable, powerful and effective for the huge audience. In order to understand it properly, perhaps a certain sympathetic contact has to be made with the popular meanings and values of 'America' as these might be threatened and destroyed by the events we witness. There is, for instance, a sentimental play on the rural landscape (farms and livestock) and on the honest and Christian virtues of hard work and family life. But there is also some serious exploration of underlying tensions within the family unit and, indeed, of broader tensions within the social order.

This combination of melodrama with social exploration as well as issue-focused shock is familiar to us from many of the best American films, and it would be wrong to underestimate the sheer cumulative force of *The Day After*'s recipe of ingredients. The ending of the film offers little hope – the Jason Robards character stumbles through a scene of devastation and debris and is sorrowfully embraced by a fellow survivor, both sinking down on their knees. In its use of popular tropes and narrative devices to engage an American audience with a crucial issue of national policy and, indeed, national destiny, *The Day After* deserves to be seen as a major television achievement.

John Corner

of the documentary–drama? This continues too, as an occasional item, but it is much more likely now to organise its looks and sounds in relation to established fictional genres (such as thriller or disaster movie) rather than to imitate documentary appearance. This is partly because of the way in which the terms of realism in television fiction have moved away from that convergence with the codes of documentary that was so apparent in the 1960s.

The manner in which television narratives can relate both to the imaginative realm of fiction and the real historical world continues to be a topic of public interest and critical fascination. As well as Paget (1998), there is an excellent collection of articles in Rosenthal (1999). The history of 'drama–documentary' is one of the most interesting strands in the whole history of television as a public medium. The questions of motive, method and form that work in this strand has posed deserve the scholarly attention that they will continue to receive.

John Corner

RECOMMENDED READING

Corner, J. (1996), *The Art of Record*, Manchester: Manchester University Press.
Paget, D. (1998), *No Other Way to Tell It: Dramadoc/ Docudrama on Television*, Manchester: Manchester University Press.
Rosenthal, A. (ed.) (1999), *Why Docudrama?*, Carbondale and Edwardsville: Southern Illinois University Press.

The Mini-Series

The increased serialisation and complexity of television drama means that it has become increasingly difficult to make clear distinctions between the series, serial and mini-series (see 'The Uses and Limitations of Genre'). However, as a crude guide, a series like *The Avengers* (see box), *Cagney and Lacey* and *Charlie's Angels* (ABC, 1976–81) are generally made up of a separate number of episodes that are usually self-contained with 'no final resolution' (Butler, 1994a, p. 29). As John Ellis puts it, 'the series implies the

form of the dilemma rather than that of resolution and closure' (1989, p. 135). This broad definition can also include an 'anthology' series like *The Twilight Zone* or *Boys from the Blackstuff* (BBC, 1982), 'a group of separate plays linked together by a theme and title' (Self, 1984, p. 25).

In contrast, the storyline within a *serial* is usually carried *over* from one instalment to another. This explains Newcomb's suggestion that they can also be referred to as 'cumulative narratives' or 'arc' shows (cited by Feuer, 1995, pp. 111–12). The serial itself can be further divided into those shows that are specifically engineered to run continuously and those that are designed to reach a final conclusion. So whereas a *continuous* serial, such as *Dallas* (CBS, 1978–91) or *ER*, is commissioned to run indefinitely (see Geraghty, 1987, pp. 9–26), a *finite* or '*closed*' serial, such as *Prime Suspect* or *Murder One* (ABC, 1996) has a fixed and *limited* number of episodes that (discounting sequels) are generally intended to reach some form of closure (however loose) in the final instalment. As Sarah Kozloff puts it (1992, pp. 90–1):

> *Series* refers to those shows whose characteristics and settings are recycled, but the story concludes in each individual episode. By contrast, in a *serial* the story and discourse do not come to a conclusion during an episode, and the threads are picked up again after an hiatus. A series is thus similar to an anthology of short stories, while a serial is like a serialized Victorian Novel. Serials can be further divided into those that do eventually end (despite the misnomer, miniseries belong in this category) and those, such as soap opera, that maybe canceled but never reach a conclusion, a new equilibrium.

Whereas the continuous or never-ending serial is frequently associated with soap opera, the finite serial or *mini-series* (a term originating from its heyday in 1970s' America) has sometimes been linked with less 'formulaic' drama. Because of its inbuilt narrative arc, it is arguable that characters and storylines are frequently given more room to change, evolve and develop. As Patricia Holland (1997, p. 114) explains, its movement towards a final resolution is 'in many ways an expansion of the creative coherence of the single play'. As a result, a mini-series like *Edge of Darkness* (BBC, 1985), *The Singing Detective* (BBC, 1986 – see box) and *Twin Peaks* (ABC, 1990–1 – see p. 10) have given the genre a reputation for frequently producing innovative, challenging and hugely popular drama.

As well as being considerably cheaper to produce than the single play, it could be argued that the mini-series more successfully exploits the fundamental dynamics of television consumption. In particular, they tend to encourage intense audience involvement through the use of multi-narrative cumulative storylines that (with the help of conventional cliffhangers) tends to bring back audiences week after week. However, like the single play, they are occasionally marketed around the name of a single writer (Lynda La Plante's *Prime Suspect*) or director (David Lynch's *Twin Peaks* – see box), delivering the prestige of

Roots

This landmark television mini-series (first shown in America on ABC in 1977 and subtitled *Triumph of an American Family*) began life as Alex Haley's work of 'faction', a novel that dramatised his own family tree, tracing his Negro descendants back to Africa. In order to raise money while writing it, Haley sold the rights to legendary television producer David Wolper, who apparently convinced him that a 'two-hour theatrical film would cut too much of the plot' (cited by Stark, 1997, p. 200). Running twelve hours long, the decision to broadcast it over eight successive nights was made as much out of caution as courage. As Wolper puts it: 'ABC was a little nervous about it so they put on all the shows in one week so if it was a disaster they'd get rid of it all in one week' (cited by Wheen, 1985, p. 152; see also Fishbein, 1983, pp. 279–80). Indeed, there was some reason for caution, as ABC's Fred Silverman later put it: 'Here's a twelve-hour story where the whites are the villains and the blacks are the heroes in a country that is 85 per cent white. It doesn't sound like a good idea at first blush' (cited by Stark, 1997, p. 200). This partly explains the inclusion of some well-known black faces such as Maya Angelou and even O. J. Simpson in the cast: an attempt to limit the alienation of white audiences (see Creeber, 2004b, pp. 23–30).

However, the mini-series (directed by Marvin J. Chomsky, David Green and Gilbert Moses) became one of the most popular television dramas in American history, the last episode being watched by 80 million people. Although its version of history was regarded by many as dubiously sensational (see Ross, 1996, pp. 97–8), *Roots* clearly touched the guilty heart of America in its bicentennial year. Despite its complex dramatisation of various generations – beginning with Kunta Kinte (Le Var Burton) in 1700s Gambia and his horrific shipment to America; the story of his daughter Kizzy (Leslie Uggans), raped by a white plantation owner, and her son, Chicken George (Ben Vereen); finally ending with Tom Harvey's (Georg Stanford Brown) emancipation – the story proved powerfully addictive. It seemed that the intensity of the scheduling produced an almost 'soap-like' familiarity with

Roots touched the guilty heart of America

characters and events. Occasional cliffhangers also kept viewers in suspense, eagerly awaiting the next dramatic instalment.

In 1979, ABC aired its sequel *Roots: The Next Generation*, taking the story from the Civil War to the present day. It also inspired a whole host of other mini-series (frequently scheduled over consecutive nights), most notably *Holocaust*, a four-part mini-series that controversially dramatised Hitler's extermination of the Jews. Wolper would later say that a successful mini-series should either be based on a bestselling novel, have 'sociological significance' or be a family saga (see Stark, 1997, p. 202). *Roots*, to its credit, had all three.

Glen Creeber

The Singing Detective

Originally a writer of single plays, Dennis Potter (1935–1994) apparently came reluctantly to the serial form. However, by the time he wrote *Pennies from Heaven* (BBC, 1978), his six-part serial set in the 1930s (which famously included characters suddenly bursting (or 'lip-synching') into song), he seemed to relish the freedom and breadth of vision offered by the cumulative narrative. Eight years later, a similar sort of innovation and commitment helped produce *The Singing Detective* (BBC, 1986), 'one of the major works of post-war British culture' (Caughie, 2000, pp. 27–8). Co-produced by his long-term collaborator Kenith Trodd, Potter's six-part 'mini-series' is essentially a first-person narrative, its famously convoluted storyline taking place primarily inside the head of Philip Marlow (Michael Gambon). A writer of 'cheap detective thrillers' (Stead, 1993, p. 108), Marlow is bedridden in a London hospital suffering from an acute case of psoriatic arthropathy, a debilitating skin and joint disease suffered by Potter himself (see Purser, 1981, p. 172; Fuller, 1993, pp. 12–13; Carpenter, 1998, pp. 125–6). During this enforced process of self-reflection he looks back on his life and childhood, retreats into a world of pulp fantasy, rages against an unjust universe and reluctantly endures therapy. In doing so, the serial takes the viewer on a remarkably complex psychological journey, gradually and teasingly revealing insights into his unstable, unhealthy and frequently unreliable mind (see Creeber, 2007).

Marlow's interior landscape is 'entertainingly' played out through a number of different and conflicting narrative levels, all competing for prominence and comprehension in his sick, acerbic and unmistakably Freudian mind (see Delaney, 1988, pp. 511–21; Lichenstein, 1990, pp. 168–72; Creeber, 1998, pp. 166–78). Hospital sitcom, lip-synching hallucinations, childhood flashbacks, film noir detective stories and misogynistic fantasies create a heady, extraordinary and frequently breathtaking mixture of narrative/generic techniques that finally forces him to face up to his personal demons (see Hilfer, 2000). The serial form proved to be a perfect vehicle for such a complex narrative structure, forcing audiences to come back week after week, desperate (perhaps like Marlow himself) to slowly piece together the shattered fragments of his troubled life (see Prys, 2007). So unusual were many of Potter's techniques that it led some critics to define the serial as essentially 'modernist' (see Cook, 1995, p. 144; Creeber, 1996, pp. 501–8; Caughie, 2000, pp. 168–71), while others preferred to interpret it as quintessentially 'postmodern' (see

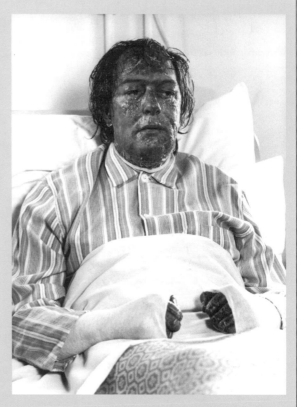

The Singing Detective: a complex psychological journey

Corrigan, 1991, pp. 179–93; Bondebjerg, 1992, pp. 161–80; Gras, 2000, pp. 95–108. See also 'Postmodern Drama', p. 54).

Many critics and journalists have tended to conceive Potter's 'serial masterpiece' (Day-Lewis, 1998, p. 24) as essentially biographical and its production as an almost solitary expression of a tortured artist (for discussion see Coward, 1987, pp. 79–87; Creeber, 1998, pp. 11–24). However, Joost Hunningher was one of the first critics to reveal the long and collaborative process that finally brought the serial to the screen. Notoriously overlooked by commentators at the time, its director Jon Amiel not only had enormous influence on how it would finally look, but even demanded that Potter rewrite important areas of the script before shooting (Hunninger, 1993, pp. 243–5; see also Gilbert, 1995, pp. 267–72; Cook, 1995, pp. 217–22; Nelson, 1997a, pp. 204–6; Carpenter, 1998, pp. 447–54). The construction of probably the most famous of all Potter scenes, the sequence when the doctors and nurses suddenly begin singing and dancing to 'Dry Bones', actually came about through intense collaboration between Amiel, Quinny Sacks (the choreographer) and

Jim Clay (the designer). However, what is clear is that the final product has become a benchmark against which some critics would argue that 'quality television' is now judged. It certainly utilised all the strengths of serialisation, taking narrative, thematic and character development way beyond what Potter had produced in the past or would sadly achieve in the future.

Glen Creeber

authorship seldom attributed to the series or soap opera. So while the series and continuous serial are often equated with the lower end of the quality divide, the mini-series has frequently (although not always) achieved a higher cultural status, sometimes compared with the serialised Victorian novel.

Not surprisingly, classic literary adaptations such as *I, Claudius* (BBC, 1976*), Brideshead Revisited* (ITV, 1981) and *Middlemarch* (BBC, 1994) have found their natural home in the finite serial form (see 'Costume Drama'). Such drama has frequently sold worldwide, enhancing its reputation as both an immensely popular and lucrative genre. Less prestigious but no less successful, *Rich Man, Poor Man* (ABC, 1976) was arguably television's first hit mini-series. Adapted from Irwin Shaw's 1970 blockbuster and originally shown in nine weekly instalments, it averaged 40 million viewers and won three Emmy awards. Other hugely successful adaptations of contemporary melodrama included *Bouquet of Barbed Wire* (ITV, 1976), *The Thorn Birds* (ABC, 1983) and *North and South* (ABC, 1985–94). Meanwhile, adaptations of contemporary novels such as *Tinker, Tailor, Soldier, Spy* (BBC, 1979), *The Life and Loves of a She Devil* (BBC, 1986) and *Lonesome Dove* (CBS, 1989) have continued to win the genre both large audiences and considerable critical acclaim.

The mini-series has also proved an unusually successful genre for dramatising large historical narratives. Whereas *Days of Hope* (BBC, 1975), *Edward and Mrs Simpson* (ITV, 1978) and *Kennedy* (NBC, 1983) took on specific historical events, others – *The Winds of War* (ABC 1983), *Fortunes of War* (BBC, 1987) and *Our Friends in the North* (BBC, 1997), for example – tended to use history as a rich and epic background (see Caldwell, 1995a). In particular, mini-series such as *Roots* (see box), *Holocaust* (NBC, 1978), *Das Boot* (Bavaria Atelier, 1982) and *Heimat* (WDR/SFB, 1984) have sometimes been criticised for turning complex historical debates into little more than soap-opera fare. In contrast, critics such as Creeber have argued that the serial's personalisation of the past creates a complex *Alltagsgeschichte* ('a history of the everyday'), providing a large and multilayered form of historical discourse rarely equalled by the single-text dynamics of either the cinema or theatre (Creeber, 2001a, 2004, pp. 19–44). Whether it resides in the form of the literary adaptation or the original screenplay, the mini-series or finite serial certainly seems to provide an important space for more complex issues and stylistic innovation than either the series or continuous serial can provide alone.

Glen Creeber

RECOMMENDED READING

Caldwell, John Thornton (1995a), 'Excessive Discourse in the Mini-Series', in John Thornton Caldwell, *Televisuality: Style, Crisis, and Authority in American Television*, New Brunswick and New Jersey: Rutgers University Press.

Creeber, Glen (2004b), *Serial Television: Big Drama on the Small Screen*, London: BFI.

Feuer, Jane (1995), 'Serial Form, Melodrama, and Reaganite Ideology in Eighties TV', in Jane Feuer, *Seeing Through the Eighties: Television and Reaganism*, London: BFI.

Costume Drama

Though period adaptations of historical novels have long been a tradition of British television, 'costume drama' might be seen as a more recent phenomenon. As designer Gerry Scott observes, 'BBC classic drama used to be a studio production, mainly broadcast on Sunday afternoons at children's teatime, and seen largely as being educational' (cited in BBC Education, 1994, p. 30). Today, costume dramas are big-budget, sumptuous productions shot on film for an audience approaching 10 million in the UK alone. Though the production phenomenon seems peculiarly British, costume dramas reach a world market. Indeed, without co-production funding, the budgets required for a multipart serialisation are unlikely to be realised.

An abstract of a 'costume drama' based on a classic novel might cite dashing heroes and attractive young women, perhaps dancing in colourful costumes, and above all a love story. There would be fine houses in verdant parklands, horses and carriages, romance and ultimately a wedding. Andrew Davies's 1995 BBC adaptation of *Pride and Prejudice* (see box) illustrates all of these generic characteristics. To unpack the broad, transnational appeal of contemporary costume drama is to reveal insights into the genre and the various meanings and pleasures it offers to a diverse audience.

The mainspring of costume drama is the classic English novel established in the canon of English literature. Though a canonical approach to both literature and television has been called into question, adaptations of Jane Austen, George Eliot, the Brontë sisters, Hardy, Trollope and Dickens continue to carry cultural capital. Other notable examples of the genre, for example *The Jewel in the Crown* (ITV, 1984), *Brideshead Revisited*, *Fortunes of War* (see 'The Mini-Series', p. 46) and, more recently *Gormenghast* (BBC, 2000), derive from substantial modern novels and often evoke moments of British 'greatness'. Drawing on Bourdieu's account of the aspirant new middle class (1979, translation 1992, pp. 11–18), it might be surmised that some viewers are buying into cultural capital with the greatest ease when they watch *Middlemarch* or *Pride and Prejudice* on television in preference to reading the novels. A process of popularisation might indeed account in part for the appeal of adaptations beyond a traditional high-culture audience. But this is just one way of experiencing costume drama.

Extending, in marked contrast, the pleasures of sensual luxury in the spectacular, other segments of a plural audience might delight primarily in the sumptuousness of the costumes and sets. From Richard Dyer's viewpoint (1992, p. 36), '*Fortunes of War* would have been worth it for Harriet's cardigans and tea-cups alone.' Stately homes typically provide the settings for the frocks and bonnets of costume dramas, affording wide-angle establishing shots of magnificent parks and buildings. A kind of 'star system' is evident in the casting of established actors (Michael Hordern, Robert Hardy, Michael Redgrave, Peter Jeffrey) with that peculiarly British upper-class acting style, while the new generation (Emma Thompson, Kate Winslet, Gwyneth Paltrow, Hugh Grant, Colin Firth, Alan Rickman) increasingly suffuse 'costume dramas' with a patina of the Hollywoodesque.

Narrative accessibility and followability are vital to popular television, and romance is at the heart of the central stories. With its convention of setbacks keeping the hero and heroine apart but leading ultimately to comedic resolution, the narrative code of romance has a strong drive motivating both characters and viewers. It also allows, however, for the breakdown of the story into serial-length sections with 'cliffhangers'. Indeed, many of the novels were originally published in instalments, but the process of selection in adaptations for television of period novels is typically one of reduction of scope and modification of structure to suit the needs of the medium.

The inevitable selectivity in compression, and the need to shorten long narrative sections for the fast-intercutting of stories in popular television's 'flexi-narrative' form (see Nelson, 1997a, pp. 24ff), has its impact on context. Personal relationships in close-ups of domestic situations – the very stuff of television's staple dramatic mode, the soap – tend to be foregrounded in costume dramas to the detriment of the broader scope of higher ideals (Dorothea's and Lydgate's aspirations to improve the world in *Middlemarch*) or of world events (the end of the British Empire in *The Jewel in the Crown*). There is, at least, a tension between the narrative pulse of the romance code and the complications of broader historical circumstances. In television adaptations, the latter tend to be reduced merely to obstacles to the hero and heroine's consummation. This may point to a significant difference between the media of popular television and the Realist novel (see Dyer, 1992, pp. 36–9, and Nelson, 1997a, pp. 142–8, for contrasting accounts).

Another attraction of costume dramas is their production values. This 'quality' is at once the presumed virtue of British costume drama production and of artefacts from the times past that they represent, a pre-obsolescence culture when things were made to last. For a segment of the audience, there may indeed be a richly conservative self-satisfaction at its own appreciation of things well done. As the accompanying 'The making of …' documentaries suggest, there is considerable viewer interest in the crafting of the serials themselves, in how the illusion of historical reality, the conviction of authenticity, was achieved. Some may even take pleasure in the cultural myth of 'Englishness', of tradition, stability and fair play constructed by some costume dramas. The rural sleepiness of the opening sequence of *Middlemarch*, underscored by Vaughan Williams's adaptation of Thomas Tallis, connotes an England that exists outside TV drama only in the historic imaginary. To non-Brits, particularly perhaps Americans and Australians who form the substantial part of the anglophone overseas television market, period costume dramas may appear to tap into deep history. That what they offer is constructs for cultural consumption, however, is evidenced in the need for clean fingernails for the American market (see Nelson, 1997a, p. 150).

In sum, costume dramas today differ from their children's serial predecessors in pursuing less a commitment to fidelity to the instigating novel (*werktreue*, as the Germans put it), or to the historical circumstances in which it is set,

Jane Austen Adaptations

There have been numerous televisual and cinematic adaptations of Jane Austen's novels over the years, but in 1995/6 alone there were *Pride and Prejudice* (BBC, 1995), *Persuasion* (Michell, 1995), *Sense and Sensibility* (Lee, 1995) and two versions of *Emma* (ITV, 1996, and McGrath, 1996). Austen's work patently resonated somehow with the 1990s but, in the market context noted, television adaptations can appeal on different grounds to a range of readers.

Austen adaptations are not identical. They range from the 'mannered watercolour prettiness of the Lee/Thompson *Sense and Sensibility*' (Matthews, 1996, p. 40) to 'Roger Michell's social realist *Persuasion*' (Fuller, 1996, p. 21). The extent to which a book's characteristics determine the nature of the adaptation is evidently as variable as those credited for the outcome (see Giddings, 1990). Although the process of adaptation is ultimately a collective one steered perhaps by the producer, director and screen playwright, television has historically credited the writer. But writers vary. Fay Weldon's 1970 television version of *Pride and Prejudice* (BBC, director Jonathan Powell), though scrupulously faithful to the book, lacks the verve and visual style that Andrew Davies (BBC, 1995) aimed to capture.

To Davies, *Pride and Prejudice*'s narrative structure needed just minor modification to lend televisual shape with episode 'cliffhangers'. The novel contains much well-crafted dialogue requiring only editing for the screen. The real challenge was catching Jane Austen's famous 'ironic style': the authorial voice must somehow be transposed into images and sounds. Davies adds a number of small but significant scenes to give access to everyday vitality beneath social form. The younger Bennet girls are frequently heard bickering. In Part 2, Lydia *en déshabillé* collides on the landing with the ponderous Mr Collins to peals of off-screen laughter. Davies delights in visualising an ironic gap between the surface manners of polite society and the animated bustle beneath. When, in Part 6, Bingley arrives at Longbourn finally to propose to Jane, all the girls hurry to dress. This highly energised scene (pulsed by Colin Davis's theme tune soundtrack that seems successfully to combine Mozart with the Keystone Cops) cuts a moment later to the drawing room where a particularly stilted exchange of pleasantries marks the ironic contrast.

Directed by Simon Langton, another feature of this adaptation involves the humanising, if not sexualising, of the otherwise formal Mr Darcy. Davies was aware (see BBC, 1995) that for the first half of the novel, its romantic hero seems an overwhelmingly proud man, partly because his image is

mediated through Elizabeth Bennet's prejudice. To soften this image and make Darcy (played with an increasingly smouldering sensuality by Colin Firth) more attractive to viewers, Davies scripts brief scenes of him taking a bath (Part 1), fencing (Part 4) and finally emerging after an impromptu dip in the pond on his return to Pemberley (Part 4). Some Austen purists resent any additions to the novel, but the above are genuine transpositions, of authorial tone in the first instance, and narrative followability on television in the second. Where the production overall evidences a commercial disposition to heritage splendour is in the treatment of material wealth itself.

In the novel, Jane Austen is interested in clothes and houses only as markers of status. Descriptions of both are remarkably limited and confined to characters the novel invites us to ridicule. Mr Collins is satirised for telling everybody of the £800 fireplace and sixty-four windows at Lady Catherine de Bourgh's Rosings Park. Preoccupation with bonnets and costume materials is part of the prattle of Mrs Bennet and her sillier daughters, Kitty and Lydia. In Davies/Langton's televisual 'costume drama', however, all material texture is captured by the camera from the embroidered peach silk folds of the titles' backdrop to the virtual catwalks of the balls and drawing rooms.

'Costume drama' treats the revelation of buildings as a dimension of narrative suspense. Though Davies's *Pride and Prejudice* opens with Bingley and Darcy riding to view Netherfield, viewers are not afforded a full-frontal mid-shot until Mrs Bennet arrives to fetch Jane home from her convalescence there (late Part 1). In the interim even the 'modest' Longbourn, home of the Bennets, looks like something from *Homes and Gardens*. In Part 3, we move up the stately home league to the grandeur of Lady Catherine's Rosings Park, shot from a number of angles. The best, Darcy's mansion, is kept to last. The audience finally sees the much-vaunted Pemberley with Elizabeth Bennet in Part 4 as her aunt's carriage sweeps up the drive and she is smitten by the panorama of the house across the lake.

Romance, however, remains the heart of the matter, but in this mid-1990s TV 'costume drama', a modern sexual chemistry is required to be anachronistically displayed through casting, costuming, location and cinematography. The décolletage revealing Jennifer Ehle's ample bosom as Elizabeth Bennet in *Pride and Prejudice* has more perhaps to do with the anticipated viewing pleasures of a heterosexual male segment of the contemporary audience than Regency English manners. Likewise, Firth/Darcy's dip in the lake had a strong appeal to heterosexual women.

In the final close-up, freeze frame on the Darcy/Elizabeth kiss as the open wedding carriage takes them to their narrative destiny, it may even be that Davies and the production team capture something of Jane Austen's irony. A viewer disposed to romance might exhale a deep sigh of satisfaction; while a postmodern reader might delight in the ironic play with a worn romantic trope (see BBC, 1995).

Robin Nelson

than an attractive heritage package of signifiers. Freed from denotational responsibility, other than to construct an internally convincing world, production teams may broaden the appeal to build a large audience conceived not as a mass but as a postmodern conflation of microcultures (see 'Postmodern Drama'). The hybrid of traditional narrative romance form and heritage splendour perhaps accounts for the effusion of costume dramas in the mid-1990s and their undoubted success.

Robin Nelson

RECOMMENDED READING

BBC Education (1994), *Middlemarch: A Viewer's Guide*, London: BBC Education.

Dyer, Richard (1992), *Only Entertainment*, London: Routledge.

Nelson, Robin (1997a), *Television Drama in Transition: Forms, Values and Cultural Change*, London: Macmillan.

The Teen Series

The teenage audience has been increasingly important to the film industry since the 1950s, and programming aimed at a teenage audience occupies a growing sector of the television schedules. There is a significant history of programming featuring and addressing teenagers and teenageness in the anglophone television landscape, beginning with the introduction of television pop music coverage. In the British context this strand of programming in the 1950s played an important part in offering breadth of provision with shows such as *Oh Boy!* (ITV, 1958–9) and *Six-Five Special* (BBC, 1957–9), and has continued to occupy a significant place in British broadcasting. In the USA, *The Monkees* (NBC, 1966–8) was an interesting precursor of contemporary teen television series. A thirty-minute crossover pop music/sitcom inspired by The Beatles' *Hard Day's Night* (Lester, 1964), *The Monkees* centred on the band's comic antics, and combined adventure and showcase musical performances with an energetic visual style. This hybrid pop/sitcom format was reworked in the 1990s, in UK–US co-productions centring on the adventures of British pop band

S Club 7 (*Miami 7* (BBC, 1999); *LA 7* (Fox, 2000); *S Club 7: Artistic Differences* (BBC, 2000)) (see 'Music on Television', p. 172).

Situation comedies, particularly those centred on family relationships, have frequently featured teenagers, such as *The Brady Bunch* (ABC, 1969–74) and *The Partridge Family* (ABC, 1970–4). The teen sitcom centred on the lives, loves and adventures of teenage characters and directly addressed to a younger teenage audience, however, has been a significant form of teen television programming since the 1980s. The popular series *Saved by the Bell* (NBC, 1989–93) followed six archetypal teen characters familiar from successful early 1980s' teenpics like *The Breakfast Club* (Hughes, 1985) – the preppy type, the jock, the nerd, the fashion queen, the cheerleader, the A-grade student – through high school, and in later seasons (*Saved by the Bell: The College Years* (NBC, 1993–2000); *Saved by the Bell: Wedding in Las Vegas* (NBC, 1994)) into college and marriage. Recently, the teen sitcom has become a primary form of television teen programming, with series set primarily in the high school and/or the family home, such as *California Dreams* (NBC, 1992–7), *Boy Meets World* (ABC, 1993–2000), *Sweet Valley High* (Syndication, 1994), *The Secret World of Alice Mack* (Nickelodeon, 1994–8), *Sister, Sister* (ABC, 1994–9), *Sabrina the Teenage Witch* (ABC, 1996–2000/WB, 2000–3) and *Malibu* (Syndication, 1998), forming the basis of narrowcasting for a young teenage audience on satellite, cable and digital through channels like the US-based Nickelodeon and the UK's Trouble TV.

Soap opera has increasingly revolved around teenage characters and is a significant context for understanding the development of contemporary teen drama. Popular Australian soaps *Neighbours* (Grundy, 1985–) and *Home and Away* (Seven Network, 1988–) have always prominently featured teenage characters, and British soaps *Coronation Street* (Granada, 1960–), *Brookside* (C4, 1982–2003) and *EastEnders* have increasingly highlighted teen issues including truancy, pregnancy and drug addiction in their address to the everyday conflicts of family and community. More recently, Channel 4's early-evening teen soap *Hollyoaks* (1995–) has taken its place alongside the American teen fare (for example, *Malibu*, *Dawson's Creek*

Buffy the Vampire Slayer

With the articulate dialogue and playful irony characteristic of 1990s' teen dramas such as *Dawson's Creek* and *Clueless* (UPN, 1996–9), *Buffy the Vampire Slayer* (WB, 1997–2001, UPN, 2001–3) depicts its eponymous heroine as she struggles to juggle her sacred birthright as a demon-slayer and the everyday demands of adolescent life. Assisted by her friends Willow (Alyson Hannigan) and Xander (Nicholas Brendon), and Giles (Anthony Stewart Head), her 'Watcher', Buffy (Sarah Michelle Gellar) encounters a different demonic foe each week, defeating them with a combination of archaic investigation, high-school savvy and impressive fighting skills. These single-episode storylines act as metaphors for the 'real' anxieties of *Buffy*'s teen protagonists, and are integrated into a continuous narrative that follows them from high school to college (in the fourth season) as they gain sexual awareness and increasing freedom from parental and institutional authority (see Billson, 2005).

A spin-off from the film of the same title (Fran Rubel Kuzui, 1992), *Buffy the Vampire Slayer* was produced as part of the Warner Bros. network's move into prime-time hour-long drama, helping to solidify its signature as the 'family' network (De Moras, 1997, p. 11) with a strong teen appeal. As such it reflects the American networks' growing interest over the 1990s in the adolescent market as a valuable niche demographic. This appeal to a teen audience is combined with the high production values associated with quality prime-time television. The series' sophisticated scripts address with wit and sincerity the enormity of growing up in contemporary America, complemented by a glossy visual style, fluid camerawork and artistically choreographed fight sequences.

Much of the series' drama (and comedy) stems from the incongruity of Buffy's position, as she wisecracks her way through fights with vampires twice her size while dressed in heels and a party dress. Her concern that she will ruin her hair or break a nail is combined with a painful awareness of the responsibilities and dangers of her powerful position. As such, *Buffy the Vampire Slayer* combines the female address of earlier series such as *Bewitched* (ABC, 1964–72) and *I Dream of Jeannie* (NBC, 1965–70) that attempted to explore the social contradictions for 'powerful' women through the introduction

Buffy the Vampire Slayer: dealing with adolescent anxieties

of fantasy into the domestic sphere (Spigel, 1991), with the potentially titillating representation of highly feminised action heroes in series like *Charlie's Angels* and *Wonder Woman* (ABC, 1976–7; CBS, 1977–9).

While *Buffy* provides men with a position from which they 'can safely indulge the male fantasy of the dominatrix and combine it with the Lolita fixation' (Forrest, 1998, p. 6), it also 'offers transgressive possibilities for re-imagining gendered relations and modernist American ideologies' (Owen, 1999, p. 24). Broadly post-feminist in its address, the series attempts to create spaces in which women can be powerful, vulnerable and feminine, and to explore the consequences of this regendering for traditional masculine roles. In its self-conscious and playful inversion of the conventions of the horror genre, *Buffy the Vampire Slayer* engages with a perceived crisis both in gendered relationships and in the place of the adolescent in contemporary American society.   *Catherine Johnson*

(Warner Bros., 1998–2003)) offered on the channel's Sunday morning teen slot T4. *Melrose Place* (Fox, 1992–9) began as a spin-off from popular teen drama *Beverly Hills 90210* (Fox, 1999–2000) (see the chapter entitled 'Soap Opera').

CONTEMPORARY TEEN DRAMA

With these precursors and companions, the quality teen television drama series appeared, developed and flourished in the 1990s, which have also seen a vigorous return of the teen film with movies such as *Clueless* (Heckerling, 1995),

She's All That (Iscove, 1999), *10 Things I Hate About You* (Junger, 1999) and *Cruel Intentions* (Kumble, 1999). Key shows have been *Beverly Hills 90210*, *Party of Five* (Fox, 1994–2000), *My So-Called Life* (ABC, 1994–5), *Heartbreak High* (Ten Network, 1994–9), *Buffy the Vampire Slayer* (WB, 1997–2001, UPN, 2001–3), *Dawson's Creek*, *Charmed* (WB, 1998–2006), *Buffy* spin-off *Angel* (WB, 1999–2004), *Popular* (WB, 1999–2001) and *Roswell* (WB, 1999–2002).

Some contemporary teen drama, though sometimes introducing and resolving a plotline in a single forty-five-to sixty-minute episode, can be understood in relation to the long-running serial form in their emphasis on repetition and deferral of resolution, and in this respect are close to soap opera in narrative organisation. At the imaginative centre of the teen drama, as in soap, are place, character and relationships, and emotional drama is often heightened through the use of close-up and (generally romantic pop) scoring (for example, *My So-Called Life* and *Dawson's Creek*), further pointing to the melodramatic nature of the genre. In these respects, teen drama can be considered usefully in relation to quality American prime-time soaps such as *Dallas* and *Dynasty* (ABC, 1981–9), the address having shifted to a teenage audience (see 'Soap Opera'). Teenageness is a significant 'in-between' period, and teen drama deals with the stuff of adolescent anxiety: friendship, love, sex and impending adulthood.

Many of these shows deal with questions of difference, otherness, increased power and the impact of these on personal and community relationships: a significant number of them draw on other cult television forms, using supernatural power as a motif through which to explore these concerns. Many shows give the sense that to be a teenager is to be not quite human. In *Charmed* (characters in their twenties, but addressing the teen audience), the Halliwell sisters discover that they have inherited the power of witchcraft (as does Sabrina Spellman in *Sabrina the Teenage Witch*); cheerleader Buffy Summers discovers that she is 'the chosen one' in *Buffy the Vampire Slayer*, and four of the main characters are teenage human/alien hybrids (see box).

Dawson's Creek, created and written by Kevin Williamson, was particularly successful. Williamson had been responsible for a number of playfully self-conscious and intertextual teenpics of the 1990s, writing *Scream* (Craven, 1996), *Scream 2* (Craven, 1997), the characters in *Scream 3* (Craven, 2000), the screenplays for *The Faculty* (Rodriguez, 1998) and *I Know What You Did last Summer* (Gillespie, 1997), and writing and directing *Teaching Mrs Tingle* (1999). *Dawson's Creek*, similarly, has featured episodes based on *The Breakfast Club*, *Risky Business*

(Brickman, 1983), *The Blair Witch Project* (Myrick and Sánchez, 1999) and *The Perfect Storm* (Petersen, 2000), and is highly self-referential with characters discussing the melodramatic plotlines and elevated, analytical dialogue that characterise their lives in Capeside, Massachusetts. In its combination of self-consciousness and intense emotionality, *Dawson's Creek*, like many teen television dramas, offers a broad address in which both engagement with the melodramatic/emotional and knowing distance can be accommodated. This was certainly the case with the more recent teen dramas such as *The OC* (Fox, 2003–7) and *One Tree Hill* (Warner Bros., 2003–6), perhaps both showing a little more irony and self-awareness than some of their predecessors. Given the intense nostalgia that surrounds the teenager and teenageness in contemporary culture, the audience for the teen drama may exceed the teenage years. What is certain, though, is that the teenager remains profoundly American.

Rachel Moseley

RECOMMENDED READING

Davis, Glyn and Dickinson, Kay (eds), (2004) *Teen TV: Genre, Consumption and Identity*, London: BFI.

McKinley, E. Graham (1997), Beverly Hills, 90210: *Television, Gender and Identity*, Philadelphia: University of Pennsylvania Press.

Shary, Timothy (2005), *Teen Movies – American Youth on Screen*, New York: Wallflower Press.

Postmodern Drama

Postmodern television drama is almost the antithesis of naturalism. Whereas naturalistic drama tends to offer an authentic-looking impression of social events in a style that seems to show the inevitable consequences of certain actions, postmodern drama adopts Lyotard's scepticism towards the 'master-narratives', which make such conclusions seem inevitable. The major world views such as Marxism or Christianity, which offer comprehensive explanations of social change, are rejected by postmodern thinkers who tend not to believe in 'final truths' and prefer to think of reality as endlessly open to further interpretation. Thus postmodern drama tends to reject historical authenticity, mixes styles and genres of television using the technique of *bricolage*, and even draws attention to its own constructedness like Brechtian theatre in order to frustrate the temptation to derive meaning from an open text (see Nelson, 1997b, pp. 235–48).

Twin Peaks

In his essay 'The Author as Producer', Walter Benjamin (1977) wrote that 'The revolutionary strength of Dadaism consisted in testing art for its authenticity.' *Twin Peaks* (ABC, 1990–1) has generally been seen as a postmodern drama that at its most effective compels viewers to reevaluate traditional genres using techniques that are often as bizarre as Dadaism. Masterminded by the film director David Lynch (although he actually only directed five episodes and co-wrote four with its principal writer Mark Frost), the series mixes the detective genre and the mythical quest with elements of soap opera (see p. 60) and other genres to create a bewildering, intertextual parody of them all which quickly achieved cult status. As David Lavery puts it (1995, pp. 6–7):

> *Twin Peaks* seems generated from, spun out of (cloned from?) precedent texts and thus cultic in origin, authority and appeal. A large part of the series' appeal to aficionados … was tracking its intertextual, allusionary quotations: the many actors and actresses reborn from the never-never land of old TV and movies, the red herring evocations of old movies, allusions to previous Lynch films, numerous inside jokes, cameos by Lynch (as Gordon Cole), Frost (as a newscaster in the first episode of the second season), and even Lynch's son Austin (as Mrs Tremond's magical grandson, Pierre). These and many other facets of *Twin Peaks* invited fanatic, cultic participation, generating discourse about discourse.

As this suggests, its convoluted narrative presents the most unexpected developments for viewers familiar with traditional genres. When FBI agent Dale Cooper (Kyle MacLachlan) investigates the death of Laura Palmer (Sheryl Lee) in the town of Twin Peaks, he resorts to dreams and intuitive methods of detection borrowed from Tibetan Buddhism. The abandonment of the hypothetical and deductive reasoning that is a necessary feature of the detective genre is the source of much of the drama's humour, but may also contain serious elements. The other characters, for instance, fail to register surprise at these bizarre events and the drama itself has a dreamlike quality, heightened by its slow pace, its hypnotic music and its sometimes startling images. Subplots that offer red herrings multiply confusingly.

Twin Peaks subverted traditional genres

Unlike detective drama, however, the solution of Laura's murder (which we are not given a fair chance to guess at until halfway through), does not conclude the narrative. A deeper underlying struggle with evil (which appears to have transmigrated from one character to another in a reversal of Buddhist philosophy) continues and Cooper has to save his lover Annie (Heather Graham) from the Red Room, where some of the coded warnings he has received from Laura and others in dreams suggest that he is really battling an omnipresent evil. Motive has little meaning for the bizarre extremes of personality that are encountered here. The warnings hinted at by, among others, the Log Lady (Catherine Coulson), who introduced the series with gnomic statements to help us 'read' the text, suggest that the search for human motives may not only be fruitless but also extremely dangerous.

The Red Room promises to hold the key to the mysterious events, but here Cooper may discover that, as the Log Lady says, 'all the characters in a dream may be yourself'. Cooper's former partner turned murderer, Windon Earle (Kenneth Welsh), may therefore possess Cooper himself in a way that turns the Red Room into a psychoanalytic (re)enactment. When Josie is killed, 'Coop' is taunted by a non-realistic vision of Bob (Frank Silva). If the viewer is also implicated and equally unable to stand apart from his or her own deep involvement in the action, the notion of truth itself is questioned and the conclusive revelations of other drama series may seem far too glib in comparison.

Adrian Page

Postmodernism is founded on the belief that signs are arbitrary and that their conventional meanings can always be abandoned and substituted. Genres are, therefore, no longer stable and can be continually reinterpreted. Hence, the value of postmodern drama is a matter of intense debate. For Baudrillard (1988), postmodern phenomena such as drama have become an interplay of simulacra, or signs that mimic reality and yield no profound meaning, but for others

Ally McBeal

Ally McBeal (Fox, 1997–2002) has been dubbed a 'dramedy'
since it is a genre hybrid embracing aspects of sitcom, soap
opera, courtroom drama and MTV. Its narrative structure,
however, is relatively conventional among series–serial
hybrids. Ongoing stories of the interrelationships between the
partners in the Fishman & Cage law firm are intercut with
episode-contained lawsuit cases undertaken by one or more of
the partners. Typically, however, the courtroom dramas
address a topical social issue from an unusual angle, subvert-
ing (on many occasions inverting) dominant social values.
'Silver Bells', for example, advocates the legitimacy of a *ménage
à trois*, a new model perhaps for the American family. In
another episode, Fish vigorously defends the case of a female
litigant charging harassment against her boss because he had
seduced all the women in the office except her. The main characters are themselves idiosyncratic. Beneath the opulent
veneer of their legal practice, Cage's lack of confidence is manifest in several nervous tics and Fish has a shoe fetish.

A range of compositional devices prevents viewers from
believing too deeply in the fictional world, opening up spaces
with critical potential. Taken as sign, Ally McBeal (Calista
Flockhart) is herself double-coded, at once an independent
professional woman in charge of her destiny and a vulnerable,
waif-like figure waiting for 'Mr Right' to come along. The play
of these two images (and the divided response it has generated
from feminists and post-feminists) suggests a productive tension (see 'Sex and the City' below). By exaggerating glamorous
character types familiar in American television, and by parodying familiar televisual tropes, *Ally McBeal* draws attention to
its compositional principles and exploits the double-coded
postmodern irony of simultaneous affirmation and subversion. Digital technologies serve to break the frame by visually
distorting the physical world. Ally's tongue pokes out and
extends grossly when she dislikes somebody. Advised to 'think
lips' when she needs to be romantically confident, Ally puckers
her lips till they expand fleshily with a pink lipgloss.

Additional appeal to the 'now' generation is made by use of
popular music. Vonda Shepard features regularly in the bar
where each episode ends up below the Fish & Cage family
home–workplace. But the music is used in interesting ways. At
times, it marks a dramatic moment, not so much by under-

Ally McBeal combined elements of the sitcom, soap opera and
MTV

scoring but by musical mood and lyric offering a counterpoint.
On other occasions, music is used directly to comment on the
action. Ally, and some of the other main characters such as
Cage, have their own private theme song. On advice from her
psychoanalyst (Tracey Ullman), Ally thinks Gladys Knight and
the Pips when she needs a boost of confidence, and they duly
appear digitised on screen as if both in and out of her head.
Thus the use of music expressionistically to articulate a character's interior thoughts and feeling has a new take.

The overall result is a multilayered, self-conscious postmodern text. Its multi-tracked *bricolage* of televisual and
musical styles affords a range of sheer pleasures to be taken.
But it also offers a provocation seriously to consider contemporary social issues by transgressing normative codes to disturb traditional sureties and invite quizzical – if not outright
oppositional – readings (see Nelson, 2000).

Robin Nelson

such as Linda Hutcheon (1989) the postmodern dissolution
of conventional meanings is a politically progressive gesture.
Hutcheon argues that in deconstructing conventional
wisdom such as that found in naturalism, mythologies are

exposed and their influence is overcome. In postmodern
drama, however, the act of deconstruction calls for a considerable effort on the part of the viewer, who has to find meanings in texts that aim to be inscrutable.

Heroes

Heroes (NBC, 2006–) is an American drama series created by
Tim Kring, a screenwriter and television producer who was
previously responsible for shows such as *Strange World* (ABC,
1999–2002) and *Crossing Jordan* (NBC, 2001–7). The series
can be read in a number of ways and through a number of
genres (science fiction, teen drama, soap opera, fantasy TV
and so on), but arguably issues of postmodernism seem to
offer a useful theoretical context in which it can be analysed
and understood.

First, *Heroes* appears to self-consciously emulate the aesthetic style of American comic books. Not only do its major
characters have superhero abilities (such as flying, teleporta-
tion and tissue regeneration), but its use of bright primary
colours, special effects, blue screens and 2D/3D animation
creates an almost artificial or even 'hyper-real' *mise en scène*.
Professional comic book artist Tim Sale was even brought in
to provide the artwork used within the series, such as the
paintings that Isaac Mendez (Santiago Cabrera) creates
during precognitive trances and the comic book *9th
Wonders!* that Hiro (Masi Oka) discovers on his first visit to
New York. Inside its covers Hiro finds his own past and
future life graphically depicted, every important event
broken down into comic book-size chunks, complete with
speech bubbles.

This comic strip aesthetic may be linked to the breakdown
in the distinction between 'high' and 'low' culture that typifies
much of postmodern culture. Hiro is just one of the characters that has the responsibility of saving the planet, but he
finds the meaning of his quest in the popular culture of the
everyday, rather than in the 'grand narratives' of philosophy,
science or high art. When asked how he has learned so much
about the time/space continuum, he replies '*X-Men* no.143,
when Kitty Pryde time travels …' (1.1). Intertextual references
such as this are also important to its postmodern sensibility,
the series awash with an almost endless allusion to other TV
shows, films, comics and so on – not least, Hiro's obsession
with *Star Trek*. As postmodernism tends to problematise any
fixed notion of the real, this inherently intertextual universe
could be read as exposing the fact that the real itself is just
another tissue of quotations.

However, it is perhaps the show's fluid representation of
identity where it seems most explicitly postmodern. In a postmodern world, the notion of a fixed and authentic self is
called into question, the breakdown of traditional subject
positions (based on nationhood, sexuality, race and even
gender) becoming increasing unstable. Hiro's ability to

Heroes: Hiro explores the 'global village'

teleport, for example, could be seen as dramatically symbolis-ing Marshall McLuhan's notion of the 'global village' (1962). The proliferation of television, air travel, mobile phones, email and the Interent not only shrinks the globe (thereby altering all our conceptions of space and time), it also transforms our very notion of citizenship from a local to a global perspective. Similarly, both pretty cheerleader Claire Bennett (Hayden Panettiere) and Internet stripper Niki Sanders (Ali Larter) appear to display and reflect traditional notions of femininity. However, Claire's ability to withstand any form of physical harm and Niki's superhuman strength and multiple personali-ties suggests a world where conventional notions of gender have become destabilised.

From a postmodern perspective, then, *Heroes* portrays a universe where human beings are no longer shackled by the limits once imposed on them by the rigid dogmas of science and religion. 'Grand narratives' such as these are challenged and shown to be malleable, open to scrutiny and subject to constant reimagining. Perhaps this postmodern deconstruc-tion of the 'truth' is indicated in the first few minutes of the opening episode by professor of genetics Mohinder Suresh (Sendhil Ramamurthy). He argues that the cockroach is the 'pinnacle of evolution' as it can resist radiation and exist for weeks without food. 'If God has indeed created himself in his own image,' he explains to his students, 'then I submit to you that God is a cockroach' (1.1). It is a suitably postmodern statement for a TV drama that appears to celebrate the break-down of traditional hierarchies; whether they are cultural, artistic, scientific, philosophical or religious. Indeed, in a post-modern universe the answers to the 'big questions' are not likely to be found in the grand pronouncements of a non-existent God, but in the seemingly superficial and shallow images of everyday popular culture. As the most famous tag-line from the show puts it: 'Save the Cheerleader, Save the World'.

Glen Creeber

The first generation of television dramatists who could be labelled postmodern were the playwrights who belonged to what Martin Esslin (1961) labelled the 'Theatre of the Absurd'. The absurdist tradition is one where drama shows the world to be devoid of dependable values and seeks what little consolation can be found. Samuel Beckett, whose play *Waiting for Godot* (1952) is sometimes identified as a founding text of postmodernism, wrote drama for television in the 1960s and 1970s such as *Eh, Joe* (1966) and *Ghost Trio* (1977). These characteristi-cally bleak and difficult dramas display the futility of human expectations in a world that cannot promise any ultimate fulfilment.

The absurdist tradition was taken up in the 1960s' cult television series *The Prisoner* (ITV, 1967–8), starring and directed by Patrick McGoohan. Here a secret agent is about to resign when he is abducted and finds himself a prisoner in a mysterious village where every attempt is made to encour-age him to surrender his autonomy and conform. The series tested the idea that the human spirit could resist the futuris-tic scenario where social control had reached its ultimate technological perfection. All efforts by the prisoner to dis-cover the identity of Number One, the supreme controller of the Village, are unsuccessful until finally he appears to dis-cover that he is Number One. The issue of whether social control is maintained by coercion or by our own conscious-ness remains open and relevant in the final episode. Chris Gregory (1997) traces strong similarities between these early dramas, *The Prisoner* and *Twin Peaks* (see box).

Such an interpretation of *The Prisoner*, however, runs the risk of sounding more like a modernist reading of the series, since it still seems to hold out the prospect of making sense of the world we know. To be truly postmod-ern, television drama must suggest multiple ironic read-ings, which undermine the stability of all our contemporary certainties. Thus, rather than categorising a specific set of dramas as postmodern, it may be more appropriate to trace the postmodern tendency of familiar genres to invite alternative readings. Dominic Strinati (1995), for example, has argued that the 1980s' cop series *Miami Vice* (NBC, 1984–9) is 'postmodern' because it drew attention to the aspects of popular culture of which it was composed. John Caughie (2000, p. 164) has also argued that the mode of irony he calls 'suspensive' is found in post-modern drama, where 'a radical vision of multiplicity, ran-domness, contingency and even absurdity, abandons the quest for paradise altogether'.

Postmodernism also tends to dissolve the distinction between 'popular' and 'highbrow' genres. In particular, postmodern drama often involves a central character's quest for truth in a world saturated with 'semiotic excess' (Collins, 1992, p. 331). In *Northern Exposure* (CBS, 1990–5), for instance, allusions to 'high' art, literature and philosophy are frequently mixed with everyday references to television, Hollywood movies and pop music. Joel Fleischmann (Rob Morrow) may dream of a failed love affair in terms of 'old black-and-white Hollywood films' (Collins, 1992, p. 332), but he also 'encounters' great figures of the twentieth century such as the founder of modern psychoanalysis, Sigmund Freud. In one heated debate, Freud even dismisses criticism of his doctrines with the ironic sentence, 'It's only a theory.' In this way, *Northern Exposure* creates comedy from the paradoxes that a search for authenticity leads to in a postmodern environment. As Jim Collins has pointed out, following Umberto Eco's ideas, the postmodern sign is 'always already said' (p. 333). The sign that is reused must be quoted knowingly in order to endow it with additional meaning.

However, *Northern Exposure* may also be an example of what Fredric Jameson (1993) argues is postmodernism's assimilation by capitalism. The endlessly unfolding questions may represent no more than an infinitely extendable 'product' whose lack of closure simply ensures continued audiences and increased revenue. Phillip Hayward (1990) suggests that this might be particularly true of a series like *Moonlighting* (ABC, 1985–9) (Hayward, 1990, p. 226; also cited by Feuer, 1995, p. 101):

> Instead of dreams of radical, analytically deconstructive television the media mutation of the late Eighties has followed hot on the prophecy of theory and witnessed an eclectic pillaging of once esoteric formal devices, pressing them into forms of popular cultural bricolage glacially unconcerned with niceties of radical schools or purist

debates. *Moonlighting's* strength, originality and challenge to aspects of avant-garde (and/or alternative) media practice is in its subtle intertextualities and formal devices being produced for a popular TV audience, within its paradigms and with none of the cares of the avant-garde and no allegiance to any movement or practice beyond that of populism.

The virtue of this, if there is one, may be that, as Robin Nelson (1997b) suggests, the viewer can come to terms with the way that media culture constitutes its own subjectivities, or it may be that the postmodern simply encourages indulgence in the pleasure of freedom from inherited categories.

Adrian Page

RECOMMENDED READING

Collins, Jim (1992), 'Postmodernism and Television', in Robert C. Allen (ed.), *Channels of Discourse, Reassembled*, London and New York: Routledge.

Lavery, David (ed.) (1995), *Full of Secrets: Critical Approaches to 'Twin Peaks'*, Detroit: Wayne State University Press.

Nelson, Robin (1997b), 'Coda – Critical Postmodernism: Critical Realism', in Robin Nelson, *Television Drama in Transition: Forms, Values and Cultural Change*, London: Macmillan.

SOAP OPERA

Studying Soap Opera

What is soap opera? What are its distinctive features as a narrative system and a way of addressing the viewer? The name itself gives us some clues. 'Soap' marks the genre's commercial origins. It refers to the fact that the format emerged from the radio sponsorship by detergent companies in 1930s' radio; indeed, the immense popularity of the soap opera in the 1940s means that it must be viewed as a central force in the rise of broadcasting as a commercial institution. 'Opera' is a clue to the kinds of judgments often made about this genre, as a well as an indication of its characteristic emotions, plots and performance styles. The word served as a way of ridiculing the high-blown sentiments of the programmes and their female audience, signalling a vulgar taste for overdramatic excess. The term 'soap opera' thus communicates something of the cultural and economic status historically assigned to this particular genre, a status we need to take into account when we study it. Yet even though the formal characteristics of the genre and the institutional conception of its spectator stem from this consumer cultural framework, the uses of soap opera for both viewers and for media scholars extend into broader territory, as we shall see.

Soap opera is, most basically, serialised narrative in broadcasting. Definitions of soap opera's specific formal characteristics vary in scope and emphasis, but they generally share some core features. To begin with, all in one way or another centre on the concept of seriality. Seriality is a narrative structure that spans multiple media and storytelling genres. Its core feature is the distinctive packaging of the experience of fiction over an extended period of time, in segments; all serial narratives thus involve some form of interruption in the flow of the story. The serial form is closely aligned with the rise of fiction as a commodity form. It achieved ascendancy in the nineteenth century in England and America with the growth of a mass market for novels and magazines (Hayward, 1997; also see 'The Mini-Series').

As Jennifer Wicke notes in a study of Anglo-American consumer culture and literature in this period, the scheduled structure of the serial narrative, as a commodity and as a space for commercial speech, encouraged a close, readerly attention. Its regularised forms of interruption and continuity rewarded readers who maintained an ongoing engagement with the text and its advertising inserts (Wicke, 1988, pp. 35, 51). The mass-market institutionalisation of serial fiction extended from magazines to motion pictures with the emergence of popular film serials in the early twentieth century. In this period the identification of serial fiction with women audiences was solidified, as ongoing film serials like *The Perils of Pauline* (1914) were actively marketed to young women consumers (Stamp, 2000).

By the time broadcasting came along, the commercial and textual conditions of serial narrative as a form directed towards a female audience were already largely in place. Radio, however, extended this narrative's reach, allowing serial drama to integrate itself into the rhythms and routines of the home and the (specifically female) labour associated with it. As a broadcast, domestic form, soap opera thus has some specific characteristics. Muriel Cantor and Suzanne Pingree note that seriality proliferates and expands in the broadcast versions of soap opera. The daily, decades-old soap opera narratives that appear today on daytime television include characteristics such as 'competing and intertwining plot-lines', each developing at an independent pace and forestalling any final resolution of conflict: 'The completion of one story generally leads into others, and ongoing plots often incorporate parts of semi-resolved conflicts' (Cantor and Pingree, 1983, p. 22). A long history of feuds and alliances between characters establishes a deep 'backstory' for all ongoing arcs at any moment in soap opera, and makes dramatic reversals, revelations and emotional reorientations a constant element of soap-opera plotting. Built-in pedagogical structures of redundancy and summary ensure that fans who are at different levels of familiarity with the action and character relations may find a point of engagement. In addition, soap-opera narrative, particularly on daytime television, tends to focus on particular communities and family groups. Over the course of a show's run, the drama, emotion and intrigue that unfolds in these settings seems to happen at seemingly the same pace as the everyday life of the viewer.

Cantor and Pingree define the soap opera quite narrowly, restricting their definition (and the extreme form of seriality included in it) to the daytime soaps that air in five-day instalments on American television. However, soap is perhaps more accurately perceived as a flexible and adaptable narrative form, capable of many kinds of variation across temporal and national contexts (Feuer, 1994, p. 552). Prime-time soap operas such as *Dallas* (CBS, 1978–91) (see box) or *Dynasty* (ABC, 1981–9) are also serials, but their weekly schedules, more closely governed by the seasonal structure of the prime-time TV schedule in America, mean that they embody a different set of serial conventions. Indeed, as Jane Feuer has pointed out, over the course of the 1970s, American prime-time television moved increasingly towards serial rather than episodic forms of narrative (Feuer, 1992). A series like *Melrose Place* (Fox, 1992–9) (which refers in its title to one of the first prime-time soap operas, *Peyton Place* (ABC, 1964–9)) might legitimately be called a prime-time soap opera in the tradition of *Dynasty*, *Dallas* and *Falcon Crest* (CBS, 1981–90). Yet at the same time it is important to point out that the serial plotting devices (cliffhangers, characterological reversals and last-minute plot twists) that link *Melrose Place* to these earlier forms are also increasingly characteristic of other forms of prime-time drama, from *LA Law* (NBC, 1986–94) to *Chicago Hope* (CBS, 1994–2000) to *NYPD Blue* (ABC, 1993–2005).

These American examples should not obscure the fact that the conditions of seriality and the history of soap opera shift from one national context to another. In the UK, where commercial broadcasting did not exist until the mid-1950s, soap opera developed relatively late. BBC drama director Val Gielgud considered serial drama vulgar and opposed its production. It was not until after the war and the programme *Mrs Dale's Diary* (BBC, 1948–67) that serial narrative entered British radio. It is somewhat ironic, in this light, that whereas radio soap opera died out in the early 1960s in the United States, replaced by daytime serial drama on television, it continues in England – the popular programme *The Archers*, aired on the BBC first in 1951 as a form of public education for the ministry of agriculture, maintains a devoted following of listeners to this day. Nor should the American origins of the genre prevent us from noting that definitions of soap opera themselves vary from one country to another. Whereas in America soap opera is a term associated primarily with daily daytime serials, in other countries programmes designated as 'soap operas' may air once a week, several times a week, or daily and at different times of day. Some, like the long-running British soap *Coronation Street* (ITV, 1960–), might have started out as weekly or biweekly programmes but now broadcast more frequently as a result of changing institutional relations between advertisers, broadcasters and other programming sectors (see box).

Peyton Place: a place for melodrama in the prime-time schedule

However, one aspect of soap opera does seem consistent across national boundaries, and that is its historical association with female spectatorship. Soap opera's narrative characteristics and institutional forms are deeply rooted in a particular, and most certainly *gendered*, cultural history of the home as a target of consumer address. In the early 1930s, when the soap-opera format first took shape, major transformations in consumer culture were in process. Alongside commercial radio came the rise of brand names, the increase in advertising and, by the late 1920s, the recognition of household markets dominated by female consumers – a recognition signalled in the titles of books such as Christine Frederick's 1929 marketing classic *Selling Mrs Consumer*. At the beginning of the next decade, radio became increasingly identified with female markets. Robert C. Allen (1985, p. 107) cites a 1932 study that found that 'the housewife in a majority of cases is the member of the family who has the most influence upon family purchases and is the one who spends the greatest amount of time in the home. She is therefore, the member of the family most easily reached by radio broadcasts.' Although it has attracted viewers from a range of demographics throughout its history, the image of the soap opera as a 'women's genre' persists to this day. As Laura Stempel Mumford points out, this persistence does not tell us much about 'actual' audiences, but it does call attention to the fact that soap-opera narratives require of the viewer 'a set of knowledge and skills normally associated with women in patriarchal culture' (Mumford, 1995, p. 45).

Perhaps because of the perception of its audience as female, soap opera was also an early and important space for women and writers in American broadcasting. *Painted Dreams* (WGN, 1932) written by Irna Phillips, is generally

Dallas

Created by David Jacobs, *Dallas*'s (CBS, 1978–91) first five-episode pilot season was aired in April 1978. Although it initially received poor reviews, it had already reached the audience rating top ten by the end of its first limited run. Centred around a saga of lust, greed, power and sex, it was the first genuinely successful 'prime-time' soap opera since *Peyton Place*. As Sue Brower puts it, 'It was the complicated stuff of daytime melodrama, done with big-budget glamour – high-fashion wardrobes, richly furnished home … office interiors' and 'exteriors shot on location' (Brower, 1997, p. 453). At the height of its popularity *Dallas* was exported to ninety countries, reaching 200 million viewers each year, and would go on to produce 356 episodes. Such was its success that it quickly produced spin-offs (*Knots Landing* (CBS, 1979–93)) and countless imitations (most notably *Dynasty*, *Flamingo Road* (NBC, 1980–2) and *Falcon Crest*).

A modern rehash of the Romeo and Juliet story, *Dallas* centred around the conflict of two oil families (the Ewings and the Barnes), with Bobby Ewing (Patrick Duffy) and his wife Pamela 'Barnes' Ewing (Victoria Principal) as its 'star-crossed lovers'. However, as popular as both these characters were, it was J. R. Ewing (Larry Hagman – also executive producer) who really caught the public's imagination. As the unscrupulous heir to the Ewing empire, J. R. became an archetypical television villain and a character the public loved to hate. Kind to his mother Miss Ellie (Barbara Bel Geddes and later Donna Reed) and to his young son and heir John Ross (James Richard Beaumont), he was nonetheless shameless and underhand with anyone who came in his way of attaining the power and money he so desperately craved. The most regular victim of his continually abusive behaviour was his business rival Cliff Barnes (Ken Kercheval) and his long-suffering and alcoholic wife, Sue Ellen (Linda Gray). This fascination with the character and the serial reached a crescendo in the 1980 season when the by now regular cliffhanger ended with the question, 'Who Shot J. R.?' With so many possible suspects, this conundrum became the talking point of the summer. When it returned in the following season, 76 per cent of all American television sets (83 million American viewers) were tuned in to find out.

Despite its incredible success, *Dallas* has also become a byword for the unbelievable and sensational elements that,

Dallas viewers responded to its 'emotional realism'

critics argue, typify contemporary television. When a speeding car killed Bobby so that Patrick Duffy could leave the soap, the subsequent drop in ratings meant that drastic action needed to be taken. The following season when Duffy returned, Pam went to the shower to find Bobby standing there. It seems she had dreamt the entire season before! Such sensational storylines have meant that critics sometimes talk about 'wall-to-wall-*Dallas*' when criticising the 'dumbing down' of television generally. However, as Ien Ang's (1985) groundbreaking study of the soap opera has shown, the way people watched it and the 'emotional realism' it produced for viewers was sometimes more important that the quality of the writing and the believability of the actual storylines (see 'Soap Operas and their Audiences'). As Ang puts it, 'It is in this world of the imagination that watching melodramatic soap operas like *Dallas* can be pleasurable: *Dallas* offers a starting point for the melodramatic imagination, nourishes, makes it concrete' (Ang, 1985, p. 80). Its final melodramatic episode was aired on 3 May 1991.

Glen Creeber

described as the first soap (Allen, 1985, pp. 110–16). It aired locally, on a Chicago radio station, but its popularity and the success of both Phillips and her protégés led to more and more serials for women. By the 1940s, soap operas were the dominant form of radio programming. As Michelle Hilmes and Ellen Seiter have shown, Phillips battled critics constantly. In her professional writings, Hilmes notes, Phillips 'tried to draw the serial back into the mainstream of radio practice and to reveal the falseness of the dichotomy between daytime/female audiences and nighttime/masculine ones so carefully drawn by the industry' (Hilmes, 1997, p. 157). Phillips's success was also the occasion for criticism; her career was marked by a constant battle with the characterisation of her work as 'unrealistic' and 'melodramatic'. As Allen points out, the cultural devaluation attached to soap opera in its heyday echoed a nineteenth-century conception of female authorship, voiced in Nathaniel Hawthorne's disparaging caricature of women authors as a 'damned mob of scribbling women' (Allen, 1985, pp. 140–1.) Furthermore, Hilmes points out, the institutional recognition of women both as a buying power and as authors of daytime programming had a double edge. In practice, it meant that women would be figured in radio's programming practices *primarily* as targets of a commercial address and as daytime listeners. Women listeners were rarely figured into assessments of the audience at other times of day and in other formats; and in the sphere of production they were gradually excluded from 'non-feminine-designated areas of production and industry management' (Hilmes, 1997, p. 165).

Soap-opera production 'crossed over' into other media before television; the radio serial *Stella Dallas* (NBC, 1938–56), for example, was made into a film with Barbara Stanwyck. However, with the arrival of television the institution of radio began to change, and soap opera moved from radio to TV. The first radio soap to be produced on television was *The Guiding Light* (CBS, 1950–) a daytime soap that still airs to this day. These first broadcasts, like their radio counterparts, were fifteen minutes long. By the mid-1970s, daytime soap operas in America were an hour in length, a fact that led not only to extremely elongated narrative patterns but also to the development of detailed studio designs and techniques for shooting these narratives. Soap-opera production since this period is a highly regimented industry. As Allen points out, the tremendous demands of the shooting schedule, in which one hour's worth of broadcast quality programme be produced per day, led to a rigid and detailed division of labour in soap-opera production. Programmes are shot quickly in 'real time', in studios built especially to accommodate quick set changes. Scripts are written according to strict guidelines and are rewritten along a particular chain of command; directors, similarly, are allowed 'an extremely limited repertoire of visual flourishes' (Allen, 1985, pp. 48–54, 55).

The serial form associated with daytime soap opera in America travelled to prime-time television in 1964, with the twice-weekly series *Peyton Place*. The programme, based on a bestselling novel, featured a high-profile celebrity cast that 'showcased the expression of female sexuality, leading to its controversial reception as part of the new "single girl" phenomenon' (Luckett, 1999, p. 75). *Peyton Place* left the air in 1969, but it established a place for melodrama in the prime-time schedule. The popularity of *Dallas* and *Dynasty* both in America and abroad in the 1970s and 1980s reflected the expansion of soap-opera conventions beyond the daytime context, as well as their transformation within more high-society fantasies of wealth and power.

Anna McCarthy

RECOMMENDED READING

Allen, Robert C. (1985), *Speaking of Soap Operas*, Chapel Hill: University of North Carolina Press.

Brunsdon, Charlotte (2000), *The Feminist, the Housewife, and the Soap Opera*, Oxford: Oxford University Press.

Mumford, Laura Stempel (1995), *Love and Ideology in the Afternoon: Soap Opera, Women, and Television Genre*, Bloomington: Indiana University Press.

Realism and Soap Opera

We often judge fictions – novels, television programmes, films – on their degrees of realism and verisimilitude, but what does the word *realism* mean? The history of realist movements in art and culture is a history of diverse aesthetic forms and constructions of reality, from social realism to psychological realism. Realism originally arose as an aesthetic movement in the nineteenth century. Its aim, art historian Linda Nochlin writes, was 'to give a truthful, objective and impartial representation of the real world, based on meticulous observation of contemporary life' (Nochlin, 1971, p. 13). As she points out, the sense of reality depicted in realist art was drawn from the philosophical and material resources of nineteenth-century networks of science, industry and artistic practice. Paintings depicting the labour process and the urbanising working class, like Claude Murillo's *Young Beggar* (1650) or Courbet's *The Stone Workers* (1849), gave aesthetic and political status to everyday life. Nochlin and other critics in a variety of disciplines emphasise that conceptions of the real have strong generic, national and historical boundaries. As a critical concept, an aesthetic strategy, a framework within which fiction is produced and consumed, realism is thus continually expanding. As John Fiske points out, 'Realism is not a matter of fidelity to an empirical reality, but of the discursive conventions by which and for which a sense of reality is constructed' (Fiske, 1987b, p. 21 – see 'Documentary Realism').

There are several reasons why realism is a useful category for the study of soap opera's textual forms and reception contexts. As Ien Ang showed in *Watching* Dallas (1985), viewers use a working model of realism in their assessments of serial drama and its pleasures. Ang found that a number of viewers judged *Dallas* to be 'realistic'. However, it was clear that this sense of reality did not emerge from the show's diegetic world, its settings, characters and plot elements; these aspects of the show were incommensurable with the reality of viewers' everyday lives. Rather, viewers derived a sense of realism from the show's apparently true-to-life depiction of psychological situations. Ang called this sensibility *emotional realism*, and concluded that 'what is experienced as "real" indicates above all else a certain structure of feeling which is aroused by the programme' (Ang, 1985, p. 47). This sense of the emotionally real does not require verisimilitude on the level of plot, character or setting. On the contrary, Ang discovered that these diegetic elements played quite a different role in viewers' engagement with the programme. She wrote that '[t]he external manifestation of the fictional world of *Dallas*' contributes to pleasure 'not because of its reality effect ... but because of its stylisation' (see box).

Insisting on the specificity of emotional realism and distinguishing between different levels of realism that are made possible in serial television is crucial for feminist approaches to the study of soap opera as a genre. Popular representations often depict it as a fantasy genre and its viewers as deluded and gullible persons, unable to distinguish between reality and fiction. This stereotypical representation of women's reception practices has a long history, dating back at least to Jane Austen's *Mansfield Park* (1814); its resilience is indicated in the popularity of a film called *Nurse Betty* (LaBute, 2000), which tells the story of a waitress who is deluded into thinking that she is a character in a soap opera. Ang's study, along with others such as those by Dorothy Hobson (1982) and Christine Geraghty (1991), contributes a richer understanding of the relationship between knowledge and belief in the viewing process. As such they offer not only a useful corrective to representations of women as deluded viewers, but also allow us to see how viewers actively manipulate the boundary between fiction and reality for pleasurable purposes.

In addition, the responses of Ang's viewers introduce another reason why it can be helpful to focus on realism as a mode of address in the study of soap opera. This is the fact that variations in the production and reception dynamics of realist forms in soap opera tend to demarcate

national differences within the genre, for both viewers and critics. When distinguishing *Dallas*'s emotional realism from its diegetic reality, Ang's respondents often focused on the latter's 'Americanness'. These viewers, like many consumers of prime-time American serial drama exported from the USA, linked the stylised elements of the programme's *mise en scène* to Hollywood production values and by extension to an 'unreal' and excessive imaginary world (Ang, 1985, p. 55; see also Morley, 1989, pp. 31–4). Similarly, Dorothy Hobson notes, British viewers of soap operas such as *Coronation Street* and *EastEnders* (BBC, 1985–) tended to oppose their 'native' soaps to American ones via the distinction between fantasy and realism (Hobson, 1989, p. 157). Such judgments signal a cultural recognition of social realism as an aesthetic strategy in British and Australian serial drama; often, they reflect a corresponding recognition of the settings and situations of American soap-opera exports as hyperbolic and hence unrealistic.

Coronation Street has been singled out in particular as a paradigmatic example of realism in British soap opera. Focusing on conflicts and struggles in the lives of working people in a small urban community in the industrial north of England, the programme uses a range of visual and narrative techniques to convey a sense of the everyday lives of 'ordinary people'. As Marion Jordan explains, in *Coronation Street* as in social realism 'the settings should be commonplace and recognisable (the pub, the street, the factory, the home, and more particularly the kitchen) ... the time should be the present ... the style should be such as to suggest an unmediated, unprejudiced and complete view of reality' (1981, p. 28). This conventionality is not invisible, however: '*Coronation Street*, though deploying the devices of the soap opera realism upon which it is based, far from attempting to hide the artifice of these devices ... asks us to take pleasure in its artistry' (p. 39). But whereas *Coronation Street* exploits verisimilitude as both a technical feat and an affective relationship for the viewer, American prime-time drama exports are less flexible. As Jostein Gripsrud notes in a discussion of the Norwegian reception of *Dynasty*, 'the historical experience with Hollywood films and TV shows made the "emotional realism" more or less the only realism expected from American screen entertainment' (1995, p. 258.)

These stark contrasts between national versions of the soap opera are reflected in the different ways critics approach soap opera's relationship to realism in different countries. Whereas British and European critics of soap opera generally pay more attention to realism as a strategy for representing social realities of class and *habitus* in

Coronation Street: social realism in British soap opera?

Soul City

Soap opera is not generally thought of as a form in public and political education, but innovative serial television drama in the Republic of South Africa has been used for precisely this purpose. In 1994, after the collapse of the apartheid system, an Independent Broadcasting Authority (IBA) was created to introduce large-scale policy reforms into the once white-dominated South African Broadcasting System. Among these was a mandate that television serve the public not only as a source of entertainment but also as an agency of free information and education during the transition to democracy (see 'Educational Programming'). This mandate reflected the overall ethos of 'transparency' that governed the establishment of state and private institutions in the post-apartheid era, and that structured the unique system of disclosure and amnesty in the judicial process established with the Truth and Reconciliation Commission (TRC).

Soul City (SABC, 1994–) has been described as 'what might result if ER (NBC, 1994–) or General Hospital (ABC, 1963–) were set in a clinic serving a sprawling black South African township'. Like many prime-time and daytime dramas in the west, it is set in a medical facility. Indeed, Soul City is almost closer to a hospital drama than a soap opera; it airs on television once a week over a fifteen-episode season, a broadcast schedule that excludes it from basic definitions of seriality. However, the programme is not only a television phenomenon. A fifteen-minute radio version, closer to the 'classic' soap-opera form, also broadcasts daily. This accommodates a broader audience, given that, according to figures from 1998, only 60 per cent of the population has access to television sets. The programme's public health goals are also reinforced through tie-ins with other media: serialised health education booklets and weekly health-oriented contests run in newspapers each week.

Seriality in some form or another is thus crucial to Soul City's public health strategies, as it provides a way of reinforcing issues and interventions over an extended period of time. In this respect, the programme seems to affirm Gledhill's characterisation that the soap opera's ability to 'chew on' social realities in its narratives lies partly in the serial form and in the emphasis on dialogue. Its weekly situations, addressing ongoing health and workplace issues in the lives of its characters through dialogue, are clearly the root of Soul City's attempts to bridge dramatic enactment and the realities of the spectator's everyday life. The serial is distributed by California Newsreel on a compilation cassette entitled Prime Time South Africa.

Anna McCarthy

popular television, American soap opera criticism brings a quite different set of questions to bear on the genre's relationship to the real. Rather than focusing on the implicit opposition between reality and fantasy, or viewerly and textual constructions of an 'authentic' class experience via mise en scène, American scholars have addressed questions that arise from the particular form of the soap opera as a daytime and prime genre in the USA. In the case of the (non-export) daytime soaps, this means examining how the studio space and the serial form set parameters on the ways that soap operas create the ongoing impression of perceptual reality, and also (and more implicitly) the ways in which the genre relates to the lived realities of the spectator, often understood to be female and almost always considered to be a devoted watcher. Robert C. Allen (1985) addresses realism's textual dimensions in quite formal terms, focusing primarily on the evolution of a conventional audiovisual language for the coherent representation of sense of time and space in daytime soap-opera studio production: 'soap opera style can be seen as a continuation, if not condensation, of Hollywood's stylistic practice, in which elements of style function in support of diegetic illusion' (p. 64; for a discussion of realism in theory construction, see pp. 225–6, n. 9).

In a more recent study of American daytime serial soap opera, Laura Stempel Mumford (1995) brings in similar comparisons with cinematic realism, focusing on the formal and political implications of soap opera's transformation of certain Hollywood realist structures, notably closure. She also points out that 'the fact that many soap opera events take the same amount of time they would occupy in viewers' lives makes their depictions especially "realistic"' (p. 29). This is compounded by the fact that soap operas tend to observe national holidays when they occur on weekdays – soap-opera plots often feature Christmas dinner on Christmas Day, for example. Mumford also notes that production budgets of soap operas, permitting fewer retakes, shape actors' performances so that characters' conversations often seem no smoother than viewers' (p. 38). Both Mumford and Allen thus address realism primarily as an issue of representational style or transparency, as a set of formal techniques that do not call attention to their own artifice.

However, as Mumford's interest in the serial form might suggest, the specificity of the daytime drama's ongoing, seemingly endless narrative structure in American television means that even when the term 'realism' is not literally used, many American soap-opera critics are nevertheless very interested in the genre's relationship to 'the real'. This can be seen in two distinct lines of enquiry. One approaches the serial form by raising questions about the relationship between the cycles of the programme and the cycles of everyday life for the spectator. Tania Modleski, for example, shows in her classic study (1982) that the ongoing, predictable schedules of American daytime soaps bring the texts of the soap opera into the conceptual orbit of everyday life and lived experience. A 'deeper' reality is thus discernible in the serial form of the soap opera, she suggests: the reality of housework, of domestic rhythms, and the endlessness of household routines for women. Similarly, Christine Gledhill (1992) implies that the ongoing, dialogical nature of soap-opera narrative gives rise to strategies of representation more realist than melodrama, soap opera's filmic relative. She writes that instead of offering '*deus ex machina* resolutions' typical of the latter form, soap opera's event structure provides a space for characters to explore 'the emotional, moral and social implications and consequences of the event' (p. 121; see also Mumford, 1995, p. 25). The seriality of daytime soap opera also shapes the ways in which it depicts certain political possibilities. As Joy Fuqua (1995) notes, writers for daytime soap operas in the 1990s found it difficult to include gay characters as ongoing, developing participants in the diegetic everyday. As one writer put it: 'It's one thing to explore homophobia. It's quite another to explore the life of a gay couple – a life that includes sex and such problems as whether or not to adopt children' (Michael Malone, quoted in Fuqua, 1995, pp. 208–9). As this indicates, gay issues were a way of injecting a sense of topical, political 'realism' into the narratives of soap operas, but institutional barriers prevented their presence in the more mundane diegetic reality of daytime serial dramas.

This example illustrates that there is no straightforward or singular relationship between realism and politics in soap opera. Rather, realist conventions and sensibilities are formed on different levels of the text and may raise political issues on one level while foreclosing upon them on another. Indeed, to refer to a previous example, American daytime soaps can present a realist and an anti-realist sense of the passage of time simultaneously. Although events seem to take place on the same calendar and seemingly at the same rate in as they might in 'real life', child characters in some soap operas can mature at a rapid rate, going from birth to adolescence (and romance plots) in a few years.

Such fractured and contradictory modes of realist social identification and critique in various national contexts reflect, to a large degree, the limits imposed upon representation and narrative by the commercial broadcasting systems in which soap operas generally air. Political speech and the representation of alternative political or communitarian realities must necessarily exist within the boundaries established by an implicit sense of the mainstream. However, in other nations, where non-commercial broadcasting predominates or where commercial television is invested with a high level of political responsibility by government policymakers, other possibilities for rendering the politics of everyday reality in soap opera become possible.

A final issue that should be addressed in any discussion of soap opera and realism is the role of technological change, and the aesthetic paradigms associated with it, in constructing new horizons of 'the real' in television. Most obviously, the rise of 'real-life' serial programme forms, like MTV's (see 'Music on Television') popular and long-running programme *The Real World* (1992–), and the spate of surveillance-based reality dramas like *Big Brother* (Endemol, 1999–) and *Survivor* (Planet 24, 1997–) (see 'Reality TV', p. 134), suggests that changes are under way with the emergence of non-fiction analogues of the soap-opera form; indeed, when MTV launched *The Real World*, it promoted the show as 'a real-life soap opera'. Although, as Mumford notes (1995, p. 32), critical clarity requires that soap opera continue to be defined as a fictional form, it is clear that emotional and perceptual realism are the point of overlap between 'actual' soap opera and these new forms of serial documentary.

In such programmes the hyperbolic and 'unreal' conditions of the production process, analogous to social psychology experiments, produce a sense of immediacy and transparency. Similarly, the artificial social engineering through which such shows are 'cast' nevertheless leads to high degrees of emotional realism as the people on screen interact with each other over time. Even though they are not technically 'soap operas', such programmes are thus interesting to consider in relationship to the soap opera because they expose the dialectical and multiple relations between transparency and hyperbolic artifice that shape the genre's modes of realism across institutional and textual borders (see 'Docusoaps' and 'Reality TV').

Anna McCarthy

RECOMMENDED READING

Fuqua, Joy V. (1995), 'There's a Queer in my Soap!', in Robert C. Allen (ed.), *To Be Continued … Soap Opera Around the World*, Chapel Hill: University of North Carolina Press.

Gledhill, Christine (1992), 'Speculations on the Relationship between Soap Opera and Melodrama', *Quarterly Review of Film Studies*, vol. 14, no. 1–2.

Jordan, Marion (1981) 'Realism and Convention', in Richard Dyer et al. (eds), *Coronation Street*, London: BFI.

Soap Operas and their Audiences

From the time of its construction and articulation among popular media genres in the 1930s, soap opera has been signified in public discourse via its 'audience'. On the one hand, for US soap companies, soap opera was fashioned as a direct route to women who controlled a household's consumption. In this domain, the most significant fact about the soap opera audience was its *quantity*. As Robert Allen says (1985, p. 30), 'Within nine years after the debut of the first network radio soap opera in 1932, the soap opera form constituted 90 percent of all sponsored network radio programming broadcast during the daylight hours … . This enormous audience today provides … one-sixth of all network profits.'

On the other hand, this clear embedding of the soap-opera form and its (female) audience within the most overt aspects of capitalism led academic and other critics into a sustained rejection of the new genre. Soap opera and its audiences were swept along on cross-currents of critical discourses that, as Allen says, were to define its image for decades. He points to two 'superintending' discourses that, almost from the beginning, positioned the soap-opera audience in a position of 'lack'. On one side, there was the deeply conservative aesthetic discourse of 'mass culture' thinking, which expressed itself in different forms (German Expressionism, the literary criticism of F. R. Leavis and so on) in the new 'mass-industrial' societies.

To the other side of this 'aesthetic' critique of the soap-opera audience, there was the 'scientific' one. Allen explains the complex relationship between soap-opera audiences and American social scientific research of the dominant Lazarsfeld Bureau of Applied Social Research, founded in 1939 with significant commercial funding. This commercial 'scientific' backing 'helped to "encrust" the meanings of soap opera within the discourse of mass communications research with a particular conception of its audience, which is felt even today' (Allen, 1985, p. 22). Lazarsfeld's research was in part designed to counter the 'anti-social' charges against soap laid by psychiatrists like Louis Berg,

who claimed that broadcasters proffered a surfeit of daytime fare that 'pandered to perversity' and played out 'destructive conflict' (cited in Allen, 1985, pp. 21–2). A more 'pro-social' message about soap opera was needed, and this was provided by pioneering research within the Bureau: for example, by Herta Herzog's definitive 1944 study of the soap-opera audience, which emphasised the psychological and social *needs* that listening to soap opera fulfilled. However, the lack of comparable work on *other* popular genres, meant that:

> Despite the clear indication that soap opera listening pervaded all groups, the methodologies of the studies suggested that soap opera enjoyment had to be explained as some kind of lack on the part of listeners: the psychological need of women for advice, a social or emotional lack, educational deprivation, the inability to enjoy other types of programming, and so forth. (Allen, 1985, p. 25)

As Allen says, work in the Lazarsfeld Bureau defined the field of academic soap-opera study for the next thirty years. But in the 1970s (as a result of the competing frameworks of uses and gratifications studies and screen theory) and particularly in the 1980s, the soap-opera audience gained a more positive face. Most important here was the work of feminists in the field of soap opera audiences.

- Terry Lovell (1981), who deployed Gramsci's distinctions between 'good sense' and 'common sense' in her study of *Coronation Street* (see box) to argue that this soap opera offered viewers certain marginalised 'structures of feeling'. 'It offers women a validation and celebration of those interests and concerns which are seen as properly theirs within the social world they inhabit. Soap opera may be … a context in which women can ambiguously express *both* good-humoured acceptance of their oppression *and* recognition of that oppression, and some equally good-humoured protest against it' (Lovell, 1981, pp. 50–1).
- Charlotte Brunsdon (1981), who drew on her work on other television genres (such as her *Nationwide* (BBC, 1969–83) study with David Morley, 1978) to resituate soap opera and current affairs in terms of gendered cultural competences. Brunsdon reassessed Bourdieu's work on class and cultural competence to point to practical and ideological knowledge systems internalised by young men and women that leads to greater attention to, and pleasure in, one popular television form than another. In the case of soap opera, programmes like

Crossroads (ITV, 1964–88) were engaging with, and extending, existing discourses of femininity.

- Dorothy Hobson (1982), whose own study of *Crossroads* may be said to have pioneered a new generation of 'ethnographic' (or at least empirical–qualitative) studies of the 'active audience'. Deliberately addressing 'the most maligned programme on British television' (p. 36), Hobson challenged head-on the 'deficit/lack' model of soap-opera audiences that had prevailed for so long. As she argues, 'It is criticised for its technical or script inadequacies, without seeing that its greatest strength is in its stories and connections with its audience's own experiences. The programme is a form of popular art precisely because it has a relevance to its audience' (pp. 170–1).

- Tania Modleski (1982), whose study of Harlequin romances and daytime soap opera argued for the relationship between these forms and a new, historically positioned, feminist aesthetic. 'Soap operas invest exquisite pleasure in the central condition of a woman's life: waiting … [S]oap operas do not end. Consequently, truth for women is seen to lie not "at the end of expectation", but *in* expectation, not in the "return to order", but in (familial) disorder' (p. 88). Why, asks Modleski, given the post-structuralist emphasis on 'decentring the subject', do we not start by acknowledging women's pleasures in a popular television from where 'women are, in their lives, their work, and in certain forms of their pleasure, already decentred' (p. 105) – the soap opera?

- Ien Ang (1985), who, in her study of *Dallas* (see box), drew (like Terry Lovell) on Raymond Williams's notion of 'structure of feeling' to argue for the notion of an emotional realism that is beyond the empiricist 'real'. Ang engages critically with both empiricist realism (where 'a text is realistic (and therefore good) if it supplies "adequate knowledge" of reality') and screen theory's concept of the 'classic realist text' (which is 'bad because it only creates an illusion of knowledge'). In both these notions of realism, 'a cognitive–rationalistic idea dominates: both are based on the assumption that a realistic text offers *knowledge* of the "objective" social reality … But the realism experienced by the *Dallas* fans … bears no relation to this cognitive level – it is situated at the emotional level: what is recognised as real is not knowledge of the world, but a subjective experience of the world: a "structure of feeling"' (p. 45). Ang is marking here a profoundly important movement in post-structuralist feminist research against the 'cognitivist/rationalist' and instrumentalist biases of modernist thinking, and towards her own later elaboration of critical ethnography (Ang, 1985). 'It is emotions which count in a structure of feeling' (p. 45); and it is the pleasurable play of 'endless fluctuation between happiness and unhappiness' (p. 46) that marks soap opera's 'tragic structure of feeling'. For example, Sue Ellen's alcoholism is a potent metaphor for a woman trapped in desperation, and her sexual affairs are a potentially appealing action with which women viewers can empathise in fantasy.

- Ellen Seiter et al. (1989), whose Oregon study also took up the 'critical ethnographic turn', discussing reflexively the 'discursive formation of women talking to women' in the research interviews conducted by Ellen Seiter, Gabriele Kreutzner and Eva-Maria Warth. Focusing on 'soap operas in the context of the everyday life for women working in the home' (p. 223), the Oregon study took to task Modleski's overtly 'textualist' analysis. Working-class women, in particular, rejected Modleski's analysis (of the 'ideal mother' inscription of the soap viewer) as middle class. Seiter et al. did, however, find 'fond admiration' (p. 237) for 'the supposedly despised villainesses' of soap opera – thus inadvertently supporting Modleski's argument that this perennial soap representation provides 'an outlet for feminine anger: in particular … the spectator has the satisfaction of seeing men suffer the same anxieties and guilt that women usually experience, and seeing them receive similar kinds of punishment for their transgressions' (Modleski, 1982, p. 97).

- Mary Ellen Brown (1990, 1994), whose emphasis on soap opera and women viewers' talk took the 'resistance' line of feminist theory (which is so evident in the contributions described above) to its ultimate, 'everyday' position. Brown recognises that women are embedded in patriarchal culture, but they are not victims of it – especially when they talk to each other about soap opera. Brown's emphasis on 'emotional critique' and 'speaking with the body' extends Ang's post-structuralist critique of the 'cognitive–rationalistic' concerns with a 'knowledgable' reality. Her emphasis that 'talk is action' also quite directly opens the way to further feminist work in two important areas: the social constructionist discourse analysis of E. Graham McKinley (1997) in her study of *Beverley Hills 90210* (Fox, 1990–2000) (see 'The Teen Series'); and the critical ethnography of Marie Gillespie (1995) in her ethnographies of Indian-produced soap operas among a Punjabi Hindu family living in Southall, London.

- Michael Stewart (1999) has argued – rightly, in my view – that Gillespie's work (and also Lisa Rofel's (1995)

A Country Practice

Production analysis is another side of the soap-opera/
audience relationship that can provide the ethnographic
'richness and detail' that Stewart (1999) is looking for.
Although serious ethnographies of television production
in Britain were being published in the later 1970s and
early 1980s, these were on the private eye, cop and
science-fiction (see p. 3) genres, not soap opera.
However, David Buckingham's important 1987 book
on *EastEnders* and its audience did show the value of a
processual analysis of production (via interviews with
television personnel about 'creating the audience'), the
'audience in the text', the circulation of publicity and
media comment about the series, and 'active audience'
analysis. Like the feminists, Buckingham also engaged
with 'pleasure', but situated socially and historically in
individual viewers.

In 1986, Tulloch and Moran produced A Country Practice:
'Quality' Soap, based on several months' ethnographic study
of Australia's longest-running and highest-rating, peak-view-
ing soap opera of the 1980s (*A Country Practice* (Seven,
1981–93), which was also the first to open up the British
market for Australian soaps). The intention here was to challenge the long history of dismissal of soap opera and its audiences in a different way from the feminist 'resistance' studies.
A soap opera was chosen that was both very high rating *and*
regarded as 'quality' professional work by all who worked on it
(the series attracted Australia's best film writers, was regarded
as their 'best work' by set designers, floor managers, sound
and vision directors and so on at Channel 7, Sydney). Each
professional worker on the series, from executive producer
through actors and studio-floor staff to station scheduling
managers and publicity, were working daily to put their particular economic and semiotic 'signature' on the show.
Consequently, by

(a)   studying several episodes through from pre-planning to
      post-editing meetings,
(b)   examining the positioning of this particular product in a
      particular commercial channel, and
(c)   conducting audience research on the episodes the
      researchers had followed,

they could explore the 'semiotic density' of the television text
(with its *range* of inscribed audiences according to multiple
and fragmented 'authorships'), and relate this to actual audience meanings.

A Country Practice: 'quality' soap?

On the audience side, it was possible to:

- Examine the meanings of both 'issues' (rural unemploy-
  ment, HIV/AIDS) and 'romance' stories among different
  viewers, according to gender, class and age.
- Assess the effect of the 'halfway-house' style (which made *A
  Country Practice* a very 'traditional', naturalistic formula for
  some of its film-experienced writers). For example, one
  writer worried that the quick 'cutaway' style (between 'laughter' and 'tears') would lessen the 'impact' of his HIV/AIDS
  story: consequently the researchers assessed the meanings of
  differently edited versions of his episode with audiences.
- Explore the meaning of different audiovisual signatures on
  audiences: for instance, according to directors' different
  visual styles (in relation to the 'legalise heroin' insertion),
  or omitting (young/old addiction) 'balancing' information
  conveyed by the music and sound score in differently
  edited versions of the same episode.
- Examine differences in the meaning of 'pleasure' over
  'romance' strands as between 'fans' and mixed family
  groups at home.
- Assess with audiences the executive producer's assertion
  that his needle-sharing, HIV/AIDS message would have
  more 'impact' if carried by a much-loved soap-opera character than via a ninety-second public service advertisement.

Like the feminist audience research, this work responded to the
long history of denigration of soap opera and its audiences, but
in different ways: (1) it went to the 'everyday' of the TV industry for its own construction of 'quality'; (2) it traced the economy and semiotics of this 'quality' into the production and

circulation of its 'texts'; (3) it examined the pleasures, meanings and (production-team intended) 'impacts' on different audiences of the show, drawing on both qualitative and quantitative methods. 'Pleasure', then, was traced both in the everyday working practices of TV professionals and in audience responses.

John Tulloch

study of the soap opera *Yearnings* (1991–) in post-Tiananmen China) marks an important new phase of analysis of the soap-opera audience. In Stewart's view, the feminist studies so necessary in the 1970s and 1980s were nevertheless considerably overdetermined by soap opera's negative historical inscription. This is entirely understandable, given the social weight and historical depth of the discourses of cultural value that have shaped soap opera's reception and within which soap opera continues to be understood. However 'in the [Modleski, Seiter et al. and Ang] studies … there's a danger that the recurring oppositions – between realism and pleasure, public and private, masculinity and femininity, activity and passivity – are inverted rather than undone' (p. 74). Speaking of Gillespie's *Mahabharata* (BRTV, 1988–90) study in Southall, Stewart says, 'The great value of Gillespie's study lies in the richness and detail of its ethnographic observation. Most noteworthy, perhaps, is how particular, binary ways of thinking about soap opera collapse when a specific cultural context is examined … . The programme's excessive, melodramatic structure does not transcend other restrictive or illusory realities; it very clearly *is* the reality, part of the "factual" history within which the Dhanis make sense of their lives' (p. 79).

Nevertheless, continuity with the feminist research of the 1980s needs to be maintained. Above all, the analysis of embodied emotionality (both in soap opera and in audience responses to it) needs to remain a central research focus. Ironically, that is where it started – in Louis Berg's psychiatry. We have come a long way from his description of the soap-opera audience as victims of 'acute anxiety state, tachycardia, arrhythmias, increase in blood pressures, profuse perspiration, tremors, vasomotor instability, nocturnal frights, vertigo and gastro-intestinal disturbances' (cited in Allen, 1985, p. 21). But the importance of bodily and emotional responses to the soap-opera 'event' is one that (as Ang and others have argued) has been almost entirely lost from view in instrumentalist academic discourse. The analysis of soap-opera audiences – in relation to the emotions of risk and fear, as well as pleasure and anger – is still ahead of us.

John Tulloch

RECOMMENDED READING

Ang, Ien (1985), *Watching Dallas: Soap Opera and the Melodramatic Imagination*, London: Routledge.

Seiter, Ellen, Borchers, Hans, Kreutzner, Gabriele and Wrath, Eva-Marie (eds) (1989), *Remote Control: Television, Audiences and Cultural Power*, London: Routledge.

Tulloch, John and Moran, Albert (1986), A Country Practice: 'Quality' Soap, Sydney: Allen and Unwin.

The Telenovela

The telenovela (or the television novel) constitutes one of the most important cultural expressions within contemporary Latin American popular culture. They are massively present in the everyday life of millions of Latin Americans, to a degree unseen in most other parts of the world. The most popular television channels show telenovelas in both daytime and prime-time broadcasting. In a small country like Nicaragua, for example, the largest television channel broadcasts eight daily Latin American telenovelas, five days a week. Latin America's largest TV network, Brazilian Rede Globo, broadcasts four telenovelas daily, six days a week (all in prime time – between 5.30 and 9.30 p.m. – only interrupted by thirty minutes of news). They run an average of 120–50 episodes, in some countries more, and they achieve ratings unseen in most other countries in the world (often surpassing the ratings of the daily TV news). Rede Globo's prime-time telenovelas reach about 50 per cent of the audience, and this in a highly competitive environment where many of the other channels compete by also transmitting telenovelas.

In addition to the cultural significance of telenovelas in Latin American societies, they are also big business on the Latin American media market (traditionally a commercial market), and have been exported to more than 130 countries worldwide. The main producers are Brazil, Mexico and Colombia, followed closely by Argentina, Venezuela, Peru and Chile. As Trinta (1997, p. 276) points out, their traditional characteristics can be found rooted in the dynamics of melodrama:

Common elements include emotional entanglements involving well-established characters and the traditional romance plot with true love triumphing over adversity; characterisation is clearly subordinated to plot and spectacular physical action predominates. The plot is developed around a sad 'love story', whose end is reached by resolving a certain number of interwoven situations. In this way, affectionate and tender devotion always wins a victory over evil.

As a melodramatic art of storytelling, telenovelas have grown out of the history of popular culture, having historical matrices in ancient oral and literary storytelling (also reflected in more recent mass-communicative narratives within newspapers, theatre, circus, radio and cinema). As

such, a joint history can be traced together with the soap operas of the anglophone world. However, the particularities of the Latin American telenovelas are obviously the result of forty to fifty years of genuine development as a Latin American genre. Furthermore, telenovelas can be distinguished by their national genre characteristics. Whereas the Brazilian telenovas tend to be more modern and socially aware, the Mexican have generally been regarded as more traditional and romanticised in tone. This has, however, been changing in recent years, not least with the growth of the Mexican TV company, TV Atzeca.

We also find subgenres in individual countries, characterised by significant differences in aesthetics, content and

Brazilian Telenovelas

The Brazilian telenovela is the telenovela of Latin America into which most resources are poured. They are the most expensive, they use the most locations, employ the best actors and tend to incorporate the most social critique within their narratives. The largest producer on the Brazilian market is Central Globo de Produção, part of the Globo corporation and owned by the legendary ninety-year-old Roberto Marinho, honorary president of the Globo companies. In the early 1990s Globo was the world's largest producer of television fiction, producing simultaneously an episode a day for four different telenovelas. The Globo companies include all aspects of the culture industry and have also spread into several other industries (telecommunications, oil, agriculture, sports).

Two major trends influenced the genre from the mid-1980s, leading to the development of the *post-realist* telenovela: first, the process of democratisation in Brazil, and second, the international orientation of Rede Globo. Democratisation in society led to an abundance of political criticism and social comment in telenovelas generally. From the mid-1980s the daily eight o'clock telenovela contained highly political subtexts, criticising corruption, nepotism and the fight for power and raising important issues (such as Catholic priests getting married, agrarian reform, racial questions and disappeared street children). These contemporary problems were massively visualised by the telenovela and transformed into issues discussed by almost all levels of society. *Roque Santeiro* (Globo) in 1985, by Dias Gomes, was the first telenovela along this line (originally produced in 1974, but censored), and has become one of the most important telenovelas in the history of the genre.

In the 1990s, political subtexts were increasingly apparent in telenovelas, reflecting the freedom of speech and marking the post-military epoch in which Brazil now lives. Simultaneously, a certain generic innovation had emerged, based partly on a nostalgic turn and focusing on rural settings and plots that unfold in some of Brazil's many beautiful natural settings. *Pantanal* (TV Manchete, 1990) was a trendsetter in this respect. It evoked the nostalgia shared by many of the first- and second-generation migrants in the huge urban centres in Brazil. *Renacer* (*Reborn*, Globo, 1993) and *O Rei do Gado* (*The Cattle King*, Globo, 1996–7) were two other major examples.

O Rei do Gado brought a very polemic issue to the screen, that of agrarian reform and the social movement of the landless in Brazil (the 'Sem Terra' movement). This telenovela took up the agrarian reform issue in the midst of serious land conflicts in Brazil. Nineteen landless peasants were killed in a conflict with landowners shortly before the telenovela went on air. The narrative, telling the story of a rich landowner falling in love with a poor landless woman, became a direct comment on the contemporary conflict in Brazil – and, indeed, sought to place itself as close to the actuality of the contemporary climate as possible. It visualised on a massive scale the struggle for land that had been a growing social movement in Brazil, turning this issue into one of public knowledge and concern, and transforming this particular struggle into a legitimate political cause. It had a tremendous effect, significantly increasing public attention, media debate and political discussion, and even encouraging the passing of several laws on the issue. As such, it is arguable that the televnovela continues to play an important and crucial role in the development of democratisation within Latin America as a whole (see Trinta, 1997, pp. 281–4).

Thomas Tufte

audience profile. This is the case in Brazil where Rede Globo has developed a six o'clock subgenre (mostly the historic epos or *novelas de epoca*); a seven o'clock subgenre (comedic, youth-oriented satire of a very national–domestic nature); and, finally, the eight o'clock telenovela (usually the flagship programme of the evening, being the most expensive, often most socially oriented and almost always based on a contemporary narrative woven around a classical melodrama).

Dramaturgically, telenovelas are 'open' works; the narrative is not concluded when the telenovela goes on air, but unfolds in a process dependent on audience response. Typically, when a telenovela starts, between twenty and thirty episodes are filmed and ready, the author has written fifteen to twenty more, and thereafter seeks to keep about twenty episodes ahead of the episode on air.

Very roughly, three major genre developments can be depicted in the history of the telenovela (the first screening in the early 1950s, as 'tele-theatre', with the daily telenovela emerging in the early 1960s). The 1950s and 1960s can be seen generally as the period of *romanticism*, being largely theatrical, thematically and aesthetically distanced from reality and primarily focused on a love story. In contrast, the late 1960s to the mid-1980s was the period of increased *realism*, when the telenovela developed into a genuine national *and* Latin American genre, culturally and thematically reflecting contemporary issues, inherently more televisual, and with the gradual introduction of ordinary dialect and colloquial language. The language of the telenovelas (especially the Brazilian, of the late 1960s and onwards) reiterated this realism, further enhancing the close relationship between telenovelas and the everyday life of Latin Americans. The Brazilian-produced *Beto Rockefeller* (TV Globo, 1968) marked the major breakthrough of this realistic subgenre. Finally, from the mid-1980s (the beginning of this phase varying somewhat according to the political developments in each country)

the genre developed into a *post-realist phase*, reflecting thematically the spirit of (re)democratisation and freedom of speech. However, all three subgenres still co-exist today.

Throughout their history, telenovelas have tackled some of the most important issues of the day, including migration, adaptation to urban life, managing rural nostalgia, struggling for social mobility and coping with and aspiring to modern consumer culture. During the years of military dictatorship in many Latin American countries it combined the dual role of being an attempted instrument of the military rulers, and at the same time respecting the audience demand for reflecting everyday contemporary life.

Today, freedom of expression is widespread and an integral element of the conditions upon which the media industries operate. Many contemporary issues are now taken up in the genre, parallel to and often woven together with the continued discourse of romantic and realist telenovelas. However, the emotionally abundant melodrama continues to be the overall rule of the game, often with the inclusion of a touch of fantasy or 'magic realism'. As such, telenovelas continue to predominate their national and regional markets, leaving American television series to more marginal broadcasting hours or to specialised television channels.

Thomas Tufte

RECOMMENDED READING

Fadul, A. (ed.) (1993), *Serial Fictions in TV: The Latin American Telenovelas*, São Paulo: ECA/USP.

Trinta, Aluizio R. (1997), 'News from Home: A Study of Realism and Melodrama in Brazilian Telenovelas', in Christine Geraghty and David Lusted (eds), *The Television Studies Book*, London, New York, Sydney, Auckland: Arnold.

Tufte, Thomas (2000), *Living with the Rubbish Queen – Telenovelas, Culture and Modernity in Brazil*, Luton: University of Luton Press.

COMEDY

Studying Comedy

Many analyses of comedy begin by noting the paucity of work in the field, and this will be no exception. Although the analysis of television is itself in its infancy, the discussion of television comedy has been categorised by fits and starts, exploring a diverse range of concerns, and arising out of conflicting histories and methodologies. Considering the sitcom's dominance of American prime-time television for nigh on fifty years now, as well as the genre's central family entertainment status in Britain and America, it seems odd that sustained analysis has not been a mainstay of media studies.

This lack arises from a congruence of factors. Most visibly, comedy's low cultural status has meant that academics coming from a humanities or literature background have often chosen to focus on more 'serious' concerns; comedy has always played second fiddle to tragedy. In addition, humour is, on the whole, popular and populist, and, although cultural studies' aims included broadening analysis out to popular forms, it is clear that much work is still carried out on 'quality' texts (see 'The Populist Debate').

More subtly, however, other factors have prevented a sustained critique of broadcast comedy. The range of the field is enormous and complex, incorporating sitcom, sketch shows, stand-up, advertising and animation, as well as the role of comedy in other genres such as drama, news, chat shows and so on. Furthermore, variations within each of these genres are vast. Where to begin analysing comedy when it encompasses mainstream sitcoms such as *Friends* (NBC, 1994–2004), surreal horror comedy like Chris Morris's *Jam* (C4, 2000), thirty-second television adverts and Jerry Springer's interjections on his talk shows? The complex and ubiquitous nature of comedy is one of its clearest defining aspects: unfortunately, this makes it notoriously difficult to get to grips with.

Furthermore, the nature of comedy itself has remained annoyingly elusive. So, while humour theory (see box) has attempted to define just what it is that makes us laugh, that theory's interdisciplinary nature and acknowledged failure in so far achieving its aims has meant that, on the whole, its work has not been taken up by media and cultural studies. This has resulted in studies of broadcast comedy that, bizarrely, almost fail to acknowledge humour at all.

In response, studies of comedy have chosen to focus on its other aspects. Predominant is the question of humour's subversive nature, representing a critique of dominant ideologies apparent within much of cultural studies. Comedy has been co-opted for such analysis precisely because of its assumed social role as a questioner of norms and a licence to say the unsayable. It is clear that Rowe's (1995) work on the 'unruly woman' legitimises certain representations and jokes precisely because they question not only the norms for comedy, but also those for society as a whole. This has also been explored in terms of representations of sexuality, in which a contradictory tone is often adopted: for example, although comedy was one of the first places to acknowledge that homosexuals exist, its predilection for camp portrayals has resulted in criticisms of stereotyping (Medhurst and Tuck, 1982). The question remains, of course, of whether we laugh with or at such portrayals.

Such analyses focus on the sitcom, and this has been a notable aspect of the study of broadcast comedy. The subsequent narrowing of the perceived role and nature of comedy has meant that, academically, it appears as if stand-up, satire, radio comedy, or anything other than sitcom does not exist. Furthermore, other aspects specific to comedy have yet to be adequately explored, such as audience readings, performance and stardom. And contemporary trends in cultural studies methodologies (particularly ethnography) have not, on the whole, been applied to comedy which, considering the social focus of both of these, would seem a fruitful collaboration.

This is not to say that valuable work does not exist. In the UK the field was kick-started by Jim Cook's (1982) edited collection in which sitcom's structure, social role and forms of representation are thoughtfully outlined. Although the collection's tone is an obviously cautious one (perhaps the authors could not believe they were writing about sitcom either), it pinpoints a variety of aspects broader than many subsequent analyses. Steve Neale and Frank Krutnik (1990) explore both film and television comedy, citing humour's potentially subversive social role in accordance with much similar analysis. They employ a rare method in which the varieties of comedy (sketch shows, slapstick and the like) are not only explored but are a central concern of their thesis.

Humour Theory

Humour theory is a complex and relatively undefined area, whose application to broadcast comedy has only recently begun to be explored (see, for example, Morreall, 1987). It is truly interdisciplinary, coalescing linguistics, sociology, psychology, maths and performance, among others, which may explain its involved and sometimes confusing nature. A central concern is the unpicking of joke structure, as well as questioning the role of humour within society generally. Like much of cultural studies, it explores the possible subversive nature of communication, locating humour as a potential site for critiquing dominant ideologies. However, unlike media and cultural studies, humour theory positions its subject as an essential and significantly radical social phenomenon.

Humour theories have traditionally been split into three separate camps: superiority, incongruity and relief. Although these have been treated as separate and conflicting it is clear that they overlap, with varying degrees of relevance to media communication.

The superiority theory dates back to Plato (tr. 1975) and Aristotle (tr. 1925) in the fourth century BC, but was given its clearest form by Hobbes in the mid-seventeenth century. He suggests that humour arises from attaining a position of 'sudden glory' (1914, p. 27), in which laughter reinforces power positions and is inevitably defined as a negative social phenomenon. This is similar to many analyses of sitcom, in which jokes have been seen to confirm hegemonic ideologies (Lovell, 1982).

The incongruity theory is traced back to Kant in the late eighteenth century, in which 'Laughter is an affect resulting from the sudden transformation of a heightened expectation into nothing' (2000, p. 209). Here humour results from the clash of incompatible discourses, which are themselves socially constructed and learned. It is this theory that has been most taken up by media studies, with Palmer drawing complex distinctions between social humour, broadcast comedy and jokes within narrative (1987, pp. 154, 167). Similarly, Morreall (1983) positions incongruity as essential not only to comedy but all social interactions, as one of the ways in which societies speak to themselves both socially and through media.

The relief theory is rooted in Freud (tr. 1976), in which humour functions socially and psychologically as a vent for repression and, by extension, questions social norms. Although it has proved difficult to relate such analysis to broadcast comedy, satire and a range of more sociopolitical comedians (Lenny Bruce, Bill Hicks, Ben Elton, Mark Thomas) could usefully be seen as lancing society's boils. The relationship between such a role and the debates on media effects are clear.

What has hindered the application of humour theory to broadcast comedy has, however, been its focus on jokes and joke structure. If cultural studies has increasingly noted the complex nature of media consumption (particularly its domestic mode and variable viewing patterns), the analysis of something as tiny as a joke seems like a backward step. Indeed, as contemporary analysis of broadcast comedy has focused on a narrow range of specifics to the detriment of a broader understanding, so has humour theory. It seems possible, then, that the developing relationship between the two is likely to open up a whole range of questions, methodologies and analyses, in which the study of both social and broadcast comedy will blossom.

Brett Mills

In the USA, much work on comedy has explored its sociopolitical nature. Darrell Hamamoto (1991) finds comedy to be a unifying, equilibrium-supporting form, noting this as different from its role in Britain. Similarly, David Marc (1989, p. 118) argues that sitcom is 'a representational art committed to harmony and consensus'. These analyses are placed within work on broadcasting in the USA as a whole, in which attempts to coalesce a geographically and ideologically disparate audience are best achieved, it seems, by comedy. There is a concurrent concern with the industrial nature of television comedy that, because of syndication and global sales, represents a significant source of possible long-term revenue unmatched by other genres. Moreover, the production of comedy is notably different in the UK and the USA, with the former based around specific solo writers, while the latter depends much more on stand-up comedians and producers.

Such critiques are indicative of sitcom's central position within academic work on comedy. This is odd, for it ignores the political nature of satire (seen by Humphrey Carpenter (2000) as responsible in Britain for the downfall of Macmillan's government in the 1960s), as well as the formal differences apparent in sketch shows and stand-up that surely offer sites for complex critiques of, and responses to, social ideologies and norms. Yet this very lack of formal structures (in both construction and reading) may be responsible for the deficiency of analysis of the full range of broadcast comedy. It appears that studying comedy is just too difficult. Yet that difficulty that has so far discouraged thorough long-term analysis of broadcast humour will, it is hoped, become its major focus and guiding principle.

Brett Mills

RECOMMENDED READING

Mills, Brett (2005), *Television Sitcom*, London: BFI.
Morreall, John (ed.) (1987), *The Philosophy of Laughter and Humour*, Albany: State University of New York Press.
Neale, Steve and Krutnik, Frank (1990), *Popular Film and Television Comedy*, London: Routledge.

Sketch Comedy

In both Britain and America, sketch comedy derives from the institutions and performance traditions associated with the professionalisation and commercialisation of theatrical entertainment in the nineteenth and early twentieth centuries. These included music hall in Britain, and minstrel shows, burlesque and vaudeville in America, all of them forms of variety entertainment containing a mix of music, comedy and other specialised acts and types of performance: magic acts, acrobatic acts, animal acts and so on (Bailey, 1986; Bratton, 1986; Toll, 1976). From 1907 onwards (the year in which music halls in Britain were first legally permitted to present them), comic sketches with dialogue (which in America had always been allowed) became part of a repertoire of comic forms that also included solo stand-up comedy and double acts. As further sites for comic performance were developed during the course of the twentieth century, comic sketches and their performers found a home not just in variety theatre but also in radio, film and television. Sometimes the shows and films in which they appeared would be dedicated solely to comedy, sometimes to a range of variety forms (Scheurer, 1985, p. 307, distinguishes between 'general variety', 'musical variety' and 'comedy variety'). Either way, and however tailored it was to the needs of these forms and the different media in which they appeared, sketch comedy, like solo stand-up and double-act comedy, continued – and continues – to thrive (Crowther and Pinfold, 1987; Halliwell, 1987; Jenkins, 1992a; Neale and Krutnik, 1990, pp. 176–208; Putterman, 1995; Toll, 1982, pp. 211–43; Took, 1976; Wertheim, 1979; Wilmut, 1980, 1985; Wilmut and Rosengard, 1989).

As the term implies, sketches are short, usually single-scene structures. They generally comprise a setting, one or more characters, and an internal time frame within which the comic possibilities of a premise of one kind or another

– a situation, a relationship, a conversation and its topics, a mode of language, speech or behaviour, or some other organising principle – are either pursued to a point of climax and conclusion (sometimes called a 'pay-off'), or else simply abandoned (a device pioneered in Britain by Spike Milligan in *Q* (BBC, 1969–82)). The brevity of sketches derives from their origins in variety, in which acts of any kind usually lasted no more than twenty minutes. (Most lasted around ten minutes and radio and television sketches are usually even briefer than this.)

Distinctions can be made between sketches that are visual in orientation (like Benny Hill's speeded-up chase sequences, in which the only sound is that of musical accompaniment) and those that focus largely or exclusively on dialogue (like the Mel Smith and Griff Rhys Jones 'head-to-head' sketches, where the only action is conversation and where the setting consists simply of a table and chairs). Wilmut (1985) further distinguishes between sketches and double acts (whose sketches are built around two equally billed performers: the Smothers Brothers, Morecambe and Wise, Smith and Jones and the like). Since double-act sketches are still sketches, the usefulness of this particular distinction is perhaps open to debate. What is important is the range of comedy made possible by what may initially appear to be a restricted form.

In the early years of television after the Second World War, sketches (and other forms of comic performance) were broadcast live, usually in the context of revues and other kinds of variety shows. It was at this time that performers like Milton Berle and shows like *The Toast of the Town* (CBS, 1948) became established in the USA. Even though programmes of all kinds were soon to be pre-recorded, the aura of 'liveness', of a 'here and now' performance before an audience, remained an important ingredient in variety, as witness subsequent shows such as *Sunday Night at the London Palladium* (ITV, 1955–67) and *Saturday Live* (C4, 1985–8) in the UK and *Your Show of Shows* (NBC, 1950–4) and *Saturday Night Live* (NBC, 1975–) in the USA. However, sketch comedy was always less dependent on this aura than stand-up. Sketches could therefore always make more overt use of recording, editing and other television techniques and could appear (whether in live, in would-be live, or in pre-recorded contexts) either as obvious inserts or as part of a pre-recorded package of items.

In the USA Ernie Kovacs and *Rowan and Martin's Laugh-In* (NBC, 1968–73) and in the UK *Monty Python's Flying Circus* (BBC, 1969–74, see box) were among the first to explore the possibilities of these techniques during the 1960s and early 1970s. They were also among the first to

Monty Python's Flying Circus

The first episode in the first series of *Monty Python's Flying Circus* was broadcast in Britain on 5 October 1969. Commissioned by the BBC, there were eventually four series overall (the last episode in the fourth series was first broadcast on 5 December 1974). The show's principal writers and performers were Graham Chapman, John Cleese (who left at the end of the third series), Eric Idle, Terry Jones and Michael Palin, with additional performances and animated titles, sketches and links provided by Terry Gilliam and regular appearances by Carol Cleveland, Ian Davidson and others.

Gilliam was American, and the show and its spin-off concerts, films and books were popular in the USA. However, most commentators have focused on the show's British (indeed, English) antecedents, sociocultural context and institutional base. Aside from the TV and radio shows on which members of the *Python* team worked prior to the advent of *Python* itself (*The Frost Report* (BBC, 1966–7), *Not the 1948 Show* (ITV, 1967–8), *Do Not Adjust Your Set* (ITV, 1967–9), *I'm Sorry I'll Read That Again* (BBC, 1964–73) and others), and in addition to the initial willingness of the BBC to sponsor a new generation of performers and writers at a time when established traditions, forms and values of all kinds were being challenged, commentators generally stress the team's background at Oxbridge and in Oxbridge revues and usually cite the BBC radio comedy, *The Goon Show* (1951–60), the stage revue *Beyond the Fringe* (1960–66) and *Q* as especially influential (Perry, 1983, pp. 9–56; Wilmut, 1980).

The humour in *The Goon Show* and *Q* in particular is often described as absurd or surreal, and this is the hallmark of *Python* as well: the elements of illogicality and playfulness to be found in most comedy are in *Python* stretched to the limit (hence the prevalence of 'silliness' as an accusation levelled at some of the sketches from within the programmes themselves). So overriding are these features that they tend to qualify those aspects of the *Python* programmes that might otherwise be viewed as straightforwardly satirical (the persistent lampooning of judges, accountants, doctors, politicians, TV announcers, military officers: all who claim, assume or aspire to institutionally established modes of authority, control and social status). Although satire, certainly, can be found in a number of otherwise similar or influential 1960s' sketch shows (*That Was The Week That Was* (BBC, 1962–3), *Not So Much A Programme, More A Way of Life* (BBC, 1964–5) and the like), the *Python* programmes themselves are perhaps best characterised by what Putterman (1995, p. 163) describes as 'a

Monty Python's Flying Circus: illogicality and playfulness stretched to the extreme

single level of burlesque that turned every manner of thought into some aspect of an all-consuming vaudeville show'.

What was distinctive about this particular show was that it encompassed a much wider range of 'thought' than had hitherto been the norm (including as it did references to Icelandic sagas, philosophers such as Jean-Paul Sartre and relatively obscure historical events), while persistently playing with the formats and forms of traditonal variety and its sketches, of popular culture and popular film, and, most notably, of TV itself (Neale and Krutnik, 1990, pp. 196–208; Wilmut, 1985, pp. 195–231). In combining these elements with a complex array of comic techniques and organisational features (repetition, interruption, digression and the like), the *Python* programmes appealed in particular to a generation of young, often university-educated audience willing to make a cult of its absurdities, and able to understand its references, to appreciate the uses it made of media formats and forms, and to identify with its comic attacks on institutional authority. As Miller points out (2000, pp. 127–38), this was its appeal in the USA as well as in the UK.   *Steve Neale* explore (and to parody) the forms and conventions of broadcast TV and to adapt the presentation of their sketch material to its segmental rhythms and structures. *Rowan and Martin's Laugh-In* in particular was marked by the rapid-fire presentation of one-line gags, regular comic characters, recurrent catchphrases and regular situations (not unlike an extended sequence of advertisements). Its sketch material was compressed, condensed and telegraphic, with variants produced across the span of a programme or series (not unlike a running gag). In all these respects, it set a precedent for later rapid-fire programmes such as *Three of a Kind* (BBC, 1981–3) and *The Fast Show* (BBC, 1994–2000).

Another type of innovation was the production of sketch and variety shows by women (Carol Burnett, Tracey Ullman, Victoria Wood, French and Saunders and others) and by ethnic minorities (*The Flip Wilson Show* (NBC, 1970–4), *The Real McCoy* (BBC, 1991–6), *Goodness Gracious Me* (BBC, 1996–2001)). However, alongside the additional innovations introduced by *The Muppet Show* (ITV, 1976–81), more traditional shows continued to be made. Morecambe and Wise, the Two Ronnies, Russ Abbot, Hale and Pace, Fry and Laurie, Mitchell and Webb and a number of others have all appeared in successful sketch shows in Britain since the 1960s. In America, on the other hand, whereas sitcoms (and stand-up) have flourished, new variety and sketch shows have been few and far between. Aside from the perennial *Saturday Night Live*, *SCTV Network* (NBC, 1981–3) and the subsequent *The Dave Thomas Comedy Show* (CBS, 1990) are obvious exceptions.

Steve Neale

RECOMMENDED READING

Neale, Steve and Krutnik, Frank (1990), *Popular Film and Television Comedy*, London: Routledge.

Scheurer, Timothy (1985), 'The Variety Show', in B. G. Rose (ed.), *TV Genres: A Handbook and Reference Guide*, Westport: Greenwood Press.

Wilmut, Roger (1980), *From Fringe to Flying Circus: Celebrating a Unique Generation of Comedy, 1960–1980*, London: Methuen.

Situation Comedy, Part 1

Situation comedy (sitcom) is one of the staples of mature broadcast television. On the genre-dial it sits between 'sketch comedy' and 'situation drama', especially continuous

serials and episodic series (see 'The Mini-Series' and 'Soap Opera'). It has had a remarkably stable semiotic history, migrating fully formed to TV from radio (does anyone remember *The Clitheroe Kid* (BBC, 1957–72)?) and continuing to the present day with few fundamental changes (see Marc, 1989). The heyday of broadcasting was made just that by classics like *The Phil Silvers Show* (CBS, 1955–9) and *I Love Lucy* (CBS, 1951–7), still revered by many as among television's best-ever creations, or *Hancock's Half Hour* (BBC, 1954–61), *Steptoe and Son* (BBC, 1962–74) and *Till Death Us Do Part* (BBC, 1965–75) in Britain.

American and British sitcoms have proved to be extremely exportable around the world, using a formula so 'transparent' that they could stand in for 'indigenous' programming for the local audience (see Olsen, 1999). This is especially true for English-speaking countries, or even for those countries where English-language programming is 'neutral' compared with, say, French programming in Germany, German in France or Holland, Dutch in Belgium and so on. The genre has also led to an excess of 'fanship' with broadcasters mounting 'fests' of just one or two shows. In Australia, Foxtel opened a special cable channel during the Sydney 2000 Olympic Games, devoted to sixteen days of non-stop *Simpsons* (Fox, 1989–), twenty-four hours a day.

The sitcom format suited the Anglo-American industrial production of TV very well. It could use a studio with one or at most two sets, and few or no film inserts. With stable characters in a given situation it could be written and produced by an in-house team of screenwriters and production staff in industrial quantities at so many pages a day. It was also tolerant of commercial imperatives, allowing for segment-length acts, interrupted by commercial breaks, fitting into the TV hour (fifty-odd minutes) or half-hour. It was even productive enough to generate spin-off shows, such as *Rhoda* (CBS, 1974–8) from *The Mary Tyler Moore Show* (BCS, 1970–7), *George and Mildred* (ITV, 1976–9) from *Man About the House* (ITV, 1973–6) or *Frasier* (NBC, 1993–2004) from *Cheers* (NBC, 1982–93).

Such shows were distinguished by combining comic talent with dramatic character and action. Sitcom could put seriously funny actors into fictional situations (like John Cleese in *Fawlty Towers* (BBC, 1975–9) and Rowan Atkinson in *Blackadder* (BBC, 1983–9) or *Mr Bean* (ITV, 1990–5)) where the 'situation' in the sitcom was a vehicle for the comedic genius of a given actor, without whose services the show would be hard to imagine. Or it could feature an ensemble of less well-known actors to bring out the comedic potential in a given situation, such as *Dad's Army* (BBC, 1968–77) or *Taxi* (ABC, 1978–82/NBC,

1982–3). Naturally, producers liked it best when a sitcom developed a 'situation' and a star comic together, as in *Roseanne* (ABC, 1988–97), *I Love Lucy* or *The Cosby Show* (NBC, 1984–92). And of course, such shows made stars out of their performers, for instance Christina Applegate, who went on to a good Hollywood career after playing Kelly, the definitive 'gormless gorgeous' dumb-blonde teenager in *Married … With Children* (Fox, 1987–97).

There were two main types of sitcom: the drama of family comportment (often mixed with sibling rivalry) and the drama of sexual exploration. The former was routinely set in a home environment, the latter in the workplace:

Family sitcoms specialised in the drama of family comportment. They were distinguished from serials and drama series by their focus on internal family roles: usually parents, children and siblings, whether they were presented as blood family (*Roseanne*), melded family (*The Brady Bunch* (ABC, 1969–74)), or metaphorical family (*Cheers*). Soap opera, on the other hand, focused on the drama of neighbourly comportment. It covered the street, neighbourhood or community. Sitcoms and soaps between them showed how families could get along internally (sitcom), and alongside each other (see Hartley, 1999, p. 172). Some sitcoms hybridised with soaps (see p. 60). The BBC's *The Vicar of Dibley* (BBC, 1994–2007) was really about neighbourliness, although it was also a 'workplace sitcom' (see below) with plenty of talk and funny business in the flirting and fancying department.

Family or domestic sitcoms were perhaps the bedrock of broadcast television. They were what you grew up on, gently and amusingly teaching two important skills: how to watch television (media literacy); and how to live in families with tolerant mutual accommodation, talking not fighting (life skills). Although the sitcom remained primarily an adult genre, its efficiency in the matter of family role play also made it a major component of children's TV.

One of the pleasures of watching sitcoms was to observe how bizarre some of the family set-ups were, no matter what their surface 'smileyness' suggested about 'family values'. It was rare indeed to get the traditional 'nuclear family' – so rare that it became a plausibly novel 'situation' for the BBC's *2.4 Children* (1991–8). More likely was a non-standard family: solo father and boys in *My Three Sons* (ABC, 1960–5/CBS, 1965–72); father and girls in *Full House* (ABC, 1987–95); father and boys melded with mother and girls in *The Brady Bunch* – with never a sexual frisson among the whole lot of them, including aunt-cum-servant Alice.

There were monster families (*The Munsters* (CBS, 1964–6)), vampire families (*The Addams Family* (ABC,

1964–6)), witch families (*Bewitched* (ABC, 1964–72)), alien families (*Third Rock from the Sun* (NBC, 1996–2001)), all of which tended to suggest that, like modernity, progress, science and reason themselves, the modern suburban family was shadowed by darker and mostly unspoken 'others' from premodern and irrational traditions (see Spigel, 1996). Within the sphere of everyday ordinariness, families were fractured at best. Cybil was divorced and menopausal, Ellen gay (see below), Murphy Brown a single parent and Victor Meldrew (in *One Foot in the Grave* (BBC, 1990–2000)) a grouchy old man. Even where families were intact they were dysfunctional, as in *Married … With Children*, *Absolutely Fabulous* (BBC, 1992–2005) or *Roseanne* (see box).

Sitcoms' attention to the 'not-quiteness' of family life, and to some of the grittier issues lurking under suburban consumerism even as audiences lived in it and endorsed it at elections, made them capable of politics. Classic in this respect was *Till Death Us Do Part*, making a national hero out of a really ghastly old bastard, whose sexist, racist, xenophobic chauvinism and insularity were mercilessly lampooned by writer Johnny Speight. Speight thought he was inoculating the English against some of their nastier 'cultural heritage'. They perversely loved Alf Garnett in their millions, and made it hard for actor Warren Mitchell to play any other role. Alf Garnett, for his part, crossed the Atlantic to become Archie Bunker in Norman Lear's *All in the Family* (CBS, 1971–9), which also politicised both 'traditional family values' and the sitcom format (see Mills, 2004a).

In 1992, the then Vice President Dan Quayle criticised *Murphy Brown* (CBS, 1988–98) – 'it doesn't help' – for promoting single parenthood instead of 'family values'. Candice Bergen, who played Murphy Brown, got a 'right of reply' in the subsequent season of the series. The media throughout America spent several months debating family philosophy and national policy priorities via a fictional sitcom persona (whose own speech on the subject, however, as right-wing 'shock-jock' Rush Limbaugh commented at the time, 'wasn't funny'). Other 'political' sitcoms included *M*A*S*H* (CBS, 1972–83), making war less than noble in the Vietnam era, although it was set in Korea (see 'Hospital Drama'). *Ellen* (ABC, 1994–8) sparked public debate about gay and lesbian issues in families just as *Murphy Brown* did about single parents. *Roseanne* put working-class life and non-standard body shapes into prime-time sitcom.

Using 'not-quite' family set-ups to teach about family comportment while attending to humourous situations and attractive characters obviously caused the format to cascade from regular TV to kids' TV. The family was intact in *Clarissa Explains it All* (Nickelodeon, 1991–4), but the perspective was that of the teenage daughter, not the parents (see Hartley, 1999, pp. 181–5). In *Sister, Sister* (ABC, 1994–9) the main characters were (and were played by) African-American twins who were supposed to have been brought up separately by different parents not married to each other. The white version of this was *Two of a Kind* (ABC, 1998–9), played by the Olsen twins (who debuted as 'the' baby in *Full House*), whose mother was absent. Then there was the highly successful *Sabrina the Teenage Witch* (ABC, 1996–2000/WB, 2000–3) (Melissa Joan Hart), who lived with two witch aunts. *Moesha* (UPN, 2001) featured

an all-black leading cast, with a teenage girl (Brandy Norwood) having to deal with her father's new partner. These shows indicated that, for teenage-oriented sitcoms especially, there was a need to 'delete' the mother from the family in order to propel the 'situation'. The same was true for *My Three Sons*, *Full House*, *Father Knows Best* (CBS, 1954–60) and the like.

Workplace sitcoms often developed characterisations and actions that undercut or even belied the 'situation' itself. Even allowing for the banal sociological fact that sexual partners are often selected from among workmates, workplace sitcoms seemed generically driven to be about sexual chemistry rather than occupational specificity. They

---

Brass Eye

Brass Eye (C4, 1997, 2001) is a series of mock current affairs programmes, covering topical issues such as drugs, sex, social violence and animal welfare. While adopting the standard format of such programming, with roving reporters, studio discussions, exchanges between experts and a main presenter who guides the viewer through the programme, it aims to lay bare the contradictions and ideologies of such programming through its stretching of these characteristics to excess. The programme is loud, brash and chaotic, resulting in a bewildering viewing experience which could be equated with the Brechtian notion of 'alienation'; in doing so, it encourages a critical approach to the verisimilitude of television, and the pompous, paternalistic attitude often adopted by factual broadcasting.

Perhaps *Brass Eye*'s most celebrated technique is the fake interview, in which real celebrities are duped into lending their fame to campaigns which are not only made up, but also clearly ludicrous. In the episode about animals, for example, celebrities such as the magician Paul Daniels, the novelist Jilly Cooper and the actress Britt Ekland all gave soundbites encouraging the viewing public to donate money to help an elephant held captive in a cage so small its trunk was stuck up its own anus. Furthermore, in the episode on drugs, the Conservative MP David Amess supported a campaign against the fictious narcotic 'cake', even asking a question about it in the British Houses of Parliament. In demonstrating well-known faces' willingness to speak on subjects for which they have no knowledge, *Brass Eye* undermines televisual conventions of authority and expertise, and is therefore an early intervention into debates about celebrity culture (Evans and Hesmondhalgh, 2005).

Brass Eye is written and performed by Chris Morris, who has made a career out of dismantling the conventions of a

range of media. Starting out working in radio, he has repeatedly been sacked by various broadcasters for his behaviour, including releasing helium into a newsroom during a live broadcast. Morris perhaps came to most prominence in *The Day Today* (BBC, 1994), a series of mock news programmes which was clearly a precursor to *Brass Eye*. In *The Day Today* Morris played many parts, most notably the main news anchor, which was a pitch-perfect amalgam of various then-current BBC newsreaders, such as Jeremy Paxman and Michael Buerk. In demonstrating the news industry's bombastic processes and prioritising of presentation over content, *The Day Today* found humour in dismantling television conventions through simple exaggeration.

While *Brass Eye* continued this project, it may also be remembered for the fuss caused over its content, and debates about offensive broadcasting. This is most obviously seen in the one-off *Brass Eye* special in 2001, which, in focusing on paedophilia, aimed to interrogate the media hysteria surrounding this most sensitive of topics. However, for many audience members the intermingling of comedy and sexual abuse was unacceptable, no matter what the programme's intention, and so this episode remains one of the most complained about British television programmes of all time. Morris has noted that the intention of *Brass Eye* was to shock, for outrage forces debate and discussion rather than acceptance (Ferguson, 2001, p. 13). The fact that the then-regulators, the Independent Television Commission and the Broadcasting Standards Commission, required Channel 4 to apologise for failing to give enough warning about the programme's content before its broadcast clearly says something about the assumed relationship audiences are supposed to have with broadcasting in general, and for comedy in particular (see Mills, 2007).

Brett Mills

routinely reverted to an almost obsessive focus on 'situations' that occurred in relationships rather than in workplaces as such, especially after a given sitcom had relaxed after a couple of seasons' ratings success. A camp, pioneering example of this format (workplace as pretext for risqué talk) was *Are You Being Served?* (BBC, 1972–85). Long-running American sitcoms like *Taxi* and *Cheers* also used the device of flirting in the workplace.

British television's *Drop the Dead Donkey* (C4, 1990–8) was set in a TV newsroom, and initially developed characters associated with that environment. The unseen but brutal owner Sir Royston and his awful corporate-speak sidekick, the preening presenters with feet of clay (one of them clearly paying homage to a real newsreader, the late Reginald Bosanquet), and the reporter who'd stop at nothing to get a story (less obviously modelled on front-line war reporters of the period like Sue Lloyd Roberts). But pretty soon, with the success of the show, characters and actions took over the comedy, leaving the situation – news-gathering and its ethical dilemmas – increasingly in the background.

The character of Joy (Susannah Doyle), for example, was a great comic creation. Joy was young, lovely and smart, but low enough in the office food chain to attract sexist and patronising treatment from the main characters. Her wonderfully viperish responses, and her increasingly implausible revenges, were a delight of the show – but they had very little to do with the situation of a newsroom. The script began to pander directly to what Joy was 'about' in viewers' minds rather than in the diegetic world of the TV newsroom, putting her into situations (the gym, the Awards Night) where sexy clothes and extreme violence might coincide.

The emphasis of the show as a whole moved inexorably towards further sexual exploration: the predatory behaviour of the 'loveable rogue' larrikin reporter; the failing marriage of the wimpish hypochondriac editor; the love life of the lesbian big-sister editor; the predilection of the snooty female anchor for one-night stands with truck drivers. Eventually, *Drop the Dead Donkey* was not about TV news at all, it was about sex.

Some sitcoms seem to be hybrids, joining family comportment (living together, couch-centric) and workplace (sexual exploration, flirt-centric). *Friends* was classic here, as was *Seinfeld* (NBC, 1989–98). These twenty-something heterosexual home-building shows sometimes went all the way and put their characters in a relationship – *Mad About You* (NBC, 1992–9) (Helen Hunt) did that, eventually producing another sitcom baby to join those in *Murphy Brown* and *Full House*. Many workplace sitcoms reproduced the

family formula, while many domestic comedies required a novel 'situation'. For example, in the BBC's *Game On* (BBC, 1995–8), the 'family' comprised three flat-sharers. Samantha Janus was the potent force of the show, pretending to be a dumb but single blonde. She lived with two inadequate men, one disabled by unrequited love of an idealised partner who was cynically ripping him off, the other disabled by agoraphobia. They talked about sex all the time, as people did in workplace sitcoms, but they lived in an internally celibate household, albeit not in a classic family.

Some sitcoms seem so full of raw, new energy that they could be counted as R & D (research and development) for the genre itself, renewing its very form for a new generation of writers, performers and audiences. *The Young Ones* (BBC, 1982–4), *Absolutely Fabulous* (see box), *Marion and Geoff* (BBC, 2000–3) and *The Office* (BBC, 2001–3) did that in the UK; *Seinfeld*, *The Larry Sanders Show* (HBO, 1992–8) and *Curb Your Enthusiasm* (HBO, 2000–) in the USA. Meanwhile, *The Royle Family* (BBC, 1998–2006) achieved the same rare trick of being 'about' TV as well as 'life', testing its genre, and any vestigial faith we may have had in 'the' family, to destruction (see 'Contemporary Sitcom' below).

John Hartley

RECOMMENDED READING

Hartley, John (1999), *Uses of Television*, London and New York: Routledge.

Mills, Brett (2005), *Television Sitcom*, London: BFI.

Newcomb, Horace (1974), 'Situation and Domestic Comedies: Problems, Families and Fathers', in Horace Newcomb, *TV: The Most Popular Art*, New York: Doubleday.

Spigel, Lynn (1996), 'From Theatre to Space Ship: Metaphors of Suburban Domesticity in Postwar America', in Roger Silverstone (ed.), *Visions of Suburbia: Symptoms and Metaphors of Modernity*, London and New York: Routledge.

Situation Comedy, Part 2

As explained above, the workplace can provide a pseudo-family of co-workers who take the place of the traditional nuclear family. Sitcoms can alternate between the home and the office (beginning with *The Dick Van Dyke Show* (CBS, 1961–6)). The home and workplace can be one and the same, as in those sitcoms set in family-owned inns or resorts or in families who live 'above the store' (for example, *Fawlty Towers*, *Newhart* (CBS, 1982–90)). Friends can

The Unruly Woman Sitcom (*I Love Lucy*, *Roseanne*, *Absolutely Fabulous*)

A subtype of the family sitcom – the comedy of the 'unruly woman' – has formed a persistent thread, running from *I Love Lucy* (CBS, 1951–7) to *Roseanne* (ABC, 1988–97) to *Absolutely Fabulous* (BBC, 1992–2005) and continuing in the more contemporary characters of Grace in *Will and Grace* (NBC, 1988–2006, see box) and Dharma in *Dharma and Greg* (see below). The term 'unruly woman' has been applied to the sitcom by Kathleen Rowe (1995) with particular reference to *Roseanne* and her image of the 'domestic goddess'. The term describes an icon of a grotesque female whose excesses break social boundaries. She is characterised by a body that is both 'excessive' and 'loose'. In the cases of Roseanne (Roseanne Barr) and Edina (Jennifer Saunders), the excess is represented by fat; but since the unruly woman is just as often tall, thin and attractive (Lucille Ball or Patsy (Joanna Lumley)), it may also take the form of excessive loudness (Roseanne's voice), excessive clothing (Edina's La Croix outfits), hairstyle (Patsy's beehive) and make-up (Lucy's mouth), excessive drinking and smoking (*AbFab*) or simply exceeding the norms of femininity at the time the character was popular.

In the 1950s, for example, Lucy could have been considered 'unruly' because she constantly sought an outlet from domesticity and because she was such a comic failure at domestic tasks. Similarly, looseness can consist in anything from Roseanne's loose tongue to Edina's tendency to lose control of her body and fall (down stairs, into graves, on to conveyor belts). The sitcom has always drawn on a tradition of physical comedy, and the unruly woman is often a female clown (Lucille Ball, Jennifer Saunders, Jenna Elfman). Yet the looseness and excess of her body is not merely funny; it represents an ideological field through which the unruly woman embodies a critique of more conventional notions of the proper behaviour for a sitcom wife.

This is why Rowe and others have viewed Lucy as the prototype for the unruly woman character in the sitcom. Rowe (1995, p. 80) believes that both Hollywood romantic comedy and the sitcom centre on the relationship between the sexes and provide a clearly delineated space for female 'disruptiveness … the unruly woman became anchored in the family like television itself, no longer a bride but a wife, a mother, a matriarch … taking up the woman's story after the high drama of courtship and the wedding that resolves romantic comedy, the domestic sitcom explores what follows'.

That is, marriage and the family act as social forces that 'contain' the 'transgressive' spirit of the unruly woman, to

Absolutely Fabulous: feminine excess in the unruly woman sitcom

borrow some terms from Pat Mellencamp's discussion of Lucy and Gracie Allen. Mellencamp (1986, p. 61) writes that 'containment' was not only a defensive, military strategy developed as US foreign policy in the 1950s; it was practised on the domestic front as well, and it was aimed at 'excluding women from the workforce and keeping them in the home'.

The issue becomes the following: just how 'transgressive' should we read these sitcom wives as being? Do their antics cause them to transcend the boundaries of their situations or does the domestic setting of the sitcom act to contain them at the end of each week's episode, sending them back to the situation of domestic imprisonment with which they begin each week? In other words, how we analyse the transgressive or critical potential of each unruly woman will determine our view of her position. If we merely look at the sitcom's 'narrative architecture', no sitcom can be transgressive because the episodic format forces us to return to the familiar status quo with which this week's episode began. In order to perceive subversion, we must look at something besides narrative closure. For instance, it is possible that the outrageousness of the physical 'gags' performed by Lucy et al. may transcend her return to being Mrs Ricardo each week. Indeed, these are the moments that one remembers from *I Love Lucy*, the comic peak of the series.

In this reading, because her gags have never been surpassed, Lucy could be read as the most subversive of all, given the constraints of her historical position. On the other hand, if we are looking to find a total critique of domesticity one must choose between *Roseanne* and *Absolutely Fabulous*, which would seem to go much further in presenting characters who lack all maternal instincts; this is exacerbated by the role reversal between Edina and Saffron (Julia Sawalha) according to which Saffron's place is in the kitchen whereas Eddie displays a surreal level of domestic ineptitude (see Kirkham and Skeggs, 1998, pp. 287–98). In this reading, farce and ideological subversion count for a lot; the exaggerated excess of the characters makes them radical. The fan culture that formed around *AbFab* would seem to indicate that many viewers identified with the bad mothers and therefore against the proper but dull daughter. Yet one can also read Eddie and Patsy as characters without any redeeming value, thus identifying with Saffron and against the lead characters. In this way a more 'realistic' sitcom such as *Roseanne*, with its proletarian setting and more lifelike characters, may be seen as providing a better critique of domesticity in its very believability.

Whereas few viewers, if any, would compare their family to the Monsoons, nearly every American could identify with the typical nuclear family populating *Roseanne*. *Roseanne*'s acts of unruliness, that is to say, mean more to the audience than do the more outrageous antics of highly stereotyped characters such as Lucy or Edina. Thus when it comes to doing ideological analysis, the sitcom is far less simplistic than its structure would indicate. The situation of the unruly woman illustrates this truth about our most common form of television comedy.

Jane Feuer

provide a substitute family in shows intended for younger audiences (*The Young Ones*, *Seinfeld*, *Friends*, *Sex and the City* (HBO, 1998–2004) – see box) The nuclear family often breaks down into odd combinations including single parents with children, step-families, even gay men and straight single women (see box). Yet in every case (even in a science-fiction setting such as *Red Dwarf* (BBC, 1989–99)), the sitcom seems to require the presence of a quasi-familial structure in order to satisfy the needs of the viewer. The TV viewer is always addressed by the sitcom as a member of a family – 'from our family to yours'; in fact, the familial mode of address permeates TV in general. In some ways, then, the title 'family sitcom' is redundant since all sitcoms involve some kind of domestic unit.

On the other hand, one could argue that the workplace or 'friends' situation is distinct from the nuclear family setting; that it appeals to a different (younger, hipper) audience; that it is ideologically more contentious. Such an argument is based on the fact that the nuclear family is considered an ideologically conservative social unit that supports the status quo of 'family values'. Therefore, to base a sitcom on a nuclear family is to affirm rather than question the status quo. Following this point of view, sitcoms that undo the nuclear family are in a sense critical of it as a social institution; the alternate families that develop are social alternatives to the nuclear family status quo. Thus *The Cosby Show*, a blockbuster sitcom coming along after a long line of successful workplace family sitcoms, could be read as an ideological regression to the traditional *Father Knows Best* ideologies of the 1950s and thus reflective of a conservative turn (despite issues of race) in the sitcom taken during the Reagan/Thatcher era. On the other hand, a show that has been considered quite radically critical of family values – Fox network's iconoclastic *Married ... With Children* – also uses a nuclear family setting.

The question of what counts as an innovative feature in the development of a sitcom is difficult because in some ways we are talking about a framework so simple and so easy to recognise that the sitcom is, literally, child's play. And yet the form shows no signs of being exhausted or of not being adaptable to all kinds of socially and comically complex circumstances. As David Marc has pointed out, the sitcom's 'narrative architecture' has remained directly traceable to the radio period. As he explains it, 'episode = familiar status quo → ritual error made → ritual lesson learned → familiar status quo' (Marc, 1989, pp. 190–1).

This 'storytelling grammar', he remarks, has 'persisted across the stylistic revisions of four decades'. Marc goes on to show how episodes of different sitcoms from each decade (*I Love Lucy*, *Bewitched*, *All in the Family*, *The Cosby Show*) illustrate this problem/resolution format. That is to say, that if we look at the sitcom in terms of what might be called its plot, we find little development or innovation. The situation has always been a simple and repeatable frame on which to hang all manner of gags, one-liners, warm moments, physical comedy and ideological conflicts.

In fact, one could say that it has been the ideological flexibility of the sitcom that has accounted for its longevity. The sitcom has been the perfect format for illustrating current ideological conflicts while entertaining an audience.

What if, for example, a family of hillbillies struck oil and moved to the richest community in the USA? What if a working-class bigot father had to live with a leftist son-in-law? What if a family of liberals gave birth to a Republican son? What if the daughter of aging hippies in San Francisco were to marry the son of a ruling-class corporate family? These are the comic premises of *The Beverly Hillbillies* (CBS, 1962–71), *All in the Family*, *Family Ties* (NBC, 1982–9) and *Dharma and Greg* (ABC, 1997–2002) respectively, and what is remarkable about this list is the wide range of ideological conflict the sitcom proves able to accommodate, even including political reversals to accom-

modate changing social and political norms (for instance, the premise of *Family Ties* is that of *All in the Family* reversed).

The US sitcom *Dharma and Greg* well illustrates the ideological flexibility found in most of these 'divided family' premises. If we look at the first scene of the first (pilot) episode, we see the binary, dualistic structure so typical of the domestic sitcom. A young boy and a young girl find themselves on an underground train. The girl and her parents, coded to signify 'hippies', discuss astrological signs. The boy and his parents, dressed in preppy attire, discuss the health hazards associated with taking

---

Sex and the City

Suggested by its twenty-five-minute episodes, *Sex and the City* (HBO, 1998–2004) was originally conceived as a traditional sitcom. However, its producer Darren Star insisted that its dramatic aspirations should not be constrained by the narrative or aesthetic limitations of the genre. He therefore insisted that the show dispense with a live studio audience, canned laughter, a fixed set and the traditional four-camera set-up (see Sohn, 2002, p. 14). In contrast, its more 'filmic' style of production seemed to uniquely suit its narrative sensibilities; never allowing the comedy or slapstick elements of the show to completely eclipse its more dramatic moments (see Creeber, 2004b, p. 142).

Sex and the City was based, in part, on writer Candace Bushnell's book of the same name, compiled from her column for the *New York Observer*. Bushnell has stated in several interviews that its central character was her alter ego, but for reasons of privacy she created the fictional character of Carrie Bradshaw (Sarah Jessica Parker), a woman with the same career and same initials as herself. Based around Carrie and the personal trials and tribulations of her three closest friends – the traditionalist Charlotte York (Kristin Davis), the career-minded Miranda Hobbs (Cynthia Nixon) and the sex-obsessed Samantha Jones (Kim Cattrall) – the show soon acquired a reputation for discussing and portraying 'female-centred' issues with sometimes surprising honesty and frankness.

The most common narrative pattern of the show revolved around Carrie as she researched her next newspaper column, each of her friends providing a personal perspective on particular topics and debates. These included questions such as: 'Is there a secret cold war between married and singles?', 'Are threesomes the new sexual frontier?', 'How often is normal?', 'Can you change a man?', 'How do you know if you're good in

bed?' and so on. In this way, personal topics such as marriage, commitment, divorce, pregnancy, miscarriages, compatibility, fidelity and (of course) shopping were discussed alongside discussions about female masturbation, the joy of vibrators, oral/anal sex, threesomes, lesbianism, sexual perversion, 'funky spunk' and female ejaculation.

Sex and the City has consequently been conceived by some critics as an example of contemporary television comedy's attempt to portray and address issues of 'third-wave feminism'. According to Astrid Henry, it reflects 'an important – if limited – vision of female empowerment, a feminism that mirrors contemporary third wave attempts to celebrate both women's power and women's sexuality' (2004, p. 82). In contrast, critics like Jonathan Bignell suggested that the show rendered invisible important issues about female liberation such as questions of economic status, work and social power – arguing that 'the central characters' fascination with clothes, shoes, hair and personal style is a focus on relatively trivial aspects of women's lives, in contrast to questions of gender equality and the difficulty that real women face in employment and opportunity' (2004, p. 217).

Whatever ideological position you take on the issues examined and portrayed in *Sex and the City*, it is difficult to underestimate just how intricate and sophisticated it allowed the sitcom to become. By taking it out of the studio and into the streets, bars and restaurants of New York (its 'fifth character'), it created a greater sense of generic realism – one that could now handle adult themes, character complexity and narrative development in a way never imagined by the genre before. If *The Office* (see box below) modernised the sitcom by making it look more like a documentary, then *Sex and City* transformed it by giving it the aspirations of cinema – both in style and content.

Glen Creeber

Sex and the City: female empowerment in the modern sitcom

public transportation. Already (before Dharma and Greg even meet in their adult personas) the basic ideological oppositions of the show are set forth in this amusing fatalistic 'flashback'. The past three seasons of the series have merely served to flesh out the details. If Greg is a government attorney, then Dharma has to be a yoga instructor. If Greg is rigid and organised, Dharma must be laid back and spiritual. However, as the episodes progress, new weekly situations must be generated from this basic premise. That is why, increasingly, the parents of Dharma and Greg have served to carry the basic ideological oppositions between conservative and radical American lifestyles.

In particular, Dharma's father, Larry Finkelstein, has remained the static character signifying (warmed over and burnt out) 1960s' radical hippie politics, whereas Greg's mother has served as a similar tentpole for high-society Republican gentility. This has freed up the other characters to indulge in more fluid and changeable behaviour, as when Greg leaves the law to become a 'free spirit' for a few episodes or when Dharma becomes increasingly materialistic. Since US sitcoms usually run much longer than British ones, the basic dualism of such shows tends to thin out as time goes by and more and more situations are required. *Family Ties*, for instance, started out with a sharp contrast between 1960s' liberal parents and neo-conservative children, but as the show continued it came to centre more and more on the popular son character played by Michael J. Fox; the ideological conflicts waned, and many believe the show was trivialised. For this reason, US sitcoms usually reveal their ideological frames much more clearly in the first season than in ensuing ones, and in studying the family sitcom, we often make generalisations based on the first season of the show's run.

Jane Feuer

RECOMMENDED READING

Marc, David (1989), *Comic Visions: Television Comedy and American Culture*, New York: Blackwell.

Mellencamp, Patricia (1986) 'Situation Comedy, Feminism, and Freud: Discourses of Gracie and Lucy', reprinted in Charlotte Brunsdon, Julie D'Acci and Lynn Spigel (eds) (1997) *Feminist Television Criticism: A Reader*, Oxford: Oxford University Press.

Mills, Brett (2005), *Television Sitcom*, London: BFI.

Rowe, Kathleeen (1995), The Unruly Woman: Gender and the Genres of Laughter, Austin: University of Texas Press.

The 'Gay' and 'Queer' Sitcom

If the family sitcom often begins with a strong ideological premise that gradually exhausts itself, the gay sitcom often goes the other way: beginning with an ambiguous or confused situation, it picks up steam as the gay characters 'come out' or as the show's 'camp' humour thereby takes over. This was demonstrated by *Ellen*, which floundered in its first seasons because the lead character, played by stand-up comedienne Ellen DeGeneres, was not convincing in a pseudo-heterosexual role. And the reason she was not convincing was that Ellen DeGeneres herself was a confirmed lesbian, a state that was always readable to her gay audience. For example, she wore trousers when she was a maid of honour at her friend Paige's wedding. This was read by lesbians in the audience as a giveaway signifier of her sexual identity. It was no doubt also read as 'off' the heteronormative path by non-gay-identified viewers.

As Ellen DeGeneres started to 'leak' news of her gayness to the media (by denying, for example, that she was 'Lebanese'), the show took on a clearer identity, culminating in the coming-out episode ('The Puppy Episode', 30 April 1997). This episode also illustrated how closely interwoven in the public's mind are the persona of a sitcom star (especially ones with a background in stand-up comedy) and the assumed life status of the actor portraying that character.

Contemporaneous with Ellen's coming out on US TV, other sitcoms started to make extensive use of jokes about gender-bending and gender confusion. *Suddenly Susan* (NBC, 1996–2000) did an episode ('A Boy Like That', 24 April 1997) in which a typical liberal statement about how 'we' need to tolerate homosexuals fronted an actually quite outrageous joke on its star, Brooke Shields. The episode traced a movement from rejection to acceptance of the gay brother of one of the supporting characters, a macho Latino male. This comic premise was not particularly humourous. But in the course of following the problem/resolution format, the brothers visited a gay country and western bar with Susan (Brooke Shields) and her female co-worker.

When a gay cowboy tried to pick her up (mistaking her for a drag queen), Susan/Brooke said to him, 'Sorry, I'm really a woman.' He replied, 'Not with those shoulders.' This flirtation with the possibility of 'troubling' Brooke Shields's gender is both the funniest and most radical moment of the show because it calls attention to the fact that Brooke

Will and Grace

When his flaming homosexual pal Jack (Sean Hayes) chides the more masculine but no less gay Will Truman (Eric McCormack) for not dating enough, he taunts Will by referring to him as 'Margaret Truman'. I want to take this very simple joke from the sitcom to demonstrate some of the issues surrounding 'queer' humour, using *Will and Grace* (NBC, 1998–2006) as a case study. You do not have to know who Margaret Truman was to laugh at this joke. The mere fact that Jack refers to Will by a woman's name represents an 'insider' form of humour among gay men similar to the appellation 'Miss' in front of a girl's name (as in calling another gay man 'Miss Mary'). There is the simple acknowledgment that this is a conversation between one gay man and another. There is an acknowledgment as well of a shared historical situation according to which effeminacy and gender transitivity were what united one gay man with another. For older (American) viewers there is also the knowledge that Margaret Truman, daughter of President Harry Truman and sometime actress and mystery author, was a celebrity who possessed the particularly minor form of fame so important to twentieth-century gay male cultural experience.

Although the joke can be read and enjoyed on a number of levels, it is in fact steeped in gay cultural experience. And yet the gender-bending nature of that culture experience seems to have penetrated sufficiently into the mainstream to allow *Will and Grace* to be an equally successful sitcom for gay and straight audiences. Just as in the earlier sitcoms, Jewish humour became American humour; nowadays it might be that 'queer' humour is American humour, that the 'camp' sensibility long cherished by closeted gay men has now become part of mainstream American humour. Following a definition of 'camp' as a 'gay sensibility', we can say that 'queer humour' embraces both identification and parody, that it paradoxically combines into one sensibility the most extreme feelings of empathy and the bitchiest kind of detached amusement (Dyer, 1986, p. 154). This is the sense of humour that *Will and Grace* so frequently invokes. Although Jack is the most overt 'campy' character, even the relationship between Karen (Megan Mullally) and her maid Rosario (Shelley Morrison) combines feelings of intense devotion with an attitude towards the Latina woman that is deeply politically incorrect.

Gender-bending is crucial to *Will and Grace*. In this regard it shares the sensibility that one author has attributed to US actress and comedienne Sandra Bernhard, saying that she refuses to accept a static sexual identity (such as 'lesbian') and that she is a woman who performs gay male drag (Williams, 1998, p. 148). Thus it is not surprising that Bernhard (perhaps best known to the general public for her supporting role as a lesbian on *Roseanne*) should turn up as a guest star in an episode of *Will and Grace* (11 January 2001) that deals specifically with star worship as a manifestation of queer culture. Will and Grace are pursuing a hobby of photographing themselves in celebrities' homes that they are pretending to buy from estate agents. Masquerading as a heterosexual couple, they get away with outlandish infertility jokes such as Grace telling the world that Will has an 'undescended testicle'. When Sandra Bernhard (playing 'herself', which is what she usually does) comes home during their visit to her apartment, she immediately wants to sell to the 'happening gay guy and the vivacious redhead'. She tells them that they are soulmates and Will is so overwhelmed that he makes a 'lowball' offer of a million dollars on the apartment, which Bernhard accepts. Then Will and Grace have to tell her they cannot afford to buy it.

At this point, Bernhard's accompanist starts mixing drinks in a blender whose sound drowns out the obscenities that Sandra Bernhard is hurling at Will and Grace. She has assumed her well-known abrasive persona and her routine about being a megastar is implanted within the format of *Will and Grace*. Like Cher, Sandra Bernhard is an appropriate guest star for a show so rooted in gay cultural practices such as celebrity worship. The episode works not because of the jokes (these are relatively few) but because of the situation and the way Bernhard's stand-up persona lends itself to the inflation and deflation of gay subculture's and now mainstream American culture's obsession with the cultivation of celebrity.

In fact, many sitcom jokes in US sitcoms assume a deep knowledge of show business on the part of the American public. *Will and Grace* differs only in that the knowledge invoked is gay subcultural knowledge. That is to say, any sitcom can joke about Elizabeth Taylor's weight, but only Jack can refer to Ricky Martin as the 'openly Latino pop-singing sensation'.

Jane Feuer

Shields could represent a drag queen's image of a woman. It thus represented a form of 'queer' comedy that acted to unsettle our normative notions of masculinity and femininity. By 'queering' Susan, Brooke Shields's status as the perfect heteronormative cover girl was called into question by the joke.

Taking as our premise a distinction between comedy and humour (comedy being the overall form a show takes and humour being what makes the audience laugh), it is possible to categorise many presumably heterosexual sitcoms as possessing 'gay humour' or a 'queer sensibility'. Shows that fool around with gender identity often have a gay sense of humour, as does cult behaviour around *Absolutely Fabulous* when fans dress up as either Eddie or (more often) Patsy. The US show *Frasier* is widely read as a 'queer' sitcom, although the producers vehemently deny it.

This raises the issue of what humour means to gay versus straight audiences. Many well-meaning heterosexual viewers find it offensive that *Frasier* and his brother Niles are considered 'queer' because of their feminine tastes and preferences for opera, fine wine, designer clothing and the like. They consider this to be stereotyping and ask: why can't a man be heterosexual and effeminate? Although many gays and lesbians share this critique of stereotyping, others take comic pleasure from reading Niles and Frasier as 'queer', thereby identifying with their effeminacy. A third viewing position here would be a homophobic one in which Frasier's effeminacy is also read as gay but the laughter is at his expense – not as an individual (for Frasier's and Niles's pretensions are certainly laughable) but as a 'fag'.

In this way, *Absolutely Fabulous* and *Frasier* (as well as that moment in *Suddenly Susan*) could be considered 'queer' sitcoms; whereas *Ellen* (final season) and *Will and Grace* as well as the short-lived *Normal, Ohio* (Fox, 2000) might be considered gay sitcoms since they began with already fully formed gay main characters. Although there has yet to be a sitcom on US television that is targeted entirely to a gay audience, *Ellen* came the closest in its fifth and final season (1997–8). Much of the humour during the final season consisted in gay 'insider' jokes that appealed to a gay or gay-friendly audience. For instance, 'Emma' (19 November 1997) featured a bizarre narrative in which

Ellen reacted to its star's 'coming out'

Emma Thompson, playing 'herself', reveals to Ellen that she (Emma) is a lesbian. This plays against her well-known image as Kenneth Branagh's (ex) wife. In 'It's a gay, gay, gay, gay world' (25 February 1998), Ellen's straight cousin Spence has a dream episode in which he wakes up in a world wherein gayness is the norm and heterosexuality is aberrant. Many of the final-season episodes dealt with the humour to be found in the more or less mundane events of a lesbian's life: coming out to friends and family, firing a gay but incompetent plumber, attending a women's music festival, dating and falling in love with a woman, being rejected by her lover's family.

In conclusion, we can distinguish between 'gay' and 'queer' sitcoms according to the relative specificity of the jokes and according to how much of an attempt the writers make to reach a heterosexual audience with their jokes.

Jane Feuer

RECOMMENDED READING

Capsuto, Steven (2000), *Alternate Channels: the Uncensored Story of Gay and Lesbian Images on Radio and Television*, 1930s to the Present, New York: Ballantine.

Doty, Alexander (1993), *Making Things Perfectly Queer: Interpreting Mass Culture*, Minneapolis: University of Minnesota Press.

Wagg, Stephen (ed.) (1998), *Because I Tell a Joke or Two: Comedy, Politics and Social Difference*, London: Routledge.

Contemporary Sitcom ('Comedy Vérité')

For much of its existence, the 'look' of the sitcom has remained relatively stable. The production methods employed for most sitcom have involved recording in front of live studio audiences, which necessitates a theatrical performance style quite different from the kind of acting common in many other television genres. In addition, most sitcoms have been filmed with cameras as if they were the fourth wall, so all the action is directed outwards towards the audience; this explains why, when sitting down for a meal, sitcom characters often arrange themselves oddly on only one side of the table. The 'theatricality' of sitcom is also evident in that much of it is shot on video, and is brightly lit, so that such series appear artificial when compared to the more 'realist' aesthetic employed by the majority of television fiction. Overall, this means that it's quite easy to 'spot' a sitcom when channel-hopping because it has a look and aesthetic which marks it out from other genres (see Copeland, 2007, for a fuller history).

However, the look of sitcom has begun to change. In Britain, series such as *People Like Us* (BBC, 1999, 2002), *Marion and Geoff*, *Human Remains* (BBC, 2001) and *The Office* don't look how we might expect sitcoms to. Each of these series instead adopts the aesthetics of another television form; the documentary or factual programme. While they may be shot on video, their colours are much more muted, undermining the artificiality commonly associated with the genre. Such series are not recorded in front of studio audiences, meaning that camera set-ups can be more complex, and narrative spaces are fuller. Actors in these programmes have no need to perform to a live audience, meaning that performances are much 'smaller'. Perhaps most importantly, these series do not have laugh tracks, which for decades have served as the most obvious reminder of sitcom's comic intent, as well as signalling the audience for whom such programming is made. In these series, then, there is the abandonment of the conventions which have traditionally defined the genre, in conjunction with the adoption of the characteristics of other, normally quite separate, kinds of programming.

For example, *Marion and Geoff* is about Keith Barrett (Rob Brydon), a taxi-driver estranged from his wife (Marion) and children after she left him for Geoff. Keith is an eternal optimist, convinced he can make a go of the new circumstances life has given him, even though he is quite clearly living a hellish life, being consistently badly treated by his family, his colleagues and his housemates. The comedy arises in the disparity between Keith's reading of his own life, and the audience's perception of the truth of his situation. While the series is a 'comedy of embarrassment' (Billig, 2005, p. 136), Barrett can clearly be placed in a tradition of similarly deluded male British sitcom characters, such as Del Boy in *Only Fools and Horses* (BBC, 1981–2003), Rik in *The Young Ones* and Tony Hancock in *Hancock's Half Hour*. Yet what is significant about the series is how it's shot. The whole is filmed as if it is Keith's video diary, with a camera placed on his taxi's dashboard as he goes about his business. The camera never leaves the cab (neither does Keith, for the most part) and so we never see the other characters who are impinging on his life. In its avoidance of on-screen conflict, *Marion and Geoff* is markedly different from traditional sitcom, which has usually relied on the interactions of multiple characters for its comedy. But more important is the aesthetic of the series, which so successfully captures the look and feel of the kinds of video diaries commonly seen in reality television and popular factual programming that it is possible for the

programme's comic intentions to be missed by those who might stumble across an episode accidentally.

Such 'mock-documentary' (Roscoe and Hight, 2001) aesthetics can be seen in all of these series: *People Like Us* is a compilation of documentaries about people in the workplace, which, over the series, reveals the incompetence of the documentary film-maker, Roy Mallard (Chris Langham); *Human Remains* is an anthology of documentaries about modern relationships; and *The Office* appears to be a docusoap following the activities in a stationery-suppliers company in Slough.

In artificially creating the aesthetics of factual television, these series can be seen as responding to developments in documentary on British television in the 1990s. The docusoap boom of the 1990s helped to bring factual programming to the mainstream, and showed that mass audiences would consume such programming if it was made in particular ways. Yet questions and criticisms concerning the production practices of such series, as well as critiques of the 'truthfulness' of the 'reality' that viewers were being offered, showed that for many this development was not seen as positive. Later developments, especially the growth of reality television, have highlighted this debate, and the collapse of the distinction between 'factual' programming and 'entertainment' can be seen as problematic if the former helps fulfil the public service requirements placed upon broadcasting.

Indeed, it is the question of the extent to which television is able to show us the 'truth' of the world which is at the heart of these comedy series. As already noted, Keith's delusions about his life in *Marion and Geoff* offer a stark demonstration of the various ways in which a life can be read, and shows that individuals are often incapable of making sense of their own circumstances. Roy Mallard's incompetence in *People Like Us* has significant effects upon those he's filming, which demonstrates the falsity at the heart of the documentary project; in addition, the fact that *People Like Us* includes scenes which 'ordinary' documentaries would probably cut – such as rows between Mallard and his subjects – gives us access to the production processes at the heart of factual film-making, laying bare the techniques for all to see. This means that these programmes don't just ape the factual aesthetics of docusoaps and factual programming; they deliberately employ them in order to question and critique the supposed objectivity and access which documentaries offer, and which distinguishes them from such 'fictional' programming as sitcoms. It is this process that has been called 'comedy vérité' (Mills, 2004a).

Harris notes how 'the use of a naturalistic or documentary look has increased across a wide range of television

The Office

The Office (BBC, 2001–3) is probably the most critically acclaimed sitcom produced in Britain in the last decade, making its writers (Ricky Gervais and Stephen Merchant) rich and its star (Gervais again) a global face. While not a massive ratings hit on a par with many popular sitcoms, it garnered a devoted audience, meaning that the series lives on in other media such as books and its record-breaking DVD sales (Roberts, 2006, p. 34). In becoming the first non-American series to win the Golden Globe for 'Best Television series: Musical or Comedy', the series managed to break into the American market where so many previous programmes have failed. The American remake of the series – *The Office: An American Workplace* (NBC, 2005–) – has similarly survived where so many other transatlantic remakes have failed.

The Office is set in a paper-distribution company in Slough, England, and focuses primarily on the office's boss David Brent (Gervais) and key workers such as Tim (Martin Freeman), Gareth (Mackenzie Crook) and Dawn (Lucy Davis). The whole is presented as if it were a 'real' docusoap, with the cameras roving the office capturing everyday interactions, often filming with objects in the way to further a sense of documentary authenticity. It also includes interviews with the characters, who discuss their workplace and events within it, in a manner common in many docusoaps. Arriving on television with very little publicity, and containing no television stars, the series resolutely refuses to demonstrate its comic intent openly, instead employing 'a rhetorical form built to convince the viewer that he or she is acting as a fly-on-the-wall in a real situation' (Casey et al., 2008, p. 41). As Hill (2007) shows, contemporary audiences are often aware of the interplay of factual and fictional television forms, but this does not necessarily prevent them from being 'fooled' by programmes that have such a 'sustained plausibility' (Ward, 2005, p. 71).

What *The Office* mines for comic effect is this relationship between television, factual representation, and audiences, especially concerning celebrity. David Brent sees himself as an

The Office: 'fly-on-the-wall' comedy

entertainer, who keeps his employees happy through his pranks and mockery. But he also sees the docusoap being made about him as a way in which he can become a celebrity, hoping to become a reality star in the same manner as Brian Dowling and Jade Goody from *Big Brother* (Endemol, 1999–), and Jane Macdonald from *The Cruise* (BBC, 1998). He constantly performs for the camera, inadvertently upsetting and embarrassing his colleagues as he does so. In this way, Brent hopes to capitalise on 'the fact that we have seen an appreciable rise in the number of "ordinary" people appearing on television' (Holmes, 2003, p. 111), and that many such people have managed to carve out lucrative careers from their personae. The programme's comedy arises from Brent's inability to understand how others see him, and his clear unsuitability for the kind of stardom he seeks.

The Office therefore represents a useful intervention into the social processes in which factual television is now commonly engaged, while simultaneously relying on those processes for its humour to work. Its successful recreation of docusoap aesthetics raises serious questions about the veracity of television representations. The fact that a programme questioning the production practices of television has been so critically lauded by the industry it critiques suggests something of note about how those who work within television might value their output.

Brett Mills

drama' (2006, p. 24) and calls this a 'postmodern aesthetic' (p. 25). That is, the collapse of the traditional fact/fiction dichotomy can be seen to indicate the dissolution of traditional objective categories, resulting in generically confused media which makes no distinction between truth and lies, between reality and fiction. Indeed, the ability of sitcoms to successfully recreate the aesthetics of documentaries has

significant implications for the ways in which genres are signalled visually. This means that 'There are three sorts of (television) comedy: traditionalist, modern, and postmodern' (Steeves, 2005, p. 264). Yet in calling this 'postmodern', Harris and Steeves both imply that this is a significant and novel development. Mittell, on the other hand, argues that 'generic blending is not a new phenomenon' (2004, p. 156), and the insistence on seeing genres as discrete categories which can comfortably be defined is evidence only of 'the "purity bias" of most genre scholarship' (p. 195). Contemporary sitcom offers a useful case study for these debates, precisely because sitcom is one genre whose characteristics are often assumed to be comparatively rigid and clear; the fact that, on the whole, audiences have had little trouble making sense of these 'new' kinds of sitcom suggests that generic rigidity may not be as apparent as often thought.

It is noticeable that America has yet to produce a slew of similar comedy programmes with the same kinds of aesthetics. This not to deny that American sitcom aesthetics haven't changed, however; series such as *Curb Your Enthusiasm*, *The Larry Sanders Show*, *30 Rock* (NBC, 2006–) and *Scrubs* (NBC, 2001–) all reject the traditional sitcom style, and have abandoned the laugh track, resulting in series with more complex narrative space and the lack of 'artificiality' which can be seen as defining sitcom for its first few decades. In the fluid, chaotic camerawork of these series, there's a surface parallel with the 'comedy vérité' programmes of the UK. However, what's significant about these American series is that none of them adopts the mock-documentary format, for in none of them do the characters behave as if they know they are being filmed. Central to all the British series is the characters' awareness of the roving camera crew, and how they might be seen by viewers at home, meaning that comedy is created in the gap between the 'real' person and how they attempt to portray themselves for the viewing public. While *Curb Your Enthusiasm* similarly mines the disparity between the 'real' self and the 'public' self to comic ends, there is no implied viewing audience that the character of Larry David is aware of. Similarly, *The Larry Sanders Show* distinguishes between Larry's on-screen and off-screen persona, but the backstage elements can only have the significance they do because the characters 'know' they are not being watched by the public.

Indeed, the only notable sitcom using the mock-documentary format is the American remake of *The Office*, *The Office: An American Workplace* (NBC, 2005–). Considering the critical success of many of the British series, it might be asked why American sitcom has not followed a similar path. This can perhaps be explained by Anglo-American television differences, in which the public service tradition of British broadcasting has consistently offered factual, documentary programming as part of its output (Bignell, 2005, pp. 8–32). The docusoap boom of the 1990s followed logically from this tradition, and 'comedy vérité' is comedy-makers' inevitable response to the form of programming that was dominating British schedules. While reality television has been a big hit in America, it did not experience the success of the docusoap in the same way as Britain, meaning that the parodying and manipulation of such aesthetics in sitcom is meaningless. This shows how genres respond to one another, for developments in British sitcom can be traced to modifications in other, quite discrete forms of programming; the lack of similar material in America gives no impetus for sitcom-makers to respond to.

This leaves the question as to where the sitcom may go next. It seems that programmes that don't employ the traditional aesthetic have become absorbed into the mainstream, as shown by the success of programmes such as *Peep Show* (C4, 2003–), *Ideal* (BBC, 2005–), *Nighty Night* (BBC, 2004–5) and *Gavin & Stacey* (BBC, 2007–). Yet it is rather too simple to suggest that the sitcom has changed forever. In Britain the most successful, highly rated and long-running sitcom is *My Family* (BBC, 2000–), which in its domestic setting, performance style, production practices and laugh track, is identical to the kind of programming being produced for decades. Similarly, in America, series such as *Two and a Half Men* (CBS, 2003–) are clearly 'traditional'. The co-existence of various kinds of sitcom shows the ability of genres to adapt and survive, with a range of programming on offer, united in their comic intent despite their differing aesthetics. To write the traditional sitcom off as 'dead' is simplistic and premature.

Brett Mills

RECOMMENDED READING

Caldwell, John (2002), 'Prime-Time Fiction Theorizes the Docu-Real', in James Friedman (ed.), *Reality Squared: Televisual Discourses on the Real*, New Brunswick, New Jersey and London: Rutgers University Press.

Mills, Brett (2004a), 'Comedy Vérité: Contemporary Sitcom Form', *Screen*, vol. 45, no. 1, pp. 63–78.

Mills, Brett (2005), *Television Sitcom*, London: BFI.

Roscoe, Jane and Hight, Craig (2001), *Faking It: Mock-Documentary and the Subversion of Factuality*, Manchester: Manchester University Press.

CHILDREN'S TELEVISION

Studying Children's Television

'Children's television' is an unusual genre in that its title is defined by the people who watch it, rather than by the characteristics of the text. This section will discuss how programmes labelled as 'children's' can be generically distinguished from 'non-children's', and some of the implications of these distinctions.

The natural opposite of a 'children's' genre ought to be an 'adults'' genre; but here, the grounds of definition shift. 'Adult' programming now usually means 'sexual' or 'pornographic'. Thus, one obvious definition of 'children's' as a genre is that there will be no sex in it. Sexuality portrayed in children's material will either be in coded form, or it will take the form of health education, designed to deter and protect the young from risk-taking behaviour: for example, storylines in the children's soaps *Grange Hill* (BBC, 1978–2008) and *Byker Grove* (BBC, 1989–2006) about teenage pregnancy, or first sexual experiences. Producers of children's television, to a much greater extent than those of adult television, analyse storylines with a view to their didactic possibilities (Home, 1993).

This protectiveness as a characteristic of 'children's television' is institutionalised in regulatory documents dealing with possible 'harm'. Article 22 of the European Commission Broadcasting Directive (UK implementation, 1991), states that: 'Member states must prevent broadcasters under their jurisdiction from broadcasting programmes which might seriously impair the physical, mental or moral development of minors, particularly those involving pornography or gratuitous violence.' The other form of regulatory control that defines 'children's' is scheduling: in the UK, 'harmful' material should not occur in programmes shown before 9 p.m. ('the watershed'), although scheduling as a regulatory tool has become less effective with satellite and cable. Controls are concerned not only with sex and violence; they include not showing dangerous examples, and limitation of advertising content, to take account of the presumed susceptibility of children to persuasive techniques and copycat behaviour (see 'Advertising', p. 178).

A major aspect of regulation defining 'children's television' as a category is that it is seen as a public good that the state must provide. In the USA, commercial stations cannot be licensed unless they provide a minimum of three hours a week of 'educational' programming (a term that has been interpreted extremely loosely); in the UK, the provision takes the form of protected slots on the terrestrial airwaves in the afternoon. These blocks of programming (Children's BBC (CBBC) and Children's ITV (CITV)) are expected to be diverse in genre, and appealing to children of different ages – producing further subdivisions of the generic label 'children's' into 'drama'; 'factual'; 'entertainment'; 'pre-school'; and 'animation' (see Messenger-Davies and Corbett, 1997).

These requirements have come about as a result of a complex range of forces (for a historical overview of UK children's provision, see Buckingham et al. 1999; for a still-pertinent review of the rather different US situation, see Palmer, 1988), which continue to change as a result of new technology, more children's channels and the arrival of computers (Livingstone and Bovill, 1999). Such institutional changes could be seen as threatening to the concept of 'children's television' as a distinct programming category. Among the changes to the structure of the BBC announced in spring 2000 by its new Director-General, Greg Dyke, was the ending of a separate Children's Department within the BBC – an experiment tried, and failed, once before in the 1960s. Children's programming has been included under one of the four new 'adult' departments – not under 'Factual and Learning' (as it almost certainly would have been in the USA) but under 'Drama and Entertainment'.

The best children's schedules, whether on the BBC or within the commercial system, have traditionally attempted to provide a microcosm of adult schedules. As with adult programming, so with children's: drama is seen as a flagship genre, and a sign of the system's commitment to 'quality'. Children's drama schedules have displayed, in Caughie's terms (1991), the dual emphases of British broadcast drama: realistic authenticity, based on drama's origins in live studio production, and prestigious literary 'heritage' drama, as in costumed adaptations of classic books (see p. 49). Children's drama schedules have been one of the most favoured homes for classic serials; according to Buckingham et al. (1999, p. 36), this derives from an ideological 'core of values in which middle-class attitudes and universal moral principles had come to be seen as one and the same thing' – a view that overlooks the fact that many classic children's books have rather radical politics (for example, the stories of the Fabian Edith Nesbit). From the broadcasters' more pragmatic point of view, classic books are useful because out of copyright, and child audiences need to be sustained to help guarantee broadcasters' economic survival.

Outside the regulatory protected children's groupings, 'children's' is an extremely lucrative commercial proposition

Goodnight Mr Tom

Goodnight Mr Tom, based on the 1982 children's novel by Michelle Magorian, was first transmitted on ITV in October 1998, and was a landmark production for 'children's television'. It was produced and financed by a children's department (in this case Carlton/Central for ITV), but was first transmitted during 'adult' viewing time, at 9 p.m. – a time when children are assumed to be in bed. It was repeated on ITV in spring 2000, in the early evening. As Nelson (see 'Costume Drama') points out, children's drama schedules have always been one of the most favoured homes for classic 'teatime' serials, but *Goodnight Mr Tom* was a scheduling departure – an experiment to see whether children's programming could hold its own during adult viewing time. High ratings and a BAFTA award suggested that it could.

The programme was also unusual in being a full-length 'feature film', rather than an episodic serial. Otherwise, it had all the regular hallmarks of a generic children's drama: literary provenance; a historical setting (during the Second World War); a child as its central protagonist; impeccable period design – all signifiers, according to Charlotte Brunsdon (1997), of 'quality' television. Other guarantors of quality included location shooting in a picturesque English village; a prestigious director, Jack Gold; and the casting of a thoroughly bankable television star, John Thaw (*Inspector Morse* (ITV, 1987–2000), *Kavanagh QC*, (ITV, 1995–2001), *The Sweeney* (ITV, 1975–8)) as the gruff, elderly Tom Oakley who has a disturbed, eleven-year-old London evacuee billeted on him.

Children's drama set in the past (or future) can serve as a vehicle for distancing, and then safely examining, social issues that may (implicitly or, as in this case, very explicitly) be critical of the adult social order. *Goodnight Mr Tom* featured violent child abuse and neglect, mental breakdown, sexual dysfunction, the shortcomings of the welfare system, and the social collapse brought about by war. Admittedly, the child in *Goodnight Mr Tom* is rescued – and it is to Thaw's credit that at no point does the viewer share the suspicions of the story's professionals of him as an elderly man who should not be looking after a child. Further, there is no sense that what happened to William Beech (Nick Robinson) in the Blitz, including the loss of a Jewish friend, is anything other than

Goodnight Mr Tom: a children's drama enjoyed by adults

appallingly traumatic. A central sequence – harrowing in the book, and unflinchingly translated by Carlton/Central's production – is the death of William's baby sister in his arms, and the final mental breakdown of his mother (Annabelle Apsion).

Goodnight Mr Tom was groundbreaking in its scheduling and brought the qualities of the best children's drama production into the adult television mainstream. The children's market for fantasies and literary adaptations is more favourable than the market for social-realist British drama, hence a subsequent spate of international co-productions of stories about magic and witchcraft, once taboo in children's programmes (Home, 1993). *Goodnight Mr Tom* combined the social-realist tradition with literary 'heritage' qualities and has achieved a successful afterlife in the video/DVD market. Showcasing the best children's dramas such as *Goodnight Mr Tom*, at times when adults can see them too, would seem to be one of the best ways of guaranteeing public support for continued funding for high-quality children's programming, however 'quality' is interpreted. Most writers on children's television agree that 'quality' must include the kind of unsentimental, but ultimately reassuring (for a child audience), treatment of painful issues told from a child's perspective, as demonstrated in this film.

Máire Messenger-Davies

if the right formula (usually in the form of animation, and hence aimed at the younger end of the market) can be found and sold round the world. Examples are *Teletubbies* (BBC/Ragdoll, 1997–2001) (see box), and toy-linked and merchandising-linked cartoons such as *Smurfs* (Hanna-Barbera, 1981–90), *Ninja Turtles* (Syndication, 1987–96) and, more recently, *Pokémon* (TV Tokyo, 1988–99). The most successful cultural business conglomeration of all time is a producer not of adults', but of children's products: Disney. Many writers, for example, Kline (1993), have lamented the effect on narrative quality when merchandising becomes the primary focus, in order to lure children to buy linked products. Such programming, argues Kline, means that the whole field of childhood has now become commodified.

As with this case, writers on children's material tend to focus not on generic content features but on regulation, effects, ideological contamination, commodification and bad examples. Children's material is also expected to aid appropriate psychological and cognitive development and to stimulate youthful imaginations (Hilton, 1996). Little critical attention has been given to content, despite the fact that children's material has unique features worthy of critical notice. Children's drama is less bound by the constraints of realism than adults'; magic, fantasy, fairytale and slapstick humour are staple ingredients, which producers, writers and performers find liberating. Genuinely innovative, even avant-garde, material may be produced, for example the 1960s' and 1970s' programme for deaf children, *Vision On* (BBC, 1964–76) and the currently iconic *Teletubbies* (see box).

A further creatively liberating aspect of children's material is its carnivalesque subversion of the respectabilities of adult authority. In children's comedy, such as *Welcome to Orty Fou* (ITV, 1999–2000), adults are the butt of children's humour, not the other way round (as in adult sitcoms like *The Cosby Show* (NBC, 1984–92)). These subversions are also seen in more serious children's drama, such as *The Demon Headmaster* (BBC, 1996–8), a sci-fi story, with political subtexts about the necessity of resisting totalitarianism (see Messenger-Davies and Machin, 2000; see also 'Science Fiction'). Animation, too, provides such subversions: series beloved by children, such as *Rugrats* (Nickelodeon, 1991–4/1997–2004) and, above all, *The Simpsons* (Fox, 1989–) (not strictly a children's programme, which exposes the ambiguity of the term), are characterised by the adult/child comic reversions that reveal the hypocrisies of adult social, commercial and political arrangements (see 'Animation' and Lurie, 1990).

Stylistically, the main distinction between children's films and family films is usefully made by Bazalgette and Staples (1995) as one of point of view. The children's drama is told (and largely shot) from the point of view of the child protagonists. Other generic stylistic features signalling 'children's TV' include brightly coloured sets, vivid graphics, multimedia presentations (print, restless camerawork, fast editing, computer graphics) and glamorous young presenters given frequent direct address to the audience (a privilege less available in adult programming) characterised by informality or 'wackiness' (see Buckingham, 1995). The most pervasive stylistic of all in children's television is animation, which, as Pilling (1997) has argued, has detrimentally been seen only as a 'kiddies' genre' because of the dominance of Disney (see p. 152).

Labelling a genre as belonging to its viewers, as in the case of 'children's', is a reminder that writers, artists and cinematic auteurs are in a cultural public sphere, writing to specific audiences who are likely to be influenced, inspired or disturbed by what these artists do (as regulatory arrangements surrounding 'children's' recognise). Classifying a branch of programming according to the group that uses it also acknowledges that different audiences 'read' cultural material differently, and position themselves in multiple roles in relation to it.

Máire Messenger-Davies

RECOMMENDED READING

Buckingham, David, Davies, Hannah, Jones, Ken and Kelley, Peter (1999), *Children's Television in Britain*, London: BFI.

Home, Anna (1993), *Into the Box of Delights*, London: BBC.

Messenger-Davies, Máire (2001), *'Dear BBC': Children, Television Storytelling and the Public Sphere*, Cambridge: Cambridge University Press.

The Child Audience

For broadcasters in the UK, children are people aged between four and fifteen, who are assumed either to be in bed by 9 p.m. and thus 'safe' from any harmful influences of 'adult' programming or to be the responsibility of their parents after that time. This model of the child audience, if it were ever realistic, has been emphatically called into question by two features of contemporary children's media culture: one, the proliferation of TV satellite and cable channels, which do not observe the 9 p.m. watershed as strictly as terrestrial channels do, as well as the wide availability of video; and, two, the growth of what Livingstone and Bovill (1999) have called a 'bedroom' culture, in which unsupervised children have autonomous access to a wide range of media, including television and computers, in their own bedrooms, whether before or after 9 p.m.

Broadcasters in both the UK and the USA are required by law both to provide material specifically for children, and to take account of the presence of children in adult audiences, at least up to 9 p.m. This is a major challenge to creativity because of the huge developmental range of the child audience. Four-year-olds have very little in common with fifteen-year-olds in terms of their interests, capabilities and experience, and even ten-year-olds do not have much more. The age range does have some characteristics in common, such as the fact that they are all legal minors, subject to the authority of parents and of teachers and protected by law from 'harmful' experiences, such as sexual relations and the consumption of alcohol and tobacco. Such protectiveness is reflected in other regulations applying to the child audience.

RESEARCH ON CHILD AUDIENCES

Children as an audience are measured separately from adults in audience ratings conducted by BARB (Broadcasters' Audience Research Board) in the UK, and Neilsen in the USA. It is important for the industry to identify their child 'customers', since they are commmercially valuable for a number of reasons: first, in commercial television, they are key targets for toy, confectionery and convenience food advertising. Second, in public service terms, a children's service (no matter how skeletal or commercially driven) gives broadcasters public credibility and, in Britain and the USA, is one requirement for a commercial licence. Third, child audiences can bring adults with them, including their own care-takers while they are children, and in the sense that they grow up to be adults themselves, often retaining channel loyalty from their youth.

Child audiences have also been the subject of a very large number of academic studies in the past forty years, mainly by social scientists but some by educators. The first group has been particularly concerned with children as potential victims of harmful effects, such as copying violent behaviour. The second group is more concerned with how, and what, children learn from media. The harmful-effects school has had by far the most research money spent on it; in the 1960s and 1970s several experiments and surveys were carried out in the USA and the UK to see whether exposure to filmed violence led to children copying aggressive behaviour. Despite some evidence of short-term imitative effects in some children (mainly, though not exclusively, boys), and some evidence of weak statistical correlations between watching television and negative

social attitudes, the effects-research tradition has never conclusively demonstrated to the rest of the academic community that media have direct, measurable, harmful effects on the young. However, this has not prevented a continuing popular belief that they do.

The phenomenon of 'moral panic' surrounding the introduction of new communication technologies, especially with regard to children's access to hitherto taboo information, has been documented by Springhall (1998) and Starker (1991). Currently, such concerns are being expressed about the latest new technology, the Internet, including children's possible access to pornography. 'Moral panics' about technological change and its impact partly reflect genuine parental and pedagogic worries, and partly long-standing populist fears both of the new and of the young. It is sometimes translated into policy and legislation, as in the case of the 1994 Video Recordings Act in Britain.

Other, more positive, research traditions have arisen from the media education movement (see Kubey, 1997), where the concern is to establish the cultural contribution of mass media to children's learning and literacy in the broadest sense, including social attitudes and identity formation. Cognitive psychologists have also been interested in the new ways offered by audiovisual electronic media to understand children's intellectual functioning – for example, how they learn to 'read' the codes, conventions, signs and techniques of the media (Hodge and Tripp, 1986; Messenger-Davies, 1997), a set of competencies sometimes called 'media literacy'. This tradition links with wider concerns in childhood studies about the relation of children to the social and political world; media literacy studies address children's understanding of reality and fantasy, their 'theories of mind' about intentionality and authorship, and their ability to distinguish differing degrees of realism, credibility and representational verisimilitude in different genres, fact and fiction.

The relationship of children to different forms of media has always been a site of cultural struggle where competing disciplines and ideologies clash. Allied to a desire on the part of many adults to keep their children safe and innocent for as long as possible, is an equally powerful tendency in growing children to want to try out taboo experiences and to explore adult 'secrets' through media. The relationship of children to culture is also part of a long-standing struggle about the kinds of messages and images that the whole of society should be allowed to have access to: hence the 9 p.m. watershed and the film and video classification system. Nevertheless, the child audience deserves to be seen, not just negatively, as people incapable of coping with

Pre-schoolers: A Special Audience

The biggest audiences in the four-to-fifteen age group usually go to adult programmes (with occasional exceptions, such as the 1996 BBC series of *The Demon Headmaster*). This is not always true for the younger end of the age group, the under-tens, and it is never true for pre-school children, the under-fives. Catering adequately for this very young audience with programmes designed to stimulate learning, social skills and imagination has been characterised as one of the primary hall-marks of a public service system (Palmer, 1988; Blumler, 1992; Messenger-Davies and Corbett, 1997). The conception of the pre-school audience has changed since the 1950s when the title *Watch with Mother* (BBC, 1950–80) assumed that very young children watching television would be at home with a full-time mother figure sitting with them. In the 1960s and 1970s, the producer of *Playschool* (BBC, 1964–88) and *Playdays* (BBC,

1988–97), Cynthia Felgate, could assert: 'Our audience is one child in a room.' Nowadays, pre-school television addresses children on the assumption that they may also be in nurseries or with childminders. However, there is also an assumption that the child may be unaccompanied by an adult, for the adult presenters always address the child (through the camera), not the accompanying adult(s). This is children's territory.

Pre-school television has a long and popular tradition in both British and American television. *Sesame Street* (NET, 1969–70/PBS, 1970–) aimed at the under-sevens, with (as its witty allusions to American popular and high culture make clear) an eye on accompanying older audiences, began in 1967. The slower, real-time, British *Playschool* began on the BBC in 1964, and was replaced by *Playdays* in 1988 and by *Teletubbies* in 1997 (see below). Both BBC and ITV have produced many programmes for pre-school children, including storytelling such as *Postman Pat* (BBC, 1981–) and magazine-type shows

Playschool saw their audience as 'one child in a room'

Sesame Street prepared young children for formal school

such as *Rainbow* (ITV, 1972–92). Although the audience for them is small, in all senses of the word, such programmes can be an extremely worthwhile investment because, owing to the fact that turnover among the under-fives is rapid (obviously, the whole three-to-five population changes every two years), they can be repeated season after season – and, indeed, revived after decades (as the BBC's 1950s' *The Flowerpot Men* (BBC, 1952–4) have been). They can also have lucrative video spin-offs and toy-marketing deals. To the extent that this is so, the market, as distinct from the audience, for pre-school pro-grammes will always be care-taking adults.

Traditionally, pre-school television assumed a linguistically competent child audience, capable of following narratives and appreciating jokes, that is primarily four-year-olds and over. This changed with the virtually inarticulate *Teletubbies*, and in 1998 a controversy broke out among children's producers, media educators and academics gathered at the second World Summit on Television for Children in London, when this pro-gramme, despite its carefully researched origins, was accused of being exploitative and harmful to the very youngest chil-dren, because, unlike earlier pre-school programmes, it was aimed at pre-linguistic children who were deemed too young to be watching television; it is still, however, the most success-ful BBC export ever (see box).

The case for specialised pre-school programming made by the originators of *Sesame Street* in the USA in 1967 is that, far from relying mainly on non-verbal material, it should include basic linguistic and numerical academic skills. This was seen as necessary in order to compensate the most disadvantaged children, who are most reliant on television, for a lack of pre-school experience (Palmer, 1988). *Sesame Street* consciously set out to prepare young children for formal school, by introducing them to classroom practices such as letter and number recognition, and the verbal expression of concepts such as size, height, distance and colour. All of this, plus a socially aware emphasis on different ethnic experiences and cultures, tended to imply an older audience than under-threes; it assumed that the watching children had some exposure to life outside the home, and some awareness of what 'school' is. In this, *Sesame Street*'s philosophy was different from that of British pre-school television, with its emphasis on play; it preferred a more directive approach and had much faster, more visually busy production styles, borrowed from American advertising techniques (see p. 178).

Despite their difference in styles, the common conception of the pre-school child audience underlying all these programmes is of a group with intelligence and interests of their own, but who lack experience and thus need to be gently introduced to basic information about the world, including life skills like tooth-cleaning and meeting new baby brothers and sisters. In all of them, the importance of learning is acknowledged – but so is the importance of play. Above all, the tone is one of kindliness and affection. In this, pre-school television's attitude to its audience is paternalistic (although it would be more correct to call it maternalistic, given the predominance of women in the field) in the best sense.

Máire Messenger-Davies

---

adult material, but as a group with special interests, talents and needs of its own.

Máire Messenger-Davies

RECOMMENDED READING

Messenger-Davies, Máire and Corbett, Beth (1997), *The Provision of Children's Programming in the UK between 1992 and 1996*, London: Broadcasting Standards Commission.

Palmer, E. (1988), *Television and America's Children: A Crisis of Neglect*, Oxford: Oxford University Press.

Starker, S. (1991), *Evil Influences: Crusades against the Mass Media*, New Brunswick: Transaction.

Moral Panics

Stanley Cohen's well-established paradigm concerning the emergence and maintenance of media-driven 'moral panics' finds special application in the always contentious field of children's programming (see 'News'). The media identifies a problem; its causes are simplified; its relevant participants are then stigmatised; a campaign accrues around the key issues that have emerged from this process; the programme-makers or the 'authorities' respond; and thereafter, a whole new frame of debate is created that perpetuates the 'panic'. From *Howdy Doody* (NBC, 1947–60) to *Pokémon* in the USA to *Blue Peter* (BBC, 1958–) and *Teletubbies* (see box) in Britain, programming for the children's demographic has been coloured by debates between parents, educationists, commercial enterprises and children themselves, largely focusing on the relationship

between broadcasters as public service deliverers (even in the commercial sector) and parent advocacy groups, addressing the pedagogic and promotional agendas underpinning the broadcast remit.

Howdy Doody, which ran for 2,543 episodes between 1947 and 1960, alienated the establishment by playing out a mock presidential campaign in which the platform of 'two Christmases and one school day a year; more pictures in history books; double sodas for a dime; and plenty of movies' won more write-in votes than that of actual independent candidate Henry Wallace. The programme was one of the first children's programmes to provoke moral and ethical debates about its content, a consideration of the commercial factors potentially affecting editorial control, and the place of the programme within a more general debate about 'television as babysitter' – issues still relevant to the contemporary era. Arguably, *Howdy Doody* was advanced in its representation of Native Americans and women, and in its anti-war stance, a counter-culture imperative taken up by *Sesame Street* (see box), but ultimately it was a victim of the 'modernisation' of children's programming, largely symbolised by the impact of the Disney studio's television output. *Disneyland* (ABC, 1954–61) and *The Mickey Mouse Club* (ABC/Syndication, 1955–96) reconciled a populist ideology with commercial imperatives, promoting family values and new franchise operations alike. The American public readily engaged with the Disney ethos, and embraced the studio's theme parks with equal commitment.

This mode of quasi-vertical integration and its implications was challenged, however, by a New York PBS producer, Joan Ganz Cooney, who through her work with the Carnegie Corporation promoted the idea of pre-school entertainment for disempowered children. Empirical research conducted by the newly formed 'Children's Television Workshop' informed innovative approaches to production in the creation of *Sesame Street*, which included using advertising techniques to promote numeracy, and the exploitation of an assumed teleliteracy in children, where parody could be used to engage with educational and social issues.

Despite receiving sustained criticism since it was first broadcast in 1969, *Sesame Street* still maintains its non-materialist, pro-environment, racially and generationally inclusive signature style, having overcome allegations that the programme did not teach children how to learn, but simply taught them how to watch more television.

Similarly, the programme came under attack for its male orientation, its over-stated political correctness, its unrealistic, almost nostalgic air and its alleged didacticism, something that saw it fall foul of the BBC, which would not broadcast the programme on these grounds. In 1996, at the Second White House Conference on Children and Television, hosted by President Clinton, however, the Markle Foundation endorsed *Sesame Street* as a significant aspect in the pre-school development of high school students who had achieved higher grades in English, science and maths courses.

While the longevity alone of *Sesame Street* may offer testimony to its success, the overall quality of children's programming in the USA has been variable and subject to

---

Teletubbies

The BBC's attempt to speak directly to children as young as eighteen months old through the figures of Tinky Winky, Dipsy, Laa Laa and Po, four colourful, rotund, part-teddy, part-television creatures, in *Teletubbies* (BBC/Ragdoll, 1997–2001), provoked outrage among parents, educationists and tabloid journalists alike. The programme, part of the BBC's strategy to create a pre-school audience that would provide a platform for an older viewer demographic as the children aged, was underpinned by an unusually high £2 million budget, and was immediately seen as a vehicle for merchandising revenue. Inevitably, this provoked concern about what was seen as a conflict of interests between fulfilling the constitutional obligations of the BBC to educate, inform and entertain, and the commercial imperatives that required the programme to compete in a market environment.

The BBC stressed the credentials of Ragdoll Productions, the programme-maker, which was also responsible for the award-winning *Tots TV* (ITV, 1993–8) (which features three puppets, one of which is a French-speaking girl), and the educational focus given to the merchandising, particularly the *Teletubbies* magazine. The 'Tubbyrage' that followed the release of the *Teletubbie* dolls and accessories at Christmas in 1997, however, undermined the programme's educational agenda, and prompted the *Sun* newspaper to scream 'Time for Tubby Buy Buy', and allege that the BBC had sacrificed its commitment to quality programme-making and the tradition epitomised by *Andy Pandy* (BBC, 1950–70), *Blue Peter* and *Grange Hill*.

The educational approach of the programme also received criticism. The verbal currency of the Teletubbies is in the delivery of partially formed words and sounds that echo the 'babble' of baby talk and seek to encourage increased expression in children through imitation and repetition. This strategy also informed the variety of live-action inserts projected through the stomachs of the Teletubbies themselves which are repeated twice in each episode to excited cries of 'Again ! Again !' These inserts have demonstrated a strong commitment to multicultural representation and the inclusion of a variety of previously marginalised models of the family and sociocultural forms and practices.

Computer-animated sequences of dancing bears, sailing ships and marching animals also enhanced the contemporaneity of the programme. Concerns were raised, however, that charged the programme with encouraging poor diction and delivery, the corruption of language and learning, the creation of a context that was alienating and provocative, and knowingly seeking a cult-oriented adult audience. The latter charge was strenuously denied, but this did not prevent extensive debate about the alleged drug-culture connotations in the programme, its affiliation to quasi-apocalyptic science fiction, the gay iconography embodied in Tinky Winky and the promotion of supposedly 'alternative' values in outlook and behaviour.

The global success of the programme may, however, speak to the view that 'moral panics' tend to be deliberately generated by specific interest groups to promote certain issues, are largely temporary and (ironically) often generate new, curious and ultimately engaged audiences to programmes they might have otherwise ignored. *Teletubbies* has survived its moment of alarmist scrutiny, and exemplified a changing media environment in which the BBC has had to engage fully with the commercial sector while seeking to sustain its public service ethos (see Jacobs, 2004).

Paul Wells

the consistent interrogation of the Action for Children's Television (ACT) committee, organised by Penny Charren. ACT campaigned against the proliferation of violence in children's shows, inappropriate advertising strategies for expensive toys and unhealthy foods (see below), the use of popular celebrities in child-directed commercials and the need for a minimum of fourteen hours per week of quality, monitored, children's programming. ACT petitions were highly effective in persuading the Federal Communications Commission (FCC) and the American Advertising Federation (AAF) to modify broadcasting policy.

Parental bodies continue to engage with broadcasters about a range of issues, most notably how the representation of the family in popular programmes sits uneasily with the model children find in their own homes – a debate specifically contested in relation to the competing disparity between *The Cosby Show* and *The Simpsons*, both programmes having strong appeal to adult/child crossover audiences. Bill Cosby's advocacy of responsible programming promoting conscious role models was resisted by James Brooks, producer of *The Simpsons*, as 'pro-propaganda and anti-art' and predicated only on a singular and potentially misleading representation of children and childhood (see 'Animation').

In Britain, broadcasters have been consistently preoccupied with this 'construction' of childhood as their programmes define it. Derek McCulloch, Head of Children's Broadcasting at the BBC between 1933 and 1951, aimed to promote approaches that sought out the 'keen, fresh, unspoilt mind of the child', promoting activity over passivity, creativity over materialism, and integration and participation over mere imitation. In the spirit of this agenda and its public service ethos to educate, inform and entertain, the BBC created *Blue Peter*, which debuted in 1958 and is still running today. Extolling the creative virtues of 'sticky-back plastic', the care and consideration of tortoises, the worldwide effects of the annual *Blue Peter* appeal and the globetrotting exploits of its enthusiastic presenters, the programme became a national institution for generations of children. Still the flagship of BBC children's broadcasting in the contemporary era, the programme has, however, struggled to maintain its ethos in the light of a changing social environment where 'activity' may now be reconfigured as 'anarchy', 'competition' or 'consumption'. Changing worlds require new kinds of programming, which in turn potentially provoke new kinds of moral panic.

Pokémon, the $5 billion worldwide industry, incorporating the original Nintendo computer game, its affiliated animated series and related playing card collectibles, has provoked a variety of moral panics. The challenge of the game in identifying, capturing and competing with a variety of 'pocket monsters', and the cajoling imperative whereby children 'gotta catch'em all', has proved highly appealing, and encouraged in children an empathy with the characters and the desire to collect and categorise. The *Pokémon* trading cards have provoked school bans because of their disruptive influence, which has included assaults and theft, while also enabling children with their literacy, numeracy and negotiation skills, and providing an inclusive culture for most children, instead of those determined by fashion, music or sport. The scale of intensity about these issues may be best measured, though, by the case of a Los Angeles schoolboy who sued a school for the loss of his confiscated trading cards and won $15,000.

Moral panic also attended the animated television series. Some 600 children were taken ill and some hospitalised during the broadcast of the now banned episode, 'Electronic Hero Porygon', in which a bright, pulsating, white light caused nausea and seizure. Further episodes have been banned in the USA because of their indigenous Japanese content (particular customs and holidays, for example) and the presence of potentially confusing sexual or violent imagery – most specifically, James, Team Rocket's camp male villain, a cross-dresser and occasional female impersonator. Ironically, these issues detract from the eco-friendly and quasi-spiritual agenda at the heart of *Pokémon*'s extended narrative, and from the fact that the *Pokémon* text has positively engaged with Japan's postwar concerns about the reconciliation of sacred traditions, the natural order, new technology and postmodern youth cultures.

Periods of 'moral panic' always reflect the desire for television to respect the needs, interests and culture of children in a non-exploitative way, while maintaining a quality output. At the World Summit on Children's Television in 1998, a 'Children's Television Charter' was drawn up to address these concerns. The summit articulated anxiety about the dispersion of televisions and personal computers within the domestic space, which, it was argued, encouraged anti-social, non-family-centred experiences, and implicitly demonstrated increasing fears about going outside. Further, concerns were raised about the escalating commodification of children's culture, especially with regard to the ways that private enterprise, in the guise of toy manufacturers, was funding the proliferation of programming for niche children's channels on satellite and cable. Inevitably, it was concluded that the public service ethos is ultimately neutered by competitive commercial agendas, and that quality thresholds were under threat. The Charter recognised, however, that children have a much more discriminating, active and critical relationship with television than is often thought, and that even the most commercially minded of producers and broadcasters recognise that making quality programmes requires conscience and commitment. Nickelodeon, the satellite and cable children's channel, for example, maintains that 'what's good for kids is good for business', and promotes social development rather than a specific curricular orientation.

Broadcasters realise that children are demanding viewers, and that their supposed passivity, and its negative effects is an overstated myth. Children for the most part move beyond the 'habit' of watching television and make choices; they know how they are watching: whether they are merely filling time, gaining reassurance and companionship, picking up ideas and cultural capital, overcoming boredom or moodiness, or simply having a pleasurable experience. Television remains a very important factor in many children's lives, and further 'moral panics' are inevitable, but should they provoke the degree of care and attention necessary to maintain high standards in children's programming, then for parents, broadcasters, academics and children alike, they will be embraced and understood (see 'The Child Audience').

Paul Wells

RECOMMENDED READING

Buckingham. D. (ed.) (2000), *Small Screens: Television for Children*, London: Continuum.

Cohen, S. (1972), *Folk Devils and Moral Panics*, London: MacGibbon & Kee.

Gunter, B. and McAleer, J. (1997), *Children and Television*, London and New York: Routledge.

Children and Advertising

As a television genre, advertising is often perceived as an 'unsuitable influence' in the everyday lives of children (Palmer, 2006). Critics argue that children are vulnerable, inexperienced viewers who are insufficiently 'media literate' to be able to make proper judgments about advertisement texts (Winick et al., 1973, pp. 7–8). Yet, never before has there been such an unprecedented assault on child audiences by seemingly relentless commercial pitches, as 'tots', 'tweens' and 'teens' become the focus of intensive market research (Lindstrom, 2003) and are coveted as an 'untapped' source of consumer spending.

According to Williams (1997), writing in *Industry* magazine, young people are perceived as a valuable '3-in-1' Youth Market (cf. McNeal's model, in Gunter and Furnham,

1998, p. 3). First, they are 'purchasers' with their own spending power (or at least the power to 'pester' their parents). Second, they are 'influencers' driven by trend-setting within peer groups. Finally, they are 'the future' lucrative adult market. An underlying rationale of this portrait is that young people are ripe for 'early capture' in a (carefully constructed) consumer culture. It is partly the consumerist nature of this portrait of modern childhood that makes television advertising a hot topic for critics and academics.

In recent years, impassioned debates have slammed the upsurge in commercial targeting at young children. In December 1996, the European Commission considered an outright ban on advertising to children under the age of twelve in the UK, in line with Swedish broadcasting policy, on the grounds that children do not fully understand the aims and intentions of advertisers (AEF, 1999/2004). Similarly, Ofcom (2004) identified a link between 'consumers' and 'citizens'. Advertising (food) to children, for example, was declared a research priority in Ofcom's Media Literacy Statement (2001, Paragraph 42). But when it concretised its regulatory ruling on this issue in 2006, with the introduction of a partial ban on advertising to children under the age of sixteen, it was subject to vehement criticism that it had not gone far enough (see Griffiths and O'Malley, 2007, p. 13). Clearly, the relationship between commercial texts and the child audience is contentious, and one might argue that the scale and direction of these debates is demonstrative of the perceived power of advertisements to 'corrupt' young children (Sigman, 2005, p. 25).

FINDING THE CHILD

During an interview conducted with an executive working for a London-based advertising agency, the 'kid sector' of the market was described as being both 'really simple' and 'highly complex'! This sentiment is echoed by Williams (1997) who described children as a 'fickle, novelty-loving bunch'. These contradictions are unhelpful when it comes to trying to decipher the strategies typically used by advertisers when targeting young children.

One thing seems clear – that 'cracking' the holy grail of the lucrative youth market has become a major concern for advertisers (Lindstrom, 2003; Acuff, 1997; Del Vecchio, 1997). The key issue is that there is no substitute for a clear understanding of children when it comes to marketing products to them. Stress is placed on understanding child psychology and stages of cognitive development as well as age, gender and social (peer group) demographics. These frameworks of understanding have a direct impact on the form and content of television advertisements, and can help explain why children's commercial texts are constructed in specific ways.

CHILDREN VIEWING ADS – ATTENTION, GENRE RECOGNITION, COMPREHENSION AND RECALL

Much is made of the 'influence' of television in the lives of young children. However, even though a television may be switched on for several hours a day in the average household, it does not automatically command a high level of attention. In addition, since they are frequently perceived as the 'annoying bits' between actual programmes, it is likely that advertisements command still less attention, despite critics like Sigman (2005, p. 25) suggesting that they are 'corrupting' (see 'Advertising').

Yet, the degree to which an individual actively attends to the screen is considered an important determining factor when assessing the potential for television (and commercial) influence. Gunter and McAleer (1997, p. 136), referring to a study by Ward et al., note the differences in attention levels between older and younger children, where the latter were believed to pay less attention to television commercials. Children between the ages of five and eight years old where thought to attend fully to the screen for about 67 per cent of the viewing time, compared with an average of 75 per cent full attention for children aged nine to twelve years old (cf. Calvert et al., 1982). The data must be carefully interpreted, however, because even though the child may not be directly looking at the screen, they may 'monitor' the content of television by attending to the audio features (Rolandelli, 1989, cited in Gunter and McAleer, 1997, p. 139; Lemish, 2007, pp. 40–2) and will therefore be aware of (commercial) content and messages.

One of the most obvious ways to determine whether children are aware of advertisements is to test whether they are able to distinguish between them and the programmes in which they are embedded. Wartella and Hunter (in Meyer, 1983, p. 149) found that younger children, particularly pre-schoolers, had difficulty distinguishing between the two genres when compared with older children. Young children's ability to perceptually discriminate between the two genres is said to occur somewhere between the ages of three and five years old (Meyer, 1983, p. 150). One study suggested children as young as 3.0 to 3.6 years old were capable of recognising advertisements (Jaglom and Gardner, 1981, p. 42; Kline, 1993, p. 169; Lemish, 2007, p. 49).

As well as levels of attention and genre recognition, children comprehend and recall certain television features more easily than others. Rice et al. (in Meyer, 1983, p. 31)

reviewed a number of studies on different types of programmes and certain common production features stood out as holding the most appeal for young children. Auditory features such as lively music, sound effects, children's voices, 'peculiar' voices, non-speech vocalisations and frequent changes of speaker are very effective in attracting and holding children's attention. Children's advertisements certainly utilise many of these techniques.

A number of studies have emphasised the significance of audio features in advertisements, with emphasis on music as a method of non-verbal communication. Winick et al. (1973, p. 37) note that music is a universal language for children because it tends to elicit spontaneous body movements, stimulates individualised association, encourages clapping and requires no knowledge of language. Macklin (in Hecker and Stewart, 1988, p. 225) argues that music is the most effective attention-grabbing device and that the advertising message may well be ignored without it. She also explains that it provides a platform for 'rehearsal', where the viewer may hum the catchy tune, so enhancing the memorability of the commercial message.

Finally, Gunter and McAleer (1997, p. 137) highlight the fact that young children have a tendency to recall single elements from advertisements such as music, characters or a 'funny bit', while older children were able to recall more product and plotline information (Lemish, 2007; Noble, 1975).

TEXTUAL DILEMMAS IN ADVERTISING TO CHILDREN

One of the main problems identified by Del Vecchio (1997, p. 212) is the difficulty that some advertisers encounter when trying to translate marketing ideas into moving televisual images. His words of caution are divided into four components, dealing with production techniques, narrative complexity, audio soundtracks and character casting.

With regards production techniques, Del Vecchio notes that some advertisers suggest there is a tendency to be carried away with the use of engrossing techniques such as loud music, computer graphics, animation, fantasy setting, characters and unusual camera angles at the expense of product focus. Others argue that such techniques do not detract focus from the product but rather attract and sustain the attention of the viewer.

The production dilemma is also considered in terms of simplicity versus complexity (Del Vecchio, 1997, p. 213). On the one hand, if an advertisement is too simplistic in its mode of address and structure then older children will consider the product 'childish'. Older children are said to prefer fast pacing, complex images and more adult forms of humour. If, on the other hand, an advertisement is too complex the younger viewers will be lost.

Advertisers, when deciding upon the use of audio features, face a further dilemma relating to a choice between speech and song (Del Vecchio, 1997); whether the advertising message should be delivered via a spoken voice-over or a sung jingle. Jingles are effective in the sense that they are often so catchy that young children find themselves singing along. However, it can sometimes be difficult to decipher the lyrics of jingles so the sales message may be lost. Most advertisers prefer a combination of the two soundtrack elements in order to create the best 'attitude' for an advertisement.

Finally, Del Vecchio (1997, p. 214) refers to character casting in the specific context of gendering and the choice between using boys or girls in advertisements. Since children between the ages of five and ten years old are very gender-focused (see Durkin, 1995/1985), distinct segregation will often occur (see Griffiths, in Buckingham, 2000; Chandler and Griffiths, 2000). It is this social pattern which seems to dictate the appearance of only boys in boy-related advertisements and only girls in girl-related advertisements. The situation only becomes complicated if a product is to be targeted at *both* sexes. It is considered safer to feature predominantly boys in mixed-appeal advertisements, on the understanding that girls do not have the same degree of extreme negative reaction towards boys as boys do towards girls, and are more 'flexible' in their textual readings (Acuff, 1997, p. 157; Seiter, 1995).

SOME CONCLUDING REMARKS: YOUTH ADVERTISING – TOTS, TWEENS AND TEENS

As interest and research in the youth market intensifies, the importance of 'getting it right' when advertising to this segment becomes all the more crucial. Various statistics are circulated to help explain what young people's relationships with the world of advertising might be and it is suggested that we all encounter somewhere in the region of 3,000 advertisements a day (Media Awareness Network; Nueborne, 2001). If this statistic is to be believed, children 'naturally' become increasingly experienced users and decoders of advertisement texts as they mature cognitively and, by association, become more engaged and independent participants in the consumer marketplace.

Issues are also shifting within a multimedia landscape. While there are very strict broadcasting guidelines governing television advertising – particularly with regards the separation of advertising and programme content to help children make perceptual distinctions (see Lemish, 2007, p. 203) – there are very few constraints (as yet) online (Kenway and Bullen, 2001, p. 92). The line between educational or informational content and product advertising on the Internet, for example, is blurred (Kenway and Bullen, pp. 116ff). Online sites use information to build brand awareness or link favourite cartoon characters to games and educational information. In fact, programme-product tie-ins are shamefully exploited on youth-targeted websites to the extent that it is difficult to make distinctions.

Advertising to children has seen a remarkable expansion in the last ten years or so, and the aims, functions and techniques of targeting products at the youth market are quickly evolving. Advertisers are acknowledging the high levels of experience that children now have as seasoned media users and tend to credit them (whether rightly or wrongly) with the ability to make their own active, informed and independent decisions and choices. Media educators and government officials would argue that being 'educated against' such targeted sales messages is the best way forward, arming children with the critical skills to see through the empty promise of material goods. Tessa Jowell (then Secretary of State for Culture, Media and Sport), for example, delivered a speech at a Media Literacy seminar in January 2004 in which she placed emphasis on significance of interaction between media understanding, education and (consumer-) citizenship. More extreme campaigners are steadfast in their conviction that a total ban on advertising to children is the only answer. Given the complexities, uncertainties and controversies attached to this subgenre, perhaps the issue of advertising to children is more a question of reason and balance that of seeking a definitive 'solution' to a 'problem'.

Merris Griffiths

RECOMMENDED READING

Gunter, Barrie and Furnham, Adrian (1998), *Children as Consumers: A Psychological Analysis of the Young People's Market*, London: Routledge.

Kenway, Jane and Bullen, Elizabeth (2001), *Consuming Children: Education-Entertainment-Advertising*, Maidenhead: Open University Press.

Singer, Dorothy G. and Singer, Jerome L. (eds) (2001), *Handbook of Children and the Media*, London: Sage.

NEWS

Studying Television News

Television news generally presents itself as a 'window on the world', in which the events of the day are transparently revealed for all to see. Although we may praise or criticise television fiction for being realistic or unrealistic, many people assume that, in the case of news, such judgments are unnecessary. Thus news is not merely seen as like reality but as unmediated reality itself, beamed directly into people's homes. If this were really so, it follows that there would be little reason for anyone to study television news, since to study it would merely be to study the world it reveals. For us to analyse the news is therefore to assume that, like other television genres, the news is a form of representation (or, as it is called in semiology, signification) and that the images and words it uses are, like TV drama, the result of creative and interpretative processes. It is to assert that making television news is, in Philip Schlesinger's phrase, a matter of 'putting reality together' (Schlesinger, 1987).

Television news (and the news media in general) has been studied from a number of perspectives. Like many aspects of media studies, these perspectives range from more social-science-based approaches (in which, for example, news is examined in terms of the role it plays in society) to forms of analysis that come from the humanities (in which TV news is examined as a text). These approaches can be understood in sociological, epistemological, theoretical and methodological terms.

In general sociological terms, we can identify three broad frameworks that inform the analysis of the social role of television news.

The liberal pluralist model assumes that television news provides useful information and thus plays an important role in strengthening democracy and citizenship. Much of the scholarship and research into television news comes from and informs this approach. Within this framework, more news is good news, both in the sense that a range of different news organisations is needed to guarantee a healthy diversity of news providers, and because it is assumed that the presence of television news in TV schedules should be sufficient to guarantee wide access to serious news programming. It was in this spirit, for example, that Newton Minow, the US Federal Communications

Commissioner in the 1960s, made increasing the length of network news broadcasts a priority. More recently, in 2000, the British Secretary of State for Culture, Media and Sport, Chris Smith, expressed concern about the BBC's decision to move their main evening news show from 9 p.m. to 10 p.m., on the basis that the move may decrease the overall number of viewers of television news.

From this perspective, structures that increase the range of outlets (such as the provision of public service broadcasting channels) are generally seen as positive. On the whole, however, the liberal pluralist approach assumes that news journalists and reporters have a certain degree of autonomy from the ownership or economic structures of television channels (see Curran and Seaton, 1991; Williams, 1998). So, for example, the demands of commercial television are not seen as incompatible with the objectives of news journalism. There is, nevertheless, a concern about what is often called the 'dumbing down' of television news reporting, with the increasing adoption of more parochial, tabloid news values at the expense of hard news stories informed by an international network of correspondents.

Two more critical approaches to television news see it as playing a more problematic ideological role. The **conservative approach** sees news journalists (particularly those working for public service channels) as a generally liberal or left-leaning social group, and therefore sees the news as a discourse that reflects a liberal or left-wing bias. This approach has often informed conservative political rhetoric, particularly in the USA, where the notion of the 'liberal media' is widely asserted and believed (Herman, 1999). Because of its emphasis on the individual views of journalists, this approach is not concerned with the influence of ownership and economic structures. Although the conservative approach often has powerful advocates, it does not constitute a significant presence in the academic literature. Its focus on the individual views of journalists (as the principal determinant of the content of news) is seen by many scholars as simplistic, and the claim that journalists lean to the left is highly contested (Gans, 1985; Naureckas and Jackson, 1996).

A more influential approach in terms of media research is what might be called **the critical framework** in which television news is seen as implicated in dominant social and ideological structures, and hence tends to represent the interests of the more powerful groups within society. This approach focuses on the influence of ownership structures and the economic pressures of commercial television, as well as on the day-to-day institutional structures of television news, such as its dependence on political, economic and cultural elites as the 'primary definers' of news events (see, for example, Cohen and Young, 1983; Hall et al., 1978; Herman and Chomsky, 1988; Kellner, 1990; Tuchman, 1978). Television news is thereby seen as playing an important ideological role in creating acquiescence or consent for elite agendas. One of the central implications of the critical framework is that access to the production of news, whether as a reporter, an expert or as a source of news, should be broadened to include a wider range of voices regardless of status or power (see 'Citizen Journalism' below).

In epistemological terms, the status of television news tends to be either understood as a reproduction of reality

'The Propaganda Model of News': Herman and Chomsky

In their book *Manufacturing Consent* (1988), Edward Herman and Noam Chomsky lay out what they call the 'propaganda model' of news production. The model suggests that the economic and ideological conditions in which news is produced means that only certain kinds of information filter through. These filters, they argue, tend to privilege information that suits the interests of powerful elites, while regularly filtering out things that might go against such interests. They identify, in particular, five filters involved in the manufacture of news.

The first filter involves **media ownership**. In an era where more news media are in the hands of a few large and wealthy corporations, they argue that we would expect aspects of that ownership structure to be reflected in news content. In brief, because owners of commercial news media are likely to be invested in a pro-business, corporate view of the world (especially on issues that directly affect their own business interests) we would expect the news divisions of these companies to be more likely to promote rather than question their owner's interests.

The second filter, which applies specifically to commercial news media, is **advertising**. On television, advertisers are paying TV companies to deliver an audience for their products. This can influence news coverage in three ways. First, because advertisers are interested in the more affluent sections of the population, news programmes that tailor broadcasts to the interests of that population are more likely to be profitable. Second, advertisers favour lighter, less disturbing kinds of programming that will keep audiences in a 'buying mood', making them more receptive to sales pitches. Third, advertisers are likely to withdraw support from current affairs programmes whose message conflicts with their corporate interests (see 'Advertising').

The third filter involves what they call **sourcing**. Journalists working to tight deadlines are dependent upon their sources for the information they report. Powerful interests, whether in government or business, are aware of this, and are able to invest heavily in public relations geared to giving journalists well-packaged information designed to meet their needs. Although the provision of well-equipped press rooms, celebrity or 'authoritative' speakers, camera-friendly images, information packs and so on make the journalist's life much easier, they also make it easier for those with such resources to get their message across. This, they argue, exacerbates the tendency of news organisations to assume that government or business sources are more authoritative than, for example, citizen advocacy groups. This principle applies to news-shapers as well as news-makers. In particular, business support for various think tanks has produced a stream of corporate-friendly 'experts' who can offer 'informed' testimony on current events, whether global warming or policy on inflation.

The fourth filter they refer to as **flak**. When news threatens powerful interests, corporate-funded lawyers or advocacy groups are able to use their resources to make their voices heard. So, for example, a news story biased against poorer sections of society will tend to generate complaints from people with little power, whereas complaints from powerful interests (such as the tobacco industry) can lead to legal threats as well as creating publicity designed to discredit negative news stories.

The fifth filter they refer to is **ideological**. During the Cold War, for example, this involved unquestioned assumptions about the superiority of capitalism over communist or socialist systems. Since then, these assumptions have evolved to a widespread belief among the more influential news media in the efficiency of market solutions and the inexorability of a global, capitalist, 'free trade' system.

(*Manufacturing Consent* is published by Pantheon (1988). A video explaining the propaganda model, *The Myth of Liberal Media*, is available from the Media Education Foundation, www.mediaed.org)

Justin Lewis

(albeit one that may privilege certain views over others), or else as a form of social construction. In the first instance, the relation between TV news and the reality it depicts is seen as unproblematic – particularly when journalists adopt principles of objectivity. From this perspective, news can be criticised if it distorts or fails to reflect reality. As a consequence, the degree to which news misrepresents or distorts the world has been a constant source of examination and study.

Approaches that regard news as a social construction see reality as something that is necessarily mediated through discourse: thus, the way we understand the world will depend upon the way we are taught or encouraged to understand it. From this perspective, for example, there is no single, essential reality that we could call 'the Middle East': for people who live in the region the meaning of the term is constructed by such things as religion and ideology, whereas for most of those outside the region the meaning of the Middle East is constructed by news broadcasts. This is not to say that there are not verifiably true or false claims that can made about the Middle East, since 'truth' and 'falsity' are evaluations based on socially constructed categories. So, for example, to say something is 'big' is to classify it within a socially constructed category of size, and to assume comparisons with other smaller objects.

Because, unlike fictional genres, TV news makes self-conscious claims about the relationship between the world outside and the world it reports, it makes a difference whether we see television news as a reproduction of reality or as a social construction. From a social constructionist framework, there is no one reality for news to capture or reproduce. Although it may still be possible to criticise the news in terms of its accuracy, the notion of objectivity becomes untenable. So, for example, a television reporter may cover a story in which representatives from the two main political parties are quoted in order to be 'objective'. And yet that reporter is, in so doing, inevitably privileging the views of political elites, and constructing a view of the world in which those views are seen as defining political debate (see, for example, Canham-Clyne, 1996, on the narrow frame of reference in which the healthcare debate in the USA was reported). To see television news as a social construction does not mean, however, that anything goes, and all accounts are equal. Within this framework questions about whose version of the world is being favoured or excluded are still at issue (see 'Objectivity and Television News').

From within each of these perspectives or epistemological frameworks there are many ways of approaching the study of television news, using various theories and methods.

THE POLITICAL ECONOMY OF TELEVISION NEWS

In terms of the production of news, a number of studies have examined the political economy of television news. This involves exploring the role played by ownership and economic structures on news content. So, for example, the economic interests of the owner (or management board member) of a news broadcaster may be reflected in the kinds of stories that get told. On commercial television, the interests of advertisers, and the need for the news programme to deliver an audience to advertisers in a 'buying mood', may also be a powerful force in structuring the nature of a news broadcast (see box). Since advertisers are more interested in wealthier audiences, we might also expect to see news on commercial channels being tailored to more affluent audiences – favouring business news, for example (see Herman and Chomsky, 1988; McChesney, 1997; Murdock and Golding, 1973). The study of production has also involved examining the institutional structures within which news journalists operate (see, for example, Harrison, 2000; Tuchman, 1978; Schlesinger, 1987). This involves examining the professional codes that news journalists employ to make decisions about the news value of events and the routines used to construct news reports.

CONTENT ANALYSIS

The content of TV news has been examined both quantitatively and qualitatively. Quantitative forms of content analysis involve the systematic measurement of media content in order to provide a picture of the overall character of news coverage. A content analysis may, for example, look at which points of view are generally represented in the coverage of issues and which tend to be excluded. One of the best-known quantitative studies of television news is the series of studies carried out by the Glasgow Media Group on the TV news coverage of industrial disputes and related political and economic issues (Glasgow Media Group, 1976, 1980, 1982), which suggested a bias in the news media against the views of trade unionists. Overall, these forms of content analysis often suggest that television news is heavily reliant upon official or elite sources, in terms of both the issues covered and the patterns of coverage.

STRUCTURE AND NARRATIVE

More qualitative approaches to news content have focused on the structure and narrative of television news

The Glasgow Media Group

For over thirty years the Glasgow Media Group (also known as the Glasgow University Media Group, GUMG) has been tracking the way the broadcast media shapes our understanding of contemporary events. These events have ranged from studies of the 1984–5 miners' strike, media coverage of Greenham Common, conflict in Northern Ireland, coverage of the Falklands war, the Gulf wars and the Israel Palestine conflict, as well as exploring media coverage of mental illness, health scares, risk and child abuse. The Group argues that television news works according to preferred meanings which themselves are replete with political and cultural assumptions and which tend to favour the status quo and extant power relationships. As such these assumptions reflect the divisions and inequalities within contemporary society and frame the news as ultimately a non-critical and non-radical form of reporting of contemporary events. The Group's work has evolved from attempts to evaluate journalistic claims to objectivity, neutrality and impartiality to the use of a more refined three-dimensional empirical analysis, which includes: a) the processes of news production, b) news content analysis and c) audience reception studies, to understand the basis of communicative relationships as one of truth and power. Intellectually they stand in contra-distinction to theories that argue that the television news media are either too trivial to matter, or deal in excessive opaqueness. Rather they have consistently maintained that for any sociological assessment of ideology, and by extension politics in general (and to a lesser extent cultural identity), the study of the media and engagement with debates about its effects is critical.

Stanley Cohen: Moral Panics

Stanley Cohen popularised the phrase moral panics in his 1972 study *Folk Devils and Moral Panics*. And as he says in the introduction to the third edition of his study, 'folk devils' remain the objects of moral panics and belong, then and now, to 'seven familiar clusters of social identity' (p. viii). These are:

a) young, working-class, violent males;
b) school violence: bullying and shootouts;
c) wrong drugs: used by wrong people at wrong places;
d) child abuse, satanic rituals and paedophile registers;
e) sex, violence and blaming the media;
f) welfare cheats and single mothers;
g) refugees and asylum seekers: flooding our country, swamping our services.

These clusters of social identity are the basis from which the media amplify and distort genuine issues and areas of political and social life into various forms of 'panic discourses'. So that, for example, European common market and internal migration policy is reduced to talk of: 'asylum free for all'; 'scroungers and beggars'; and Britain as a 'haven' or 'soft touch' for 'spongers'. What Cohen attempted to identify was the process by which moral panics are in part created and generated by the media. Today, he is aware that methodologies for studying the media have dramatically improved since 1972, that there are models other than his own process model for explaining moral panics, even that the phrase has passed into common parlance. Nevertheless, his recognition of the media and their part in the consistent identification and pursuance of 'folk devils' and their role in initiating and sustaining 'moral panics' remains an important sociological insight.

Jackie Harrison

and current affairs. Work by Galtung and Ruge (1965, 1983) examined the structural imperatives, routines and rituals that inform news production, and the use of semiotics in media analysis has led to a number of detailed explorations of news programmes as texts (Brunsden and Morley, 1978; Hartley, 1982; Jensen, 1987). These approaches have stressed the importance of understanding how the form and content of television news programmes prefer certain meanings of the world over others (see also Morley, 1980).

AUDIENCES

Understanding the meaning of television news has also led to research on audiences. The influence of news on the way people think about the world has been a focus of media research for some time, and although questions of media influence were initially somewhat elusive, there is now a body of evidence to suggest that the news is influential on public opinion in a range of specific and measurable ways. So, for example, a number of studies have demonstrated that news clearly sets an agenda that is then reproduced in responses to surveys about people's priorities and opinions (see, for example, Iyengar, Peters and Kinder, 1982; McCombs and Shaw, 1972).

Overall, audience studies focusing on television news in particular (now the dominant news source for most people) indicate that people watch television news more inadvertently and with less attention than other forms of television (see Lewis, 1991). This has led researchers to use various qualitative methods to explore in some detail the way in which television news does impact on viewers. So, for example, Iyengar's research suggests that what he calls the 'episodic' framing of most news stories (which focus on events themselves rather than the causes or history of those events) makes it difficult to understand the social causes of issues like crime or poverty, and instead to attribute blame only to the individuals themselves (Iyengar, 1991); these findings are in keeping with studies by Lewis (1991) and Philo (1990), which suggest that television news can be important in creating or reinforcing fairly simple associations (such as Saddam Hussein with Hitler or striking workers with violence) that stick in people's minds.

Justin Lewis

RECOMMENDED READING

Cohen, S. and Young, J. (1983), *The Manufacture of News*, London: Constable.

Glasgow Media Group (1982), *Really Bad News*, London: Writers and Readers.

Iyengar, S. (1991), *Is Anyone Responsible?*, Chicago: University of Chicago Press.

Analysing Television News

The analysis of news requires us to begin by understanding the processes involved in making television news. Just as Hollywood producers decide that certain aspects of life are worth making films about whereas others are not, so news producers make, on a very basic level, decisions about what is news and what is not. Most TV news producers also share with Hollywood producers the need to entertain audiences – in order to gain viewers in a competitive market. Although this applies more clearly to commercial television companies, public service broadcasters such as the BBC also have indirect but tangible pressure to get respectable ratings in order to justify their level of funding.

Nevertheless, we still tend to think of news as an information rather than an entertainment service. Since most of us are well accustomed to the routines of television news programmes, and since news journalists often share a sense of which events have 'news value' and which do not, decisions about what news is often take on the air of inevitability. As a consequence, the first question we need to ask is this: why do some stories receive a great deal of coverage and others receive less, little or none?

Most people would agree that news coverage should bear some relation to the importance of an event, but the definition of importance will vary depending on who we are and how we view the world (see Galtung and Ruge, 1983). So, for example, should television news be concerned with the personal lives of public figures (whether politicians or celebrities) simply because they are in the public domain, or should such figures only be of news value when they do something that has an effect on significant numbers of people? How important is it for us to know about events in other countries, even if those events have little direct influence on our lives? Does TV news always have to be about an 'event', or can it be about trends or more general topics? Should television news reflect the unusual, such as plane or train crashes, or more typical events, such as car accidents?

Once we begin to think about these questions, it becomes clear that the decisions taken by news producers about news value are open to scrutiny. It may be that our notion of citizenship, and what it is important for citizens to know, is not adequately addressed by the norms of television news. So, for example, we may feel that it is important for citizens to know the details of things that affect them (whether it is changes in the environment, or debates around government policy on digital television) so that they might, as citizens, have some say on these issues. But we may feel it is less important to know about the personal lives or publicity stunts of politicians, if those matters have no significant influence on public policy or our understanding of issues. The consequences of such a judgment, needless to say, would involve a radical shift in the news values of much contemporary news programming.

Once we have looked at what is included and excluded from television news, we should consider how stories are told. Whose point (or points) of view is represented in the story, and whose voice is excluded? Where there are different points of view, are these views given equal weight by the form or context in which they are represented? There are many ways to do this: for example,

- We can count who is quoted or able to speak on news programmes, in order to establish whether certain categories of people (who we can call 'primary definers') are more predominant than others. So, for example, who is quoted on stories about the economy? Is it, for example, government representatives, business representatives, or people representing consumers or wage earners?

- We can look at the sources of a news story. Does that source have an interest in promoting a certain point of view, and does the news programme point this out? So, for example, the release of a report by a business group is likely to reflect a business-oriented view of the world. Is this source balanced by an opposing view?

- We can examine whether the story itself tends to create a certain view of the world. So, for example, do crime stories reflect the real world of crime, or do they create an impression that unusual crimes are more prevalent than they really are?
- We can examine the way in which a story is told. Does the narrative construction of the story prefer some meanings over others? Does the use of visual information or live footage lead towards a certain impression? So, for example, if two different interpretations are presented, but only one of those interpretations is accompanied by visual information, does this make that interpretation seem more persuasive as an account?
- We can look at what information is presented in the story. Do the facts presented tend to favour some views over others, and, if so, is this a fair representation of the facts available?

Most of these forms of analysis demand not only a detailed examination of television news, they also require us to know more about the topics represented than we can glean from the newscast. In order to evaluate what is being represented, in other words, we need to know what information or perspective is being excluded from the story.

METHODOLOGY

We also need to consider a number of *methodological* questions. In particular, if we want to make any general observations, we need to ensure that the news programmes we look at are typical rather than unusual. This means gathering a *sample* of news programmes that is large enough to establish clear patterns, and to minimise the chance of examples we look at being untypical of news coverage as a whole. If we are looking at coverage of a particular event, it is helpful to look at coverage of other comparable events as a point of comparison. If we are looking at more general features of television news, then we need to ensure that our sample is spread across a reasonable period, so that the nature of the coverage will not be distorted by any one (possibly unusual) news event.

Once we have chosen a sample, we need to establish a systematic procedure for analysis. This may involve developing a coding frame, which comprises a set of criteria for categorising each news item or news programme. So, for example, if we are looking at who is represented, we might want to have various categories of appearance such as:

- quoted without being seen;
- quoted next to photograph;
- shown speaking on camera, etc.

and various categories of person such as:

- government representative;
- member of pressure group;
- business person;
- academic expert;
- member of think tank, etc.

Before we develop our coding categories, we should ensure that these categories are pertinent to the question or issue we are pursuing, as well as being a useful way of summarising news content. We might find, for example, that there are significant types of people or statements whose presence in television news we had not anticipated (and who therefore get coded or classified under opaque categories like 'other'). To limit this possibility, it is advisable to test the coding frame on a selection from your sample (often referred to as a 'pilot study'), and, if needs be, modify it accordingly.

Once we have studied television news as a text, we need to consider the contexts in which it is produced. The authorship of television programmes is complex and diffuse: there are a number of levels of decision-making and a variety of institutional, professional or ideological pressures on programme-makers.

In the case of television news, simply at the programme level, reporters, editors and other news professionals will all have some role in what gets produced, but in an environment in which political and corporate leaders are becoming increasingly skilled at anticipating what journalists want, news-makers also play a role in constructing the news. So, for example, Ronald Reagan's adviser Michael Deaver regarded himself as a news producer, because he knew the images he created would be perfectly targeted to the needs of television news (great pictures, good copy) and therefore irresistible to the makers of television news broadcasts. Thus, when Reagan started one of the best-known car races in the USA (the Daytona 500), it was the lead item on all three main US networks – even though the event itself had little effect on anyone.

There are also pressures that come from the ownership and control of a television channel. It is possible, for example, that Rupert Murdoch's various satellite news channels (such as Sky and Fox) may reflect Murdoch's conservative, pro-business ideology. Private newscasters

How to Analyse a TV News Programme

As we have seen, television's dominant generic domains of actuality (including news) and drama have been studied by widely differing methods. Textual analysis, derived from literary/linguistic models, for instance, is applied to drama. However, news has tended to attract sociological approaches, dominated by 'content analysis'. Textual analysis was suited to analysing individual stories qualitatively, whereas content analysis was developed for quantitative research, seeking regularities and frequencies across many stories.

Textual analysis (humanities, criticism, critique) and content analysis (social science, research, policy) were used to investigate opposing realms:

- news: the public sphere, citizenship, political economy, truth;
- drama: the private domain, audiences, everyday life, emotion.

There was a gendered aspect to this distinction; news and social science seemed 'masculine' compared with soap opera and textual criticism, but textual analysis of actuality genres has become an important component of TV studies.

How to do it (adapted from Hartley, 1999, pp. 229–31)

1. *News as an industrial commodity*

- *Journalism*: news values – conflict, importance, recency, nearness, human interest, novelty, celebrity.
- *Competition*: news as commercial commodity. Sources, agencies. Compare rival news media.
- *Entertainment*: how to retain viewers while telling them things they do not like. How does news appeal and appal simultaneously?
- *Regulation*: licensing, defamation, 'decency', 'self-censorship'. For example, violence may be shown (between strangers, not intimates), dead bodies may be glimpsed (but not in close-up).

2. *News as a generic form*

- *Visual elements*: studio anchor and decor; graphics and design; actuality footage.

- *Verbal/sound elements*: institutional voices (reporters, commentators, anchors); accessed voices ('real' people); effects (music, dubbed sounds).
- *Narration*: the 'plot' of stories; characters ('we' and 'they' personifications, heroes, villains, victims); action and dialogue within and between stories; sequence as a dramatisation of 'our democracy today'.
- *Differentiation*: how news is both like and unlike surrounding genres (advertising, talk shows, drama) and media (newspapers, radio, Internet).

3. *News as a dramatisation of democracy*

- *Our representatives*: talking heads (decision-making), visualised by location (reporters hanging around in doorways); celebrities (actions and comments), based on bodily recognition.
- *Vox pops*: 'ordinary' (i.e. anonymous) people's views – the grab and the sound bite as the chorus of politics.
- *National identity*: myths of who 'we' are; policing the boundary of the social ('we' have a government, 'they' have a regime; 'we' love children, 'they' are paedophiles; 'we' are free, 'they' are illegal immigrants).

4. *News as a regime of truth*

- *Impartiality versus bias*: how can you tell one from the other?
- *Conflict*: truth as a product of 'both' sides of a story; truth as violence.
- *Eyewitness ideology*: news stories are often based on reports, statistics, media releases. But trustworthy reporting is associated with being there in the thick of the action. In practice, the information comes from a 'handout', while the reporter stands in front of something visually relevant.
- *Fact versus fiction*: news has eye contact but not music; drama has music but not eye contact.

5. *Who wants to know?*

- What are you looking for that you do not already know? The research question will shape your findings, and your methods will determine your results.

John Hartley

may also have links (whether through ownership, directorships or shareholders) with other business interests, which may be influential in pressuring news companies not to jeopardise their corporate interests (see, for example, Herman and Chomsky, 1988 (see box, 'The Propaganda Model of News'); Lee and Solomon, 1990). Public service channels, such as the BBC, are less subject to pressure than privately owned media, but can also be influenced by political appointments (to Boards of Governors), and by the need to rely on government support in revenue-raising decisions (such as the level of the licence fee). The use of advertising as the main source of revenue on commercial channels may also be a source of pressure on TV news broadcasters.

Understanding the economic, social, institutional and cultural contexts in which television news is produced illuminates our study of the content of news, in the sense that it may illuminate patterns we discover in our study of the form and content of news. This understanding may also lead us to ask certain questions of the news programmes themselves: so, for example, we might ask whether commercial television news tends to play down negative news about companies linked to the TV channel, or that routinely advertise on that channel.

Finally, if we are concerned with the social impact of news, we might conduct an audience study. There are many ways to do this (see, for example, Lewis, 1991): we might adopt a more qualitative approach (interviewing small groups of people) or a more quantitative approach (in which surveys are used to reach larger numbers of people). In either case, as with content analysis, we need to be aware of the degree to which we can generalise from our audience sample. There are also ways in which we can explore the power of television news by comparing patterns of news coverage with data generated by public opinion polls (see Lewis, 2001; McCombs and Shaw, 1972). Since TV news is still one of the prime sources of information in the process of democratic decision-making, the study of the genre remains a critical issue.

Justin Lewis

RECOMMENDED READING

Cohen, S. and Young, J. (1983), *The Manufacture of News*, London: Constable.

Lee, M. and Solomon, N. (1990), *Unreliable Sources*, New York: Lyle Stuart.

McNair, B. (1999), *News and Journalism in the UK*, London: Routledge.

Constructing News Values

The ideological role of the news media is used by some commentators to refer to the way that symbolic messages are used to establish and maintain power relations in society. According to this way of viewing the news media they play an important role in influencing the way we perceive the world, they 'control' what we see as 'natural' or 'obvious'. Others argue that a journalist picks up cultural values in stories and presents them back to the audience as a matter of course. Here the media's production of news values is not necessarily political, deliberate or conspiratorial, but is systematic and routine. In both cases it is recognised that embedded in journalistic language and news are taken for granted assumptions about what we value and do not value. In short, mainstream news values are all constructed within a common framework of understanding, for example, agreement about the desirability of democracy. Generally speaking though news values are produced by two broad sets of factors, first tangible forces external to the news organisation, second by beliefs within the news organisation and the increasing involvement of audiences with news agendas.

The first can be summarised as:

- the type of sources accessed by journalists for expert evaluations of events;
- the use of news agencies, which influence the news agenda;
- the importance placed by journalists on the output of other news organisations;
- the need to deliver large audiences to advertisers.

The second involves the way contemporary news organisations are being forced to reevaluate their news priorities and consequently their news values in the light of market pressures, technological developments and the growing competition for audience share. Because of ratings pressures, news organisations sometimes prioritise what they know audiences want to watch rather than always making the editorial decision for them. Also audiences are being encouraged to participate by contributing pictures, text or opinions on stories and are becoming increasingly involved in the creation of news agendas and the subsequent dissemination of news. Technological developments and commercial pressures continue to compromise the public service broadcasting remit in Britain and throughout Europe, forcing a reevaluation of news values and a search for new ways to engage the audience in many public service broadcasting organisations.

The construction of news values also depends on organisational values which usually differ between organisations. Different news organisations have different editorial approaches and house styles resulting in different news values. The differences in approach can be related to the ownership of the organisation, its remit, its contractual obligations and the type and size of audience it needs to attract. These factors shape the organisation's news policy and its news values. In most organisations, while the key goal is to make a profit, there are other goals, such as to produce a quality product, serve the public and achieve professional recognition. Within news organisations there has to be a mechanism in place to ensure that there is agreement from journalists about the type of news values the organisation or news programme holds. A study by Warren Breed in 1955 (see Breed, 1997) showed how agreement on news values is achieved from journalists through a process of socialisation. Often this occurs through assimilation of newsroom mythology which is communicated down by experienced journalists and by a general absorption of the organisation's remit and news policy. This produces a shared belonging to the profession with a clear and identifiable set of skills, practices, values, pressures, constraints and expectations within which journalists work. Gaye Tuchman (1997) revealed how journalists employ a set of routinised conventions in choosing and selecting news to cope with a variety of problems and pressures such as time and space limitations, financial, bureaucratic and legal restrictions, logistical difficulties and the particular constraints of the television medium itself, such as the need for visuals.

So what exactly are the dominant news values used by news journalism? Research has shown that audiences tend to find stories interesting if they are human interest stories, show conflict or controversy, cover unusual happenings, cover events that are news and are happening now and are culturally and geographically relevant. These, and the news factors identified by Galtung and Ruge, 1965, and others (see also Ostgaard, 1965; Sande, 1971; Tunstall, 1971; Bell, 1991) have been used to attempt to identify the properties of news stories that audiences will find appealing and are likely to want to watch.

Television news events have 'news value' if:

- they contain good pictures;
- they contain short, dramatic occurrences which can be sensationalised;
- they have novelty value;
- they are open to simple reporting;
- they occur on a grand scale;

- they are negative or contain violence, crime, confrontation or catastrophe;
- they are either highly unexpected, or contain things which one would expect to happen;
- the have meaning and relevance to the audience;
- similar events are already in the news;
- they contain elite people or nations or if they allow an event to be reported in personal or human interest terms.

Journalists do not look everywhere for news but work in what Fishman (1997) called 'beats' and Tuchman (1997) refers to as 'news nets'. These are areas from which news is expected to arise at certain times and with some frequency. Fishman likens working on a beats to using a road map which helps a journalist to navigate through events successfully. Mastering areas of news such as council meetings, court reporting and news conferences indicates a basic acquisition of journalistic skills. These skills are driven by routine processes such as the daily phone calls to the police, double-checking facts and figures, checking court lists, council notices, the parliamentary diary and the wires. A journalist has to able to recognise news value, a skill which is intrinsic to being a journalist. This lets them 'join the club' and excludes non-journalists.

Importantly though this 'way of working' is being threatened by recent developments in news coverage that require global coverage twenty-four hours a day (see below). The contemporary news marketplace is dominated by deadlines, urgency, live feeds, twenty-four-hour news channels, Internet news and new news consumption patterns, which facilitate instantaneity. While news deadlines are nothing new, the emphasis on being first has assumed economic significance of a kind not previously known. As the marketplace for news expands and has become global, so the economic benefits of 'being ahead of the game' are concomitantly greater for both television news and press news. This poses threats and risks to the accuracy of news journalism since being accurate in news that is often disseminated globally has to embrace and work with the constraints of new time pressures.

Overall, it is only possible to explain the construction of news values by combining and understanding the external and internal factors that influence a news organisation and the conditions in which news journalism operates.

- The ideological context within which journalism operates;
- the influence of sources, owners, advertisers, audiences, technological change and other news organisations;

Gatekeeper Studies

'Gatekeeper studies' have played an important part in helping us to understand the way in which news values are constructed. David Manning White (1950) applied Kurt Lewin's (1947) term 'gatekeeper' to journalism practice to try to understand why a journalist chooses one story over another. White's US-based research centred on the role of an individual wire editor in a press newsroom. The wire editor, who White named 'Mr Gates', selected stories to be printed from the large amount of wire copy provided every day by three large news agencies. White believed him to be the most important gatekeeper of all, as he alone was able to reject the majority of stories coming into the newsroom, thus shaping and constructing the organisation's news values. Although his aim was to try to find a way of predicting journalistic behaviour, White's research raised more questions than it answered.

Snider (1967) used White's gatekeeper theory to see if Mr Gates's selection criteria had changed over time. His study showed that in 1949 Mr Gates chose more human interest material than any other type of story, followed by national politics, international politics, state politics, national farming and international war. In 1967 international war (due to Vietnam War coverage) was the most common story type, followed by crime, national economics, human interest and disasters. Snider concluded that in both 1949 and 1967 Mr Gates picked the stories he liked and believed the readers wanted, but by 1967 Mr Gates's news values had changed to include a wider variety of stories.

The concentration on individuals as gatekeepers, however, was challenged by studies that revealed that individual journalists were not actually the key characters in decision-making. Decisions were made, not on individual assessments of newsworthiness, but on other journalistic and organisational criteria and external pressures. The American study of the organisation of news selection at NBC by Bailey and Lichty (1972), showed that, in fact, news production involves a chain of journalistic activity from the initial event to the final news product, and that story selection does not lie solely in the hands of a specific individual. The organisation is the gatekeeper, not the individual journalist.

Further gatekeeping research has shown that journalists are only passive transmitters of information, as their work practice is routinised. Staab (1990) argued that it is not necessary to discuss separately the role of different gatekeepers in the news process, as there is little reason to believe that their perception of newsworthiness differs radically according to whether they are in the collecting, transmitting or presentation stage of the news process.

Gatekeeper research has made an important contribution to our understanding of the construction of news values, as it has shown that news selection does not take place on the basis of the whims of an individual journalist in an organisation but is built into an organisation's ethos and rationale. Journalists work together within organisational constraints to produce a news product that reflects a shared agreement on what has news value.

Jackie Harrison

- the needs and goals of the news organisation;
- the routine nature of journalistic practice; and
- the importance of news factors as an explanation of the properties inherent in events

are all important and relevant. No single one, however, will serve as a stand-alone explanation of the construction of news values.

Jackie Harrison

RECOMMENDED READING

Berkowitz, Dan (1997*), Social Meanings of News*, London: Sage.

Harrison, Jackie (2000), *Terrestrial Television News in Britain: The Culture of Pro*duction, Manchester: Manchester University Press.

Harrison, Jackie (2005), *News*, London: Routledge Introductions to Media and Communications.

Shoemaker, Pamela (1996), *Mediating the Message: Theories of Influences on Mass Media Content*, New York: Addison Wesley Longman.

Objectivity and Television News

In the UK, the requirement for both the BBC and ITN to produce impartial news is a legal one and is a part of the constitution of the two systems laid down by government from their inception. The news programming of the ITV system is regulated in terms of serving the public interest impartially. The Broadcasting Act 1990 states that 'any news given (in whatever form) in its programmes is presented with due accuracy and impartiality' (Broadcasting Act 1990, 6(1)6).

The BBC and Impartiality

Impartiality at the BBC (British Broadcasting Corporation) originates from its founding principle of public service broadcasting: the detachment of the BBC from vested interests and government. The BBC is funded through the licence fee to ensure that it is free from direct governmental or direct commercial intervention. Its first Director-General, John Reith, believed that an impartial BBC could flourish and promote an enlightened and informed public only if it was not required to pass on the views of the government directly to the public. The role of the BBC is to act as interpreter of public affairs and arbiter of public tastes and standards. Over the years, however, the BBC has not been immune from political pressures. The General Strike of 1926 tested the relationship between the Government and the Corporation. The Government argued that the BBC should recognise the strike as illegal and not allow strikers' views to be heard on the radio, contradicting the BBC's requirement to be impartial.

Other governments have since tried to influence BBC content. In particular, the Thatcher Government tried to prevent the BBC from taking an impartial view during the Falklands War in 1982. In May 1982 a *Panorama* (BBC, 1953–) programme was heavily criticised for including dissenting views on the Conservative Party's war policy. BBC2's *Newsnight* (BBC, 1980–) was accused by the Government of being too detached and not supportive of the British side. The BBC has defended its position on numerous occasions, arguing that conflicts such as the Falklands War, the Gulf War and the invasion of Kosovo are not total wars, and consequently it is in the public interest to give an impartial account of events.

Impartiality is intended to be at the heart of all the BBC's programming, as it reflects two public service principles: serving all interests and ensuring that minority interests are represented. The BBC's public service broadcasting principles are codified in the BBC's *Producers' Guidelines*, which contains scrupulous requirements for news programming. The BBC is forbidden in Clause 13(7) of its Licence and Agreement from broadcasting its own opinions on current affairs and matters of public policy.

The BBC, however, is not always impartial when reporting terrorism or racism, and will only conduct interviews when it feels there is a public interest in doing so that outweighs the offence it would cause. In 1996 Martin Bell, then a BBC journalist, called for the abandonment of neutrality in war reporting and genocide in favour of a 'journalism of attachment'. Criticising the traditional form of BBC war reporting as 'bystander's journalism', Bell argued that journalists should show they care as well as know about the events they are covering. His view raised controversy; taking an impartial stance in news reporting is a central tenet of good journalism at the BBC. Its public service requirements mean that it must seek to serve the whole nation, reflecting and responding to differing tastes and views. At the BBC the maxim is that 'good journalism (which is impartial) will help people of all persuasions to make up their own minds' (BBC, 1996 p. 21).

Jackie Harrison

The Annex to the Licence and Agreement in 1964 states that the BBC accepts a duty 'to provide a properly balanced service which displays a wide range of subject matter … [and] to treat controversial subjects with due impartiality … both in the Corporation's news services and in the more general field of programmes dealing with matters of public policy' (BBC, 1996, p. 21). Regulation of television news content has an important implication for audiences. In the UK most people use television as their primary source of local and world news, and it is the most trusted source of news information (Gunter and Winstone, 1992). Audience trust has been gained via the application of journalistic objectivity norms.

However, many of the criticisms of objectivity and impartiality in journalism are generally underpinned by the assumption that objectivity and impartiality are always relative. In other words, ideas of what should be reported and in what way varies from society to society and from issue to issue. Those who argue that objectivity as a professional journalistic ideology is flawed believe that social reality is humanly produced and consequently is a social construction. Judith Lichtenberg (1991), however, argues that we cannot simply state that objectivity is impossible, and that critics of objectivity do not actually do so themselves. Although they appear to reject objectivity they are covertly relying upon it as a benchmark or ideal against which to assess deviations from it.

Completely objective television news is seen by many as impossible, owing to the subjective nature of journalistic value judgments, and by others as being undesirable, because it works against journalistic responsibility for content and against the watchdog role of the media (see box). However, despite the problems inherent in the meaning of objective news and the difficulty in achieving it, objectivity is an important professional aspiration and central to the task of television news as a whole. Indeed, journalists claim to use a set of devices that ensures that they can argue that their reporting is unbiased, such as:

- use of verifiable facts;
- clear separation of fact from opinion;
- expression of professional judgment but not personal opinion;
- inclusion of opposing sides in a debate (or different truth claims of sources);
- separating different sources' views from the report by using either quotation marks in the press, or via sound bites on television;
- use of live television pictures or live two-ways where a journalist speaks live to a newsreader from a location, showing that something is actually happening or has happened and showing reports packed with facts and figures.

However, using these devices to achieve an appearance of objectivity has raised several concerns from critics, such as:

- the routine use of sources means that mainstream views are generally allowed greater access to television news than radical views, reducing the diversity of opinion;
- responsibility for the content of the news can be levelled at the sources, allowing journalists to be relatively free from the responsibility of justifying or defending the content of their stories;
- the use of sources as experts may allow journalists to avoid the acquisition of expert knowledge, while at the same time sources have become increasingly adept at information management and 'spin';
- the growth of live news reporting on location, which gives the appearance of more objectivity because the audience can see events unfold, may be confusing, deceptive and told out of context;
- the increasing use of live and often dramatic pictures means even relatively unimportant events are sensationalised, making it more difficult for the audience to assess their significance.

Regulators aim to ensure that journalists do not unwittingly distort the news. However, the word 'objectivity' is rarely used by regulators, but is substituted by words such as 'impartiality', 'accuracy', 'balance' and 'fairness'. Here, impartiality implies a disinterested relationship to news content, whereas objectivity has broader demands than this.

However, objectivity remains valuable as an ideal against which bias can be evaluated, but is problematic as a method. Any attempt to be objective impossibly implies the feasibility of somehow removing values from news content. Of concern is the compromise position that journalists take up between playing an active role in a democratic society and the attempt at 'objective' reporting using a variety of practical devices. The attempt at objectivity in broadcast journalism may also not be the best form of journalism as it serves broadcasters' interests rather than the public interest and reduces plurality of news information. Although it is important that television journalists continue to provide accurate and reliable news information, it is not necessarily the same as providing objective news reports.

Jackie Harrison

RECOMMENDED READING

Lichtenburg, Judith (1991), 'In Defence of Objectivity Revisited', in James Curran and Michael Gurevitch (eds), *Mass Media and Society*, London: Arnold.

McQuail, Denis (1992), *Media Performance*, London: Sage.

Tuchman, Gaye (1999) 'Objectivity as Strategic Ritual: An Examination of Newsmen's Notions of Objectivity', in Howard Tumber (ed.), *News: A Reader*, Oxford: Oxford University Press.

The Infotainment Debate

The infotainment debate (as opposed to infotainment itself) is an argument about the relationship between television and public life. The debate, if not the phenomenon of infotainment itself, has been much more prominent in the UK and continental Europe than in the USA, largely because many European countries have maintained a commitment to what is known as 'public service broadcasting' as a national cultural policy (see box above). Public service broadcasting in this context means television channels financed primarily from the public purse rather than from commercial (advertising) revenues. The purpose of such arrangements is to use broadcasting to inform the public and to educate the citizen, rather than to entertain the consumer.

The beginnings of the debate occurred during the 1980s and early 1990s, when the buzzwords of deregulation and privatisation swept across the Reagan–Thatcher political universe, from the airline industry to telecommunications. Applied to broadcasting, this political reform had two consequences:

- the privatisation of previously state-owned TV channels (e.g. ORTF in France and RAI in Italy);
- the relaxation of legislative controls over content.

Both led to what seemed to some observers to be a far too relaxed attitude to the presentation of public affairs on television.

TV overtook newspapers as the primary source of news for popular audiences in developed countries sometime in the 1970s. As an emergent medium, television news paradoxically had to grow out of a professional and cultural context that was suffused with the values and habits associated with the press, the very medium that TV was in the process of supplanting.

According to the prevailing wisdom, TV news ought to conform as much as possible to the existing generic format of a serious newspaper, and look as little as possible like television. This idea is as old as the press itself: it originated in the political philosophy upon which modern liberal democracies are said to be based. In countries where voting was universal, freedom of speech and access to information had to extend to the whole adult population in order for an 'informed citizenry' to make rational judgments and decisions about public affairs. The information communicated to them ought to be accurate, unbiased and impartial, on the model of the nineteenth-century broadsheet newspaper: the *Washington Post*, the *New York Times*, *The Times* and so forth.

'Free press' advocates presumed that commercial TV companies were incapable of delivering such information unless they were under regulatory duress. Further, they thought that television was almost the binary opposite of the great civic freedoms: its appeal was to the emotions not to reason, its location was private not public life, and its purpose was entertainment not decision-formation. Indeed, television had some generic characteristics that were very challenging for a modernist understanding of what constituted good news reporting.

TV developed information formats along the following lines.

- *A talking medium*: words were heard one at a time, so a given current affairs show could only contain so many words, as opposed to a newspaper, where many more words could be printed, even if only a minority of them were read by any one reader.
- *A video medium*: moving pictures were more telegenic than talking heads. Having videotape of an event to hand tended to determine its inclusion in a news show, over and above any editorial assessment of its overall importance in a news story. Conversely, events of great significance for which there was no footage were less likely to reach the top of the news agenda.
- *A hybridising medium*: TV was very prone to evolution by spin-off. Successful formats were compulsively copied. In this very active semiotic environment, 'information' could never be 'pure' – it would always be presented via the techniques and generic formats that were regarded as most appealing at the time.
- *A porous medium*: TV contained an unusual mixture of incommensurable types of programming, especially fact and fiction, rubbing up against each other. Its formats were very porous to each other. News was constantly borrowing generic characteristics from non-news formats.

Television evolved its own time-based, audiovisual, hybridising aesthetic. Along the way it produced various conventions for generic differentiation whereby viewers could tell almost at a glance whether they were watching news or some other genre.

'Public service' news was especially committed to such distinctions. Semiotically, it was self-consciously authoritarian, often giving it a middle-aged male sort of feel, as opposed to the more energetic and 'feminised' genres around it. Journalists were often preferred as presenters, even rather than cute-looking personalities who nevertheless proliferated in children's, music, lifestyle and talk shows. News shows were often protected from advertising slots by 'news bumpers' (bits of continuity that ensured that a commercial did not lead straight into or out of a news story).

But news was never exempt from the imperatives of its semiotic surroundings. Throughout television and even print-media history, it has had to balance two contradictory necessities. Its mission to inform the public and educate the citizen meant that it had to give priority to the facts and to the due weight of stories on the day's news agenda. But simultaneously, the need to attract and retain large audiences of those same citizens (who were not compelled to attend) meant that news had to appeal to them, otherwise they would not watch it. This is an inescapable need in popular journalism (Hartley, 1996). Television had always to serve two masters – 'information-' and '-entertainment', as it were.

Exactly how much should informational programmes appeal to their audience's desire just to 'watch TV'? Viewers were 'trained' by long habituation to accept that news might be boring but still be of some importance – hence their willingness to put up with the news staples of talking heads and people waiting outside doorways. But still editors had to decide just how much foreign news could be tolerated on a popular news show, as opposed to local crime, traffic and sport stories, or how many 'human interest', celebrity and showbiz stories to balance those about conflict, war and opposition.

Meanwhile, beyond the comparatively inflexible environment of the news, television experimented with presenting information in entertaining ways that suited its status as television. Many such infotainment formats were successful:

- Lifestyle: cooking, gardening, travel, house improvement, antiques (see 'Daytime TV', p. 176);
- Reality: traffic-camera shows, home-video shows, neighbours from hell, street interviews. This format has evolved into 'survival' shows (see 'Reality TV', p. 134);
- Tabloid: consumer stories, crime, celebrities, scandal, hidden cameras and chequebook journalism;
- Investigative: most popular where the reporters put themselves in physical danger of assault by the subjects of the investigation;
- Talk: including celebrity chat shows, Oprah and Springer, late-night variety shows (see 'The Confessional Talk Show', p. 167);
- Animal: vet shows, nature documentaries; environmental stories.

On the fictional side of the divide, drama series were produced that exploited the documentary or informational mode of address to make satirical commentary. Comedy shows also made relentless use of news formats and personalities to send up people in public life and television itself.

In such an environment, news and current affairs formats inevitably hybridised. Editors tried to make their talking heads appealing. News anchors that could smile desirably and also carry descriptions of death, disaster and war were able to command high fees. Studio decor had to be appropriate – warm but not frivolous. Sometimes a newsroom staffed with eager news-gatherers could be glimpsed; other editors preferred the authoritative Big Desk. The format was occasionally revamped to maintain viewer interest. Thus, single newsreaders evolved to multiple anchors (especially older man/younger woman pairs), who moved from desks to sofas; then a vogue for single presenters returned, sometimes sitting casually on the desk. Singing or stripping news presenters were not entirely unknown.

In current affair shows the gravitational pull of infotainment was much more pronounced. Emotional scenes, such as a sporting victory or a homecoming, might be rendered with music and slow motion. Private conflicts were dramatised (often literally via 'reenactments') to produce public narratives. Facts were still routinely respected, but their status was subordinated to the mythic or symbolic resonance of a story.

Meanwhile, what happened to civil society? Some commentators lamented what they saw as 'dumbing down'. Infotainment was about identity and celebrity, not power and decision-making. Private life and personal emotion seemed to have triumphed over rational discourse about public affairs.

But this is not the whole story. Many of the criticisms levelled at infotainment formats were based on a cultural or taste hierarchy – a preference for modernist forms of political communication, and an equal but opposite prejudice against popular media. The idea that democracy might be conveyed and even extended by commercial and corporate means has been slow to gain acceptance among media theorists, even though commercial democracies have been manifest realities for a century or more.

Commercial communication – television is still the pre-eminent example – reaches citizens (including women, children, migrants and minorities) who have not been well served by the modernist communications technologies. Far from 'dumbing down' a once-knowledgeable populace, it could be argued that 'democratainment' extends the public sphere to places other media cannot reach (Hartley, 1999; Hartley and McKee, 2000). 'Infotainment' is just as active in public pedagogy and citizen-formation as was the serious press. The only difference is that its generic form belongs to television.

John Hartley

RECOMMENDED READING

Atkinson, Dave and Raboy, Marc (eds) (1998), *Public Service Broadcasting*, Paris: UNESCO.

Epstein, Edward Jay (2000), *News from Nowhere: Television and the News*, Chicago: Ivan R. Dee.

Hartley, John (1999), *Uses of Television*, London and New York: Routledge.

The Globalisation of Television News

Globalisation of everything is as old as the hills; it is the first thing *Homo sapiens* achieved, long before the invention of

CNN (Cable News Network)

Launched on 1 June 1980, CNN pioneered the 'rolling update' format, where twenty-four-hour broadcasting required something different from the self-contained news bulletin of broadcast TV. 'Rolling update' news, in contrast, was generically innovative in three ways:

- *Distension*. Each new element of a running story was taken as a separate event in itself, thereby massively distending the story by prolonging the content of a paragraph to the length of a segment or even a show.
- *Repetition*. On the presumption that viewers watched CNN in segment-length chunks, rather than continuously, it was also able to recycle the same material relentlessly, often over several days.
- *News-talk*. CNN also pioneered 'news-talk', which was not the same as the established quasi-news format of current affairs. News-talk was the habit of introducing a story from the anchor's desk, perhaps with a brief throw to the scene via a taped report, but then returning (at length) to a studio discussion about the story, frequently with another CNN employee or journalist, and occasionally a professor from NYU or MIT. This way a one-and-a-half-minute item could fill an entire segment.

But what annoyed 'anti-globalisation' critics about CNN was not its generic endlessness, but its socioeconomic provenance. Owned and controlled by entrepreneur Ted Turner until he sold it to Time Warner, CNN told its news stories from an American perspective for American subscribers. When the format was internationalised, via hotel chains and local cable providers, the content jarred for viewers habituated to their own national or state perspective on world events. From outside the USA, it seemed as if American national interests took precedence over an accurate impression of what may actually have occurred on the ground.

CNN was trusted (that is, tuned in) most at times of unfolding international crises, the paradigm instance being the Gulf War of 1990–1, when popular participation in the unfolding event, in all countries, was authenticated by watching it on CNN rather than on other providers. It was not just because CNN scooped the world with a reporter and camera in Baghdad; the very format suited the event (Wark, 1994). In Australia, which did not have widespread cable provision at the time, free-to-air broadcasters took CNN directly to bring the authentic experience of the continuously breaking story to the home screen. Similarly, more recently, the events of 9/11

CNN: the face of global news

impelled viewers around the world to tune into CNN, not rivals such as Sky or the BBC. However, such trust was strictly limited: it extended only to seeking the authentic American perspective from CNN. That point of view needed triangulation with others, including one's own national carriers, before anything like understanding could be achieved.

Other providers, such as News Corp's Fox/Sky/Star and BBC World, began to compete directly with CNN as global providers of news in the 1990s. There was also competition between these corporations for the supply of satellite/cable news services to new markets such as India and China. In those markets, local political sensitivities came into play, often at the expense of the BBC, which was regarded as biased against the Chinese government in particular.

One of the ironies of the critique of 'globalisation' was that those who lamented the globalisation of news looked on its opposite, the localisation of news, with equal alarm. The tendency for television news to offer less foreign news in favour of more domestic, human interest and crime stories has been widely criticised as an instance of 'dumbing down' in the media. The alternative, to offer everyone news from everywhere, was already available via the Internet, but this innovation did not satisfy the critics, who saw it merely as evidence of a growing 'digital divide' in the information society. The same critics, however, organised themselves globally, using the Internet, to stage protests such as those in Seattle (1999) and Melbourne (2000) at the World Economic Forum. It seemed that globalisation was emancipatory when practised by political activists, but imperialist when practised by American corporations (see Andersen and Strate, 2000).

CNN's supremacy as the fastest source of news was brought to an end by the Internet. Funnily enough, the decisive moment was televised by CNN. Court decisions and news-sensitive information relating to the unfolding Monica Lewinsky affair were released on the Internet, for instance by Matt Drudge. On the publication of the Starr Report, TV viewers around the world saw CNN's own coverage reduced to pictures of a computer screen with a reporter scrolling down pages of Internet text to find newsworthy references to non-standard uses for cigars. The rolling update continuous 'breaking news' format of cable TV had become a mere servant of the instantaneous Internet. But in fact, CNN got into trouble even for this second-hand timeliness, as commentators expressed discomfort at seeing the unexpurgated account on a TV screen, although they seemed happy for the full text of the Starr Report to appear on the Net itself (Hartley, 2000, pp. 11–36).

Hence, 'globalisation' migrated to the next-fastest medium, where it could speciate and flourish for producers and consumers alike. Specialist providers such as Reuters Financial or Bloomberg.com could follow the movement of international capital itself, and consumers could buy books from Amazon.com, or wartime memorabilia via Yahoo, whatever local legislation decreed.

Finally, however, it is worth remembering that the most impressive 'globalisation' of all still belonged to television. No other medium gathered such immense populations as broadcast TV could. This was demonstrated every four years in the Olympic Games, which counted their audiences in the billions. During some moments – opening and closing ceremonies, perhaps, or an icon race such as indigenous athlete Cathy Freeman's gold-medal performance in the 400 metres in Sydney, 2000 – perhaps even a majority of the human population of the earth were watching the same thing at more or less the same time. The species reintegrated globally, 'prehistorically', as it were (see Hartley, 1999, pp. 8–11).

John Hartley

agriculture, cities, writing and thence history. Communication of commodities, money, spouses and language across geodemographic boundaries, whether communal, civic, national or imperial, was of course a condition of those boundaries. More to the point, literally global exchanges of meaning have characterised every age and affected every region. In short, globalisation was not an invention of 'late capitalism', nor even of modernity.

Globalisation may be understood more narrowly as the exchange of capital and commodities across international boundaries by transnational firms trading for privately accumulated profit. In the sphere of information, even that narrow definition means that globalisation is at least as old as printing with moveable type. News has been global in terms of content since the first 'Intelligencers' and 'Mercuries' began to appear in the seventeenth century, to say nothing of 'news' conveyed by folk ballads and the like. Although they tended to be printed in and for the literate decision-makers of one country, newspapers brought to those readers' attention news from Tartary, Turkey and Timbuctoo, as well as from the local courts (see the contents of a 1736 English newspaper in Hartley, 1992b, pp. 154–7).

So what's new? Not much – even the politicisation of globalisation derives from a century-old Marxist rhetoric of capitalist/worker adversarialism in social theory, and leftist opposition to liberal democratic commercial expansion (imperialism). Thus, those who worried about the international political hegemony of America worried also about the internationalisation of American firms. Military colonisation may not have been imminent, but 'Coca-colonisation' was widely feared.

The temporal coincidence of technology (e.g. satellite broadcasting capacity), politics (the collapse of the Soviet Union), the Clinton era stock-market boom in the knowledge economy (software, media and telecommunications), alerted critics to the internationalisation of technologically mediated information on a new scale. What was new about it may have been nothing more than the attention of these critics, but the political fact was that 'anti-globalisation' emerged in the 1990s as a new-left, new-radical slogan to replace the lost adversarialism of the Cold War. Globalisation was criticised for inhibiting the economies of developing countries, deepening the 'democratic deficit' in the accountability of transnational transactions (especially in a period when company law was still largely nation-based) and environmental damage, often of countries remote from multinational corporations' centres of profit or of consumption.

Globalisation in the context of news, however, is not quite the same as the more general socioeconomic concept. In the television environment, it refers to the international deployment of news formats (not stories), on the model of CNN (see box). Actually, even formats had been traded or copied internationally over a long period in TV news: for instance, British television derived its news format from American models imported by ITN in 1955; competition soon obliged the antediluvian BBC to catch up. The chief generic features of broadcast network news were that it should (a) be dramatic but not be mistaken for drama, (b) be comprehensive while not exceeding half an hour and (c) be distinguishable from, while closely resembling, the news shows of competing networks (also see Hartley, 2006).

John Hartley

RECOMMENDED READING

Boyd-Barrett, Oliver, and Rantanen, Terhi (eds) (1998), *The Globalization of News*, London: Sage.

Miller, Toby, Lawrence, Geoffrey, McKay, Jim and Rowe, David (2001), *Globalization and Sport: Playing the World*, London: Sage.

Wark, McKenzie (1994), *Virtual Geography: Living with Global Media Events*, Bloomington: Indiana University Press.

Citizen Journalism

Citizen journalism is sometimes known as, 'participatory journalism', 'public insight journalism', 'public journalism', occasionally and more recently 'open source journalism' or 'crowdsourcing journalism' and, by professional organisations, as 'user-generated content'. Citizen journalism occurs where people who either do not work for a professional media organisation, or are themselves usually untrained journalists, contribute to the creation of news agendas and the subsequent dissemination of news in two main ways: either by a variety of peer to peer methods, or by passing on their own news stories, sources or views of news stories to a professional news organisation. The overlap and competing usages of the above list of terms is not salient and as a summative embracing descriptor the phrase 'citizen journalism' significantly entails the core idea of it being a variant form of news based upon a democratically free, truth-directed discussion of contemporary events.

How new or recent citizen journalism is, is an important question for media, particularly press, historians. Evidence of a history of a politically motivated citizenry's direct involvement in the activities of the press can, it is argued, be garnered from the time of the seventeenth-century Royalists, Parliamentarian disputes and civil war and the corresponding establishment of a partisan press. For example, Conboy (2004) notes that there were 722 newspapers of various forms by 1645, which allowed free expression and criticism of one side by the other. More generally Harcup (2003) makes the point that the historical

persistence of an alternative press (from the mid-seventeenth century to today) demonstrates citizen press activism as a consistent theme of political critique, the pursuit of free expression, the disclosure of 'cover-ups' and a point of criticism of mainstream or establishment journalism. Harrison (2005) notes that more prosaically the establishment of a provincial press in Britain saw a movement towards localism which increasingly involved local journalists with the disassociation of local or regional news from purely London news.

Correspondingly there is of course a vast amount of historical evidence of the exclusion of the 'common view' or of 'citizen involvement' in the news process. This is sometimes referred to as the decline of the public sphere, the failure to achieve a common communicative space, the rise of the manipulation of public opinion and is usually explained in terms of the ascendancy of a certain kind of press dominated by corporate constraints and the view that the news is a financial product or commodity and is controlled by powerful owners. One thing is clear; the debate about the origins and history of citizen journalism and its rise and demise will persist.

What is interesting about the contemporary flurry of activity calling itself citizen journalism is its reliance on two relatively new phenomena: first, the availability and popular use of genuinely robust and powerful mobile communication appliances which use a globally networked technical infrastructure and, second, parallel changes in the culture of the newsroom, in particular in relationship to news-gathering. The former provides for a new communication ethos of one to one, many to one, one to many social networks and sharing, accompanied by a political rhetoric which describes and justifies the uses of file sharing, open sources, open archives and public access rights, self-regulation and freedom, interactivity, participation and engagement. The latter is the willingness of news organisations to use citizen journalism. The contribution from citizen journalists can either take the form of primary content, which may break a story, or completely change an already running story (and involves the stimulation of further investigative activity by the mainstream news provider); or it can be in the form of secondary content, which is used to thicken an already running story. Secondary content is simply requested so that it can be used directly and is often film or pictures of an event which often has been witnessed by people and captured on their mobile phones. Eye-witnesses may actually be involved in an event or arrive just as the event is taking place. The footage and pictures they provide are often the first pictures of the event and precede those taken by news organisations whose crews arrive later. The pictures provided on mobile phones from inside the carriages of the London tube following the suicide bombings of 7 July 2005 inaugurated in Britain a new era of public contribution to news stories. Since that date many television news organisations have specifically encouraged people to send in their pictures of a given event and television news programmes will, alongside early footage, show pictures gathered by individuals which show how an event continues to affect them.

Optimistically citizen journalism is regarded as:

- heralding a golden age of news journalism through the increased democratisation of news;
- stimulating an active civil society;
- representing an extension of public service journalism (civic journalism);
- marking the establishment of genuine investigative, independent and critical news values;
- being free of corporate pressures.

Pessimistically citizen journalism is dismissed as:

- a fad that is already in decline;
- unprofessional rubbish;
- cheap journalism;
- licensed voyeurism;
- unethical;
- dangerous;
- evidence of the final 'dumbing down' of news.

In both cases views run strongly and tend on either side to be more impressionistic than empirically researched. Indeed, at the moment empirical evidence is scarce and what little there is of it is at best provisional and at worst tendentious. However, the views of the more reflective discussants are worth noting more for their analysis of the future of news and use of technology than anything specifically empirical.

On the one hand, Bowman and Willis (2003) are advocates of citizen journalism and write of a new media ecosystem which sees news customers becoming news contributors; the rise of new experts and commentators (even new watchdogs) being drawn from the public. This new type of participation facilitates the rise of communitarianism and ultra-local journalism and most importantly enables significant improvements to the quality of news itself, as online communities extend and develop stories or reveal hitherto concealed information. Websites such as NowPublic let anyone with a digital camera or a camera-enabled mobile telephone upload images or news for dissemination via the Internet, and via these contributions aims to become one of the world's largest news agencies.

On the other hand, Rebecca Blood (2003) argues that having the equivalent of a printing press on one's desktop does not make one a journalist, indeed it would be better for all concerned if the term journalist were dropped in this context, or at the very least not constantly inflated to include everyone who writes about current events. She suggests that while blogging is a participatory form of media it does not require of itself to foreswear the mandate to be either accurate or fair, which journalism does (or should do). For Blood, transparency is (or should be) the touchstone for ethical blogging. The two enterprises, journalism and blogging, are different and should remain so. It may even be the case that blogging is in decline. Tony Allen-Mills (2007) cites researchers who suggest that blogging has peaked and will level off to 100 million worldwide in 2007 and may even fall to 30 million. If this decline does occur the significance of this for citizen journalism would be difficult to evaluate. The effectiveness of the Web in terms of what type of penetration and impact a news story posted by a citizen journalist actually achieves over a period of time is difficult to assess systematically. But even here, these unknowns do not refute the claims made on behalf of citizen journalism. The reason for this is that citizen journalism is also used as a term of approval for a certain kind of democratic activity and it is this rather more than other understandings that have captured the idea of a new relationship emerging between citizens and the press.

Jay Rosen is perhaps the most articulate advocate of citizen journalism as a form of rapprochement between citizens and the press and as an explicit and self-conscious form of democratic activity. He writes in an introduction to his website, PressThink (1 September 2003), that 'today we say media instead of "the press." But it's a mistake. The press has become the ghost of democracy in the media machine, and we need to keep it alive' (see Rosen, 2003). The inclusive 'we' refers to those of us who are concerned citizens, concerned that is with what we perceive to be media dissembling and that the press is showing itself to be untrustworthy. For Rosen, and others like him, citizen journalism rests on its ability to reconnect the press and the people. The old journalistic monopoly on news has been shattered by the impact of the Web, and yet the Web, Rosen argues, is ultimately too complicated to be successfully manipulated by ordinary citizens. What is required is for both professional journalists and non-professional

Al-Jazeera

Launched in 1996, views about Al-Jazeera range widely. For some it is a mouthpiece for terrorists, part of the armoury in the clash of civilisations, systematically anti-west (and Israel), unprofessional and unethical. For others, it plays an important part in the democratisation of the coverage of the Middle East, redresses an imbalance in the reporting of the Middle East (and Muslim countries in general), provides a platform and forum for reciprocal understanding and debate and is imbued with the standards and professionalism of a public service broadcaster. For a relatively small media company, based in Doha Qatar, such brickbats and compliments testify to a significance way beyond its corporate size.

The Al-Jazeera network consists of seven channels supported by numerous websites, and while accurate viewing figures are difficult to obtain it has been estimated that in 2007 Al-Jazeera had a minimum of 40 million viewers for its Arabic channel, while in 2006 Al-Jazeera claims to have had 80 million households worldwide for its English channel. Currently the network is subsidised by the present Emir of Qatar, though the stated aim of Al-Jazeera is to be financially independent and for each of its channels to be self-financing through the conventional mix of advertising revenues, sponsorship, selling programmes and related services and subscription charges. In short Al-Jazeera seeks to have its corporate finances structured in the same way as any other private sector media company, an aim which appears to challenge the charge that it is an exclusive political entity. And yet its fame is derived from its perceived political and cultural stance.

On the one hand Al-Jazeera is demonised as Arab news for the cultivation of extremism, on the other hand it is said that it has the same explicit amount of ideological baggage as any public service broadcaster (say, the BBC), no more and no less. So, for example, it is useful to compare some of the stated aims of the BBC with those of Al-Jazeera. The BBC exists to serve the UK public interest and its main object is the promotion of its public purpose which includes: sustaining UK citizenship and civil society; representing the UK, its nations, regions and communities; and bringing the world to the UK and the UK to the world. The stated aim of Al-Jazeera is to develop and to stimulate a pan-Arab consciousness through news and debate about its meaning and significance. Unlike the BBC, Al-Jazeera is not bound by considerations of a single nation-state. Overall though it is reasonable to say that Al-Jazeera has led the way in revolutionising Arab news. Its coverage has thus far included critical assessment of western foreign policy, the scope and significance of Islamic fundamentalism, the contemporary meaning of Islamic law (Sharia), human rights, the role of women, the persecution of political dissenters and minority groups and blunt interviews with government leaders from all over the world. In this it behaves very much like many other news organisations. Al-Jazeera's demarcation of itself, around the promotion of a pan-Arab consciousness (sometimes described in terms of contextual objectivity) and the differing views on the legitimacy of this and the way it is undertaken (in particular the issues of taste and decency raised by the type of footage shown by the broadcaster) means that Al-Jazeera and the different perspectives it offers on events raise new and interesting questions about the way freedom of expression is exercised and justified in news reporting.   *Jackie Harrison*

journalists to work together, sharing their sources (open-source journalism) to produce better stories. For Rosen this is the real meaning of citizen journalism, a joint contributory relationship between the concerned amateur and the open professional. Rosen concludes that citizens must engage with journalists who are trained and best equipped to evaluate and interpret information and that the press should engage with citizens to obtain such information, restore trust in journalism and to enhance democratic activity.

Jackie Harrison

RECOMMENDED READING

Allen-Mills, Tony (2007), 'Lost for words online as blog craze falters', *Times Online*, 25 March.

Blood, Rebecca (2003), 'Weblogs and Journalism: do they connect?', *Nieman Reports*, Autumn, pp. 61–3.

Bowman, Shayne and Willis, Chris (2003) 'We Media: how audiences are shaping the future of news and information', *The Media Center at the American Press Institute*, available at: <http://www.hypergene.net/wemedia/> (last accessed March 2008).

Conboy, Martin (2004), *Journalism: A Critical History*, London: Sage.

DOCUMENTARY

Studying Documentary

The study of documentary has only recently become an established feature of film and media studies programmes internationally. Film studies has always, and understandably, had as its primary concern the study of cinematic fictions, chiefly the 'art cinema' of European cinema and the popular cinema of Hollywood. Media studies has also been very interested in fiction too, but its concern with television non-fiction has been dominated by a focus on news. In order to understand what studying documentary might currently involve and what developments we might expect, it is helpful to look at three different contexts for academic interest. We can then move on to look at some key ideas and approaches.

Perhaps the oldest strand of interest in documentary history and analysis is that displayed by vocational film schools in various parts of the world. Here, the engagement is governed by a wish to learn techniques of production and to develop the craft and creative skills for making successful documentary films and programmes. Any form of study that cannot be seen to contribute to the ends of practice has figured only marginally, if at all, within this perspective. However, a great deal of clear and focused thinking about the nature, form and function of documentary work has developed from such teaching. The wish to make good documentaries has been a great motivator of analysis and criticism (Rabiger, 1998, is a notable example).

A second strand of interest emerged from within film studies, where this label describes a body of study more closely connected with literary and dramatic analysis than with training in film practice, although there are often interconnections. In film studies, the chief if not exclusive concern is with questions of aesthetics and textual form. A highly developed and often dense analytic agenda surrounding the organisation of the image, narrative structure, *mise en scène* and the symbolic and imaginary conditions of spectatorship provides the focus of study. Some of this analytical apparatus is carried over from the study of fiction, some of it was generated around the specific circumstances of documentary practice (see Nichols, 1976, for an early outline and Nichols, 1991, for a major, influential commentary; Renov, 1993, is an excellent collection centred within film scholarship). Film studies has

tended to regard documentary film as constituting a special case of 'realism', one in which complex questions of ontology and epistemology (the status of the filmed image and its use as a means of knowledge) are linked to particular political and social intentions. Both British and American writers within film studies recognised the creative achievement of documentary (Hiller and Lovell, 1972, is a pioneering text). Moreover, the lively strand of independent cinema in the USA allowed many American writers to see it not only as a project with a 'classic' past but one with continuing social potential. This view was in some tension with the move towards a more sharply anti-realist approach in film studies, coinciding with the rise of a Marxist perspective in the whole subject field. This gave prominence to questions about 'ideology' and the means of its reproduction. From such a position, documentary was interesting in so far as it was yet one more device of illusion and misinformation. For a while, the dominant tone became denunciatory. As I shall suggest below, this is now changing quite rapidly.

The third strand of study we can identify is that which comes out of interdisciplinary media studies and therefore, in part, from cultural studies. Here, the emphasis is more on documentary as a media product, to be considered in relation to other widely circulated products such as the news and (more recently) soap opera. Film studies had almost entirely ignored television documentary, but within media studies, where documentary figured (it was still a marginal interest), it was in its television forms. These importantly included fly-on-the-wall formats (see 'Observational ('Fly-on-the-Wall') Documentary' below) as well as the full variety of documentary journalism, including the current affairs series. The connection with journalism opened up a whole set of questions not asked much, if at all, within the film studies perspective. These questions concerned the institutional order of television, the professionalisation of its practices, the development of its generic system and, possibly most important of all, its routine requirement (both social and economic) to engage with popular audiences.

Kilborn and Izod (1997) provide a good introduction to documentary from within a media studies perspective, and the analytic commentaries in Corner (1996) largely draw on media studies approaches. In the UK, the sense of documentary achievement was supported, not so much by work in the independent film sector, as by the long and distinguished tradition of public service broadcasting. Discussion of documentary was thus an aspect of the developing debates, throughout the 1990s, about the future of public service broadcasting in an increasingly commercialised broadcasting ecology. More recently still, the emergence of the forms of reality television and docusoap (see, for instance, Dovey, 2000, on this) have put questions of documentary form and value right at the centre of the debate about 'infotainment' and the risks of 'dumbing down'.

We have, then, three broad strands of study, each with its different intellectual character but all of them considerably reinvigorated by changes in the nature of audiovisual documentation itself (of which the 'reality television' phenomenon is just one notable part). Although the study of documentary is showing stronger signs of interconnection across the three areas (there are many courses, for instance, that try to relate to the film tradition as well as to television work and then to the development of practical video skills), it is not yet possible to talk of a coherent 'documentary studies'. One of the reasons for this is the particular way in which study of documentary raises the question of the relationship between form and content.

John Corner

Form and Content in Documentary Study

Documentary has always been defined in a loose, contingent kind of way (Winston, 1995, is the best historical account). 'Documentary' is an adjective that has been turned into use as a noun and, although the term still gives a useful indication of an area of practice and a range of programme types, it escapes any tight generic specification. What we understand by 'documentary' is always dependent on the broader context of the kinds of audiovisual documentation currently in circulation. For John Grierson in the 1920s, this presented a very different setting for his documentary ambitions than that within which a television producer today has to work; consequently, the word now points to something rather different both in its forms and its purposes. However, one common feature has been an interest in using images and sounds to provide an exposition or argument about the real world. This directness of address to something outside the 'text', this special level of

referentiality, is one of the things that distinguishes documentary from fiction, that also points outside itself but much more indirectly. In fiction, the imagined world of the story is primary.

One of the consequences of this characteristic is that study of documentary, any documentary, has to engage directly with what the documentary is about. It has therefore to consider the question of, for instance, health policy on AIDS, international arms smuggling, labour relations in Japan, loneliness in the student population, the history of forensic science or whatever else a documentary chooses as its topic. The precise extent to which enquiry pursues this engagement will vary with the motivation of the researchers but it will also vary, predictably, with the kind of documentary under scrutiny. Here we can distinguish between 'thick text' and 'thin text' documentaries. A 'thick text' documentary is creatively dense. This is as a result of its mode of use of such features as narrative design, subjective voice, symbolic suggestiveness and the dynamics of depicted action (including dramatisation). Its status as an authorial artefact can, in analysis, be given primacy over its status as an intervention in a specific field of knowledge or debate.

'Thin text' documentaries, however (and this would include many television documentaries), work with a more directly reportorial and observational discourse. Analysing these documentaries requires that the subject matter itself be given close attention in a manner that can route the analysis out of strictly discursive matters quite quickly. Often, such extra-textual enquiry is necessary in order to say anything useful about the text, let alone about the terms of its production and its function for audiences. In some ways, the first kind of analysis described above is close to that applied to screen fictions, and the second kind is close to that applied to the news. The interplay between the discursive–aesthetic and sociological poles, their respective aims and methods of enquiry, is a significant variable in documentary study.

Analysis of documentary, simply because of the referential character of the material under scrutiny, has on the whole resisted a tight formalism of approach. But it has often been unsure as to how best to proceed with enquiry into contexts. For instance, it might seem that study of different documentaries addressing the same topic could often be more productive than study organised according to different documentary modes or production settings. However, the question of how far to take investigation into the non-televisual world of documented topics and events, and then of what kind of analytic relationship to set up between representation and represented, has been a challenge. Quite apart from the difficulties sometimes involved in collecting detailed and accurate extra-textual data, most critics have wanted to avoid any kind of 'reflectionism' whereby a documentary is judged chiefly by its correspondence with an independent account of external events and circumstances. Such a view would run counter to the whole swing towards a view of mediation as involving a good deal more than a 'relay' process. But commentators have also wanted, particularly in more recent writing, to locate documentaries more firmly in both their discursive and their material settings, and to trace their function as referential and knowledge-yielding practices. There is a new extra-textual, empirical ambition at work in documentary study, complementing its theoretical liveliness.

Corner (1995, pp. 79–81) outlines a view of documentary as a series of transformations. This is not by any means an original view but it can help in organising both study and research. First of all there is the transformation by which a particular topic in the world becomes, in the planning process, a given range of locations, interviews, archive clips and thematic emphases. Then, there is the shooting process itself and the whole range of audiovisual decisions that go into crafting footage from various kinds of settings, circumstances, events, actions and speech. Following this, there is the editing process, when the combinatory logics of documentary are variously applied, narrative coherence is achieved, evaluations are established, emphases marked, closures made, moods set. Finally, there is that transformation by which viewers take the screened material and turn it into sense and significance, which will be broadly social and yet at that same time, depending on the topic, quite closely personal too. It is across these transformations, here only sketched, that the real magic of documentary as what I have called 'the art of record' (Corner, 1996) is to be found. It is here that its classic controversiality lies too, in the apparent fusion of index (recorded image and sound) and rhetorical and aesthetic ambition.

There is no doubt that study of documentary practice is becoming popular and that it is widening its scope too, if sometimes cautiously (the references list some of the more recent additions to the literature). It is taking on questions of pleasure more directly and examining the links between pleasure and knowledge. It needs to retain its strong sense of history, including the history of photography as well as of film. At the other end, it cannot afford to ignore the way in which the Internet is reconfiguring the possibilities of documentation, both in form and mode of use.

'Documentary' as a category has always been leaky and unstable, but there are good reasons for thinking that it is now in a stage of radical dispersal. There will continue to be 'core' work, certainly, but there will be an increasingly wide range of television, video and Net-based practice that does not fit easily under the label even though it has strong 'documentary' elements. The new and sometimes messy depictive energies now at work in televising the real will be a stimulus to documentary study, and at the same time they will encourage us to rethink the generic assumptions that underpin both practice and critical enquiry (see Corner, 2006).

John Corner

RECOMMENDED READING

Corner, J. (1996), *The Art of Record*, Manchester: Manchester University Press.

Dovey, J. (2000), *Freakshow: First Person Media and Factual Television*, London: Pluto.

Kilborn, R. and Izod, J. (1997), *An Introduction to Television Documentary*, Manchester: Manchester University Press.

Documentary Realism

'Realism' is a central and much-contested notion in painting, literature, theatre and in both film and television drama (see Corner, 1992, for a critical review). Basically, it points to how what are essentially 'fictions' can seem, in different ways, to reproduce dimensions of the real as a result of their procedures of depiction or their mode of engagement with real-world issues. There is much confusion about the use of the term 'realism' in the arts, but this sense of 'real-seemingness' and of how an effect of the real is produced is generally a primary. Clearly, there will be major differences between how a painting, a novel and a television play achieve 'realism'. Moreover, the capacity of photography, film and television to 'show things realistically' as a function of their nature as visual recording systems is something that simply cannot be paralleled in the concerns of literature (see 'Realism and Soap Opera').

'Realism' is also a term that has a long attachment to work in documentary, but here we have to be very careful in our application, for it is clear that most documentaries make quite direct and serious claims as to the reality of what they represent. They frequently do this both at the level of the image (this is the ship that brought survivors back, this is the captain of the ship) and at the level of general exposition (these are the known facts relating to the shipwreck, this is the judgment it is most sensible to make as to what happened). Their 'display' of the real world is

Documentary Fakes

The question of 'faking' in documentary has recently received a lot of press attention in Britain, largely because of the greatly increased range of 'Reality TV' formats, often shot on limited budgets and with an imperative to be visually entertaining. However, the issue of fraud and deception in documentary goes right back to the early days of documentary film-making, since it has always been clear that a degree of 'staging' is often a necessary part of giving coherence and continuity to documentary accounts. Winston (1995) is excellent on developments in practice and in principle here. In shooting a sequence of fishermen unloading their catch, for instance, what could be considered wrong with giving some directions as to their positioning and movement with respect to the camera? And, perhaps causing more pause for thought, why not reshoot it with their cooperation if it does not quite work first time? The sheer technical limitations on early actuality filming made such choices easy. In the classic 1930s' documentary *Night Mail* (Watt, 1936), for instance, the need for good shots required that the travelling post office depicted was actually a studio set, not part of the train that we see in other shots. This is a move towards what one can see as part-dramatisation, extensively used in many film documentaries.

It is helpful, at least provisionally, to think of a sliding scale of fakery. At one end of this scale there are the minor bits of intervention and fiddling that go to produce a satisfactory shot and a nice level of depictive coherence. This may mean a degree of direction and repeat shooting. At the other end there is the wholesale fabrication of persons and events, still offered within a 'documentary claim'. In between, there are a number of practices (for instance, combining shots from two separate events to give the impression of a single event; cross-cutting between two events shot at different times to suggest their simultaneity; specifically requesting people to perform actions that, in the camera's absence, they would not have performed on that occasion). These remain the subject of debate, often in relation to specific contexts and programme aims.

Two strands of documentary raise the issue of faking in an especially sensitive way. First of all, the tradition of 'fly-on-the-wall' film-making (with its roots in cinéma vérité) has set up a number of expectations about its 'direct truth' to the events portrayed (see 'Observational ('Fly-on-the-Wall') Documentary' below). There is sometimes a purist literalism about the claims made by this kind of project – everything you see really happened just as if the camera was not there at all. Again, Winston (1995) provides a useful discussion, with a strong historical perspective. This grounds the question of the integrity of the programme at a very demanding level of primary truth, one that has to take in the self-consciousness of the people being filmed. It is not surprising that 'breach of trust' becomes an ever-present concern here. Many of the new 'reality' formats, including docusoap, base themselves on this observational technique, with its distinctive, often rather voyeuristic, character (see 'Reality TV'). This has undoubtedly contributed to the intensified concern about unacceptable faking.

The second strand that needs special attention is journalistic documentary. A large number of television documentaries are still made within one version or another of journalistic investigation, perhaps with a reporter in shot, perhaps with only voice-over commentary. Broadcast journalism has its own protocols in relation to accuracy, truth and the scope for 'creativity'. These are problematic and often loosely applied, but they are different from those shaping the main development of documentary, even if the two modes are related. The journalist, usually the employee of a broadcasting organisation, occupies a public role. The claims, often explicit, made about circumstances, events and people in journalism work within tougher criteria than those surrounding documentary per se, even allowing for the difference between 'news' and 'feature' journalism. This point has sometimes been forgotten in recent debate in the newspapers, where, for instance, fakery in a docusoap about driving instruction has been placed alongside its presence in serious investigative programmes (see 'Docusoaps' below).

Once we have moved beyond the minor, 'technical' level of fakery designed to produce coherence and continuity at the level of the shot, a key question will concern the extent to which the viewer is made aware of the status of what they are watching vis-à-vis 'the real'. If we take the example of recent docusoaps, the indications are that many viewers fully realise the extent to which high levels of self-conscious performance are an intrinsic part of the speech and action in such formats. As a condition of this performance, there is often likely to be some 'rigging' of the circumstances in which filmed people find themselves. This may be acceptable but, even within docusoap, if it is found that the people are not who they claim to be and did not 'in reality' do anything like they are seen to do on the screen, then there is likely to be a popular feeling of resentment against bad practice. In a current affairs programme, such deception would be extremely serious.

At the present time, as documentary energies disperse across a whole range of innovative and hybridised formats, the question of faking will be raised more often, renewing discussion about what is legitimate and what is not across different kinds of documentation. Winston (2000) and Dovey (2000) are two recent and thoughtful attempts to debate this issue.

There is one kind of faking that has developed its own respected place in film and television. This is what is often now called the 'mockumentary', in which documentary devices are imitated and/or parodied for comic effect. The fun of 'mockumentary' usually comes from the subversive delight gained from aping documentary's discourse of seriousness, combined with an engagement with a particular topic thought ripe for comic exploration in its own terms. Rob Reiner's brilliant *This is Spinal Tap* (1983) mixes spoof rock-vérité with a hilarious exploration of band culture across a number of years and fashions. More recently, the wonderful New Zealand film *Forgotten Silver* (Costa Botes and Peter Jackson, 1995) spoofs historical documentary techniques with a comic sideswipe at film scholarship. On television, there has been a whole range of comic/parodic developments, ranging from the level of the sketch through to entirely faked programmes (see 'Contemporary Sitcom'). The fact that documentary discourse is now seen as a fit subject for parodic attention is a healthy sign for television culture as a whole, and it will certainly do no harm at all to have the newer, more duplicitous formats exposed to ridicule in this way.

John Corner

frequently accompanied by spoken propositions about it (in commentary, voice-over or in-shot talk).

Although the point has not been noticed quite as much as it deserves to be, this means that the business of making a 'realistic' television play is likely to be very different from that of making a 'realistic' documentary. We may slip into a number of confusions if we do not recognise this from the outset.

It can help matters if we distinguish between two forms of realism in documentary practice. First of all, there is what we can call observational realism (see below). This is essentially a set of formal markers that confirm to us that what we are watching (which might be in a 'fly-on-the-wall' documentary or a sequence from, say, a current affairs programme) is a record of an ongoing, and at least partly media-independent, reality. Important here will be a sense of spontaneity of action and a movement of camera that presents us with something which is perceptually coherent but which is following developments beyond the control of the crew. Some observational sequences will be shot in a 'raw' style, gaining their realism from their lack both of smoothness and of immediate significance when compared with television fiction. However, others may be shot in such a way as to imitate at least some of the scopic range and lucid continuity of fictional sequences (many early film documentaries had scenes like this, primarily because the 'fly-on-the-wall' effect was not then a technological option). We would not expect a documentary to look precisely like a scene from fiction (subjective point-of-view shots, shot reverses and so on) except at the cost of undermining its credibility. Of course, a documentary shot entirely in 'dramatised' mode (see 'Drama–Documentary') is likely to conform much more closely to the principles of dramatic realism as part of its general strategy.

It is important to notice that in both the above examples, any 'realist' effect is working to confirm what we have already been asked to assume by the more general claims made by documentary work. The 'realism' does not itself generate this assumption, as it does in dramatic fiction.

The second kind of realism we can call expositional realism. This is even less like the realism of fiction. It might be best to see it as a 'rhetoric of accuracy and truth' that many television documentaries variously draw on. Here, we are talking about the way in which an overall exposition and/or argument is structured across the various components of image and sound. We might think of a current affairs documentary claiming to expose the operation of international arms smugglers. What is the fit between what we see and what we hear? How are contesting interpretations of the evidence organised and weighed? How does the symbolic dimension of what we see bear on our emotional responses and our evaluations? In what ways are particular scenes offered as 'typical' of more general circumstances? What different relations of proximity and distance do we have to what we see and what we hear? Questions such as these will direct us to a close analysis of the way in which particular pictures and words combine to 'win the viewer' for the particular case that the documentary is making. This is a case that might be explicit (and that, rather than enforce a judgment, might encourage viewers to exercise critical independence), but it will often have an implicit level of working too.

One way of broadly distinguishing between realism in screen fiction and realism in documentary is to see the former as essentially provoking a distinctive kind of imaginative relationship between screened events and viewing consciousness. We can then see the latter as essentially provoking an inferential relationship between the two. What this means is that the narrative of the realist fiction is designed to engage imaginatively (and selectively) with viewers' perceptions of the real world and what can happen in it. There is often a pleasing play-off here between fantasy and reality. In the documentary, we are offered bits of evidence and argument and we have to construct truths from them, truths of fact and perhaps truths of judgment. However, we should remember that imagination plays a part here too.

The specific conventions of 'realism' in television drama are always changing (which is why the idea of 'realisms' is sometimes to be preferred). The particular ways of relating the viewer to the real in documentary are changing too, and the rise of popular factual entertainment (as in the emergency services series and the 'docusoap' – see below) has increased the rate of change.

The special kinds of linkages with the real to which documentaries aspire ensure that the question of 'realism' will continue to surround work under this heading. Kilborn and Izod (1997) draw out the main factors and their interconnections usefully. But in addressing these issues we should be alert to how documentary practice differs from fictional practice, however fashionable it may have become to underplay or even to ignore this difference.

John Corner

RECOMMENDED READING

Corner, J. (1996), *The Art of Record*, Manchester: Manchester University Press.

Dovey, J. (2000), *Freakshow: First Person Media and Factual Television*, London: Pluto.

Kilborn, R. and Izod, J. (1997), *An Introduction to Television Documentary*, Manchester: Manchester University Press.

Observational ('Fly-on-the-Wall') Documentary

Stephen Mamber (1972a, p. 79) described direct cinema, the American observational documentary movement of the 1960s, as 'real people in undirected situations'. The idealism and impossibility contained within Mamber's definition of observational cinema at its zenith no doubt now seems quaintly outmoded: how can a filmic representation ever be 'undirected'? How can that film ever just be a 'way of looking' as opposed to a way of altering or manipulating the reality it is looking at? These are problems that have vexed both the history and the theorisation of observational cinema since its emergence as a documentary genre

in the late 1950s to its multiple current refigurations in contemporary television.

The first problem facing anyone attempting an overview of observational documentary is that of naming. 'Observational' is the catch-all but 'unsexy' term for several substrands. 'Direct cinema' (equally unattractive and really rather nebulous) refers specifically to the film-making of Robert Drew, Richard Leacock, Donn Pennebaker, the Maysles, Fred Wiseman and their protégés working in America in the 1960s and after; 'cinéma vérité' derives from Dziga Vertov and refers specifically to the reflexive, anthropological work of, for example, Jean Rouch in France, again in the early 1960s; 'fly-on-the-wall', a term universally disliked, is the term most readily applied to observational work in British television by, among others, Roger Graef and Paul Watson (see below).

Although 'direct cinema', 'cinéma vérité' and 'fly-on-the-wall' possess certain essential differences, the conflation of the terms is principally a matter of convenience that arose out of a recognition of a common root to films otherwise as dissimilar as *Chronique d'un été* (*Chronicle of a Summer*) (Morin, Rouch and Brault, 1961), *Salesman* (Albert and David Maysles, 1969) and *The Fishing Party* (BBC, 1986). The attribution of the term 'cinema' in this context is also problematic as, apart from *Chronique d'un été*, the notable examples of observational documentary have been made for television. There were also distinguishing cultural and historical differences between the American, French and British observational documentary movements; they derived from different national documentary traditions, possessed different antecedents and dealt with different subject material. The assimilation of direct cinema, cinéma vérité and 'fly-on-the-wall' into the generic term 'observational cinema' is arguably the result of documentary theory perceiving form to dominate history or content.

The pre-eminence of form is upheld by the fact that all 1960s' strands of observational documentary share a unique technical–historical moment, namely the advent of lightweight 16mm cameras and portable, synch-sound recorders. Despite Annette Kuhn having argued that 'certain types of equipment were developed and marketed expressly to make a specific type of film-making possible' (Kuhn, 1978, p. 75), this is to put the cart before the horse. Instead, it seems logical to conceive of such technical advancements proving the necessary catalyst to a new type of documentary rather than vice versa. A comparable set of innovations (DVC cameras, digital editing suites) proved equally significant factors in the 1990s' revival of observational documentary in Britain in the form of the populist 'docusoap' (see below), but it would be perverse to argue that docusoaps created the need for DVC.

Observation documentary tends to deal with current events, events that are unfolding in front of the camera and to which the makers of the programme do not know the outcome. Likewise, the new observational style has led to a greater interest in the personal and the intimate: people-based documentaries that are less preoccupied with the staple content of more didactic documentaries such as historical analysis. A charge levelled at many observational documentaries, therefore, is that they are superficial and apolitical. One can challenge this view in two ways: by following the lead of the editors of *Cahiers du Cinéma* who argued in the aftermath of 1968 that all films are political, even those that on the surface appear not to be, or by suggesting that the focus upon personality and character in many observational films simply offers political insight of a different, covert kind (see Comolli and Narboni, 1976).

The hidden or masked ideology of observational documentary remains one of the movement's more significant traits: the criticism through exposure of a class-riddled British society in *The Fishing Party*, the brutality of 1960s' psychiatric care in Wiseman's *Titicut Follies* (1967), the severity of America's army training regime in Broomfield and Churchill's *Soldier Girls* (1981) (see box). It is always tempting to ignore the more naive protestations of the key direct cinema exponents when professing to have no substantial influence upon the events they filmed and to look instead at the truth that results from the very interventions these film-makers so studiously repress. Robert Drew and his followers believed they were striving for (and able to create) a pure documentary: that is, one that remained faithful to its subject matter through its responsive (as opposed to proactive) editing, camera and sound and through its eschewal of voice-over and interview (see Waugh, 1985).

The observational documentary movement has developed enormously since its conception in 1960, and yet the legacy of direct cinema is substantial. In Britain the style has continued to dominate, in a variety of modified forms, television output in particular. Out of direct cinema, cinéma vérité and its British contemporary Free Cinema (films such as Lindsay Anderson's *Every Day Except Christmas* (1957) and Karel Reisz's *We Are the Lambeth Boys* (1959)) came the use of observational techniques for the purposes of drama in films (for both cinema and television). *Cathy Come Home* (BBC, 1966) (see 'Drama–Documentary'), directed by Ken Loach, was just one of several 'kitchen sink' or gritty realist dramas to emerge out of British cinema and television that adopted

and adapted the techniques of direct cinema. In the 1970s and 1980s Paul Watson made *The Family* (BBC, 1974) and Roger Graef made *Police* (BBC, 1982). Both series derived from or were reminiscent of earlier American predecessors: *The Family* was based on *An American Family* (PBS, 1972), while *Police* echoed the concerns of Fred Wiseman's institutions films. In the 1980s, the BBC2 strand *40 Minutes* was dominated by observational documentaries, and even its more style-conscious replacement *Modern Times* conformed to many observational ideals. With the genre's proliferation and diversification throughout the 1990s, stylisation and reflexivity have increasingly crept into the observational documentary form (see box).

What is distinctive about the manner in which British observational documentary has evolved is its ability to assimilate widely differing and frequently contradictory conventions. Having started as an anthropologist, film-maker Chris Terrill, for example, continued the 'fly-on-the-wall' tradition with series such as *HMS Brilliant* (BBC, 1995) before being a pioneer of the most popular and long-lasting reincarnation of the observational mode in Britain: the docusoap (see below). In the series *Soho Stories* (BBC, 1996), *The Cruise* (BBC, 1998) or *Jailbirds* (BBC, 1999), however, reflexivity and self-consciousness (the clear integration of the camera, Terrill's voice and presence or the subjects' performances for that apparatus and director) have burst into 'fly-on-the-wall' formats (see box). With British television's continued prioritisation of observational documentary comes the realisation that, if the genre is to be sustainable, it needs to acknowledge both the impossibility of direct cinema's aim and the essential voyeuristic impulse that still make observational documentary universally appealing.

If one thinks briefly of the British 'fly-on-the-wall' tradition, one senses immediately that what is most interesting about the films of Watson, Graef or those that came in their wake are the moments of disruption that no amount of observation can suppress. Watson has said that, 'when I made *The Family*, I had an agenda, my own voice, a point of view ... I made the films with a clear idea of the story I wanted to tell and in the hope of providing genuine insights into the human condition' (cited by Bruzzi, 2000, p. 79). This interaction between Watson's point of view (or 'manipulation' as Fred Wiseman contentiously put it during an interview at the National Film Theatre) and the documentary subject is what realistically constitutes observational documentary. Andrew Bethell, talking about his series *The House* (BBC/Double Exposure, 1995), commented that, after an initial observation period in which the subject matter dictated the filming, he developed a

New Reflexive Documentary – The 'Broomfield Film'

Nick Broomfield is the 'star' director of British documentary – perhaps more famous than the films or programmes he makes. So much so that in 1999 he appeared in a series of television advertisements for the Volkwagen Passat in which he performed a pastiche of what journalists readily refer to as the 'Broomfield film'. The essential ingredients of this by now caricatured formula are: Broomfield as sound recordist brandishing boom and sporting 'Mickey Mouse' earphones, a rambling investigative quest of an elusive subject, the unconventional but often compromising interview with the protagonists, a relaxed camera style and an ironic, retrospective voice-over. Along with other documentary-makers such as the American Michael Moore, the British Molly Dineen and Louis Theroux, Broomfield has helped create a subgenre of the observational mode: the 'fly-in-the-ointment' or reflexive documentary in which the director appears (part investigative journalist, part nemesis, part comic turn) to prise the truth out of unwilling subjects.

Broomfield began far more conventionally with straightforward observational films such as *Tattooed Tears* (1978) and *Soldier Girls* (1981), both of which he made with Joan Churchill, his then partner, who had worked as camerawoman on *An American Family*. His debt to vérité techniques is, however, clear from more recent statements such as: 'Feature films may be taken more seriously as works of art and as pieces of entertainment, but only the documentary can really capture the spontaneity and immediacy of real life' (Macdonald and Cousins, 1997, p. 364). At a recent question and answer session at the London Film Festival, Broomfield directly acknowledged his debt to direct cinema, naming Pennebaker, the Maysles and Wiseman as the greatest influences on his work.

In these early Broomfield documentaries, with their emphasis upon detailed observation and character, it is easy to see this legacy, particularly in the films' interest in the workings of institutions and the fraught situations the confrontations in such institutions promote. Both *Tattooed Tears* (about the California Youth Training School correction centre) and *Soldier Girls* (about the women US Army recruits of Charlie Company, South Georgia) are intensely moving in their sympathy for and empathy with the inmates and trainees. However, in retrospect, the documentaries hint at Broomfield's frustration with the traditional 'fly-on-the-wall' form. This frustration was cogently expressed in relation to the later and aptly named *Driving Me Crazy*: 'I'd become sort of disenchanted with the narrow parameters of this style of film-making. All too often what you look at on TV is very cleaned up and dishonest' (Paterson, 1989, p. 53).

It was during the making of *Driving Me Crazy* (1998) that Broomfield first appeared on camera, exasperated by his planned film beginning to implode. From this moment on, his films changed from 'fly-on-the-wall' to hybrid 'anti-documentaries' in which the conventional observational documentary co-existed with the anti-film elements that most documentary producers would leave on the cutting-room floor: abortive phone calls, chats with marginal characters, Broomfield and crew setting up. The co-existence of the conventional and the reflexive observational documentary illustrates Broomfield's predilection for dismantling the form itself. In doing this, Broomfield further forces his audience to reassess the whole notion of what constitutes a documentary. However, perhaps the radical has now become the mainstream, not only in the case of Broomfield but also in his imitators, not least Louis Theroux who in 2000 made a film about Eugene Terreblanche using remarkably similar tactics to those found in Broomfield's *The Leader, his Driver and the Driver's Wife* (1991).

Stella Bruzzi

sense of what he wanted to capture in the series and so arrived for later filming 'with a shopping list' of confrontations, events, insights he needed and would seek out, if not directly engineer.

The problem remains, however, of how unbiased 'fly-on-the-wall' can be and whether or not 'observational' can ever be synonymous with 'objectivity'. The work of Graef, Watson and Broomfield (see box) would, in their different ways, suggest that it can never be. What direct cinema ignored was precisely the value of the author's voice to observational documentary (a 'voice', ironically, that was there even in the films that ostensibly eschewed authorial

intervention). One of the men featured in *The Fishing Party*, for example, had an injunction placed on the BBC film when he realised that even an observational documentary (that traditionally 'leaves the driving to us', as Bill Nichols has characterised it) could offer an intensely critical portrait of its subjects. Observational documentary is as full of bias and subjectivity as any other form of documentary; it is only recently coming to terms with integrating this realisation formally into the films themselves. Indeed, it could be argued that its spontaneity is but a useful masquerade for achieving its aims.

Stella Bruzzi

RECOMMENDED READING

Bruzzi, Stella (2000), *New Documentary: A Critical Introduction*, London and New York: Routledge.

Macdonald, Kevin and Cousins, Mark (eds) (1997), *Imagining Reality: The Faber Book of Documentary*, London: Faber and Faber.

Winston, Brian (1995), *Claiming the Real: The Documentary Film Revisited*, London: BFI.

Educational Programming

The Roper Starch 1995 Global Consumer Survey found that 'educational' was the second most important description by respondents (after 'interesting') to describe the attributes of the television programmes they watched (Taylor, 1997, p. 56). The notion of 'educational' television is not at first as self-explanatory as it seems. Television has always had a consistent current that has seen its social function as being an educational tool, and this persists, even in the face of hard-nosed commercial interests, although it has caused radical changes to its form, moving away from traditional education 'from the top' (Quinn, 1997, p. 14).

The whole notion of public service broadcasting rests partly on the idea of education. Whereas television in the USA developed along commercial lines with only marginal public service, in the UK public service was at the centre of the BBC's remit. The whole conception of education has changed over the years along with television itself. Arguably, a large part of children's television is educational one way or another, and children clearly now receive a large part of their social education from television (see 'The Child Audience'). In a related development, the proliferation of 'infotainment' has increasingly become the preferred form of educational television, or informational television at the turn of the millennium.

In the early 1950s, the Ford Foundation sponsored many small educational channels in the USA, granting them money to set up the Program Production Center in 1952 (which later became national Educational Television). By 1956, there were only two educational stations, mostly broadcasting British programmes and Canadian Broadcasting Corporation programmes, despite the Federal Communication Commission (FCC) reserving 242 channels for educational television in the early 1950s. The Carnegie Commission of 1965 looked into the possibilities for an educational television service and, concluding that the networks could not be displaced, conceived the new Public Broadcasting Service (PBS) as an add-on to the current system. The Corporation for Public Broadcasting (CPB) was formed as the administrative body that would unify and protect the new stations, while overseeing the whole system. PBS was formally inaugurated in November 1969, with the CPB administering and coordinating the network of local stations.

The 'big five' educational broadcasters in the USA are WGBH (Boston), KCET (Los Angeles), WNET (New York), WETA (Washington, DC) and WTTW (Chicago). These supply most of the American programmes that appear on PBS stations, as well as exporting many programmes overseas. Some of the most successful PBS-produced programmes include *Sesame Street* (1970–), *Vietnam: A Television History* (1983), *The Civil War* (1990) and *Savage Skies* (1996). *Savage Skies*, a series about weather, was a co-production between WNET (New York) and the British broadcaster Granada. WGBH (Boston) has gone in for a number of international co-productions, particularly of the sort that adapts a literary classic. *Nostromo* (1997) was a co-production between WGBH, the BBC and RAI (Italian television). Similarly, WGBH has co-financed many British costume dramas, such as the BBC's *Great Expectations* (1998). PBS programmes have also included *American Playhouse* (1982–) and the current affairs programme *Front Line* (1983–). In the 1990s, there have been calls for PBS to be disbanded, and its future has long been precarious (Katz, 1989, p. 203).

The provision of educational television has always targeted children. Children's educational television is embodied in *Sesame Street*, a programme that always had an entertainment aspect despite nominally being about teaching children spelling and simple maths. British productions included the *Watch with Mother* (BBC, 1950–80) slot, with puppet or animated dramas broadcast immediately after lunchtime, extensive programming for schools on weekday mornings and youth television shows such as *Blue Peter* (BBC, 1958–). The latter was hosted by presenters who resembled parents or scout leaders, and this same programme format and strategy was evident in programmes that addressed both children and adults. A good example from Britain is *Tomorrow's World* (BBC, 1965–2003), a popular science and technology programme where, it could be argued, adults are regularly addressed as if they were children.

Formal education on television in the UK expanded with the advent of BBC2 in 1964. More recently, the BBC has endeavoured to sell its 'educational' television abroad, discovering that there is a massive international market for

The Discovery Channel and *Walking with Dinosaurs*

The Discovery Channel was founded in the USA in 1987 by John Hendricks. Early on, the channel struggled. Its central aim was to merge learning and enjoyment, unlike the traditional form of education embodied by schools (Taylor, 1997, p.58). Discovery also owns the Learning Channel and has a worldwide reach to sixty countries, including over 11 million homes in Europe (Taylor, 1997, p. 55). Discovery is a niche channel, providing high-quality, factual and accessible programming. Its schedules rely heavily on documentaries, commonly on subjects such as the natural world, history (including war), people's lives (from surfers to firemen to famous celebrities), anthropology (such as the programme *Disappearing World* (original broadcast, ITV, 1971–7)) and instructional programmes (telling audiences how to fish, cook or travel). The channel tends to have very repetitive scheduling, showing similar things at the same times each night, thus ensuring a regular audience. Some of the documentaries are produced by other channels and are repeated on Discovery, others are co-productions between Discovery and other channels.

One such co-production was *Walking with Dinosaurs* (1999), made as a junior partner with the BBC and billed as 'the biggest thing on television in 160 million years'. On the one hand it was clearly a signpost to the future capabilities of television, but on the other it was simply a further evolutionary stage in the television nature programme. It strictly followed the strategies of this genre, although it harked back to age-old desires for humanity to commune with dead and mythological creatures.

Through the use of a computer graphics interface (CGI), the programme was able to bring the dead back to life, animating dinosaurs against a background of actual landscapes. Not only were the images diverting by their very spectacular nature, but also the programme aimed to induce empathy in the audience through establishing certain 'characters' we could follow, and dramatising and narrativising their existence. Its format was based explicitly on this television genre, with the programme constructing a vista upon various dinosaurs' lives, as if they were living animals today being portrayed in a nature documentary like any other.

Each episode of *Walking with Dinosaurs* had a distinct theme and was set in a particular era, some of them aeons apart. The opening episode was about the start of the dinosaurs' ascendancy in the Triassic period, and was called 'New Blood'. The final episode was called 'Death of a Dynasty' and focused on the *Tyrannosaurus Rex* in the Late Cretaceous period. While unity was ensured by the voice-over declaring a 'scientific' analysis of the activities on screen, the narratives followed individual animals, constructing them as distinctive characters in order to elicit the audience's empathy and provide dramatic continuity to the events of each episode. *Walking with Dinosaurs* may never have existed without Steven Spielberg's *Jurassic Park* (1993) and its sequel *The Lost World* (1997). The irony was that *Walking with Dinosaurs* created the very theme park that is never completed in the films (see Donnelly, 2004).

K. J. Donnelly

high-quality programming. The BBC used to be satisfied with brief public information films, targeting children crossing roads, AIDS and drug abuse. It began a partnership with the Open University that involved extensive showings of its programmes, although in 'graveyard slots': first after midnight and more recently on Saturday mornings on BBC2. The range of BBC educational programming for adults went from adult literacy programmes of the 1970s such as *On the Move* (1978), to the high-prestige intellectually inclined BBC2 series *The Ascent of Man* (1973), presented by Jacob Bronowski, and John Berger's *Ways of Seeing* (1972).

Educational programmes that court a general audience, of both adults and children, have adopted the modes of 'infotainment', marking the union of informational and entertainment programming. Programmes are made as engaging as possible, and in an audiovisual language that spectacularises what a few years earlier might have been fairly dry discourses of information. The final product is educational television that uses an audiovisual language originally associated with mainstream entertainment television, such as sensationalism, fast pace, spectacle, enhancing music and narrativisation.

The BBC has reinvented its public service remit through the production of 'quality drama', usually based on a literary 'classic' (see 'Costume Drama'), and infotainment (see 'News') culminating in the landmark series *Walking with Dinosaurs* (1999). This merged the tradition of the nature documentary with the spectacle of prehistoric monsters, conjoining adult and child audiences. The co-producer of *Walking with Dinosaurs* was cable/satellite Discovery Channel (see box). Along with the History Channel, it has developed a provision dominated by documentaries. Archive material used for historical programmes and documentaries is often cheap, and programmes relying on such material are certainly made more cheaply than drama shows of similar length. The success of the Discovery Channel and the History Channel parallels the perceived decline in education, certainly a decline in its status and prestige, in Britain. As television now provides large amounts of integrated information, perhaps education's principal functions have been absorbed by television as a whole.

K. J. Donnelly

RECOMMENDED READING

Katz, Helen (1989), 'The Future of Public Broadcasting in the US', in *Media, Culture and Society*, vol. 11.

Quinn, Jane (1997), 'Getting Closer to Audiences: The BBC Experience', in Manfred Meyer (ed.), *Educational Television: What Do People Want?*, Luton: John Libbey Media/Luton University Press.

Taylor, Joyce (1997), 'Success in Cable Networks: The Discovery Channel', in Manfred Meyer (ed.), *Educational Television: What Do People Want?*, Luton: John Libbey Media/Luton University Press.

REALITY TV

Introduction

The 1990s saw 'factual' television became one of the most dynamic, successful and rapidly evolving fields of production. In genre terms it is now characterised by a very high degree of hybridisation between what would formerly have been discrete programme types. This new mix is often referenced by the idea of 'infotainment' television, in which the primary public service goals of entertainment and the provision of socially useful information are assumed to dissolve into one another. Across the schedules of British TV the proportion of factual television increased between 1989 and 1999, often in prime-time pre- and post-watershed slots, mainly at the expense of sitcoms (see p. 65), game shows and quizzes (see Dovey, 2000 p. 18).

'Reality TV' has become the description used by both popular and academic critics to describe some of the most high-impact examples of the new factual television. The precise use of the term 'reality TV' has shifted since it was first applied to news magazine programmes based round emergency service activities. It has subsequently also been used to describe talk shows, docusoaps (see below) and now 'constructed' documentaries such as *Castaway*, shown by the BBC in 2000 and 2007.

As a descriptive term it was first used in the early 1990s to describe the particular genre of magazine-format programmes based on crime, accident and health stories, what we might call 'trauma TV' (see Kilborn, 1994; Dauncey, 1996; Nichols, 1994). Reality TV is generally historically located as beginning in the USA with NBC's *Unsolved Mysteries* (1987–2002) (Kilborn, 1994, p. 426), followed closely by other networks' imitation and reproduction of the form with CBS's *Rescue 911* (CBS, 1989–96), *Cops* (Fox, 1989–), *America's Most Wanted* (Fox, 1988–) and in the UK with shows such as *Emergency 999* (BBC, 1992–2003). Also in the UK, *Crimewatch UK* (BBC, 1984–) has been seen as central to the development of the form, particularly in respect of debates around criminology and the media (see Schlesinger and Tumber, 1994). The UK also had a range of other police and emergency service programmes such as *Police Camera Action* (ITV, 1994–2002) and *Blues and Twos* (ITV, 1993–), as well as its proportion of coincidental accident programmes such as *You've Been Framed* (ITV, 1990–). Through the early years

of the 1990s the genre made inroads into TV schedules all over North America and Europe, running in prime-time pre- and post-watershed slots achieving fiction and variety show audience ratings. In the UK programmes such as *Crimewatch UK*, *999*, *Blues and Twos* and *Police Camera Action* regularly attracted audiences over the 10-million mark (Hill, 1999).

Reality TV is a compelling mix of apparently 'raw', 'authentic' material with the gravitas of the news magazine package or informational programme, combining the commercial success of tabloid content within a public service mode of address. At the level of construction, reality TV is characterised by:

- camcorder, surveillance or observational 'actuality footage' (see above);
- first-person participant or eye-witness testimony;
- reconstructions that rely upon narrative fiction styles;
- studio or to-camera links and commentary from 'authoritative' presenters;
- expert statements from emergency services personnel or psychologists.

These elements are often framed by a magazine format in which a number of stories will be covered in each programme. The in-depth emergency service programme in the UK, such as *999*, often featured just one dramatic rescue story per fifty-minute episode. The more explicitly observational *Blues and Twos* usually offers three stories per half-hour. The relentless pace of *Police Camera Action* offered an average of around thirty individual video clips in a TV half-hour, loosely grouped into different commentary-led sections.

The way the material is packaged is essential: the disparate elements are strongly narrativised in ways that conform to conventional fictional police dramas or to the form of melodrama. In turn, the individual stories are structured within an overarching public service narrative address. In the case of 'trauma TV' we are given to understand that our viewing pleasures are safely contained by an explicit appeal to a communitarian logic of security (that is to say, how to avoid becoming a victim of crime or how to participate in crime-detection processes). Hill (1999) has argued that this narrative structure is reflected strongly in audience

Big Brother

Footage from surveillance cameras or from covert taping have been a mainstay of the 'reality TV' programmes described in this section, such as *Crimewatch UK* or *Police Camera Action*. Concealed cameras have also formed the basis for a number of investigative documentary programmes, including *Undercover Britain* (C4, 1993), *Private Investigations* (Granada, 1994) and *MacIntyre Undercover* (BBC, 1999). These programmes have used undercover reporters equipped with hidden mini-cams to entrap subjects such as bad employers, bad landlords, sex workers and so on. This dissemination of surveillance-type images across the factual TV schedules is based on a widespread acceptance of the idea of CCTV as visual evidence. The CCTV image appears to simply calibrate visual perception: it is operated by machine, and no human mediation is involved in its production of 'pure' evidence. It has the additional power of a kind of voyeurism, in that its broadcast on television allows the viewer to see things that were never intended to be seen.

By 1999 there was already a widespread acceptance of CCTV footage as a 'natural' part of television output. The stage was set for the triumph of the global broadcasting phenomenon of *Big Brother* (Endemol, 1999–). Created in 1999 by the European transnational entertainment group Emdemol, *Big Brother* was first and foremost a brilliant marketing phenomenon for the way in which it combined a number of different elements into a seemingly unassailable combination. First, it took the 'ordinary people' aspect of 'reality TV', exploiting the appeal of watching ordinary people interacting, with the permanent possibility of intimacy revealed. Second, it used CCTV techniques: the subjects were under constant camera observation, producing the impression of an indexical representation of reality with a chaser of voyeuristic pleasure. These two pre-existing elements were combined with three genuine innovations: first, the game show format. This was indeed a piece of factual television, though very few 'facts' or information were imparted: this was pure entertainment, a game, a competition. Second, it was a game with a peculiar psychological twist in that the participants were called upon to act as a team: the idea of the team was constantly invoked by the participants themselves, yet they were simultaneously called upon to 'betray the team' by voting out some of its members. This combination of collectivity and competition created the drama.

To the innovation of the game show the producers added the elements of interactivity. This functioned in two ways. The first and most obvious was through the telephone voting system that the public used to make the weekly eviction decisions. The revenues from the phone lines were enormous and made Emdemol an even bigger profit on their investment. (If television was once about delivering audiences to advertisers, it may soon be about delivering callers to phone lines.) The second element of interactivity that Emdemol utilised was the Internet, in so far as the user could log on to video streamed

Big Brother: a combination of reality TV and the game show

camera feeds from the house, plus audio, at any time of the day or night. However, the programme itself is perhaps the first example of a genre crossover from online to broadcast: since the first Web cams came on stream in 1996, the Internet has been the place where this surveillance of the everyday has truly developed. Web cams had already proved that the public performance of the intimacies of everyday life could be a revenue-earning hit. This use of the Net by *Big Brother* created a core of user involvement with the programme, points of

activity and identification for the audience that in turn fed into the most important marketing network of all – the word-of-mouth network.

For *Big Brother*, although often excruciatingly boring to watch, provoked conversation, argument and intense investment on the part of its audiences. This fascination proved to be the basis for the first truly international new TV genre of the twenty-first century.

Jon Dovey

responses to reality TV programmes based in the work of the emergency services. Here the fear occasioned by exposure to crime or ill health is balanced by the resolution offered in the outcomes of the featured cases. In the case of programmes constructed around the drama of everyday life we may be offered the interpretation of psychologists to lend general insight into the particular experiences being represented (for example, *Big Brother* (Endemol, 1999)). In either case, the 'public service' utility of the programme is often awkwardly at odds with the entertainment-based drive of the narrative structure.

Since the first wave of ratings-friendly factual programming based on the emergency services, usage of the term 'reality TV' has widened somewhat. Popular use of the term 'reality TV' may also refer to programmes that use 'ordinary people' framed within a variety of 'first-person' or confessional modes of speech, such as the chat shows and docusoaps dealt with elsewhere in this volume. The different kinds of programme described as 'reality TV' are unified by the attempt to package particular aspects of everyday life as entertainment.

'Reality TV' is now used as a genre description of any factual programme based on an aesthetic style of apparent 'zero-degree realism' – in other words a direct, unmediated account of events, often associated with the use of video and surveillance-imaging technologies. During the 1990s the low-gauge video image, grainy, under-lit and often unsteady, became the pre-eminent televisual signifier of truthfulness. After a hundred years of moving-image culture we can now understand how each epoch has its own privileged style for the delivery of visual evidence. For the first 'actuality' audiences, the flickering images of everyday street scenes were astonishingly truthful and accurate. Later the Griersonian documentary tradition, very formal, constructed and poetic, became the standard for the portrayal of the everyday. This tradition in turn was overthrown by the observational film-makers of the 1960s and 1970s with their lightweight cameras and their mission to 'convey the

feeling of being there'. The new standard for visual evidence within factual television is the video image itself. It is worth noting that the widespread success of programmes based in this appeal to authenticity occurs at the same time as the widely acknowledged triumph of simulation and spectacle (see, for example, Baudrillard, 1983). An image-saturated culture appears to have produced a greater hunger than ever before for an astringent aesthetic of visual realism.

Jon Dovey

RECOMMENDED READING

Bonner, Frances (2003), *Ordinary Television: Analyzing Popular TV*, London: Sage.

Hill, Annette (2007), *Restyling Factual TV: Audiences and News, Documentary and Reality Genres*, London: Routledge.

Holmes, Su and Jermyn, Deborah (2003), *Understanding Reality Television*, London: Routledge.

Murray, Susan, and Ouellette, Laurie (eds) (2004), *Reality TV: Remaking Television Culture*, New York: New York University Press.

Studying Reality TV

As outlined above, the term 'reality TV' is a container for a variety of hybrid genres – particularly factual entertainment content. It is a useful term that instantly says this television programme is a hybrid of non-fiction and entertainment elements. Reality TV is also a value-laden term, and its association with entertainment, information, authenticity, performance and other conceptual values ensures it means different things to different people. Thus, when studying reality TV we need to acknowledge there is no one definition of the genre, nor do people agree on what they think is reality TV. Rather than see this as a problem, the challenge of defining reality TV is part of its power as a genre.

The reality genre is constructed through production and reception processes (Mittell, 2004). Programme-makers draw on production traditions, referring to previous practices to construct a reality programme similar to, or a variation on, another type of programme; and audiences draw on their knowledge of previous programmes to recognise it as a distinctive genre. All television genres become mixed up with others, and in this sense all programming is based on multiple generic participation. However, the development of a range of popular factual genres in the 1980s and 1990s has ensured hybrid genres are associated with what is most commonly described as reality TV, a term that, like misdirection in a magic trick, is not quite what it claims to be (Hill, 2004).

Reality TV, or 'popular factual', is a catch-all category for a variety of different one-off programmes, series and formats that follow real people and celebrities and their everyday or out of the ordinary experiences. Reality TV subcategories include infotainment about crime or emergency services; docusoaps about institutions or groups of people; lifestyle, often about how to do gardening, or making over someone's home or personal appearance; life-experiment programmes where people experiment with different social experiences; reality game shows where a game element is introduced to a group of people in a controlled situation; reality talent shows where members of the public or celebrities audition for and perform music, or other artistic endeavours; and the reality hoax, a mock situation that usually mocks those deceived by an elaborately staged set-up. There are other emergent categories within reality TV, such as reality business series like *The Apprentice* (BBC, 2005–), and the wide range of their formats shows how all-encompassing this type of hybrid content can be. The industry term 'reality event' sums up the scale and influence of hybrid genres such as *The X Factor* (ITV, 2004– see box) that can run for up to twenty weeks, delivering a large audience share over a long period of time, and forcing competing genres to work hard

Audiences and Reality TV

There is a common assumption that people who watch reality TV are stupid. This assumption is based on people's perceptions of reality TV as 'trash TV'. Junk food provides a common reference for reality TV. As this viewer explained: 'Reality TV, I get this ghastly feeling occasionally, you know, you just sometimes feel like eating a large bag of crisps and some bars of chocolate. It's junk food television' (Hill, 2007, p. 105). In previous research I conducted on reality TV audiences (Hill, 2004) the main finding was that viewers were like computer games players, in that they had learned to play the game of reality and expected the rules of the game to change on a regular basis. The other key finding was that viewers possessed a default critical mode when talking about reality TV, often criticising the genre for being 'mindless entertainment', and criticising themselves for watching it. This research was based on a representative sample of around 10,000 viewers in Britain. It is fair to say that these viewers were not stupid, and indeed there was much evidence to show their critical engagement with the genre of reality TV.

Research suggests audiences have a general understanding of reality TV's presentation of people and their experiences in an entertainment frame. This creates a contradictory viewing experience. On the one hand, some viewers can criticise reality programmes for being sensational and staged. They criticise themselves for watching reality programmes, for consuming what they perceive as fast-food television. On the other hand, there are aspects of reality TV some viewers like. For example, the attractions of reality TV may include crossing boundaries between fact and fiction, a playful approach to ordinary people and celebrities, the spectacle of emotions, the intensity of experiences. There are certain kinds of reality programmes that are perceived as 'good' because they are so 'bad', inviting 'a guilty pleasure' in watching them. And there are also certain kinds of programmes that are perceived as 'good' because they deal with particular issues in a way that some viewers can relate to in their everyday lives. As this viewer explained, some programmes 'contain things about the ordinary drive of life. Ambition, envy, relationships. What actually does go on in reality in some people's lives' (Hill, 2007, p. 106).

Alongside general criticism of the genre, audiences are aware of variations within reality TV. Given the large range of formats it is hardly surprising that people make distinctions between different types of programmes. The various different hybrid formats, and the additions within ongoing formats, also means audiences are subject to increasingly complicated generic content. Research on reality TV audiences around the world indicates many viewers/users have a great deal of knowledge about genres. Therefore it could be said that many viewers are engaged in regular discussion about the generic cross-fertilisation that is so distinctive to this genre. In this sense, they are rich in genre knowledge.

Annette Hill

to retain a place in the schedules. Reality TV is therefore a wide-ranging category that makes television top heavy with reality entertainment-led programming (see Holmes and Jermyn, 2003, and Murray and Ouellette, 2004, for further discussion).

There are two broad distinctions within reality TV – programmes that film situations already taking place, and those that create the situation for the purposes of the programme. One type of popular factual is more observational in nature, the other is more constructed. Sometimes production and commissioning departments separate the two into formatted and non-formatted, implying there is a distinction between formatted constructed reality TV and more non-formatted observational programmes. The boundaries are not clearly marked, and the nature of reality TV is to continuously blur boundaries and rely on hybrid genres. But it is useful to bear in mind that a distinctive feature of observational reality programmes is that they rely on filming people in their normal environment, and any changes that occur would mainly have happened if the cameras were not there. The distinctive feature of constructed reality programmes is that someone is removed from their normal environment and placed in a new one, and any change that takes place would not have occurred without the proactive and deliberate intervention of the production company (for example, *Big Brother* – see box). All documentary filming alters 'real-life' situations but that alteration is the raison d'etre of these programmes, rather than something that producers seek to minimise. We might call these programmes 'made-for-TV reality', and it places them close to other non-fiction genres such as sports or light entertainment, and other fictional genres, such as soap opera or melodrama.

Reality TV also includes television programmes with interactive elements, such as voting, and related websites or mobile content. The interactive and multi-platform elements of various reality programmes are part of the story of the reality genre. *Big Brother* was described by Peter Bazalgette, former Chief Creative Officer of Endemol International, as 'the most perfectly converged piece of entertainment ever conceived' (2005, p. 284). The format has been shown all over the world, since its original transmission in Holland in 1999. Countries airing a fifth, sixth, or seventh series include America, Mexico, Brazil, Britain and many European countries. *Big Brother* has also been locally produced in South Africa, pan-Africa, Argentina, Ecuador, Columbia, Croatia, Poland, Serbia, Thailand and the Middle East, among others. According to Bazalgette, 'viewers have switched *Big Brother* on eighteen billion times. More than a billion

votes have been cast via telephones and interactive TV. Six and a half billion page views have been recorded at *Big Brother* web sites' (2005, p. 284).

In summary, the power of reality TV as a genre is in its ability to work across factual and entertainment content. Reality TV is a feral genre (Hill, 2007). This metaphor of reality TV as 'feral' suggests it is a genre experiment gone wild. Reality TV is wildly opportunistic in its desire to attract popular viewers around the world; it is de-territorial in its ability to cross generic boundaries; it is disruptive in the production and scheduling of existing genres; and above all it is resistant to containment. Whether we like it or not, reality TV is a powerful genre in that it has an ability to make and remake itself within the contemporary entertainment industry.

Annette Hill

RECOMMENDED READING

Bazalgette, Peter (2005), *Billion Dollar Game: How Three Men Risked it all and Changed the Face of Television*, London: Time Warner.

Hill, Annette (2007), *Restyling Factual TV: Audiences and News, Documentary and Reality Genres*, London: Routledge.

Murray, Susan, and Ouellette, Laurie (eds) (2004), *Reality TV: Remaking Television Culture*, New York: New York University Press.

Docusoaps

Docusoaps were the television documentary find of the 1990s. For the first time factual programmes, put out in prime-time slots, could rival their popular drama counterparts. At its peak *The Cruise* (BBC, 1998) achieved approximately 11 million viewers per episode, and *Driving School* (BBC, 1997–2003) peaked at 12.5 million. Even long-running series such as *Vet School* (BBC, 1996) and *Vets in Practice* (BBC, 1997–2002) have retained audiences of around 8 million. The term 'docusoap' itself was coined by journalists keen to dismiss this new brand of factual television that, in their estimation, contaminated the seriousness of documentary with the frivolity of soap operas (see p. 60).

In certain respects, docusoaps resemble their more conventional 'fly-on-the-wall' antecedents (see 'Observational ('Fly-on-the-Wall') Documentary'). For example, like the films of Wiseman, Graef or Watson, they feature the lives of ordinary people sharing a common experience. The difference between docusoaps about ordinary lives and a Wiseman film about equally mundane existences is not

The Family: a precursor of the modern docusoap

instead worked in the office of Southwark Council and had been picked for the series on the basis of his potential appeal to audiences. Likewise, some sequences in *Driving School* were shown to be faked for dramatic effect (see 'Documentary Fakes').

Docusoaps, like earlier forms of observational documentary, were made possible by specific technological advances. By their very nature, observational series are bound to amass a higher-than-average shooting ratio, and working on 16mm film (for so long the preferred choice of television as well as cinema documentary film-makers) was becoming prohibitively expensive. With the arrival of new digital cameras and editing suites it has become at once easier and cheaper to film and cut material, thus allowing for the needs of observational documentary once more. In 1998, Paul Hamann, as head of BBC Documentary Features, commented that docusoaps could be produced three times as cheaply as comparable light entertainment. Coupled with the fact that, for the first time in British television history, factual programmes regularly obtained a higher share of the viewers than drama, docusoaps proved irresistible to channel controllers and commissioners alike. It is also significant that the docusoap's similarity to popular drama has enabled it to retain much of the same audience.

There are several series that are repeatedly named as the direct precursors of docusoaps, the most commonly named being *The Family* (BBC, 1974) or Watson's later *Sylvania Waters* (BBC, 1993), *HMS Brilliant* (BBC, 1995) and *The House* (BBC/Double Exposure, 1995). These more traditional BBC 'fly-on-the-wall' series were all relatively costly to make, but all proved unexpectedly popular. *The House* stands apart in this quartet and most explicitly paved the way for docusoaps in general. The series was more proactive than reactive, giving priority to drama and crisis over serious commentary; it was clearly intrusive and meddlesome and was swathed in an arch, forceful commentary narrated by Jancis Robinson. Although the film-makers did not manufacture crises (as they later did with *Driving School*), they did appear voyeuristically interested in them. This detail in itself spawned several imitators, most notably *Hotel* (BBC, 1997), a series about the Adelphi in Liverpool, which almost exclusively revolved around crises and arguments among the staff, usually involving the manageress Eileen Downey or the chef Dave Smith. In every case, the reason for these heated confrontations is marginalised in favour of capturing a protracted 'slanging match' on screen. The producers of *Driving School* similarly admitted that Maureen and Dave Rees were chosen as the series' star couple because their naturally argumentative relationship would transfer well to a thirty-minute prime-time slot.

essentially one of subject, although people having driving lessons is perhaps a less inherently 'worthy' subject than patients on a ward for the terminally ill; the real difference is one of tone. What truly sets docusoaps apart from their predecessors is their prioritisation of entertainment over social commentary. This is in part a formal issue. One docusoap convention borrowed from drama is the focus on 'characters', usually known by their first names and introduced during jocular opening title sequences. Allied to this is that docusoaps, like soaps (that also putatively tackle serious contemporary issues), are more interested in characters' personalities than in their social roles or profession.

Also reminiscent of soap opera is the docusoap's fast-paced editing style, chopping together short sequences and alternating between a limited number of narrative strands per episode. However, this bias towards drama and sensationalism has frequently got the genre into trouble. There were, for instance, the substantiated allegations that Ray Brown, the 'star' clamper of *Clampers* (BBC, 1998), was no longer a clamper when the series was being made, but

'Accidental Footage'

Linda Williams has detected, in what she terms the 'new' (that is, more reflexive) documentary, a loss of faith in 'the ability of the camera to reflect objective truths of some fundamental social referent' (Williams, 1993, p.13). Television's ability to represent the truth in the way that observational documentary film-makers argued it could, has recently been replaced by an acceptance of the medium's limitations and an awareness that, as Williams puts it, what can be shown is a series of 'competing truths' rather than one overarching one. This has become so much the way in which factual representation is interpreted that Andrew Britton states, as if it is a foregone conclusion, that 'there can be no such thing as a representation of the world which does not embody a set of values' (Britton, 1992, p. 28).

However, the subject of this section is a form of factual film-making that is, by its very nature, less prone to distortion than others, and that is 'accidental footage'. By this I mean film or video material collated by individuals who do not set out to record the events they find themselves filming, which thereby lack premeditation and hence 'authorship' in any conventional sense. Examples of 'accidental footage' would be Zapruder's 8mm film of the death of President Kennedy, the assassination of Kennedy's brother Robert in 1968, George Holliday's home-video footage of the beating of Rodney King, live transmission of the Shuttle disaster or the terrorist attack on the Twin Towers in New York in 2001.

These examples are strictly speaking newsreel (see p. 104) as opposed to 'documentary', the latter, as Soviet film-maker and pioneer of the compilation film Esfir Shub argued, being the consciously, subjectively conceived final film into which raw material might be placed (Leyda, 1996, p. 59). The important factor linking the above cases of 'accidental footage' is that they were not premeditated or prepared for except in the split second it takes to turn a camera on and point it. Because of this, all possess an amateurish intensity even if, as in the case of Robert Kennedy's death, the cameras were operated by news professionals.

In the case of someone such as Abraham Zapruder, what he immortalised on 8mm on 22 November 1963 was entirely unexpected. 'The Zapruder film' (as it is commonly known) exemplifies the uniqueness of film as accidental record. Its most significant feature is the discrepancy between technical quality and the importance of its content. Zapruder is not an adept cameraman, and at one point, just before Kennedy receives the fatal shot to his head, threatens to lose the President from view altogether. His iconic twenty-two seconds of home-movie footage, however, has captured for posterity one of the most monumental events of the last century. The significance of the 8mm film is not simply its content, however, and 'Zapruder' became shorthand in New York film schools of the 1960s for a piece of film of extremely low technical quality whose content was nevertheless of great significance. Zapruder's film lacks 'value' as defined by Britton but has an impact upon its audience that any documentary film-maker craves by seeming as unadulterated as the moving image can be. The few frames of film offer no perspective on or understanding of the day's events in Dallas. In fact, it is deeply, tantalisingly ironic that this most graphic of material is incapable of yielding the answer to the most important question of all: who killed Kennedy?

Although it is these home movies that best deserve the tag 'cinema of truth', it is the very 'authenticity' of such material that also renders accidental footage inconclusive. To return to Shub's distinction between newsreel and documentary: such material as the Zapruder or 9/11 are more often than not recontextualised within, for example, a news bulletin or documentary. The representational world is forever making sense of and explaining the real world, and the instinct is not to leave raw footage alone but to attempt to explicate it. Conversely, the dual impetus now is towards being wise to the inauthenticities of documentaries as Williams et al. are, while revering the most 'authentic' types of factual image-making. The two (the reflexively self-conscious and the spontaneous) have, in a further irony, become formally synonymous, as both fictional and factual television have adopted the shorthand of wobbly cam, blurred shots, crash-zooms and inaudible dialogue to signify greater truthfulness. The logical conclusion to the conundrum of the factual image is a series such as *Big Brother*, filming ten down to two contestants, twenty-four hours a day, for a prize of £70,000. The boundaries between the 'real' and the 'reel' no longer seem to hold much interest.

Stella Bruzzi

The docusoaps' penchant for drama has manifested itself in a variety of forms, the clearest being its reliance upon stars and performers. Again, however, this echoes concerns of earlier direct cinema documentaries about performers and the vérité preoccupation with the performances of their subjects in front of the cameras. The Adelphi, immediately following the transmission of *Hotel* on BBC1, became immensely popular as people wanted to see the 'real' Eileen and Dave; Maureen Rees got an agent, cut a record and appeared on *This is Your Life* (BBC,

1955–64/ITV, 1969–2003) and Jane McDonald, the cabaret singer featured in *The Cruise*, has become an immensely successful recording artist and television presenter.

What clearly sets docusoaps apart from their immediate predecessors is their open acknowledgment of the importance of performance to factual as well as fictional programmes. So, in *The Cruise*, Jane McDonald chats to director/cameraman Chris Terrill while he is filming her, pushing the series beyond impersonal observation. One of the paradoxes of docusoaps is that they purport to be interested in the excessively ordinary, while at the same time having reached the level of success and notoriety they have done by the discovery and promotion of 'stars'. In this context, the stars of docusoaps are hyper-ordinary people, those who can transcend and achieve an identity beyond the series that created them. Consistent with this contradiction is the docusoap's reluctance to engage with what could be termed the theoretical permutations of the relationship between factual broadcasting and performance. Latterly, docusoaps have become a caricature of themselves: vehicles for larger-than-life performers who have intentionally sought the new fame that factual television can offer.

It is this perceived 'shallowness' that has prompted much of the media criticism of the genre. The journalist Allison Pearson comments that, 'In the hands of its most serious practitioners – directors such as Molly Dineen and Roger Graef – documentary aspires to tell us something about the human condition. The docusoap, by contrast, tells us something only about the condition of human beings who know they're on television' (Pearson, 1998). Interestingly, Graef himself has vigorously defended docusoaps in the press, and Paul Watson has argued that 'there is no analysis, no insight … their only function seems to have been to turn the rest of us into peeping Toms' (McCann, 1998). At a time when documentary is more popular than ever, it has also come in for the sharpest criticism.

Stella Bruzzi

RECOMMENDED READING

Biressi, Anita and Nunn, Heather (2004), 'Just being themselves: from docudrama to new observational drama' in Anita Biressi and Heather Nunn, *Reality TV: Realism and Revelation*, London and New York: Wallflower Press.

Bruzzi, Stella (2000), *New Documentary: A Critical Introduction*, London and New York: Routledge.

Kilborn, Richard (2003), 'Performing the Real: the rise and fall of the docu-soap', in Richard Kilborn, *Staging the Real: Factual TV Progamming in the Age of Big Brother*, Glasgow: Bell and Bain.

Reality Talent Shows

The reality talent show is based on the premise of ordinary people or celebrities taking part in a competition. The contestants sing, dance, act, while undertaking physical and mental tests that ensure they are fighting to stay in the competition. The format involves backstage reportage of their training each week, followed by the performance itself, comments by a selection of outspoken judges and an invitation to the audience to vote for their favourite contestant. Each week one person is voted out, until eventually there is a high-pressure showdown in the series finale. Series such as *The X Factor* involve ordinary people who have a chance to become a star, and indeed are trained by music industry professionals to become pop stars of the future. Series such as *Strictly Come Dancing* (BBC, 2004–) involve celebrities who can transform themselves with professional training from an actor, or sportsman, to a dancer. The key elements within this type of reality TV are talent, competition and transformation, where the viewer can watch and indeed influence the journey of the contestants from day one to the finale.

Reality talent shows highlight the international reach of reality TV formats made by production and format houses and sold to countries worldwide for local production. Reality formats have been described by Moran as examples of 'new television' (2005). He claims that 'a unique intersection of new technologies of transmission and reception, new forms of financing, and new forms of content' has led to a global type of television programme, 'drawing upon but transforming older practices of transnational adaptation, the format is simultaneously international in its dispersal and local and concrete in its manifestation' (2005, pp. 291, 305). Reality event formats such as *Idol* have been phenomenally successful worldwide. FremantleMedia (with 19TV) own the *Idol*s brand and the details on their official website promote it as an international bestseller. They sold the format to over thirty territories, including among others the UK, the USA, Australia, France, Germany, Sweden, Poland, Iceland, Kazakhstan, Russia, the pan-Arabic regions, South Africa, India and Singapore. The original series (*Pop Idol*) shown in the UK on ITV1 in 2001 aired for sixteen weeks, with the finale attracting 14 million viewers, and a 57 per cent share (72 per cent among sixteen- to thirty-four-year-olds). There were almost 9 million votes cast in the finale, which saw the winner and runner-up begin a nationwide tour and produce albums and top ten-selling singles in the same year. The American version of *Idol* (*American Idol* (Fox, 2002–)) has been very

Strictly Come Dancing

Strictly Come Dancing (BBC, 2004–) is a perfect example of how reality talent shows mix the traditional and the new to make a successful format. The show is based on the long-running series *Come Dancing* (1949–98), a light entertainment series based on traditional ballroom dancing competitions. The series ran for five decades, a classic of public service entertainment, filming ballroom dancing across the nation, adding a touch of glamour to postwar Britain. *Strictly Come Dancing* was the BBC's new vision for an old Saturday-night favourite. It takes the tradition of ballroom, mixes it with contemporary celebrity culture, and adds successful elements of reality TV, such as behind the scenes footage, voting and live performances. One BBC producer called it 'post-reality TV', reflecting the next development in reality entertainment formats.

The format has all the hallmarks of what Moran calls 'new television'. It has been sold to over 25 countries worldwide, with *Strictly*, or *Dancing with the Stars* (BBC, 2006–) locally produced in America, India, New Zealand and many European countries. The essential ingredients include fourteen celebrities paired with professional dancers. Each week they learn a ballroom style, from foxtrot to tango. A panel of judges scores the performances, and viewers vote for their favourites. The live Saturday show is based around the dance routines and voting; the Sunday dance-off sees one couple depart; and the weekly spin-off series *It Takes Two* (BBC, 2004–) includes training footage and studio discussion. There is great potential for drama, romance, anger, disappointment and sheer pleasure in dance. Series five (2007) saw the hottest competition in the history of the show. The series finale attracted 12 million viewers, making it the third most watched show on the BBC that year. Two celebrities, Matt Di Angelo, actor in the BBC

Winning *Strictly Come Dancing*

soap opera *EastEnders* (BBC, 1985–), and Alesha Dixon, a pop singer, went head to head in the final with a repertoire of challenging dance routines. Each celebrity had gone through an emotional journey to get to the final – Matt started strongly but suffered from nerves later in the series, forgetting his routine in show ten and saved from elimination by public vote; Alesha had given it her all from the start after a publicised separation from her husband who had been caught in an affair with another singer. Alesha won the crown, crying at the result, and telling her dance partner Matthew Cutler 'I love you'. The presenter Bruce Forsyth said, 'You could become the biggest female star in this country'. Dixon plans to release a solo album, present a television series for the BBC and continue with her new dancing career. *Strictly* is an example of a global format that makes and remakes itself within the entertainment industry, crossing over from traditional ballroom dancing to celebrity culture, and from light entertainment to reality talent show.

Annette Hill

successful, with the fourth series averaging 26 million viewers, a 23 per cent share, and 500 million cumulative votes. In Singapore *Idol* had a market share of 60 per cent in 2004. Network 10 showed *Idol* in Australia in 2004 and the series ranked as its highest since 2000. Ten million people voted for *Idol* in South Africa (third series in 2005), and the winner and runner-up got to meet Nelson Mandela. There was even a *World Idol*, in 2003, with series one winners from eleven different countries taking part during a Christmas special.

What is the appeal of reality talent shows? In one sense these shows are talent spotters, with panel judges and viewers working together to find the next singing or dancing

star. *Dancing on Ice* (ITV, 2006–), which won the British Broadcast award for best international programme sales (2008), has a spin-off show *Make Me a Star* (ITV, 2008–), where the successful ice-dancing champions Torvill and Dean search the nation for stars of the future. The show asks 'Are you the next Torvill and Dean?' followed by clips sent in by the public showing embarrassing ice-skating moments, for example, one man wanted to be the first magician on ice. Clearly, the expectation is that only a few lucky people have star quality, and for most of us the opportunity to talent spot stars of the future is the closest we will get to being a star. In another sense, these shows offer an emotional journey. We begin at the audition stage, and watch the participants as they go through an intense learning experience, training, performing, bonding with their team mates, or falling out with the trainers or judges, fighting each week to stay in the competition and improve their vocal or dance performances. The contestants may have natural talent, but they have to want to win, want to be a star.

Yet another reason for the success of these shows is their event status. Typically, each season sees one or two series go head to head in the ratings, with a long run-up to Christmas, or Easter when the finale occurs, and a week-by-week debate in the popular press and in everyday life about the twists and turns in the show. The reality talent show event is typically shaped by the weekend show, followed by the results of the voting, and then the weekday reports of training in the run-up to the next show. In 2007 ratings in the UK for *The X Factor* and *Strictly Come Dancing* were around 10 million, with a 40 per cent share, which means that most of British audiences were watching one or the other show. The live broadcast adds to the event status of the shows, creating a drama where anything can happen, and we can be there to witness the success or failure of the performances as they happen. We may not be in the studio, but the audience is made to feel they are a vital part of the show – we are constantly told to 'Vote now!' to save our favourite contestants. It is a reality show where the audience is led to believe they can change the course of events by the touch of a button. Part of the appeal of reality talent shows is that viewers can feel like the real stars of the show.

Annette Hill

RECOMMENDED READING

Biressi, Anita and Nunn, Heather (2004), *Reality TV: Realism and Revelation*, London: Wallflower Press.

Holmes, Su and Jermyn, Deborah (2003), *Understanding Reality Television*, London: Routledge.

Moran, Albert (2005), 'Configurations of the New Television Landscape', in Wasko (ed.), *A Companion to Television*, Maldon, London and Victoria: Blackwell, pp. 291–307.

Makeover Shows

The makeover is the success story of lifestyle television. Lifestyle programmes traditionally address topics such as homes and gardens, or food and drink. Lifestyle uses a combination of presenters, experts and ordinary people to offer advice and ideas about contemporary living. Broadly speaking there are two types of lifestyle, instructional and makeover programmes. Instructional programmes offer straightforward advice, makeover focuses on the transformation of an object or person. In the 1990s, lifestyle television moved away from its didactic roots to embrace the makeover. The popularity of makeover series such as *Changing Rooms* (BBC, 1996–2004) in the evening schedules highlighted a significant shift from traditional lifestyle to the contemporary makeover. The makeover focuses on an individual or group of people who are tackling a lifestyle project, be that a home or their fashion sense. Presenters and experts help with their progress as they transform their homes with the latest interior design, or their appearances with fashionable clothes. The common narrative is 'before and after', as we follow ordinary people through the makeover process, seeing the transformation of these people through their chosen lifestyle project.

As makeover has become ever more popular it has taken the idea of transformation to the limits of lifestyle. There are makeover shows about dirt and clutter, where experts transform a grubby house into a germ free, clutter free home. The theme of transformation is extended beyond the change in appearance to touch on 'self-improvement' and makeover of your 'inner self'. A makeover series such as *How Clean is Your House?* (C4, 2003–) is a hybrid of instructional programming and psychological drama. Dirt is not only a physical element of the programme, it is also a psychical element, where it comes to represent values and emotions associated with cleanliness and order. The dust, grime and germs found in the home are symptomatic of something emotionally deeper, and the more they clean the more the experts uncover the personal issues at the heart of the problem of dirt. In the fashion makeover series *What Not to Wear* (BBC, 2001–) the experts even use a psychologist's couch to uncover the emotional problems of women with bad fashion sense. The psychology of makeover is taken to the limits in body transformations such as *Extreme Makeover* (ABC, 2002–7), where a person undergoes cosmetic surgery to achieve 'the ultimate makeover'. The people who feature in the series are deeply troubled by their appearances, such as childhood trauma about being overweight, or obsession with a minor disfigurement. Cosmetic surgery offers a medical solution to their perceived problems, along with expert counselling and life-coaching. The expectation is that physical transformation can lead to emotional well being, a transformation of 'the inner and outer you'.

Frances Bonner (2003) suggests that lifestyle and makeover series offer ordinary people the opportunity to be seen and heard on television, to put forward their point of view, to share their lifestyles with viewers. Experts are an important element of the makeover format, but as Bonner suggests it is ordinary people and their lifestyle transformations that make the show. The trend in the psychological transformation connects with this emphasis on ordinary people in makeover. Without these personal stories there would be little to connect with, one show would blend into another, but by emphasising the transformation of ordinary people the makeover offers viewers an opportunity to see inside other people's homes and compare them with their own. In some cases, a makeover series invites viewers to identify, or sympathise, with ordinary people. For example, *Extreme Makeover: Home Edition* (ABC, 2003–) is about people in truly tragic domestic circumstances, their homes are often falling apart and their family life is threatened by poor living conditions. The expert team transforms these people's lives, bulldozing the existing home and building a bigger home for a better future. The

makeover is almost an act of charity; these people need help and their emotional journey is by far the most important part of the programme. Here, the makeover becomes a hybrid of property development and melodrama, an emotionally powerful lifestyle genre.

Critics have highlighted how makeover shows offer templates for living, often templates that conform to middle-class aspirational values about bigger homes, the latest consumer products, a perfect body. Experts may offer their advice, but ordinary people also get a chance to reject this advice, or modify it to suit their lifestyles. In series such as *Changing Rooms* people openly criticise the experts' interior design choices. Women in *What Not to Wear* do not always follow the advice of the presenters. A series such as *Grand Designs* (C4, 1999–) focuses on the personal tastes of ordinary people with extraordinary dreams of property development. In the same way viewers may follow tips and advice given by experts, but they can also reject this advice. One producer described the

Supernanny

Supernanny (C4, 2004–) is a part of a trend in the makeover format that addresses parenting and child behaviour. There are various modern parenting methods available with different advice for child rearing. *Supernanny* is based on an approach to parenting that emphasises boundaries and rules. Jo Frost is a 'modern-day Mary Poppins' who spends three weeks with families who have troublesome toddlers. Her mission is to bring the family together by solving behavioural problems through simple techniques, such as the 'naughty step'. The transformation comes from the parents adopting Jo's approach to childcare and, through this experience, they improve not only their child's behaviour but the family dynamic as a whole. *Supernanny* is a parenting makeover – combining child behavioural advice with family soap opera.

A typical episode follows the story of a family in crisis. The source of the crisis is usually that the child, or children, have a problem listening and relating to their parents because the parents have a problem in parenting. For example, in one episode a toddler has problems sleeping, eating, using the potty and cries all the time. 'Supernanny' helps the mother, a former professional ballroom dancer, establish a bedtime routine, family mealtimes, regular potty training. When the child cries and has tantrums, Supernanny advises the mother to ignore their cries, instead using a reward system for good behaviour. After three weeks, the transformation is complete and mother and child are bonding in a different way than

before. In another example, Jo criticises the parents of five children for deciding not to parent – chaos rules, their children do what they want, the family spend little quality time together. After three weeks with Supernanny they have established order and started to bond as a family. The transformation from chaos to order is the central theme of the show.

Supernanny is an international hit. It attracts 3 million viewers in Britain, the series performs well in other countries, and Jo Frost stars in an American version of the show. Her childcare book topped the bestseller lists in the USA off the back of the first series. In Britain, her series inspires devoted followers. For example, there is an official online community for the show, with advice, regular blogs and behaviour management tips, such as the car drill technique. According to a poll by the National Family and Parenting Institute (NFPI), parents are using television programmes such as *Supernanny* to teach them how to manage their children. Other child-rearing experts have criticised the series for its approach to parenting. The emphasis on strict discipline and routine is at odds with other approaches to parenting that emphasise the child's needs and emotions. Some psychologists argue that controlled crying can cause damage to a child's development. Thus, the show touches on issues within makeover concerning lifestyle choices. It offers one approach to parenting, a 'modern-day Mary Poppins', but such an approach is open to comparison, debate and criticism by experts and viewers.

Annette Hill

makeover as 'takeout' television where viewers take away tips on interior design, fashion, relationships, parenting and so forth (Channel 4 Producer Notes, 2005). Viewers can just as easily throw away this advice. Indeed, perhaps one of the reasons makeover works so well as a format is that viewers can compare their lifestyle choices with other people just like them, and in doing so feel better about themselves – 'well, at least I'm not like that'. The element of criticism that is such a feature of makeover, where the expert tells someone to change their bad habits, is also an element of the reception experience, where the viewer can criticise other people and their lifestyle choices. In understanding makeover television we begin to see how lifestyle choices are connected to personal, social and emotional issues in contemporary living.

Annette Hill

RECOMMENDED READING

Bonner, Frances (2003), *Ordinary Television: Analysing Popular TV*, London: Sage.

Heller, Dana (ed.) (2007), *Makeover Television: Realities Remodelled*, London and New York: I. B. Taurus.

Hill, Annette (2007), *Restyling Factual TV: Audiences and News, Documentary and Reality Genres*, London: Routledge.

Moseley, Rachel (2000), 'Makeover takeover on British television', *Screen*, vol. 41.

ANIMATION

Studying Animation

Over the last twenty years, Animation Studies has grown as a discipline, encompassing all aspects of the form from the traditional cartoon, to CGI features, to 3D stop-motion and experimental works. Still comparatively little attention has been given to animation on television, however, often casting it as merely 'the Saturday morning cartoon' or *The Simpsons* (Fox, 1989–). It is clear, though, that an increasingly rich vein of animated programming informs the television schedules and deserves critical engagement. This might be achieved in the following ways:

- Looking at TV animation as a distinct form in its own right, related to, but significantly different from the 'classical' achievements of the Disney Studio, particularly in its 'golden era' between 1928 and 1941, and the theatrically distributed cartoons by Warner Bros. and MGM in the 1940s.
- Engaging with the specific role that animation has played in children's programming, acknowledging its pertinence in educational and public information strategies.
- Addressing the particular 'language' of animation as a unique form of expression, and the ways that it has, therefore, subverted or radicalised established television genres.
- Assessing the extent and nature of animated programming in the multi-channel era, and as a 'leading-edge' component of contemporary digital culture.
- Evaluating animation as a fundamental part of global programming dedicated to speaking to indigenous audiences and yet, using the seemingly 'universal' commonality of animated forms to reach international markets and viewers.

By engaging with these core themes and topics, it is possible to identify the historical, cultural, economic and aesthetic factors that have defined animation on television.

Studying animation is, of course, closely allied with the study of film and television, in general, but because of its cross-disciplinary and multi-disciplinary nature, it also invites address from other areas, most notably from the perspective of fine artists, graphic designers and illustrators.

Though much television animation is still fundamentally related to its status as a 'cartoon', particularly in the cable and satellite multi-channel era (though it is important not to neglect the plethora of 3D stop-motion and computer-generated animation), the very nature of the cartoon has changed. As the historical overview that follows stresses, there is a fundamental difference between the 'full animation' of the golden era of theatrically distributed cartoons of the 1930s and 1940s, to the 'reduced animation' of the television era of the 1950s through to the 1990s, to the 'digitally' enhanced animation of the contemporary era. This, in itself, affords an opportunity to take one example of contemporary TV animation, as a brief case study to exemplify the model of analysing animation stated above.

To view Genndy Tartakovsky's *Samurai Jack* (Cartoon Network, 2001–4) within the context of TV animation as a form in its own right, for example, is to recognise a significant milestone in that the bold outline around characters which came to become a regular feature of many animated series, was abandoned in preference to full colour design idioms. This represented a significant shift from 'block' graphic design-styled characters and environments to fully drawn quasi-illustrative work, using a range of visual sources and approaches to fine art from a variety of national cultures. Consequently, such work also set itself apart from the cartoon aesthetics of the 'golden era', in the sense, that classic Disney and Warners' cartoons in drawing from comic strips and Vaudevillian performance, defined their own increasingly self-reflexive full animation styling, focusing on the cartoon itself as a film form, rather than the relationship to other models of visualisation. *Samurai Jack* appealed to its children/adult crossover audience, therefore, by engaging with a contemporary model of visual literacy, which at one and the same time, was aware (albeit often unconsciously) of the anime aesthetics, but more significantly, deployed a modified version of 1970s' TV animation, updated with progressive graphic forms and illustration. This was more pertinent to contemporary audiences who were more versed with Hanna Barbera cartoons (see below) and Japanese imported shows (see below) than the classic theatrical cartoons.

This leads on significantly to the ways in which *Samurai Jack* uses the distinctive language of animation. Metamorphosis – the seamless transition from one state to another without edit – embodied in Jack's arch enemy, the shape-shifting, Apu. Condensation – the maximum degree of suggestion in the minimum of imagery – exhibited in the design of characters from different cultures: for example, aboriginal characters defined through primal dream art, or Chinese characters through calligraphic art. Fabrication – the construction of imagined environments and contexts – facilitated through the series' play with different time periods, and mythological narratives. Symbol and metaphor – primarily shown through the series' prioritisation of creating long sequences without dialogue (influenced greatly by the work of Akira Kurosawa and Sergio Leone), and the use of figures and creatures from folktales epitomising a particular skill, attitude or outlook. Penetration – the capacity to depict and illustrate seemingly unimaginable interior mechanisms, organic forms and psychological states – often seen in dream sequences, supernatural contexts and heightened dramatic conflicts. The manipulation of time and space – most often seen in the series' use of split-screen devices and the staging of extended 'moments' over long periods of time – and, finally, sound, key in creating mood and atmosphere.

The series operates as a state-of-the-art exhibition of the animated form using a core design principle centred on the look of Jack himself, but thereafter, using many design sources and references from *Quick Draw McGraw* (Syndicated, 1959–62) to Frank Miller (American writer, artist and film director best known for his film noir-style comic book stories). This enables the work to speak to a range of audiences, and to discourses not merely in western popular culture, but worldwide. *Samurai Jack*, like many contemporary TV animation series, uses digitally enhanced traditional methods, but most significantly, makes play with the 2D graphic space in a self-conscious way that engages at many levels with the history of TV animation.

The following overview takes into account the dominant work which underpinned the evolution and development of animation for television in the USA and the UK.

Paul Wells

TV Animation – A Brief Overview

The emergence of television in the domestic home in the mid-1950s was to change many aspects of social life, but its impact on cinema was especially pronounced. The American animated cartoon, though extremely popular in theatres, was always regarded as a marginal entertainment, and mainly as children's fare, and with the changing economies of production, it was inevitable that it would be a casualty of tightening studio belts. With the closure of departments at Warner Bros. and MGM, who were dedicated to the production of theatrically distributed cartoons, it was necessary to revitalise the industry through the redefinition of animation as a form. Though veterans of the stature of Chuck Jones were highly critical of the early TV era, dismissing it as 'illustrated radio', the necessary constraints in technique and approach meant that commercials and animated programming had to adapt to much reduced budgets and, ultimately, drew more heavily on comparatively minimalist contemporary idioms in graphic design and modern art.

Though in the UK, this working practice emerged much earlier in the wartime and postwar work of the Halas and Batchelor and W. M. Larkins studios, and across Europe, with the fledgling 'limited animation' of the Zagreb studio proving influential, it was UPA (United Productions of America) who radicalised the cartoon in the USA, and created the template for the reduced animation of television work. UPA was formed in 1943 by three 'breakaway' artists from the Walt Disney studio, Steve Bosustow, Dave Hilberman and Zack Schwartz, who all wished to develop the animated cartoon in a different way from the Disney style. Employing new approaches, the studio went on to international success with innovative films like *Gerald McBoing-Boing* (1951), *Rooty Toot Toot* (1952), *Tell-Tale Heart* (1953), *The Unicorn in the Garden* (1953) and, most famously, through the films featuring *Mr Magoo*. Though successful companies emerged in the USA – like Pintoff Productions, John Sutherland Productions, John Hubley's Storyboard studio and Briton John Wilson's Fine Art Films, all influenced by the work of modernist illustrators and designers, Saul Steinberg, Stuart Davis, Robert Osborn and Raoul Dufy – it was Hanna Barbera who successfully industrialised the new conditions of the cartoon for mainstream broadcasting. With its oft-repeated and limited movement cycles, Hanna Barbera created animation that was necessarily more character and performance driven, and relied on witty scripts and amusing vocal deliveries. With the success of *The Huckleberry Hound Show* (NBN, 1958–62) and *Yogi Bear* (Syndicated, 1958–62), Joe Barbera was justified in his view that 'the kids don't give a darn if there is 4000 or 40,000 drawings, so long as the entertainment is there'.

As Hanna Barbera went from strength to strength, producing cheaply made but viable cartoons, the company essentially revitalised the animation industry. This led to the creation of *The Flintstones* (ABC, 1960–6) as the first 'prime-time' cartoon, and with its playful take on established 'sitcoms' like *The Honeymooners* (CBS, 1955–6), created a model which has passed down into the contemporary era with shows like *The Simpsons*, *King of the Hill* (Fox, 1997–) and *Family Guy* (Fox, 1999–2002/2005–). Animation enabled these erstwhile sitcoms to become more surreal and subversive, prioritising fantastical and oneiric interpretations of everyday life, offering an ironic critique of the foibles and assumptions of middle-America. In Britain during this era, most companies had become commercial service providers for the fledgling ITV, and for the Saturday morning cartoons first shown in the USA.TVC (Television Cartoons), for example, made *The Beatles* (1965–9), a series preceding *Yellow Submarine* (Dunning, 1968), but capitalising on the British pop 'invasion' of the early 1960s. While studios like Halas and Batchelor did their share of service production, they also spoke to the reinvention of the cartoon within the British context by combining caricature, satire and sight-gags in the BBC-funded *Tales of Hoffnung* (1964), using the graphic puns of Gerard Hoffnung, which gently poked fun at classical music culture and the upper classes. Halas and Batchelor were also to innovate in the *Habatales* (Syndication, 1959) during the 1960s, simply through the

'Symphony Orchestra', one of the *Tales of Hoffnung*, sending up the culture of classical music, helped Halas and Batchelor reinvent the cartoon for British audiences in the 1960s

use of the chinagraph pencil in the simple designs for the *Foo Foo* (ITV, 1959–60) series.

Though shows like *The Jetsons* (ABC, 1962–87), *Jonny Quest* (ABC, 1964–5) and work by Gene Dietch at the reinvented Terrytoons had successfully innovated in the form, the commitment purely to a 'Saturday morning' market prompted an inevitable decline. *Scooby-Doo, Where Are You?* (CBS, 1969–76/ABC, 1976–91/WB, 2002–5) proved a major hit, though, and the enduring Filmation studio successfully adapted comic books, including *The Archies* (CBS, 1968–9), which spawned a hit single in 'Sugar, Sugar' in 1969, and reworked DC and Marvel Comics' superhero stories in series like *The Adventures of Superman* (Syndicated, 1952–8). Television's voracious demand for material, particularly in America, however, led to the escalation of imported productions; the creation of poorly conceived series, actually produced more cheaply abroad; and schedule fillers. The impact of Penny Charren's Action for Children's Television (ACT) lobby also had a considerable effect in changing the character of cartoons, making them less violent and more banal. Though many in retrospect claim affection for the plethora of 'pop group'-related cartoons like *Josie and the Pussy Cats* (CBS, 1970–1), *The Jackson Five* (ABC, 1971–3) and *The Osmonds* (ABC, 1972), it was clear that television cartoons had become formulaic and unappealing.

Ironically, only with the impact of a 1982 strike by animation screenwriters, producers and practitioners in protest against the amount of service work going overseas did the situation slightly improve. Filmation effectively saved the American animation industry for those working in television by breaking the monopoly of the broadcast networks, producing first-run shows, broadcast daily: the now fondly remembered *He-Man and the Masters of the Universe* (Syndication, 1983–4) and *She-Ra: Princess of Power* (Syndication, 1985–7). Such a model was later to be adopted with the development of niche cartoon stations in the global, multi-channel era. This also provided opportunities for independent production, with animated inserts constituting part of *Pee-Wee's Playhouse* (CBS, 1986–90), and the creator-driven material like *Mighty Mouse – The New Adventures* (CBS, 1987–9), produced by Ralph Bakshi, the legendary maker of the first recognised 'X'-rated feature cartoon, *Fritz the Cat* (1975), and Canadian director, John Kricfalusi, later the creator of the controversial *The Ren and Stimpy Show* (Nickelodeon, 1991–6) (see box). Ironically, as finance declined for mainstream commercial television production, the emergence of MTV in 1981 provided a new opportunity for animators to make promotional pop videos, and revive the long-standing cartoon tradition of animation illustrating songs. The Fleischer studios produced *Screen Songs* as early as 1929, which encouraged sing-alongs in theatres as an animated bouncing ball alighted on lyrics. The animated pop video also recalled the pop band cartoons of the 1970s, and in the work of, among others, Erica Russell, Zbigniew Rybczynski, Jim Blashfield, the Quay brothers and Aardman proved especially engaging as an expression of art sensibilities in a popular form.

In Britain, though, with the emergence of Channel 4 in the early 1980s, there began a halcyon era in animation production. Inspired commissioners and producers, Paul Madden and Clare Kitson, responding to the station's remit to reclaim the margins of culture, and speak to different models of cultural representation, invested in British animators, funding films by Nick Park, Joanna Quinn, Barry Purves, Alison Snowden and David Fine, the Quay twins, Candy Guard, David Anderson, Vera Neubauer and Phil Mulloy, among many more. These films proved groundbreaking and fully established British animation on the world stage at festivals, but more significantly, found a major domestic television audience. Most popular, were TVC's adaptations of Raymond Briggs' work, including the Christmas perennial, *The Snowman* (1982); *When the Wind Blows* (1986), a challenging story of two senior citizens, survivors of World Wars, who find their naive investment in the government's advice in the event of nuclear attack is painfully inadequate when such an attack actually occurs; and *Father Christmas* (1991), about a grumpy Santa Claus. At the same time, 'Animate!' was established by the late Dick Arnall, seeking to ensure that experimental animation would be produced, also for a television audience. Animate! has endured into the contemporary era, and has helped advance the careers of Chris Shepherd, Run Wrake and Ruth Lingford, as well as providing a platform to question the very definition of animation as a moving-image practice in the digital era.

The emergence of *The Simpsons*, first on *The Tracey Ullman Show* (Fox, 1987–90), and in a Christmas special, broadcast in 1989, returned animation to American prime time. In a direct challenge to the increasingly right-wing agenda of *The Cosby Show* (NBC, 1984–92), which it was scheduled against, *The Simpsons* championed a left-leaning liberal position, and presented the dysfunctional, blue-collar family as an intrinsically American family, which implicitly challenged established and accepted moral and political authority (see box). Working on multiple levels, *The Simpsons* has endured as an example of television programming which consistently 'takes the temperature' of American culture, pointing up the foibles and fantasies of a nation preoccupied with its own mythologies and political

TVC's adaptation of Raymond Briggs' *The Snowman* has become a Christmas institution on Channel 4, lyrically capturing the uninhibited spirit of a child's imagination

rhetoric. It was little wonder that Bart Simpson countered President George H. W. Bush's assertion that 'We need a nation closer to the Waltons than to the Simpsons' with the view that 'Hey, we're just like the Waltons. We're praying for an end to the Depression, too' (see Mills, 2004c, p. 181).

While the sitcoms that followed in the wake of *The Simpsons* met with mixed popularity and critical success – *South Park* (Comedy Central, 1997–) being an obvious exception in further radicalising subject matter for television broadcast – much work became increasingly self-reflexive about animation culture. Spielberg's *Tiny Toon Adventures* (Fox, 1990–4) and *Animaniacs* (Fox, 1993–8) harked back to Warner Bros. cartoons of the 1930s and 1940s; Kricfalusi's *The Ren and Stimpy Show* looked back to the work of Bob Clampett; *Johnny Bravo* (Cartoon Netwoork, 1997–2004) was deliberately stylised to be like a Hanna Barbera cartoon of the 1970s; while the Paul Dini-scripted, and Bruce Timm and Eric Radomski-created *Batman – The Animated Series* (Fox, 1992–5) referenced the Fleischer Bros. wartime *Superman* (Universal Studios,

TV Anime and Japanese Aesthetics

In the first instance, animation for television in Japan was
purely created as educational material. Otogi Pro's *Otogi
Manga Calendar* (*Otogi Manga Karendā*) (TBS), three-minute
vignettes on various topics, ran for 312 episodes between 1961
and 1964. In 1963, though, Mushi Productions, established by
the 'Disney of Japan', Osamu Tezuka, to produce animation
based on his own extremely popular 1950s' manga, made
Astro Boy (*Tetsuwan Atomu*) (Fuji TV, 1963–6), which proved
enduringly successful both in Japan, and when syndicated in
America. Four early series prefigure any number of reflexive
tensions which were to emerge as Japanese animation influenced the American cartoon, and vice versa. *Gigantor* (*Tetsujin
28-gō*) (Fiji TV, 1963–5), again based on a manga story, was
Japan's first giant robot cartoon, and proved to be the progen-
itor of many narratives engaging with the interface between
humankind and progressive technologies, sometimes in a
spirit of utopian achievement, more often in the tradition of
an apocalyptic imagination that characterised popular storytelling in post-Hiroshima Japan.

Sally, the Little Witch (*Mahōtsukai Sarī*) (TV Asahi, 1966–7)
was targeted primarily at a girls' market, and featured what was
later to become the staple of Hayao Miyazaki's feature films,
and many other shojo anime – the 'magical heroine' – whose
adolescent identity belies the power and affect of her powers
and, most notably, her ability to facilitate spiritual reconciliation in the communities she inhabits. *Speed Racer* (*Mach
GoGoGo*) (Fuji TV, 1966–8), made by Tatsuo Yoshida, founder
of Tatsunako Productions, was based on his 'Superman'-styled
designs which he had mastered in the Japanese manga version
of the American superhero's stories. It was later parodied by
the J. J. Sedelmaier studios in fond recollection of its popularity
in the USA. Finally, the first colour television animation in
Japan, Tezuka's *Kimba the White Lion* (*Janguru Taitei*) (Fuji TV,
1965–78), which has become extremely well known in the west
as part of a series of high-profile debates in which the Disney
studio were accused of plagiarising the series as the source for
their feature, *The Lion King* (1994). Though this was denied by
the studio and its artists, who argued that they had no knowledge of Tezuka's work, even though it had been regularly
broadcast in America, the parallels are too close to be mere
coincidence. These debates and the already established impact
of anime in the west, drew into relief the profound influence of
Japanese animation on American cartoon aesthetics in the contemporary era.

It had been long established that Japanese studios under-
took service work for American television – MOM

Productions, for example, making Rankin/Bass's 3D stop-
motion Christmas favourite, *Rudolph the Red Nosed Reindeer*
(1964) – but this relationship would eventually lead to a
hybrid production, *Battle of the Planets* (Syndicated, 1978–85)
which was a re-edit and adaptation of Tatsuo Yoshida's
Gatchaman series (Tatsunoko, 1972–4), made some six years
earlier. New material was added to reduce the violent and
indigenous aspects, and to echo characters from George
Lucas's all-conquering *Star Wars* (1977). This in itself had
been influenced by Japan's TV science-fictional output,
including Toei Doga's *Mazinger Z* (Fuji TV, 1972) and Leili
Matsumoto's *Space Battleship Yamato* (*Uchū Senkan Yamato*)
(Yomiuri TV, 1974–5), and in turn, *Star Wars* was to inform
Fujio Fujikpo's *Doraemon* (TV Asahi, 1979–) and Yoshiyuki
Tomino's *Mobile Suit Gundam* (*Kidō Senshi Gandamu*)

Akira, the 'breakthrough' anime, which effectively introduced
numerous forms of Japanese animation to western audiences,
was essentially a feature informed by science-fictional themes,
long the staple of imported TV shows like *Astro Boy* and
Gatchaman

(Animax, 1979–80). While inevitably American cartoon animation influenced a great deal of work across the world, for example, Bruno Bozzetto's *Mr Rossi* (1960–74) series in Italy, and in Australia, the Zagreb veteran, Zoran Janjic's series, *Arthur! and the Square Knights of the Round Table* (1966–8), American and Japanese animation continued to share a very particular call and response, which affected all aspects of animation production from art films and features to TV series.

Akira (1988) is acknowledged as a key breakthrough film in bringing anime fully to the attention of western audiences, and though its dystopic action-driven story characterises a great deal of spectacle-orientated anime features, it is the more character-centred series which became popular on television. *Macross* (Studio Nue, 1982–3) and *Dragon Ball* (*Doragonbōru*) (Studio Nue, 1984–95) were informed by science-fictional elements, and points of extended conflict, but their dramatic interest remained in the moral and ethical quandaries of the characters. Goku, the warrior martial artist in *Dragon Ball*, and its sequel *Dragon Ball Z* (Fuji TV, 1989–96) must collect

seven legendary orbs to be granted a wish from the Dragon God, and this quest narrative pits his allies against villains from his own and alternative worlds. The free play of many Japanese narratives with the juxtaposition of past and present, supernatural and material worlds, and demons and ordinary folk, often children, suggests an engagement with spiritual and ideological issues. *Macross* explores the very nature of what it is to be human in its story concerning the warlike giant Zentraedi, who does not understand notions of love – expressed through the songs of Chinese pop star, Lin Minmei – or friendship, when retrieving an errant aircraft from Earth.

The Toonami and Jetix cable strands focus on Japanese anime and anime-influenced shows, and anime storylines and aesthetics continue to influence American cartoons. This effectively ensures a continuing engagement with the preoccupations of youth cultures, an address of the impact and effect of technologies, and a vision of current trends and future worlds.

Paul Wells

1941–3) series, and the work of graphic artists, Will Eisner and Jack Kirby. Challenge to such traditional fare came in the guise of the first fully computer-generated television series for children, *ReBoot* (YTV, 1994–6). It was created by a British group of artists and animators known as 'The Hub': John Grace, Ian Pearson, Gavin Blair and Phil Mitchell. Its key achievement in the first instance was to produce each twenty-two-minute episode in a six- to eight-week period, challenging the limited capacity of computer animation at that time.

Inevitably, the rise of satellite and cable channels in the early 1990s saw the development of new programming strands that drew upon work made in the past, and encouraged new graphic design-led work, most notably, that of Genndy Tartakovsky and Craig McCracken, in *Samurai Jack* and *The Powerpuff Girls* (Cartoon Network, 1998–2004). From 'Cartoon Network', to 'Boomerang', to 'Toonami' to 'Nick Jnr', animation has flourished, and is increasingly recognised as an extraordinarily versatile medium that remains responsive to the needs of contemporary television and its ever-increasing global audience. If television animation from the USA has grown – even if actually made by service providers in Korea and India – then television animation in Britain has become parochial. While preoccupied with personal embarrassment during the 1990s in 'Britain's answer to *The Simpsons*' – sitcoms like Candy Guard's *Pond Life* (C4, 1998–2000), Sarah Kennedy's *Crapston Villas* (C4, 1994–7) and Snowden and Fine's *Bob and Margaret* (C4,

1998–2001) – the noughties have seen a much more anti-establishment approach to adult animation. Jon Link and Mick Bunnage, following on from the dark satire of Baby Cow's *I Am Not An Animal* (BBC, 2004) and the BBC's *Monkey Dust* (2003–5), privilege vignette-led, character-based humour, in *Modern Toss* (C4, 2006), produced with limited animation and challenging in its 'bad taste' comedy. Crucially, though, this is not insobriety for its own sake, but a well-observed take on British social types, and satiric, rather than subversive in nature.

I Am Not An Animal was Baby Cow Animation's attempt to create animation for adults in the tradition of British satire and caricature

Having survived and developed over fifty years, television animation has developed its own subgenres, and transcended its seeming limitations in economy and market restrictions. Many series and programmes have stood the test of time, and are now recognised as distinctive, aesthetically progressive and socially relevant, often offering incisive critique of political and arts cultures.

Paul Wells

RECOMMENDED READING

Furniss, M. (1998), *Art in Motion: Animation Aesthetics*, Sydney: John Libbey.

Pilling, J. (1997), *A Reader in Animation Studies*, Sydney: John Libbey.

Wells, P. (1998), *Understanding Animation*, London and New York: Routledge.

Children's Cartoons

Cartoons have played an intrinsic role in children's television programming on both sides of the Atlantic, and have become a significant aspect of its overall economy and profile. Since the early 1950s, the three dominant networks in the USA, ABC, CBS and NBC, have competed for the children's audience predominantly through the culture of cartoons. In Britain, the dominance of the BBC provided a platform for animated children's programming, most obviously in its *Watch with Mother* (BBC, 1950–80) and teatime strands, until the emergence of ITV in 1955 provided the context for both regular cartoon series and animated commercials. The political economy of broadcasters and the aesthetic and thematic outcomes of cartoons are profoundly interrelated, and much that has been achieved in the television field has been about the buoyancy of the marketplace as much as the talents of the animation studios.

Faced with budgets one-twentieth of the amount used to produce a six-minute *Tom and Jerry* (1940–57) in the MGM studio era, Hanna Barbera reconfigured the cartoon for television in the USA. After the initial effort of *The Ruff and Reddy Show* (NBC, 1957–60), *The Huckleberry Hound Show* debuted in 1958 and featured Huckleberry, Pixie and Dixie and Yogi Bear, some of Hanna Barbera's most enduring characters (see above). This type of 'reduced' or 'planned' animation necessarily prioritised its scripts, sacrificing any complex motion in the imagery to repeated cycles of movement and simple design strategies. Dialogue was more important than the visual elements, and the producers thus sought to create popular catchphrases – 'I'm

smarter than the average bear' (Yogi Bear), 'I hate meeses to pieces' (Jinx the Cat) and so on – and focus on distinctive vocal idioms in performance that supported the verbal interplay between characters.

Voice artists like Daws Butler, Don Messick, June Foray and Mel Blanc were, in effect, the real stars of the shows. Children and adults clearly embraced this simplicity; its reward, ironically, the creation of *The Flintstones* for prime-time broadcast. The Hanna Barbera series, from *The Huckleberry Hound Show* to *Scooby-Doo, Where Are You?*, have proved, however, to be the high point of early TV animation, and the standard overall plummeted dramatically to the point that by the late 1960s the Action for Children's Television committee, led by Penny Charren, actively campaigned for better cartoons.

Significantly, in the British context, the 'cartoon' has not taken precedence, and its animation aesthetic has been much more informed by the three-dimensional puppet films of figures like Bura and Hardwick (*Trumpton* (BBC, 1967), *Chigley* (BBC, 1969), *Camberwick Green* (BBC, 1966)), Oliver Postgate (*Bagpuss* (BBC, 1974), *The Clangers* (BBC, 1969–74), *Ivor the Engine* (ITV, 1975–7)) and Ivor Wood (*The Herbs* (BBC, 1968), *Postman Pat* (BBC, 1981–), *Paddington Bear* (BBC, 1975)). Rather than embrace the 'gag' and 'chase' orientation of the American cartoon tradition, and its self-reflexive relationship to television and popular culture (still readily evidenced in *The Simpsons* and its imitators), British animation opted to create parochial, community-oriented vehicles that foreground benign paternalism, eccentric heroes, domesticised heroines and consensual modes of living. This kind of animation is grounded in more realist codes, and draws upon shared knowledge and nostalgic mythologies about 'localness', 'middle-England pastoralism' and 'ritual'. Whereas the American television cartoon paled against the graphic freedoms of its 'golden era' antecedents at Disney, Warner Bros. and MGM, British animation drew upon its literary and artisanal arts traditions to create a distinctive kind of 'cartoon'; one that explored the foibles and follies of character and situation rather than the open vocabulary of the cartoon idiom.

In the contemporary era, the overall boom in the production of animated feature films and quasi-sitcoms, and the emergence of niche children's channels and dedicated broadcast outlets like the Cartoon Network, has necessitated a reevaluation of the place of cartoons and animated films in aesthetic and commercial terms. The emergence of Nickelodeon, the Disney Channel and the Fox network competing head-to-head against the majors in the children's market significantly reduced licence fees

Cartoon Controversies

Cartoons in the television era have often been subject to criticism, complaint and censorship. The Broadcasting Standards and Practices (BS&P) departments, drawing from the 1952 TV Code of Standards of the National Association of Radio and Television Broadcasters, have been the main arbiters of broadcast material in the USA. Advocacy groups such as the National Coalition on Television Violence and the National Federation for Decency, as well as sponsors and advertising agencies, have also been vigilant in monitoring graphic freedoms in animation, because of its assumed children's audience. The threat of 'anarchy' in the cartoon remains the enduring legacy of the studio era. Shorts produced for cinema exhibition, for example, were often recut for television, excising any contentious race representation, sexually provocative movement, scenes of excessive drinking or smoking, or unorthodox behaviour that might encourage imitation. Walter Lantz syndicated fifty-two theatrical cartoons to television and was required to cut twenty-five sequences.

Beavis and Butthead: adult animation with few limits

Animators were fully aware of the constraints placed upon them by the medium within which they now worked, and practised self-censorship that was only further modified in the instance of justifiable complaint. Jay Ward's deliberately playful *Rocky and His Friends* (NBC, 1959–73) challenged these boundaries, however, with satirical subject matter and 'smuggled' impropriety that attempted to provoke the censor. *Mighty Mouse: The New Adventures* (CBS, 1987–8) cartoons of the late 1980s, directed by Ralph Bakshi, also became a cause célèbre, when the Reverend Wildmon of the American Family Association alleged that one episode, 'The Littlest Tramp' (1989), depicted drug abuse (the act of inhaling cocaine), though to more innocent eyes this may look like the sniffing of a crushed flower. This event did irreparable damage to the series, for in spite of the fact that the offending three and a half seconds were removed and, somewhat ironically, the series won an award from another parent watchdog group, the Action for Children's Television (ACT) body, *Mighty Mouse: The New Adventures* were cancelled. Later, in 1995, *2 Stupid Dogs* (TBS, 1993–5) was subject to a small cut when a voice artist sought to include the word 'fuck' in a gabbled monologue.

Significantly, however, in the contemporary era, *The Simpsons, Beavis and Butthead* (NBC, 1993–7), *The Ren and Stimpy Show* and *South Park*, in uniformly challenging the consensual apparatus of institutional and utilitarian perspectives, have tested the arbitrariness of the BS&P guidelines. In relaxing some areas of what may be addressed and represented, the BS&P departments have responded to changes in contemporary attitudes without sacrificing their responsibility. As recent Independent Television Commission studies in Britain have demonstrated, children are far more tele-literate and discriminating about the intended effects of cartoons than

The Simpsons: a dysfunctional American family

they have often been given credit for, and recognise the difference, for example, between that which frightens them in an exciting and pleasurable way, and that which intimidates and alienates them. Further (and this is also supported by a number of American studies), children see the artifice and excess of cartoon language in a way that enables them to distinguish between the harmlessness of *Tom and Jerry*'s slapstick violence and the harmfulness of everyday brutalities in real life.

Paul Wells

and production budgets for new work. Further, this necessitated new pre-sales and distribution agreements for animation houses worldwide. This has created an eclectic mix on all broadcast channels of 'classic' cartoons from the 1930s to the 1950s, previous 'home-produced' television animation, imported series from other countries (most notably Japan (see box)), but increasingly Britain has a foothold in overseas markets with programmes like *Make Way for Noddy* (PBS, 2002–), *Maisie* (Cartoon Network, 2001–) and *Bob the Builder* (BBC, 1999–), and new work produced in recent times on much reduced investment.

The Hanna Barbera back catalogue and a range of Warner Bros. *Looney Tunes* and *Merrie Melodies* have found their place on the Cartoon Network, seeking its original audience of 'baby boomers' and, now, their children. Original series like *Jonny Quest* have been updated as *The Real Adventures of Jonny Quest* (Cartoon Network, 1996–7) in order to accommodate computer-generated animation and 'modernise' the science-fictional premise of the series. A fully computer-generated series, *Roughnecks: Starship Troopers* (Syndication, 1999), contemporises this aesthetic further, echoing the graphic space and violent confrontational thematics of many computer games and their virtual environments. The often neglected *ReBoot*, made in the USA by British artists, was a pioneer in this area by setting its narrative within a computer environment, aping Disney's feature film *Tron* (Lisberger, 1982). The popularity of mainstream Japanese feature anime is reflected in the presence of Pokémon, Digimon and Dragonball Z in the schedules, and may be traced in many elements of contemporary American cartoons. Ironically, many 'American' cartoons have often been made in Japanese production houses.

The popularity of these cartoons is well evidenced, and still speaks to the view that the graphic freedoms available in animated film are still profoundly innovative, even when potentially compromised by the production context. The 'cartoon' can facilitate the depiction of seemingly impossible actions, extraordinary metamorphoses, narrative acts of condensation (the maximum degree of suggestion and association in the minimum amount of imagery) and modes of caricature that offer insight, clarity and amusement in relation to complex ideas. This is self-evidently appreciated, but perhaps only partially understood, by the children and adults alike who embrace the form. Its very language, and its capacity to change with the sociocultural and economic conditions of its production, assures its longevity and continuity.

Paul Wells

RECOMMENDED READING

Peary, D. and Peary, G. (eds) (1980), *The American Animated Cartoon*, New York: E. P. Dutton.

Pilling, J. (ed.) (1997), *A Reader in Animation Studies*, London: John Libbey.

Wells, P. (1998), *Understanding Animation*, London and New York: Routledge.

Adult Animation

The importance of design, voice and music mark animated programmes' difference from the dominant conventions of mainstream cinema and television, eschewing the whole notion of 'realism' and embracing zany activities to keep the wandering attention of child audiences (see above). Yet animation has also aimed at adult audiences, and in the 1990s there was a proliferation of successful television cartoons aimed more at adults, or at least aimed less specifically at children.

The predominant form of animation has been drawn and painted. This is called cel animation, as originally an outline was inked on to a sheet of acetate, or cel, and then painted by hand. Thousands of these cels made up a cartoon, photographed painstakingly one by one in succession to give the impression of motion. Another form of animation that is noteworthy is clay animation, where models are constructed of clay or Plasticine and moved very gradually as successive frames of film are exposed. Both of these processes are most laborious. More recently, the use of computers has entered the field of animation. Although it is responsible for the kind of CGI (computer-generated imagery) that graces live-action films, computers have

Adult Swim

Early in 2001, Cartoon Network premiered its spin-off delivery, *Adult Swim*, creating an 'adults only' strand of animation broadcasting, which was predicated on the core concept of 'all kids out of the pool'. Now a global phenomenon, and characterised by a range of cross-platform deliveries, *Adult Swim* has become extraordinarily successful, and proof of the attraction of animated programming to mature audiences worldwide. Essentially, *Adult Swim* programmes, including *Aqua Teen Hunger Force* (2000–), *Robot Chicken* (2005–), *Harvey Birdman, Attorney at Law* (2000–7), *Squidbillies* (2005–), *Metalocalypse* (2006–) and *Minoriteam* (2005–6), all exploit the surreal and subversive opportunities afforded by the freedoms of the animated form, and speak directly to the more taboo aspects of adult culture. Often made by, and appealing to a 'baby-boomer' generation, or driven by new post-MTV creator-led visions, such cartoons are less predicated on sophisticated animation, and more on crude aesthetics. It is also true, though, that such programming seeks to affiliate itself not merely to the limitations of the form defined by the 1970s 'Saturday Morning Cartoon', but also to the dynamic idioms of popular comic books and politically charged underground graphic narratives.

Though *Aqua Teen Hunger Force* – featuring the adventures of a trio of fast-food items living in New Jersey – is *Adult Swim*'s longest-running show, it is the Emmy Award-winning 3D stop-motion show *Robot Chicken* that has garnered most plaudits. Created by Seth Green and Matthew Senreich, *Robot Chicken* is a sketch show parodying popular cultural forms, celebrities and artefacts, using material corruptions of well-known toys and action figures. Senreich himself worked with Wizard Entertainment on various toy-lines, and many initially were created as merchandising for cartoon shows. Here they are effectively 'recycled' and recontextualised – superheroes living together in everyday house-sharing conditions; religious figures recast as samurai; characters created for children's stories effectively living adult lives. The character Optimus Prime from *The Transformers* (Syndication, 1984–7) series, for example, plays out a narrative ultimately advising audiences to get checked out for prostate cancer.

Though many of the programmes in the *Adult Swim* strand are not overtly political, their alternative perspectives inevitably mount a critique of the contradictions and hypocrisies in American culture. Particular targets are fundamentalist extremists, self-righteous educators and the spin-strategies of the commercial sector. Inevitably, sex and violence feature regularly in many of the series, and references to drug culture proliferate, but the core focus of the humour is the incongruity between the original meaning and intention of iconic character-types and situations, and the ways in which this is altered, repositioned, or played out on more literal terms and conditions. Of particular interest in this respect is *Minoriteam*, which does have an explicit ideological agenda. The show features five superheroes who are each based on a racial or ethnic stereotype, battling against villains who essentially embody issues of racism or discrimination.

Fully coloured, *Minoriteam* pays particular homage to the comic-book aesthetics of Jack Kirby, and the *Marvel Superheroes Show* (Syndication, 1966). In the figures of paraplegic Chinese laundryman, the Fu-Manchu-like Dr Wang; Mexican oil baron-cum-leafblower wielding, El Jefe; turbo-charged, pot-bellied, sexual predator, African-American, Fasto; part Jewish mailman, part volcano, Jewcano; and Non-Stop, the bullet-proof, Indian corner-shop owner, deeply embedded tensions between the everyday realities of racism and the rhetorics of political correctness are addressed.

At one level, this follows on from graphic work by Alan Moore (*The Watchmen* (DC Comics, 1986–7)) and Frank Miller (*The Dark Knight Returns* (DC Comics, 1986)) in presenting superheroes in crisis, trapped by the disparity between their personal identity and their expected social role. Or in Brad Bird's *The Incredibles* (2004), where superheroes are forced to repress their superpowers to lead normal suburban lives, before once again finding socially acceptable heroic purpose. At another level, *Minoriteam* is sending up white, left-leaning liberals, and the rhetorics of corporate elites, but is actually searching for more innocent times when superheroes were less preoccupied with themselves. *Minoriteam*'s main nemeses are the Dick Cheney-esque *The White Shadow* (CBS, 1978–81), a Powerpoint-mad bureaucrat, fearful of nothing but the Inland Revenue Service; 'Standardised Test', an eraser-headed robot, champion of white-biased school testing; and 'Racist Frankenstein', despiser of black-coloured objects.

Crucially, then, *Minoriteam* in using 1970s' naivety to bypass individualised late millennial angst, actually returns to an engagement with insidious kinds of social evil and injustice, rather than the neuroses of identity. Instead of fighting egocentricity or megalomania, these superheroes expose pointless bureaucracy, economic disparity and disadvantage, and the contradictions of sexual and cultural politics informing everyday relationships. As becomes clear, in many instances, the supposedly innocent language of animation is used for subversive and socially challenging effects.

Paul Wells

aided the production process for traditional animation, allowing faster working through computerised camera movement and coordination.

What often is referred to as the classic period of animation took place under the Hollywood studio system (Wells, 1998, p. 208), and was led by such inspired animators as Chuck Jones and Tex Avery, and cartoon characters such as Bugs Bunny, Mickey Mouse and Road Runner. Until the 1960s, short animated comedies or cartoons were fillers on a cinema schedule that would have included a number of items. Cartoons such as those produced by Disney and Max Fleischer's *Betty Boop* (1930) were produced to fill cinema schedules yet had a far longer shelf life than expected. *Betty Boop* also included some very risqué moments. When cartoons were simply part of the cinema bill, there was a need to engage adults as well as children, but with the wholesale move of the television cartoon in the early 1960s, they aimed more directly at children. As the decade of the 1960s started, television began to require so much in the way of cartoons that more were made expressly for the small

The Fleischer brothers' Betty Boop, though made famous in her 1930s' cartoons, found a renewed career in television in less sexually provocative shorts, and as part of the multi-channel delivery recycling 'golden era' animation

screen as the demand from the large screen waned with changing patterns of film exhibition. However, the quality of animation dropped as more programmes were made, at a faster rate and more cheaply than had previously been the case.

William Hanna and Joseph Barbera were paramount to developments in comedy animation on television during the 1960s and 1970s (Erickson, 1995, p. 22 – see 'Children's Cartoons'). Some of their shows recast adult live-action television programmes for children, such as the very successful *Top Cat* (ABC, 1961–2), known as *Boss Cat* in the UK to avoid connection with a branded pet food, which was loosely based on the characters in *The Phil Silvers Show* (CBS, 1955–9). Hanna Barbera dominated the market for children's cartoons, producing only isolated adult fare. One show was *Wait Till Your Father Gets Home* (Syndication, 1972–4), which was similar to *All in the Family* (CBS, 1971–9) (see 'Situation Comedy'). It centred on Harry, wife Irma and their children, college drop-out Chet, overweight sixteen-year-old Alice and nine-year-old hustler Jamie. Adult cartoons seem to return perennially to the theme of family strife, and ultimate unity. Indeed, it is easy to see a direct line of descent from *The Flintstones* and *The Jetsons*, through *Wait Till Your Father Gets Home* to *The Simpsons* (see box) and *Family Guy*.

In the 1990s, a greater number of cartoons have aimed at a more adult market, sometimes through appealing to the juvenile in adults. MTV produced animation such as Mike Judge's *Beavis and Butthead*. It saw successful spin-offs in *King of the Hill* and *Daria* (MTV, 1997–2002), both of which lost the cruder edge of the original, through a focus on middle-aged men and young women respectively in place of juvenile males. *Beavis and Butthead* evolved from a short animation on MTV's seminal weekly 'Liquid Television' slot in the early 1990s. This programme showcased animation with no limits and primarily courted an adult audience. Later MTV animation included such cult successes as *The Head* (1996) and *Celebrity Death Match* (1998–). The latter evinced a cruel sense of humour, pitting clay models of well-known stars against each other in an arena, in a no-holds-barred fight to the death.

As this illustrates, sex and violence were often on the agenda in animations in the 1990s. *The Ren and Stimpy Show* reinvigorated the classical style of crazy cartooning, and both *The Simpsons* and *South Park* broke new ground for television cartoons. British animation has never attained the success or volume of production of American products, although it has produced international successes such as the Wallace and Gromit short clay-animation films: *A Grand Day Out* (BBC, 1992), *The Wrong Trousers* (BBC,

The Simpsons and South Park

The Simpsons (Fox, 1989–) and *South Park* (Comedy Central, 1997–) inaugurated a new phenomenon, seeming in essence to be children's cartoons although they were aimed more at adults, and both exhibiting witty storylines imbued with massive amounts of popular culture references. *The Simpsons* was a groundbreaking cartoon series. One of its great strengths was that it worked on two levels: on one it was a comic 'sitcom' about a family, while on the other it was a riot of popular culture references and self-reflexivity. It was created by Matt Groening (born 1954), and first appeared as a regular small animated section in *The Tracey Ullman Show*. The series debuted in 1989, and got massive ratings. It was shown on prime time by the Fox network, becoming the first animated prime-time series in twenty years. In the UK, *The Simpsons* was central to the expansion of BSkyB satellite television, which retained it and only later allowed it on to national terrestrial television, where it found a home on the BBC. In the UK it was nurtured for an audience that included younger children, hence the significant number of more 'adult' moments edited out of British broadcasts of the show by both the BBC and Sky.

The Simpsons was premised upon a number of seemingly universal attractions, based on a dysfunctional family, that made it popular with diverse audiences. The father, Homer, is selfish and ignorant, while mother Marge holds the family together. Son Bart, like his father, is none too intelligent, having trouble at school and being destructive in the home. Daughter Lisa functions as the social conscience of the family and is mentally gifted, although her parents rarely recognise this. The final member of this nuclear family is Maggie, the baby. Examples of shows include 'Natural Born Kissers', where Marge and Homer's love life is reinvigorated by dangerous situations, while Bart and Lisa discover the alternative ending of Casablanca when using a metal detector. In 'Rosebud', parodying *Citizen Kane* (Welles, 1941), Mr Burns wants to find his childhood teddy bear, which now belongs to Maggie Simpson. The show's satire has included mutated fish caused by a nuclear power plant, corrupt politicians and media manipulation. Added to this is the propensity for rapid-fire cultural references and intertextuality, including appearances by media mogul Rupert Murdoch (the owner of Fox network), Mulder and Scully from *The X-Files* (Fox, 1993–2002). *The Simpsons* broke new ground for animated television shows, opening the way for *South Park* and *King of the Hill*. Its place at the centre of American popular culture was underlined when, in the 1992 election campaign, George Bush declared: 'We're going to

South Park dealt with adult and controversial themes

keep on trying to strengthen the American family. To make them more like the Waltons and less like the Simpsons' (see Mills, 2004c).

South Park appeared on television to voices raised in protest by moral guardians everywhere. For parents with young children, it represented a threat in that it was about young children, looked like a cartoon for young children, yet dealt with adult and controversial themes such as sex, Charles Manson, murder and suicide: material clearly for an older audience. The show's originators, Trey Parker and Matt Stone, created *South Park* to look like the most primitive cartoon possible, with very simple character design, which proved particularly suited to being made into tied-in products like stuffed toys.

The show's protagonists are a group of third-grade children who live in a small Colorado town called South Park. They are Stan, Kyle (the Jewish one), Cartman (the fat one) and Kenny (the poor one). Although Stan and Kyle are the 'best friends' at the centre of many of the stories, the other two proved more popular with audiences. Whereas Kenny always wears a coat with the hood up so that his dialogue is muffled, the obese and anti-social Eric Cartman proved very popular with children, to their parents' chagrin. Apart from basic and crude humour, the programme was very stylised. In each episode, for example, Kenny has to die in some way or another, prompting a repartee between Kyle and Stan: 'Oh my God, they killed Kenny!'; 'You bastards!' Satire was more evident in other *South Park* characterisation. The children's accomplice on many of their adventures is 'Chef', voiced by soul singer Isaac Hayes, who serves them dinner at school. School, and authority more generally, is represented in rather negative terms. The children's neurotic teacher, Mr Garrison, is always accompanied by and speaks with a vent glove puppet called 'Mr Hat'.

An example of the unpredictable trajectory of an episode is 'Pinkeye', where Russian space station Mir falls to earth, landing on Kenny's head. He dies but returns as a zombie, as the town is overwhelmed by zombies straight out of George Romero's film *Night of the Living Dead* (1968). At the conclusion, Chef sings Michael Jackson's 'Thriller' in a parody of the pop video. The show has a fine sense of popular culture references, as well as (usually spurious) celebrity cameos in unusual situations. Actual guests included George Clooney (voicing a dog), Jennifer Aniston, the band Korn and Elton John, and other celebrities have been crudely fabricated, including Streisand, Celine Dion and Saddam Hussein, not to mention Jesus, who regularly appears with his own television talk show.

However, *South Park*'s roster of guests fades into insignificance in comparison with that of *The Simpsons*.

Their show has included comedians Bob Hope and Ricky Gervais (who has even written his own episode), singer Tom Jones, scientists Stephen Jay Gould and Stephen Hawking, artist Jasper Johns, basketball player Magic Johnson, and musicians such as Ringo Starr and Sting voiced by the stars themselves. A principal attraction of both *The Simpsons* and *South Park* is that they allow a kind of regression to childhood for their adult viewers. This is stronger in the case of *South Park*, where there is additional perverse enjoyment of the child characters' precociousness as well as their misunderstanding of the adult world. Although *The Simpsons* has become one of the most popular television cartoons ever, *South Park* has managed to gain more notoriety for its bad taste, often bordering on the insulting, although its success did lead to the production of a feature film, *South Park: Bigger, Longer & Uncut* in 1999.

K. J. Donnelly

1993) and *A Close Shave* (BBC, 1995). Similarly, Japanese cartoon animation, anime, was very popular in the Far East and by the mid-1980s started to appear on western screens, although it ended up becoming a cult rather than a mainstream item (Erickson, 1995, p. 36, and box above).

Since the mid-1980s, animation has almost all been contracted out to Asiatic studios, not only because of their expertise but also because of their cheap labour costs. European art-animation, such as three-dimensional work by Jan Svankmajer (*The Death of Stalinism in Bohemia* (*Konec stalinismu v Čechách*) 1990) and the Quay brothers (*The Street of Crocodiles*, 1986), received great acclaim. Art-animation never reached the degree of international impact exhibited by series like Fox's *The Simpsons*, for

example, which was the first cartoon scheduled on US prime time for decades. The Cartoon Network was launched in the USA in 1992 and, despite commissioning the production of new cartoons, still relies heavily on reruns of the massive volume of cartoons from the past.

K. J. Donnelly

RECOMMENDED READING

Erickson, Hal (1995), *Television Cartoon Shows: An Illustrated Encyclopedia, 1949–1993*, Jefferson: McFarland.

Lenburg, Jeff (1981), *The Encyclopedia of Animated Cartoons*, New York: Da Capo.

Wells, Paul (1998), *Understanding Animation*, London: Routledge.

POPULAR ENTERTAINMENT

The Populist Debate

'Popular entertainment' could be judged as a misleading title, in the sense that it might suggest that other TV genres are neither 'popular' nor 'entertaining'. This is clearly not the case. Soap opera, for example, is probably one of the most consistently popular forms of television entertainment the medium has yet to produce, and comedy is almost always based (at least, in the first instance) on its ability to entertain its audience and make it laugh. However, for the purpose of clarity and organisation alone (and not, we hope, any hierarchical undercurrent), the title seems to suit a number of different and assorted genres individually addressed here under this rather broad but useful umbrella heading. It could be argued that included here are a variety of different (and perhaps even miscellaneous) programmes that can be seen as sharing a number of inherent forms and characteristics – not least, their tendency to be downgraded and despised by critics for their unashamedly populist and frequently commercial aspirations.

At its most basic level, television is a scientifically managed institution for the mass production of entertainment, a bureaucratically organised regime of pleasure that systematically produces permutations of the everyday and the spectacular. These permutations are designed to capture audiences and deliver them to advertisers, in the case of commercial networks, or government, in the case of public stations. Genres combine the memorandum and the commodity; one ensures standardisation, the other marketability. They also provide benchmarks for aesthetic taste and pedagogic direction.

The populist debate revolves around the question of pleasure and consumption. In particular, it centres on the issue of whether some forms of 'popular entertainment' purely pander to an audience's 'baser' tastes and desires (simply designed to keep advertisers happy); or whether programmes such as the quiz or talk show can actually provide audiences with more than simply 'standardised' and 'formulaic' fare. Central to this debate is the issue of whether television viewers are primarily 'passive' or 'active' in their viewing habits. Whether they passively accept television's commercial imperatives or whether they actively produce meaning and resistance in their complex production of pleasure and entertainment (also see 'Soap Operas and their Audiences'). Because certain programmes are judged to be inherently 'formulaic' or driven by mass desires (for instance, the consumerist imperative of the quiz show), particular genres face the wrath of public and critical scorn more than others. As a result, 'popular entertainment' on the small screen quickly came to the attention of politicians, academics and influential pressure groups, all eager to promote their particular ideological crusade.

One hundred and fifty years ago, it was taken as read that audiences were active, given their unruly and overtly engaged conduct at cultural events. But the emergence of public education in the west in the nineteenth century, allied to the disciplines of literary criticism and psychology, shifted critical rhetoric about audiences (Butsch, 2000, p. 3). Since the advent of the mass media, especially television, much energy has been devoted to evaluating the active versus passive sides to media audiences. Television programmes are 'symbols for time' (Hartley, 1987, p. 133), and the alleged misuse of time has become integral to the desire to police everyday television-watching. Various critics have in turn defended audiences against these charges of inactivity, arguing that 'the people' engage in resistive readings of TV programmes that reference viewers' social struggles rather than adhering to television producers' preferred responses.

Widespread anxiety is expressed by social critics about the supposed lack of 'active choice' in watching television (Carson, 1983). This concern dates back a long way: the modernist American architect Frank Lloyd Wright called TV '[c]hewing gum for the eyes' (quoted in Kellner, 1990, p. 1). Today, communitarian philosophy and sociology rail against rampant individualism, secular selfishness and the absence of civic responsibility. An allegedly active public is contrasted with a putatively inactive TV audience (Bellah et al., 1992, p. 49):

> we are not happy when we are watching television, even
> though most of us spend many hours a week doing so,
> because we feel we are 'on hold' rather than really living
> during that time. We are happiest when we are success-
> fully meeting challenges at work, in our private lives, and
> in our communities.

Hence the link to panics about education, violence and apathy supposedly engendered by (popular) television and routinely investigated by the state, psychology, Marxism, neo-conservatism, the Church, liberal feminism and others. The audience as consumer, student, felon, voter and idiot engages such groups. Sometimes the criticisms are about particular genres, TV wrestling is degrading, info-tainment is commercial, and talk shows trivialise current affairs; in contrast, 'real' sport binds the nation and 'real' journalism informs the electorate. Sometimes the criti-cisms are about TV as a genre (its audiovisual form makes it inappropriate for education or its commercialism/sta-tism scar its democratic potential).

These anxieties have in turn drawn critique. In the 1960s, Harold Garfinkel (1992) developed the notion of the 'cultural dope', a mythic figure 'who produces the stable features of the society by acting in compliance with pre-established and legitimate alternatives of action that the common culture provides'. The 'common-sense rationali-ties … of here and now situations' used by ordinary people are obscured by this condescending categorisation (p. 68). When the audience is invoked as a category by the indus-try, critics and regulators, it becomes such a 'dope'. This is often a gendered invocation, as Michèle Mattelart (1986, p. 65) explains:

> in the everyday time of domestic life … the fundamental
> discrimination of sex roles is expressed. … The hierarchy
> of values finds expression through the positive value
> attached to masculine time (defined by action, change
> and history) and the negative value attached to feminine
> time which, for all its potential richness, is implicitly dis-
> criminated against in our society, interiorised and lived
> through as the time of banal everyday life, repetition and
> monotony.

Quiz and talk shows are deemed inferior because they are associated (contradictorily) with both passivity and high emotion. These criticisms have supporters on both left and right, across both the social sciences and the humanities, and such denunciations continue to flourish.

The active-audience tradition picks up on Garfinkel's cultural-dope insight. Instead of issuing jeremiads, it claims that audiences are so clever and able that they outwit the institutions of the state, academia and capital-ism that seek to control and measure them and their inter-pretations. In one sense, this position has a venerable tradition, via literary theorists like old Nazism man Hans Robert Jauss's (1982) aesthetics of reception and old Marxism man Jean-Paul Sartre's (1990) philosophy of the

mutual intrication of writer and reader in making meaning (Mattelart and Mattelart, 1998, pp. 119–20, 123). In com-munications and culture, especially television, the idea really spread with Umberto Eco's mid-1960s' development (published in English in 1972) of a notion of open texts and processes of encoding–decoding. This was picked up by sociologists Frank Parkin (1971) then Stuart Hall (1973) on the left, and on the right by uses-and-gratifications functionalist Elihu Katz (1990). It is often associated today in television studies with John Fiske (1987b).

This counter-critique attacks criticisms of television for failing to allot the people's machine its due as a populist apparatus that subverts patriarchy, capitalism and other forms of oppression (or diminishes the tension of social divisions, depending on your politics). Popular TV is held to be subversive/relieving because, almost regardless of content, its output is decoded by audiences in keeping with their own social situation (Seiter, 1999). The active audi-ence is said to be weak at the level of cultural production, but strong as an interpretative community. Consider the special skills of cultish fans. They construct parasocial or imagined connections to celebrities or actants, who fulfil friendship functions or serve as spaces for projecting and evaluating schemas that make sense of human interaction. In addition to adoring the text, cult audiences domesticate the characters, removing them from the overall story and quoting their escapades and proclivities as if they were part of the fan's world, a world opened up to other followers through quizzes and rankings. References to favourite episodes, the behaviour of actants, or the qualities of stars, catalyse memories. Sequences and tendencies are disarticu-lated from screen time, reshaped and redisposed to con-trast with one's own social circumstances (Leets, de Becker and Giles, 1995, pp. 102–4; Harrington and Bielby, 1995, pp. 102–4, 110; Eco, 1987, p. 198). In addition, the despised genres listed earlier are recuperated: wrestling (see 'Sport', p. 170) becomes carnivalesque, infotainment legitimises the pleasures of shopping and talk shows address hitherto suppressed topics of public debate.

Meaghan Morris (1990) glosses, enacts and criticises the active-audience tradition in her account of I Love Lucy (CBS, 1951–7) as seen on 1950s' Australian television. This isolated image of women evading patriarchal control had dramatic effects on the Morris household – mother and daughter revelled while father absented himself. But the programme was also a sign of political economy and diplo-macy: it represented a resiting of Australian geopolitical culture away from Britain and towards the United States (pp. 15–16). This captures the duality of television as a cap-italist and governmental technology that is also populist. It follows that the idea of this apparatus as a sign of freedom is an ambivalent fable for cultural democracy. Popular TV is certainly amenable to a notion of localism, resistance and feminism working via the 'subversive pleasure of the female spectators' to produce an active engagement with both the text and the family. But this can become a critic's alibi for social speculation. Our suspicions should be aroused when academic theory cites 'the people' as demotic supports for its own preoccupations, because when 'the people' become one more text to be read and interpreted, they stand for the critic's own practice of reading. Far from being sources of information, 'the people' have been transmogrified into delegates that endow the critic's own account with a populist ring (Morris, 1990, pp. 21–3). Aberrant decoding by fans becomes a means of making the output of the culture industries isomorphic with a professor's anti-capitalist, anti-patriarchal, anti-racist politics.

Today, this active-audience position may be the most visible aspect of television studies. Virginia Postrel wrote a 1999 op-ed piece for the right-wing US financial newspaper the *Wall Street Journal* welcoming active-audience research, describing it as 'deeply threatening to traditional leftist views of commerce' because notions of active media consumption by fans were so close to the sovereign consumer beloved of the right: 'The cultural-studies mavens are betraying the leftist cause, lending support to the corporate enemy and even training graduate students who wind up doing market research.' Todd Gitlin (1997, p. 32) argues that some sectors of cultural studies are indeed in synch with neo-classical economics and the right: 'What the group wants, buys, demands is ipso facto the voice of the people. Supply has meshed with demand.' As Herbert I. Schiller puts it (1989, pp. 147–8, 153), the direct opposition that is frequently drawn between political economy (production matters) and active-audience theory (interpretation matters) assumes that the fragmentation of audience niches and responses nullifies the concentration and reach of economic power in mass culture – pluralism ensures diversity. But is this credible? Perhaps a 'shared interest in [a] show is an end in itself and seldom leads to some action beyond that interest, some larger political purpose' (Butsch, 2000, p. 291).

In reaction to both the cultural-dope and active-audience models, Alec McHoul and Tom O'Regan (1992, pp. 5–6, 8–9) criticise the idea that 'local instances' of people 'embracing' or 'refusing' the dominant interpretations preferred by global producers makes any general statement about textual meaning. Instead, they propose a 'discursive analysis of particular actor networks, technologies of textual exchange, circuits of communicational and textual

Lucille Ball: breaking the boundaries of female comedy

effectivity, traditions of exegesis, commentary and critical practice'. In other words, the specific 'uptake' of a text by a community should be our focus; but not because this reveals something essential to the properties of TV genres or their likely uptake anywhere else or at any other time. We can only discern a 'general outline' of 'interests', applied to specific cases 'upon a piecemeal and local inspection'. For television is an instrument of instruction and response that varies with place, time, genre and audience (O'Shea, 1989, pp. 376–7).

As Justin Lewis says (1991, p. 49), 'TV viewing is a cultural practice, and like all cultural practices, it involves not only "doing it" but "ways of doing it".' For those of us schooled in pub talk or Leavisite talk, whether it be about sport, art, politics, literature, friends or television, there is nothing necessarily new or socially subversive about evaluations by fans. None of which is to say that, on the other side, the anti-populists are correct in their infantalisation of audiences. As Pierre Bourdieu suggests (1998, p. 48), 'paternalistic–pedagogical television' is 'no less opposed to a truly democratic use of the means of mass circulation than populist spontaneism and demagogic capitulation to popular tastes'. Dan Schiller (1996, p. 194) suggests a way beyond such graceless antinomies. TV production need not be thought of in opposition to consumption, with one practice 'productive' and the other not, or one side trumping the other. Instead, the work of television employees is one moment of labouring activity, and the work of television audiences is another moment. This suggests that rather than embarking on either active interpretation or passive reception, audience members' labour includes self-understanding – but that labour cannot and should not be conceptualised in isolation from their day jobs, or the work of others in bringing TV to them (Maxwell, 2001).

Toby Miller

Author's note: My thanks to Marie Leger and Richard Maxwell for their comments.

RECOMMENDED READING

Fiske, John (1987b), *Television Culture*, New York and London: Routledge.

Harrington, C. Lee and Bielby, Denise D. (1995), *Soap Fans: Pursuing Pleasure and Making Meaning in Everyday Life*, Philadelphia: Temple University Press.

Schiller, Herbert I. (1989), *Culture Inc.: The Corporate Takeover of Public Expression*, Oxford: Oxford University Press.

The Quiz Show

The quiz (or game) show genre has played an important and sometimes controversial role in the history of television in the USA and elsewhere. Legendary quiz show executive Mark Goodson, whose company has been responsible for over 22,000 hours of quiz show programming on US television, called quiz shows and soaps 'the great indigenous television forms', and the two genres have several common features. Like soap operas, TV quiz shows in America grew out of a popular radio format of the 1930s; and both genres have been aimed principally at a daytime, and largely female, audience. Unlike the experience in many other nations, in the USA only rarely have soap operas or quiz shows had a significant presence in network prime time. The chief exceptions for the US quiz show are the period between 1955 and 1958, when the *$64,000 Question* (CBS, 1955–8) sparked a short-lived, high-stakes quiz show boom in prime time before revelations of fraud in many of the most popular programmes nearly killed the entire genre. The second exceptional period of prime-time game show popularity followed the phenomenal success of *Who Wants to Be a Millionaire?* (UK, Celador, ITV, 1998–) as a summer replacement series in 1999, spurring the current proliferation of prime-time game shows in American TV network schedules.

The subject of little scholarly attention, the quiz show genre has endured long periods of critical disdain and indifference, interrupted by infrequent moments of generalised and often hyperbolic critical reaction to the spectacular success of a specific show or format, before the genre recedes again into fringe-time invisibility and critical obscurity. Unlike the soap opera, the subject of sustained and sophisticated scholarly attention over the past two decades, the critical literature on TV game shows remains dominated by fan tributes, sociological reflectionism and elitist scorn.

As John Fiske has pointed out, soaps and quiz shows share a climate of critical hostility, a tendency towards stylistic excess and parody (the precise differences between a straightforward quiz show and the many parodies of quiz shows across TV history are sometimes difficult to identify, and a popular image of their audience as highly – perhaps pathologically – involved in their viewing styles). Although Mark Goodson argued that the successful quiz show should have the viewer talking out loud to his or her TV set, the narrative and character structures of the genre are arguably the most distant from those of

Who Wants to Be a Millionaire?: 'England's most successful cultural export in the last 30 years'

literary-based TV genres. As nearly authorless texts, the quiz show has frustrated traditional auteurist and generic methods of analysis imported from literature and film studies.

If neglected by critics, the quiz show has proved to be one of the most flexible and resilient of television formats. Cheap and easy to produce, the format has thrived at diverse levels of the television food chain, from low-budget, local, live origination and fringe-time syndication to network prime time and cable networks as diverse as Nickelodeon, the Playboy Channel, MTV and the Food Network. It is not uncommon for a long-extinct quiz show from decades past to be revived with a new host or minor revision in format, or for a successful programme quickly to spin off multiple sequels and imitators. Quiz shows have run the gamut from the low-stakes, high-prestige contests of official knowledge of *Mastermind* (BBC, 1972–) in the UK and *GE College Bowl* (NBC, 1958–9, 1969–70) in the USA, to the carnivalesque celebrations of consumer desire of *The Price is Right* (NBC, 1956–65) and *Supermarket Sweep* (ABC, 1965–7). In the USA, the genre is robust enough to have supported a number of so-called 'misery shows', including *Queen for a Day* (NBC, 1956–64) and *Strike it Rich* (CBS, 1951–8), where down-and-out

contestants compete for sympathy from members of the studio and home audiences.

The genre has also proved to be an extremely exportable one, less in the form of programmes themselves than in the licensing of programme formats. Indeed, the 1999 success of the UK programme hit *Who Wants to Be a Millionaire?* for the ABC network in the United States, followed by the similar success of *Survivor* (CBS, 2000–) the following year, created a minor buying frenzy among US programmers for new game show formats. The exploding trade in programme formats, driven principally by the game show and 'Reality TV' genres, has at least temporarily weakened traditional US network hostility to foreign programming and American domination of global TV markets (see 'Reality TV').

The quiz show genre is a highly diverse one, ranging from straight contests of knowledge, to audience-participation games featuring outlandish and sometimes humiliating stunts, to programmes built around stumping a panel of celebrities, where the emphasis is less upon a specific outcome than on the humourous or risqué banter between celebrity and civilian. Contests of knowledge range between 'official' and vernacular knowledge, from arcane facts of history or science to the prices of everyday commodities. Other popular shows, including *The Dating Game* (ABC, 1965–2000), *The Newlywed Game* (ABC, 1966–99) and *Family Feud* (ABC, 1976–85/CBS, 1988–), depend upon the success of contestants in correctly surmising the responses of others to a range of questions. Perhaps inevitably, the extremely popular high-stakes quiz shows of both the late 1950s and the late 1990s provoked widespread critical musings about how such get-rich-quick dramas reflect cultural attitudes about class, knowledge and upward mobility.

The various television quiz formats turn around differing calibrations of luck, knowledge and skill, and almost all offer the spectacle of ordinary people facing life-transforming decisions in extended real time. Indeed, although several episodes of a series are typically taped back-to-back some weeks before their air dates, contemporary high-stakes quiz programmes expend a great deal of effort to create a sense of 'liveness', supporting an analogy to televised sporting events. Most game show formats depend heavily on the figure of the host, almost always male (of the thirty-five national versions of the current global hit programme *Who Wants to Be a Millionaire?*, only three are hosted by women), who functions as something between the contestant's sympathetic helpmate and cruel inquisitor. The visual design of the game show ranges from the quotidian opposing tables and podiums of the school

Who Wants to Be a Millionaire?

Described by the *New York Times* as 'England's most successful cultural export in the last 30 years', the high-stakes quiz show *Who Wants to Be a Millionaire?* (UK, Celador, ITV, 1998–) has demonstrated the power of a single programme to reshape prime-time schedules and broadcast competition around the world. After two years of fruitless pitches to British broadcast networks by its production company, Celador, *Millionaire* was picked up by ITV in the autumn of 1998 and became an immediate hit, gaining as much as 72 per cent of the television audience. By the end of 2000, the programme was on the air in thirty-five countries and sold as a format to forty-five more; Celador's managing director told a journalist, 'It's a bit like the old days of the British Empire. We've got a map of the world in the office coloured in pink where we've placed the show. Most of the world is pink.'

The British production company maintains tight control over the franchise, and the format of various national versions is identical: after being selected via a series of telephone and studio qualifying quizzes, individual contestants answer a series of fifteen questions of escalating difficulty while seated opposite the programme's host in the middle of a high-tech amphitheatre. Contestants may draw upon assistance three times, electing either to poll the studio audience, phone a friend for advice, or eliminate two of the incorrect answers. Top prize-winners are rare across the world, most frequently occurring in the USA, where six contestants have won $1 million over two seasons of the programme. The show's Indian version, *Kaun Banega Crorepati* (Star Plus/Zee TV, 2000–), broadcast five nights a week in the 2000 season, gained an 87 per cent audience share and was responsible for vaulting Rupert Murdoch's Star Plus satellite channel from third to first place across India; Star's profits from this one programme were more than the combined earnings from all the other Star TV channels in India.

The success of *Who Wants to Be a Millionaire?* (ABC, 1999–) in the USA has been equally spectacular. Picked up for a limited-run summer replacement series in August 1999 by Disney/ABC, it reached as many as 22 million viewers per broadcast and was responsible for boosting the overall summer audience ratings of the largest four US networks by 9 per cent. In the 1999–2000 television season, it lifted ABC from third to first place in network competition, the first time that had been accomplished in US television history. For the February 2000 sweeps period, when advertising rates are set for the ensuing quarter, ABC filled 18 per cent of its entire prime-time schedule with multiple episodes of the show.

Its success at ABC brought many imitators, and by January 2000 quiz shows consumed six and a half hours of weekly prime time, more than at any point since the 1950s. By May 2000 it was among the top ten US network shows for each of its three weekly broadcasts, and ABC's overall audience figures were up 20 per cent for the season. ABC's revenues were up 30 per cent for the season, with the network demanding up to $400,000 per thirty-second commercial in the programme (production costs are estimated at between $500,000 and $1 million per episode); industry estimates placed ABC's annual profits from the show between $400 million and $600 million, an amount greater than the typical total annual profits of an entire US TV network (see Creeber, 2004b).

William Boddy

spelling bee to the video game- and science-fiction film-inspired *mise en scène* of the contemporary big-budget *Who Wants to Be a Millionaire?* and *Winning Lines* (BBC, 1999–2004). Indeed, it is not unusual for producers to spend more on the programme's set than upon any other element of the programme, including prizes.

William Boddy

RECOMMENDED READING

Fiske, John (1987a), 'Quizzical Pleasures', in John Fiske, *Television Culture*, New York and London: Routledge.

Goedkoop, Richard (1985), 'The Game Show', in B. G. Rose (ed.), *TV Genres: A Handbook and Reference Guide*, Westport: Greenwood.

Schwartz, David, Ryan, Steve and Wostbrock, Fred (1999), *Encyclopedia of TV Game Shows*, New York: Checkmark.

The Celebrity Talk Show

The child of vaudeville and radio variety, TV celebrity talk shows have been a staple of American TV since *The Tonight Show* (NBC, 1954–) premiered in September 1954. Pat Weaver, the famed NBC producer in the 1950s, is credited with originating the genre. He changed the focus of late-night programming from a variety show emphasising performance to a talk show with a series of conversations interspersed with performances.

Since its start, the set on the stage replicates a living room with a desk for the host and a couch for the guests (with a curtained performance stage to the right). The format, too, has remained the same: an opening monologue by the host, a segment with the studio audience

The Tonight Show

The Tonight Show has aired uninterruptedly since 27 September 1954 on NBC as the pre-eminent late-night talk show. It remains the most profitable series on American television. It was never seriously challenged for its authority as the leading celebrity talk show until *Late Night with David Letterman* which began in 1982 on NBC and the *Late Show with David Letterman* which began in 1993 on CBS. The programme has gone through a number of hosts, but its success is most closely associated with Johnny Carson, a mild-mannered comedian who perfected the good-natured humour and light conversation that characterises American celebrity talk shows.

Nightly after the news, the programme would announce itself with the upbeat sound of swing music as Ed McMahon, the sidekick, would sing out 'Heeerrrrrrrrrrrrre's Johnny!' Carson would appear from behind a curtain in a sports jacket to wild clapping and howls. After thanking them for their generous applause, he began his monologue, a humourous combination of joking about current events and interaction with

the audience. His style reflected his Midwest background: cool, casual and clean-cut but still mischievously charming, which made going 'to bed with Johnny Carson' an American pastime. His humour was self-consciously fashioned on the work of Jack Benny, who emphasised comedic timing such as the pause and slow burn. Carson conversed with celebrities with the air of cocktail party repartee. He kept the conversation light assiduously avoiding confrontation and political controversy. But he also kept it flirtatious as he kidded his guests about their lives and work. The programme's popularity relied on the unerring uniformity of the programme and Carson's humour for over thirty years.

The various incarnations of *The Tonight Show* are distinguished by the personalities of the different hosts. The programme originally began under the title *Tonight!* in 1954 with Steve Allen as the host. Although he established the basic format of *The Tonight Show*, Allen as a musician created a more musical show with musical guests as regulars. His method was improvisation, and he would often jump up and run into the audience or out on to the street, invent narration

The Tonight Show with Johnny Carson: 'cool, casual and clean-cut'

to the imagery of a remote camera, or compose a song sponta-neously based on audience suggestions. Jack Paar, the second host (1957–62), was not a comic but an expert conversational-ist who could joke. As a result the programme was more issues-oriented and acerbic and ultimately controversial. When NBC censored a joke of his, he walked on stage the next night and announced his anger with NBC's decision and walked off the programme. In 1961 he took the show to West Berlin and filmed in front of the Berlin Wall, which was less than a month old. The Defense Department deployed a group of soldiers to stand between the Wall and the filming. The department launched an inquiry into Paar's action, leading ultimately to the host's resignation in 1962 when Carson came on.

In 1992 Jay Leno (a stand-up comic and frequent guest) took over after Carson's thirty-year stint. Although David Letterman, a popular but acerbic guest host, was the heir apparent to the permanent position, he lost out to the softer and warmer humour of Leno, a closer model to the light tra-dition of Carson. In 1994 Letterman was the first to compete successfully with his own celebrity talk show on CBS by carv-ing out a younger audience with his irreverent humour. By 1995 the late-night celebrity talk show audience split.

Jane Shattuc

(interviews and games), and a set of interviews and per-formances with well-known guests on stage. Each host is paired with a sidekick who functions as an announcer but also a foil for humour and an ideal listener. The pro-grammes are recorded with a live studio audience in the daytime and aired at night. *The Tonight Show*, *The Dick Cavett Show* (ABC, 1968–86), *The Arsenio Hall Show* (Syndication, 1989–94) and *Late Night with David Letterman* (NBC, 1982–1993/CBS, 1993–) represent the most successful examples in the USA. The programmes have a cultural cachet, given their centrality in the late-night schedule of the networks. They serve as important publicity venues, which have made the careers of guests by increasing the visibility of the individual or group. *The Mike Douglas Show* (Syndication, 1962–82) and *The Merv Griffin Show* (NBC, 1965–86) were daytime celebrity talk shows and became the prototype for confessional talk shows (see below) when the daytime genre began to shift in the 1970s and 1980s to average Americans as the 'celebrity' guests and their social and personal issues as topics.

The genre focuses on interviews with entertainment luminaries (actors, musicians, popular artists and televi-sion personalities) but sometimes politicians, authors and average citizens whose lives merited public recognition. Each programme establishes a set list of celebrities who 'drop in' regularly, much like neighbours for a chat. The host and guest (often with mugs of coffee) carry on a lively slightly rehearsed conversation focused around a specific object or media event that the guests want to promote (film, TV programme, CD or tour). In exchange for the publicity, the guest usually divulges intimate details of their lives or work to please the audience. Much like domestic hospitality, the host treats the guest as if s/he is 'royalty' or a celebrity in the case of American culture. 'In this form, entertainment is sacred, providing viewers release from the frightening events and less-than-desirable life conditions in their everyday experience. Fun is functional. Entertainers are elevated to the status of cultural heroes' (Himmelstein, 1994, p. 343).

The celebrity talk show is also marked by its interaction with the studio audience. After a five- to ten-minute humourous monologue that warms up the audience's response, the host often steps into the audience. The inter-action serves numerous functions. It allows for a seemingly 'democratic' moment as average people are given a similar treatment to the celebrity guests. The audience interaction also creates a more emotive response from the audience, and the rest of the programme becomes more dynamic. The audience members are frequently called on by name and asked to interact with the host. Although the studio audience is seen and called upon, it still functions similarly to a laugh track (although less predictable) as passive 'inscribed viewers' whose main role is to represent the at-home viewer by following the programme's rules of good viewership. They embody the immediate 'you' to whom the hosts refer in their monologues as they address the camera. They laugh and applaud to a degree voluntarily out of appreciation for the entertainment. Nevertheless, the pro-ducers attempt to prescribe the emotional tenor of the show through studio signals – flashing signs or gesturing personnel – telling the studio audience to laugh and applaud.

The history of celebrity talk shows is defined by slight variations in the prescribed formula of light entertainment established in the 1950s. *The Dick Cavett Show*, the ABC celebrity talk show of the late 1960s and early 1970s, posed as the 'intellectual' alternative to *The Tonight Show*. Partially because of Cavett's Yale University education and interest in language, the programme attracted a more high-brow audience and set of guests. It was famed for the verbal sparring between guests and sometimes host: bouts between Norman Mailer and Gore Vidal, Cavett and Lester Maddox (a southern anti-civil rights politician) and TV actor Chad Everett and Lily Tomlin (who walked off the stage when Everett objectified his wife). The programme never retained a large viewership.

The Arsenio Hall Show in 1988 was the first to attract a younger audience than *The Tonight Show*. With the first black talk show host, the programme was able to book soul and rap groups on TV (McNeil, 1996, p. 58). David Letterman followed Hall's youth-orientation when he competed successfully opposite *The Tonight Show* in 1993. With his irreverent humour ('Top Ten Lists' and 'Stupid Pet Tricks'), ribbing of everyday New Yorkers (often working-class and immigrant Americans) and sardonic sparring with women celebrities, Letterman offered an iconoclastic alternative to the staid slower style of *Jay Leno's Tonight Show* (NBC, 1992–). By 1995 the late-night celebrity talk show audience split: *Letterman's Late Show* retained the all-important demographics of young viewers, but *The Tonight Show* regained its overall ratings lead as the voice of light entertainment in America (see box). However, Letterman's irreverent style quickly spread to the UK, 'borrowed' by presenters such as Jonathan Ross (*Friday Night with Jonathan Ross* (BBC, 2001–) and Chris Evans (*TFI Friday* (C4, 1996–2000)).

Jane Shattuc

RECOMMENDED READING

Himmelstein, Hal (1994), *Television Myth and the American Mind*, Westport: Praeger.

McNeil, Alex (1996), *Total Television: A Comprehensive Guide to Programming from 1948 to the Present*, New York: Penguin Putnam.

Munson, Wayne (1993), *All Talk: The Talk Show in Media Culture*, Philadephia: Temple University Press.

The Confessional Talk Show

The confession or the baring of private feelings and acts in public is what most people associate with American talk shows between about 1980 and 2000. An episode of *The Oprah Winfrey Show* (Syndication, 1986–) on 3 May 1994 typified this when a rape victim confronted her alleged rapist. On one level, Winfrey's graphic description of the rape relegated the topic to the cheap thrills or voyeurism of a tabloid. She carried on the tabloid tradition of exploiting these two people's misfortune for corporate profit. Yet on another level, the dramatic and individualised account on the programme allowed ordinary citizens – in the studio and at home – to enter a debate about sexual power in their everyday lives. These confessional talk shows, whether the topic was transsexuality, incest, interracial sex or wife beating, took up the feminist slogan of the 'personal is political' and gave it a commercial forum. They gave feminine or race issues normally labelled private, personal or domestic a public airing, reaching women of all classes, races and ages. The tension between commercial tabloid exploitation and the politicisation of the private sphere stands as the central debate in the reception of these talk shows.

This talk show genre is more complex than a label such as 'confessional' or 'tabloid' reveals. The form is divided from the other types of talk shows by the following five distinct characteristics:

- it is 'issue-oriented'. I choose this term over 'confessional' to avoid the sensational inference involved in the word 'confession' (for example, revealing taboos). The content of these programmes emanates from social problems or personal matters that have a social currency, such as rape, drug use or sex change;
- it is distinguished by the centrality of active audience participation;
- the subgenre is structured around the moral authority and educated knowledge of a host and/or an expert who mediates between guests and audience;
- it is constructed for a female audience in that women were the overwhelming majority of viewers until the mid-1990s, when the producers created a more masculine, youth-oriented form;
- this kind of talk show is usually an hour-long syndicated programme produced by non-network production companies to be sold for broadcast to network-affiliated television stations in the USA.

The first generation of talk shows or four top A. C. Nielsen-rated programmes in the 1980s fit these generic traits: *Geraldo* (Syndication, 1987–98), *The Oprah Winfrey Show* (see box), *The Phil Donahue Show* (Syndication, 1970–96) and *Sally Jessy Raphaël* (Syndication, 1983–2002). Such unanimity allows them to be characterised as a distinctive cultural group. The issue-oriented content of the first generation differentiates daytime talk shows from other interactive TV forms such as game shows and other talk shows (see above). Talk shows are not the news. But even at their most personal and emotional, the topics of these shows

The Oprah Winfrey Show

Although Phil Donahue originated the genre of the confessional or issue-oriented talk show in 1970, *The Oprah Winfrey Show* (Syndication, 1986–) is responsible for its international success. By 1993 it attracted a greater number of women viewers than network news programmes, nighttime talk shows, morning network programmes and any single daytime soap opera in America. It was seen in sixty-four foreign countries. Over 15 million American people were tuning in daily to watch Oprah Winfrey and her female audience debate personal issues with as much fury as an old-time revival meeting. For its first nine years the programme typified the genre: a social issue was individualised as a personal problem at the top of the hour ('How do girls lose self-esteem?' 'Toxic Prozac?' or 'Violence in high schools'). A series of guests who characterised the issue, often representing two sides of the matter, were invited to discuss it with the host Oprah Winfrey, an expert and the studio audience. A debate would usually take place between various factions on stage and/or in the audience.

Winfrey's success as a host lay in her ability to posit herself as a 'typical' American woman in her beliefs and experiences (despite her $50 million yearly income). *The New York Times* described her as 'everywoman'. She continually called on her personal experience as a source of evidence, and in the process became famed for her confessions: being born out of wedlock, childhood sexual abuse, childhood poverty, HIV brother and her own cocaine addiction. Her on/off battle with her weight evolved into a leitmotif for the talk show as she staged her weight problem with programmes on weight control, dieting, cooking and exercising. She carted in a wagonload of fat on stage to indicate her reduction, to the emotional applause of her studio audience. 'If Oprah can do it, you can do it', or self-empowerment, became a central theme. Yet such emphasis on self-help was often criticised in the press as masking the financial difference between Winfrey's and her average viewer's ability to be empowered.

More importantly, Oprah Winfrey was the first black woman to host a daytime talk show in America. Although the programme focused on the private sphere, it staged more women's and racial issues than the other talk shows. The degree to which one can consider these to be political debates depends on the definition of 'politics' used. Winfrey tended to focus on the personal problems emanating from current societal issues. Amid shows on celebrities and makeovers, typical feminine/feminist topics were rape, the glass ceiling, girls and self-esteem, and spousal abuse. A number of academics see the

The Oprah Winfrey Show: 'a typical American woman'?

early years of *The Oprah Winfrey Show* as embodying populist feminist politics as she staged the 'personal as political' (Carpignano et al., 1990; Livingstone and Lunt, 1994; Masciarotte, 1991). The power relations of the domestic or traditionally feminine world got a public airing. Average women of all colours were given a rare voice to complain about their treatment.

However, critics protested that the programme sensationalised social issues by revealing the private lives of unsuspecting guests. Other critics saw her programme as reproducing 'self-contained individualism' where the audience and guests depoliticise problems and can only change themselves personally (Peck, 1994, 1995; McLaughlin, 1993). Overtly race-based discussions were less common. In 1987 the programme went to a small town in Georgia to stage what became a famed debate about racism. The programme produced a thirteen-part series called 'Racism 1992'. Other episodes discussed issues about, for example, 'What colour are you?' and 'Why the black man is the most feared individual'. As a commercial product, the programme more often deflected the possibility of larger political change or movements. For all their airing of angry social debates, the programmes would end on Winfrey invoking the power of the individual and/or a 'higher power'.

In 1995 Winfrey went on air and renounced the tabloid nature of talk shows in general and her own talk show in particular. She pledged she would go on a 'spiritual quest of moral uplift' with her programme. As promised, the programme changed radically. The subjects became directed at personal self-improvement without a social connection with topics such as 'Tipping and gift-giving anxiety' and 'Advice to Oprah letter-writers'. Interviews with celebrity standard-bearers became routine. The programme also returned the bourgeois expert to central stage and created star new-age experts such as 'Dr Phil' McGraw and Gary Zukav (who is 'dedicated to the birth of a new humanity'). The programme began 'Oprah's Book Club' in order to get 'the country excited about reading'. Within months, Winfrey's monthly picks would make the books instant bestsellers – proof of the programme's ability to guide tastes. It was an idea later 'borrowed' in the UK by the likes of *Richard and Judy* (C4, 2001–8).

Importantly, the role of the audience declined, switching from a town hall debater to deferential question-askers with this new top-down structure. The programmes focus on

established 'bourgeois' authority, whether it is Winfrey, an expert, a celebrity or a novelist. The audience has evolved into a school of acolytes in this personal and moral self-improvement quest. The political dimension of social problems has moved to the background if not disappeared. Oprah Winfrey expanded this new-age media empire in 2000 by launching *O, the Oprah Magazine*, Oxygen.com and a cable network – all generically dedicated to a nebulous notion of 'a woman's view of the world' (Oprah.com).

Jane Shattuc

emanate from a current social problem or issue. They can be considered the fleshing out of the personal ramifications of a news story: the human-interest story. There needs to be a cultural conflict around which the drama of the show is staged. The subjects are culled from current newspaper and magazine articles, viewer mail and viewer call-ins. The producer deems whether the issue has opposing sides and is socially broad enough to be applicable to a large audience. In fact, local stations categorised them as 'informational' programmes for their licence renewals in the 1980s.

On one end you have programmes staging classic social policy or public sphere debates such as 'Mystery disease of the Persian Gulf War' with army personnel (*The Phil Donahue Show*, 23 March 1994), 'Press actions on Whitewater' with reporters (*The Phil Donahue Show*, 16 March 1994), 'Strip-searching in schools' with school administrators (*Sally Jessy Raphaël*, 14 March 1994), or even 'Do talk shows and self-help movements provide excuses?' with lawyers and cultural critics (*The Oprah Winfrey Show*, 22 February 1994).

More typically, the social issue is placed in a domestic and/or personal context such as 'Arranged marriages' (*The Oprah Winfrey Show*, 10 March 1994), 'When mothers sell babies for drugs' (*Geraldo*, 17 March 1994), 'Custody battles with your in-laws' (*Sally Jessy Raphaël*, 22 April 1994) and 'Domestic Violence' (*The Phil Donahue Show*, 1 February 1994). Such domestic social issues are often further broadened to deal with perennial behaviour problems such as 'You are not the man I married' (*Geraldo*, 14 February 1994), 'Broken engagements' (*The Oprah Winfrey Show*, 31 January 1994), 'Ministers who seduce ladies' (*Sally Jessy Raphaël*, 19 April 1994) or 'Jealousy' (*The Phil Donahue Show*, 3 March 1994). These topics are still social; they involve the breaking of a cultural taboo (for example, infidelity, murder, seduction or non-procreative sex).

Because of the phenomenal popularity of *The Oprah Winfrey Show*, a second wave of programmes in the 1990s

emerged from the historical need of commercial television to repeat success. These are what can be clearly classified as 'confessional talk shows'. To create a different market, the new programmes reached out to a younger audience and constructed a new form based on the sheer pleasure of breaking social taboos – especially those maintained by an older generation of 'serious' talk shows. Scores of new talk shows aired: *The Jerry Springer Show* (Syndicated, 1991–), *Maury Povich* (Syndication, 1991–), *Montel Williams* (Syndication, 1991–2008), *Jenny Jones* (Syndication, 1991–2003), *Ricki Lake* (Syndication, 1993–2004), *Gordon Elliott* (Syndication, 1994–7), *Carnie* (Syndication, 1995–6), *Tempestt* (Syndication, 1995–6), to name but a few.

With this shift, topics moved from personal issues connected with social injustice to interpersonal conflicts that emphasised the visceral nature of confrontation, emotion and sexual titillation. The expert disappeared as the number of guests proliferated, each programme staging a whirlwind succession of five-minute sound bites of conflict, crisis and resolution. Topics were more baldly about conflict: 'They're out of control … sex', 'Sister! Stop stealing my man', 'Women confront ex who cheated and warn new girlfriend' and 'Now that I slept with him, he treats me like dirt'. Fights between the guests, guests and audience members and audience members became a staple. Reacting to this shift towards greater 'tabloidisation', both the political left and right in America exploded in anger.

Liberal to left magazines (*Ms*, the *New Yorker* and the *Nation*) decried the lack of social consciousness of the programmes. William Bennett, the neo-conservative former Secretary of Education, launched a campaign against the new talk shows in October 1995. He labelled them as a form of 'perversion'. This controversy around the new talk shows caused them to be universally labelled 'confessional'. By January 1996 many talk shows were cancelled. Phil Donahue quit. *Geraldo* and *Oprah Winfrey* changed format under social pressure. Only *The Jerry Springer Show* succeeded in carrying on the tabloid banner by taking the conflict to extremes with ritualistic on-stage profanity and brawls. Any connection to the original claim of talk shows of staging the political issues of the identity rights movement had disappeared (see Roscoe, 2004).

Jane Shattuc

RECOMMENDED READING

Carpignano, P., Andersen, R., Aronowitz, S. and Difazio, W (1990), 'Chatter in the Age of Electronic Reproduction: Talk Television and the "Public Mind"', *Sociotext*, no. 25/26.

Livingstone, Sonia and Lunt, Peter (1994), *Talk on Television: Audience Participation and Public Debate*, London: Routledge.

Shattuc, Jane M. (1997), *The Talking Cure: TV Talk Shows and Women*, London and New York: Routledge.

Sport

Sports television does not constitute a single genre, but rather a mix of different forms of television production practice. First, television coverage of major sporting contests belongs to the category of media events (Dayan and Katz, 1992) alongside royal weddings and funerals, state occasions and live music concerts, sometimes sharing the same outside broadcast production facilities. The most important of these – the Olympics, the soccer World Cup and the Super Bowl – play a role in encouraging a sense of national identification. Second, the news reports, interviews and discussion panels that are integral to television sports broadcasts represent a specialised form of journalism, framed by a distinctive set of news values shared with newspaper and radio sports journalism. Third, sports television often performs an explicitly promotional role. Title sequences and video segments promote sporting events through constructing narrative conflicts between participants, using techniques that are similar to those used in advertisements, pop videos and movie trailers.

SPORTS TELEVISION AS MEDIA EVENT

Although the first moments of live television sports coverage occurred before the Second World War – in the UK a Wimbledon tennis match in 1937, in the USA a college baseball game at Columbia University in 1939 (Barnett, 1990, pp. 5, 19) – it was not until the late 1940s and 1950s that the conventions of sports television that we now take

for granted were established. In general, television presentation of many sports events continues to follow the rules of the 180° system: cameras are all positioned on one side of an imaginary line running from one end of the playing area to the other, as if to transgress this rule would disorient the viewer. Whatever presentational changes there have been over the years – faster editing and the use of more camera positions and new technologies (mobile, tracking, miniature and blimp cameras, for example) – this basic principle is still largely adhered to.

Sports television involves the deployment of a range of routines that have been developed to react to events as they unfold. The biggest disaster that can happen in sports broadcasting is to miss crucial moments in the action, and these techniques have developed to try to make sure that this does not happen. Accordingly, sports television production is based on a division of labour whereby editors, camera operatives and technicians are assigned specific, clearly defined tasks. Personnel are employed on the basis of their skills and experience in applying tried and tested conventions (Gruneau 1989; MacNeill, 1996).

Following radio, the conventions of television commentary have also developed to respond to uncertainty in the action. Commentary is organised around a distinction between a commentator (UK) or play-by-play announcer (USA), and a summariser (UK) or color announcer (USA). Typically, the former will be an expert in narrating the event and take responsibility for controlling the commentary, whereas the latter will be an ex-athlete and provide a participant's perspective. Although commentary is improvised and unscripted, commentators prepare through compiling extensive background notes, using information provided by sports journalism.

SPORTS TELEVISION AS JOURNALISM

Much of the content of sports telecasts is in the form of reports and interviews conducted by sports journalists. Sports journalism is a specialised branch of journalism with its own distinctive hierarchy of news values. The preoccupations of sports journalism routinely involve stories concerning sport issues exclusively: disciplinary issues, contract negotiations, levels of motivation and commitment, tactics, injuries and the like. Occasionally, stories relating to the financial or public policy aspects of sport will be covered, as will scandals around betting or drugs. Even more exceptionally major crime, sex or violence scandals involving sports stars will intrude, although these stories are less likely to be covered by sports journalists. However, most of the time sports journalism produces news that is predominantly about how sporting

The Super Bowl

Since its inauguration in 1967, the National Football League's Super Bowl has provided the paradigm example of television's role in the increasing commodification of sport. In the USA many of the highest-rating television events ever are Super Bowls, the 1996 game between Dallas and Pittsburgh peaking at 138.5 million viewers. The Super Bowl has become a festive ritual linking households with the abstract community of the nation through a shared viewing experience, providing an ideal opportunity for the articulation of hegemonic representations of American values (Wenner, 1989). The Super Bowl provided a prestigious showcase for new advertisements from blue-chip companies. The fees that broadcasters have commanded have been estimated at $1 million for a thirty-second spot in 1995, increasing to $2 million in 2000. And competition for the broadcasting rights to the package of which the Super Bowl forms a part is fierce, the cost of rights escalating exponentially with each new contract negotiated. The package the NFL sold to ABC, CBS and Fox in 1998 amounted to $2.2 billion a year. American football also provides one of the earliest examples of how the rules of sport have been modified as a result of the growing economic power of television: it was as long ago as 1958 that the television time-out was introduced to provide extra spots for advertisers.

The Super Bowl broadcast exemplifies sports television as a hybrid genre. The build-up to the Super Bowl starts up to two weeks before the event. The NFL, the two participating teams, the host city's organising committee, sponsors and other interested parties all provide journalists with story material through press conferences, controlled access to the players and other stage-managed events (Schwartz, 1997). This journalism provides many of the frames of reference for the ensuing promotion and coverage of the Super Bowl.

Promotion constitutes a crucial element of this coverage. Video segments are used to promote the Super Bowl through innovative use of editing, computer-generated effects, sound and music. By contrast, television presentation of the actual game typifies that of other sporting events in relying on conventional, tried and tested techniques, although American football is distinctive for its stop-start action – the ball is 'in play' considerably less than it is in similar sports (Real, 1989). Breaks are filled by detailed analysis of replays and statistics and, of course, advertisements (see p. 178). Close-ups of players are also regularly featured, although American football is different from other sports in that the protective headgear used prevents television from conveying the player's emotions through the demonstration of facial expressions; almost as if to compensate, the aggressive or celebratory gestures performed by the players appear exaggerated.

Rod Brookes

performance is directly affected by any of a limited range of predictable and routine matters.

SPORTS TELEVISION AS PROMOTION

In the context of the escalating costs of sports rights, broadcasters not only cover events, they also aggressively promote them. Title sequences and video segments typically set the scene for television coverage of major sporting events through using a variety of post-production techniques. Slow-motion action, sound effects, computer-generated graphics and effects, music, voice-over, colourisation, all enhance the construction of narrative conflicts between the participants to be resolved, at least temporarily, in the contest to follow. Further, broadcasters promote those events where they own the rights through promos or spot advertisements in advance of the broadcast itself. This is as crucial for public service broadcasters needing to attract high ratings to justify the financial outlay of acquiring sports rights, as it is for pay TV or pay-per-view broadcasters seeking to persuade viewers to subscribe to their services.

Additionally, frequent advertisement breaks are integral to commercial sports broadcasts as broadcasters seek to maximise, within regulatory constraints, the revenue that can be generated. In the case of major events the subject of advertisements is directly related to the event in the course of which the advertisements are scheduled – for example, for the 1998 World Cup Nike produced a series of skits featuring the stars of the tournament playing beach football. The individualist values embodied in Nike advertisements accentuates the status of sports stars as celebrities, and tends to present even team sports as contests between star individuals.

Although sports television can be described as a hybrid genre, in practice it is impossible to identify clear boundaries between the different televisual practices that constitute it. A typical sports event broadcast will unfold seamlessly from introductory titles through an opening video segment, to a news feature segment on the teams or individuals involved, then perhaps to a pre-game ceremony, back to expert discussion panels, into the game proper and, finally, interviews with the participants. Yet analysing sports television as a complex mix of different genres is useful in understanding the changing tensions that characterise its production and consumption. There has always been a conflict between television's role in purporting to cover or report sports events and television's role in promoting those events by enhancing their entertainment value through a variety of techniques (Whannel, 1992), but this conflict has intensified in the context of increasing commodification of sport since the 1980s.

Similarly, sports television has always had to reconcile serving the different interests of the knowledgeable sports fan and the uncommitted 'general viewer'. How these conflicts are resolved in different ways can be exemplified by comparing the BBC's and NBC's coverage of the 2000 Olympic Games. Whereas live coverage was prioritised by the UK public service broadcaster, even though this meant events were transmitted when many viewers were asleep or at work, the US commercial network withheld live coverage, preferring instead to provide extensively packaged recorded highlights during prime time in order to generate maximum revenue from advertisers (see Brookes, 2004a).

An analysis of television sport as comprising a hybrid mix of genres is useful in addressing a range of contemporary issues: the changing relationship between media and sport, the significance of the processes of commodification and globalisation, and the role of sport in the construction of identities around nation, gender and 'race' (Brookes, 2002; also see 'The Globalisation of Television News').

Rod Brookes

RECOMMENDED READING

Barnett, Steven (1990), *Games and Sets: The Changing Face of Sport on Television*, London: BFI.

Rowe, David (1999), *Sport, Culture and the Media*, Buckingham: Open University Press.

Whannel, Garry (1992), *Fields in Vision: Television Sport and Cultural Transformation*, London: Routledge.

Music on Television

Like its close sibling radio, television has always been part of the transmission of music, converting music from a live form into a recorded form, and stimulating the sales of recordings. The development of music on television broadly has seen the trajectory of a move from simple live performances of songs and musical pieces, to a situation where the music is accompanied by enhanced and often elaborate visuals. This spectrum includes performances enhanced by lights, camera effects, props and editing, although the proliferation of music television has inaugurated a new audiovisual form, the pop video, that has furnished a new style to television, seeping out of specialist channels and into commercials and action films.

Live television broadcasts relied upon the performance of musical numbers as much as they relied upon other 'turns' from the stage, offering the opportunity for audiences to see stars from close quarters. With the arrival of rock 'n' roll, popular music became more stridently visual, embodied by the impact (both real and imagined) of seeing Elvis swinging his hips. The visual aspect has always been tied closely to fashion, and the role of singers in influencing youth consumer choices has been a central way for pop musicians to differentiate their products in a very competitive market. The 'image' of the musician and the music spilt over into clothing, record covers and later into pop videos.

In the 1950s, shows appeared that were based on popular music, such as *Your Hit Parade* (NBC, 1950–9) and in its wake shows like *American Bandstand* (NBC, 1957–87/Syndication, 1987–9), *Top of the Pops* (BBC, 1964–2006) and *Soul Train* (Syndication, 1971–). All music shows were based on having musicians appear in the studio and perform hit songs of the day. ABC's *American Bandstand* ran for three decades; it was hosted by Dick Clark and made its debut in May 1957, running until 1989. It had a live audience and featured live acts as well as filmed performances. With its neat teenagers and rather staid Dick Clark, *American Bandstand* was notable not only for making rock 'n' roll acceptable to parents but also for its 'integrationism', including black musicians and audience members at a time when other shows refused. Other shows like *Your Hit Parade* played more 'adult' music, as did variety shows with occasional musical appearances. *The Ed Sullivan Show* (CBS, 1948–71), for example, famously would only show Elvis from the waist up, and the Doors contravened orders and persisted with the 'suggestive' lyrics to 'Light My Fire', although the show broke viewing records during The Beatles' appearance.

In the USA, radio was paramount for records reaching audiences, but in the UK television took on this function, as there were fewer radio stations. Television shows became a central means of marketing singles, and a record could be made a hit by simply managing an appearance on *Six-Five Special* (1957–8), *Oh Boy!* (1958–9) or, later, *Top of the Pops* (1964–2006) or *Ready Steady Go!* (ITV, 1963–6). *Ready Steady Go!* was the first television programme to serve the new generation of 1960s' youth in Britain (Hill, 1991, p. 103);

Ready, Steady, Go!: 'The weekend starts here!'

presented by the young and fashionable Cathy MacGowan, it always commenced with the catchphrase, 'The weekend starts here!'.

Pop musicians' appearances on television were important for publicity, directly stimulating record sales. Initial television appearances were nakedly about publicity. The Beatles made their first 'pop videos' in 1965 in order to facilitate multiple TV appearances but without the expense and effort of live performance in the TV studio (Neaverson, 1997, p. 120). This led the way forward, ultimately to music television's channels of pure pop promo. In the 1970s, there was a more diversified programming of music on television. 'Rock' programmes appeared that, as a symptom of progressive rock, were more 'serious' about their content. In the UK, *The Old Grey Whistle Test* (BBC, 1971–87) became an institution, consisting of live studio performances as a reaction to the endemic lip-synch 'miming' on most pop shows. The range of groups appearing was far wider than the pop chart, and many appeared briefly before returning to obscurity. In its ethos of musical authenticity, the show was similar to the *MTV Unplugged* (MTV, 1989–) of the 1990s.

MTV (see box) started in the USA in 1981 and changed the whole landscape of music on television. Not only was it the first full television station dedicated to music, but it

Top of the Pops: a central means of marketing singles

Music Television (MTV)

MTV went on the air for the first time on 21 August 1981 announcing itself with The Buggles' *Video Killed the Radio Star*. The record had been released two years earlier, but audiences got the point. MTV, as a television station playing only pop music, had developed out of Warner's pop music shows such as *Pop Clips* (Nickelodeon, 1981), *Video Jukebox* (HBO, 1981–6) and *Sight On Sound* (Qube, 1977), which allowed viewers to decide on the videos that would be screened on the programme. At first, it showed many promos by British groups (Rimmer, 1985, p. 71). One reason for this was that British and other European acts had already been producing videos, to take advantage of the opportunities for publicity on television that Europe had and the USA lacked. The British 'New Romantics' and 'new pop' broke into the American market at this point, and video and MTV were central in their success. New styles could be showcased by promos and the distinctiveness of British groups like Culture Club (featuring cross-dressing Boy George) and the bravura of videos like Duran Duran's *Rio* were compounded by the New Romantics' unique visual character.

The early 1980s simultaneously saw the proliferation of video technology, and the outlet of MTV inspired the use of the gamut of video processing effects, as well as offering almost limitless possibilities for imagination. The pop video allowed another dimension to pop music's product differentiation in a market that was increasingly competitive, and against a background of declining music industry sales over the long term. At first, record labels allowed pop videos to be shown by MTV at no cost. After all, they were simply a form of publicity or advertising, inspiring audiences to run out and buy records. Fairly quickly, however, the music industry worked out that promos were popular in their own right, and thus could be sold on video and MTV could be charged a licence fee for showing them.

Upon its inception, MTV had worked largely to the principle of keeping up a steady flow of pop videos, although in the later 1980s its slots became scheduled in a more traditional manner for a television station (Goodwin, 1992, p. 132). The channel has set the norms for pop and rock music, inspiring the notion of the 'MTV-friendly' video (Banks, 1996, p. 175), and certain types of musical genres, such as light heavy metal and adult-oriented rock, tended to dominate broadcasts. The channel's narrow marketing strategy simply ignored many musical genres. Local television started to exploit the areas of popular music not reflected by MTV, with rap, soul, country music and jazz having their own minority channels.

By 1985, Viacom, MTV's parent company, decided they wanted a channel to attract some of the older generation, specifically the baby-boom generation, who had grown up with pop and rock music and wanted a diet of older 'classics' as well as more album-oriented material. This led to the introduction of MTV's sister channel VH-1 ('Video Hits One'). Despite increasing competition from other music television channels such as Video Jukebox Network's *The Box* (BoxTV, 1992–), MTV is still massively successful and now has channels in Europe, Asia and Latin America.

K. J. Donnelly

became the arena for a new form of stylistic combat between pop groups. Throughout the decade, pop videos often differentiated their product through a distinctive video, such as Madonna's *Like A Virgin*, which portrayed her individual fashion sense as well as her sensual image. Europe did not get MTV until 1 August 1987. In the UK at this time, an innovative music show called *The Tube* (C4, 1982–7) was bringing MTV's style to terrestrial television as well as proving inspiring to later music television generally.

1985 saw the musical television event of the twentieth century, the Live Aid concert in aid of the famine in Ethiopia. It was broadcast live all over the world, and cut between stages at Wembley in London and Philadelphia. The roster of stars was notably conservative, including a re-formed Led Zeppelin and Paul McCartney, the spectacle amplified by Phil Collins singing on the stage in London, then flying on Concorde to the USA to take the stage again.

Probably the most memorable moment was a montage of starving Ethiopians accompanied by the Cars' song 'Drive'. This was very affecting, yet ambivalent in that the profound images were altered through their accompaniment by a banal pop song. Live Aid reinvigorated the flagging careers of a few older pop stars, and the music industry in the later 1980s reflected this turn to conservatism. In the 1990s, classical music has been the recipient of the same processes as pop music, with the Performance Channel on cable and satellite television showing operas, ballets and full classical concerts, as well as shorter pieces. The proliferation of channels made possible by digital television has already opened the gates to many specialist music stations, catering for very specific and fragmented audiences, unlike the mass audience that once sat enthralled in front of *American Bandstand* or *Top of the Pops*.

K. J. Donnelly

RECOMMENDED READING

Banks, Jack (1996), *Monopoly Television: MTV's Quest to Control the Music*, Boulder: Westview.

Goodwin, Andrew (1992), *Dancing in the Distraction Factory: Music Television and Popular Culture*, Minneapolis: University of Minnesota Press.

Rimmer, Dave (1985) *Like Punk Never Happened: Culture Club and the New Pop*, London: Faber and Faber.

Ordinary Television

At times it is possible to see across a number of individual genres certain continuities and regularities that bring them into a closer relationship with each other. Such is the case with the grouping 'Ordinary Television' (see Bonner, 2003). The term describes non-fiction television made in the first instance to be entertaining but also usually (though not invariably) to provide some information as well. Jeremy Tunstall's term 'edinfotainment' (1993, p. 80) and the popular term 'infotainment' both note this conjunction. Time of day shows – morning, afternoon or 'tonight' shows – together with quiz and game shows, lifestyle programmes, talk shows, reality shows and television magazine shows (like the comedic consumer car show, *Top Gear* (BBC, 1977–) or the Australian science programme, *Catalyst* (ABC, 2001–)), are members of the grouping. What they share is precisely a concern with the ordinary, the mundane, the domestic. *Top Gear*'s fondness for displaying supercars may seem contrary to this, but this is a show that enacts the fantasies men invest in cars and in this way is indeed ordinary.

As television fragments into more and more channels, which become in the process individually less profitable, this usually cheap form occupies more and more of the schedule. The programmes' strong presence in daytime programming is one indication of this, but they occur across the schedule. As Charlotte Brunsdon (2003) has argued, the 8–9 p.m. slot on British television was long devoted to lifestyle shows concerned substantially with cooking, gardening and interior design. Quiz shows are often stripped across the working week and the more substantial reality show franchises like *Big Brother* (Endemol, 1999–) occupy large swathes of time across more than one channel, extending online, to recoup the costs of licensing the format.

It is a central characteristic of the programmes that they actually involve the screen presence of ordinary people. They may be present in a studio audience or more centrally on-camera, perhaps as quiz contestants or people whose houses or even bodies are being made over. Their presence on a programme may momentarily lift them out of the ordinary, and for a tiny minority of reality show contestants that prominence may last a little longer. In recent years the practice of producing occasional celebrity versions of ordinary programmes like *Who Wants to Be a Millionaire?* (ITV, Celador, 1998–) 'Celebrity Special', has been extended to whole shows following the generic patterns of an ordinary television-type of show but using celebrity contestants. The reality challenge show *I'm a Celebrity … Get me out of Here* (ITV, 2002–) exists only in a celebrity form and with challenges far from the mundane, but as Su Holmes (2006) indicates, a touchstone of ordinariness persists.

Across the range, it is customary for these programmes to involve at least one presenter, often with additional reporters or experts. The two-hour ITV programme *This Morning* (ITV, 1988–) has two hosts, a roster of fifteen experts, including an agony aunt, who are called on variously across the week. Each episode interviews a mix of ordinary people and celebrities about matters that have brought them to prominence, as well as using them to test out products, receive gifts or makeovers and chat about issues of the day. Furthermore the majority of it is broadcast live and mirrors the situations viewers find themselves in: the studio setting is designed to resemble a living room and real-world occasions like the January sales or school holidays are marked in both. And what is being talked about across this quite significant portion of the week are overwhelmingly domestic concerns – health, families, food, personal appearance, relationships and leisure pursuits.

On this show and others, the presenters' interchanges with their guests are structured to reveal what Paddy Scannell calls 'the most fundamental aspect of broadcasting's communicative ethos' – sociability (1997, p. 23). This talk for talk's sake precedes the quiz show questions, frames the practicalities of the home makeovers or pet-care instructions and may constitute the whole of a chat show presenter's interchange with a celebrity. Sociable talk ignores social distinctions and assumes everyone is similarly located, most readily through its attention to the family.

This is one of the most pervasive discourses of ordinary television. Ordinary people appearing on television are identified in family terms and their domestic relationships may be the focus of the programme, as is the case with *Wife Swap* (C4, 2001–) or *Trinny and Susannah Undress* (ITV, 2006–), both of which sanction the varieties of humiliation they inflict on the subjects by concluding assertions of their having strengthened the original family bonds. Sentimentality about the family pervades even those shows most centred on its dysfunctionality, like talk shows, while cosmetic surgery programmes enjoy showing a mother and daughter simultaneously undergoing similar operations.

The other discourse which pervades ordinary television is that of consumption and here social distinctions, especially of class, are very evident. This is hardly surprising given the centrality of lifestyle programmes arguing that a person's appurtenances reveal their identity. Programmes looking at and making over homes, gardens and personal appearances combine with those considering cars, food and holidays to provide ample occasions for product placement or service boosting. The prizes offered and gifts given operate similarly and a rhetoric of the importance of continual turnover and renewal dominates. A very small counter-discourse about excessive debt has recently become evident, as in the British show *Your Money or Your Wife* (C4, 2006–), and a range of green programmes contesting consumption more generally is occasionally screened. Both are, however, isolated and apart from some reference to organic practices which may link the latter with food and gardening shows, there is not much of the interweaving of the ordinary television universe that sees products, practices and personnel moving from one show through a number of others.

What is least evident on 'ordinary television' is an attention to the kind of work that most of the viewers engage in everyday. There is a much wider range of occupations present in drama shows. Those shown working on ordinary television engage in a very narrow field, primarily within service industries – chefs, architects, designers of gardens and interiors, and, because of the strong presence of health, medical personnel. The considerable labour that gardening involves or the demanding and time-consuming nature of child-raising is subsumed into play or self-gratification.

On free-to-air broadcasting, 'ordinary television' is usually locally (meaning nationally) produced. It may be made to a licensed format, but very little is directly imported. The ordinary people shown and the minutiae of their domestic concerns produce a picture of ordinary life with discernible national inflections.

Frances Bonner

RECOMMENDED READING

Bell, David and Hollows, Joanne (2005), *Ordinary Lifestyles: Popular Media, Consumption and Taste*, Maidenhead: Open University Press.

Bonner, Frances (2003), *Ordinary Television: Analyzing Popular TV*, London: Sage.

Hill, Annette (2005), *Reality TV: Audiences and Popular Factual Television*, London and New York: Routledge.

Daytime TV

Classic daytime TV was a by-product of the successful establishment of the concept of 'prime time', especially in the USA during the late 1940s and early 1950s. This was a period when sex-role stereotyping was all the rage. It was just after the Second World War, during which millions of women had been mobilised, not only to join the armed services but also to take up employment in factories and elsewhere. 'Rosie the Riveter' was a vital part of industrial and economic production. After the war, some ideological effort was made by government and commercial agencies alike to persuade women to be satisfied with home duties and domestic life – the rationale being partly a 'return to normal', partly to open up job opportunities for demobilising GIs. A commercial craze for domesticity was evident that had no precedent; certainly it had not occurred after the First World War.

Having established prime time as the default setting of television entertainment, daytime TV became a site of anxiety for programmers and audiences alike. The anxiety centred on the role of the housewife, and women more generally. They were cast as home-makers, and that role was understood as productive (not leisure). Work included cleaning, both wet (laundry, dishes) and dry (polishing, vacuuming), cooking and, after that was done, parenting and 'wifely duties' – not only sexual, but also keeping the family mood up. But at the same time women were cast as consumers, in particular purchasing 'freedom' from housework drudgery, 'earning' leisure for themselves by choosing products that would, often as if by magic, cook and clean for them (see Spigel, 1992).

But being at home in the day was meant to be productive. Naturally, television executives wanted to capture larger audiences for their commercials, increasing capacity not least by extending the length of the broadcasting day (using programming that was dirt cheap compared with prime-time drama). There was no way of stopping daytime TV, which therefore had to promote the amelioration of housework while maintaining the housewife as a productive worker whose reward for wise consumption was leisure. What would they do with this leisure but watch TV? In this anxious, not-quite balancing act, daytime TV became somewhat different from its prime-time sibling. It was more useful.

The presumed audience profile (isolated suburban housewives at home, with children at school, husband at work and a home to make) was not a mere demographic fact, although such people were available as audiences.

More to the point it was a desire both of television networks and of commercial organisations more broadly. The era of 'mass persuasion' was as much about trying to get people to take satisfaction from their role as domestic consumers as it was about selling individual brands and products. Hence, daytime television was not only a conduit through which domestic product could be promoted, chiefly orificial and alimentary items like food, cleaning agents for body and house, and capital items for the home such as fridges (Hartley, 1999, pp. 99–103). It was also the means by which the very 'ideology of domesticity' that would make such things acceptable and even attractive could be communicated on a society-wide scale.

What emerged from this was a psycho-profile of 'the housewife' and the desires projected on to her, which daytime TV then sought to satisfy. Home-making and emotionality were the chief characteristics, leading very quickly to the broadcast forms that brought those characteristics together. Women at home could take time out from the pursuit of food and cleansing products through their loved ones' alimentary systems, and of germs and dust out of the home, then:

- put their feet up to enjoy soap opera's emotional dilemmas (while relishing the vicissitudes of neighbourliness);
- prepare neat culinary and cleansing surprises for the family while watching help shows;
- take note of the hints offered by TV experts to make the household economy more efficient;
- reflect on the politics of the personal with talk shows (see above);
- be updated on desirable products and their purposes in commercials and sponsors' segments;
- bring the children back into focus in the afternoon with shows aimed at pre-schoolers (later afternoon shows for older children would not assume a parental co-viewer; see 'Children's Television').

These functions were mixed and matched through the daytime period, supplying it with an internal rhythm it may otherwise have lacked. Daytime TV became a kind of metronome, pacing the progress of the day. It also performed this function for viewers not directly addressed by the 'housewife' scenario, including seniors, unemployed workers, rich people and people in institutions and shops.

Here, then, was a textual system geared to TV viewing as domestic work. And hard work it was, for both sides of this Faustian bargain. Daytime TV was teaching people to devote themselves to a practice of self-definition and self-affirmation based on resolving anxiety about their status as

housewives with desire for products. Those products were both semiotic (TV shows) and in the shops (advertised commodities and services). It was not easy for TV shows to 'interrogate' or address a viewer who was simultaneously watching TV and working, consuming and producing (no wonder they were 'distracted'). And perhaps it was not so easy for women to internalise the 'ideology of domesticity' required to sustain their domestic labour. Certainly, daytime TV quickly attracted the critical attention of the resurgent feminist movement in the 1970s (see Lopate, 1976), and many women never recognised themselves in the 'imagined community' of daytime TV viewers even as they watched daytime TV (see Brunsdon, D'Acci and Spigel, 1997). The work of Lynn Spigel (see, for instance, 1992) is exemplary in tracing domestic fantasies of suburban consumption and isolation in television history.

Daytime TV eventually matured as just one segment of a 'family' programming schedule that was consciously constructed by the TV networks on both sides of the Atlantic, and wherever commercial television took hold in consumer cultures:

- breakfast TV for children preparing for school (and their carers);
- daytime for women (and 'unproductive' persons);
- afternoon for children;
- early prime time for family (channel choice exercised by children);
- late prime time for family (channel choice dictated by 'dad');
- late-night television for men or non-family (single) adults.

This orderly sequence could be disrupted by sport (see above), news events, specials ('telethons', for example) and blockbuster movies. But in general the 'family schedule' purported, over time, to address all members of 'the' family, making a composite 'normal citizen' anew every twenty-four hours, even though such a beast was never being addressed 'whole' at any one time. But the combination of daytime and prime-time TV left little room for conceptions of the audience other than the family (Paterson, 1980; Feuer, 1983).

The networks did not compete with each other by counter-programming against this scheduling regime until the 1980s, after the advent of BBC2 and Channel 4 in the UK and Fox in the USA. The family schedule's long-term supremacy was also threatened by cable, although some cable channels distended the daytime format further by stripping particular soap operas (*Days of Our Lives* (NBC,

1965–), *Dallas* (CBS, 1978–91), *Dynasty* (ABC, 1981–9) – see 'Soap Opera') over the whole week, or particular genres ('shopping') over the whole day (and night).

Daytime TV was for most of its heyday a 'despised' area of programming, little watched by politicians, academics and moral entrepreneurs. It was never policed for moral, political or sexual deviation quite as heavily as were news, current affairs or prime-time drama series. As a result, daytime TV was often able to address topics and debates that would not have found clear expression in prime time. Talk show guests, soap opera characters, women presenters with strong characters, all were able from time to time to 'push the envelope' of the sayable and seeable (see Lumby, 1997).

Even in more routine sequences, daytime TV was often very close to the slower, more 'anthropological' rhythms of life, starting afresh each week on the perennial lack of fit between expectations and performance of the self, the family and interpersonal relations. It was an early mechanism for bringing private life into the public domain. Sooner or later the issues of gender, neighbourliness, personal identity and sexual politics in which it dealt would loom much larger in the 'public sphere' (see Lumby, 1999).

Daytime TV may not survive the post-broadcast era as a distinctive 'genre', although many of its elements will persist (not all of them during the day). But its dispersal into other forms can only mean that its counterpart – prime time – is also facing radical changes. As interactive and multimedia applications mature, and view-on-demand becomes more available, there is no need for audiences to sit down together at one time in one country to see particular shows. They can view whatever, wherever and whenever they choose from digitised archives to which they subscribe. People may prefer to see 'women's' genres in big daytime swathes, in the knowledge that others in their imagined community are doing the same things to the same temporal rhythm. But they will not have to. They can watch them any time, or use the daytime for other things, like watching the shows that cable TV already offers throughout the day.

John Hartley

RECOMMENDED READING

Lopate, Carol (1976) 'Daytime TV: You'll Never Want to Leave Home', *Radical America*, vol. 11, no. 1.

Lumby, Catharine (1997), *Bad Girls: The Media, Sex and Feminism in the 90s*, Sydney: Allen and Unwin.

Spigel, Lynn (1992), *Make Room for TV: Television and the Family Ideal in Postwar America*, Chicago: Chicago University Press.

Advertising

A television commercial is an audiovisual item of non-programme material typically recognisable by its brevity (thirty seconds being most common) and by its primary perceived intent: to advertise or persuade rather than simply to inform or entertain. Commercials are in fact the first televisual genre that children identify – at around three years of age – primarily because they interrupt programmes. From this age, children request products advertised in commercials (so they may be aware of ads offering information about availability) although the persuasive intent of commercials is not normally understood until at least the age of five (Jaglom and Gardner, 1981).

As a genre of persuasion the advertisement is tailored more strongly than most televisual genres to establishing a preferred reading and to positioning the demographically targeted viewer. However, contemporary ads are not always characterised by an explicitly persuasive intent. Grabbing the target consumer's attention is the first priority for the ad makers. In one British study, over a quarter of viewers who had watched an edition of *News at Ten* (ITV, 1967–) had seen *none* of the commercials (Clark, 1989, pp. 62–3). Consequently, it is hardly surprising that ads seek to entertain as well as to persuade. In Britain, ad agencies are conscious that the hard sell is not popular (Clark, 1989, p. 46). Furthermore, it may not suit the medium: it has been argued that television involves 'low involvement learning' that does not directly persuade consumers but that a kind of 'sleeper' effect operates when they are shopping (Clark, 1989, pp. 107–8). Ads for certain product sectors and target markets avoid direct persuasion and pursue what marketing psychology calls 'the peripheral route', relying more on symbolism, connotations and formal stylistic features than on product information (Arens, 2002). It is a reductionist fallacy that the only intended function of advertisements is to lead to direct and immediate sales of a particular product or service. This ignores a key marketing function – namely, to establish, maintain and extend the identity and status of a brand. Ads sell values as well as products – as well as ads collectively promoting consumerism, specific ad campaigns promote particular values in order to differentiate a brand from its competitors.

Leiss et al. (2005, pp. 170–98) identify four basic focuses in ads: information, symbolism, personalisation and lifestyle. They note that while all of these can still be found in ads (some being more closely associated with particular products), the primary focus of ads has shifted historically

The Levi's 501 'Launderette' Commercial

The commercial most widely discussed in the literature of cultural studies is without doubt the Levi Strauss 'Launderette' ad, first shown in 1985. Charged with revitalising the brand, the advertisers in the UK targeted sixteen- to twenty-four-year-old males and employed nostalgic US iconography, in this case loosely evoking the era of James Dean and Elvis Presley.

Catchy retro music grabs us from the start of this fast-paced twenty-eight-shot mini-narrative: *I Heard it Through the Grapevine* (leading Marvin Gaye's 1968 version to re-enter the Top Ten). Model Nick Kamen walks into a laundromat, emptying a bagful of stones into a machine, stripping confidently down to his boxers and throwing his jeans into the wash, ignoring but fully aware of his audience. John Hegarty, a founding partner of BBH, was the creative mind behind this ad and a series of Levi's ads. The whole series relied heavily on the 'peripheral route', employing a shared iconography (lighting, colour, clothing and music) and a common theme of highly charged sexual voyeurism. The focus of these ads is emotional and symbolic rather than rational and informational. Information is confined to the last two shots (simple products shots appended to the narrative with the captions 'The original shrink-to-fit jeans' and 'Now available stonewashed'). In the familiar formula, juxtaposition implies that it is the jeans themselves that are erotic and that this quality will transfer to the wearer.

The primary reason why this ad is so often discussed as a cultural document is that it reflects a significant shift in popular representations of masculinity, representing the 'new man' by utilising traditionally feminine codes of representation (Goffman, 1979) in its fragmentation of a sexy body offered in intimate close-ups as the passive object of the viewer's appreciative gaze (Mort, 1988). In commoditising the male body it also challenges the stereotypical alignment of male with active and female with passive – opening up the male body not only to the female gaze (Moore, 1988), but even more markedly

Levi's 'Laundrette' commercial, 1985 (Bartle Bogle Hegarty for Levi Strauss & Co.)

inviting the *male* gaze (Mulvey, 1975) in a narcissistic or homoerotic manner previously confined to gay erotica – straight viewers being offered the reassurance that this performance is really for the benefit of the giggling girls (Simpson, 1994).

Reminding us that the definition of genres in terms of textual features alone is reductionist, this groundbreaking ad is thus important for the way in which it involves the negotiation of a new 'contract' with the viewer. It also illustrates the potential of commercials as props for the rehearsal of identities. Sales of Levi jeans increased by 800 per cent in five months – sales of white boxers soared too (viewers don't always accept the preferred readings, even of ads).

Daniel Chandler

in this same sequence, so that they can also be seen as phases in advertising (they allude also to a fifth focus on 'demassification' observable since the late 1980s). Historically, television advertising emerged within the phase in which personalisation tended to be foregrounded (around 1945–65). Ads began to be directed increasingly toward people's needs and desires. Ernest Dichter's influential *Handbook of Consumer Motivations* was published in 1964.

In Britain, the first commercial shown on television was a minute-long ad for Gibbs S R toothpaste – first

transmitted at 8.12 p.m. on 22 September 1955, twelve minutes after ITV broadcast its first television programme (to only 100,000 homes). Though it had elements of personalisation, it was primarily both symbolic and informational. It began with the atmospheric images and sounds of an icy mountain stream, fluty music and a male voice-over using a lot of repetition of 'tingling' words before shifting to a more traditional didactic informational focus. It famously featured a tube of toothpaste and a brush symbolically embedded in a block of ice in this snowy landscape, so that one might infer that using the toothpaste would lead to breath as fresh as a mountain stream and teeth as white as snow. It has long been a staple in ads for a product to be juxtaposed with a person or an object that the advertisers would like targeted consumers to regard as possessing some relevant and desirable quality that they might consequently associate directly with the product itself. 'We no longer buy oranges, we buy vitality,' as Vance Packard put it in his book *The Hidden Persuaders* in 1957.

The richly symbolic world of advertisements, their persuasive intent and the brevity of the form have rendered them attractive and amenable to semiotic analysis (e.g. Leymore, 1975, Williamson, 1978, Goldman, 1992). Cook offers an illustrative structural analysis of a Wrigley's commercial in terms of binary oppositions (Cook, 1992, pp. 54–8). Even the hard-headed marketing industry has employed semiotic principles in designing its campaigns, for example in British Telecom's 'It's Good to Talk' (1994), Guinness's 'Good Things Come to Those Who Wait' (1999) and Persil's 'Dirt is Fun' (2005–7). Semiotics has been productively combined with quantitative content analysis in academic research into commercials. Jhally (1987) charted variations in the codes of the genre according to whether commercials were broadcast in network prime time or in the breaks in (more male-oriented) broadcast team sports. Camerawork and editing codes have been shown to be key features in the gender-targeting of toy commercials: for instance, those directed at girls show a strong tendency to be slower-paced, having shots of longer duration and significantly more soft dissolves than ads for boys; ads targeted at mixed audiences tend to share the formal features of those for boys, making the female target market a marked category (Chandler and Griffiths, 2000). Children as young as six years old can distinguish ads targeted at males from those aimed at females by their distinctive formats and visual styles (Huston et al. 1984) (also see 'Children and Advertising').

The primary persuasive functions of the commercial are sometimes in tension not only with those of viewers whose primary purpose is to be entertained but also with the aesthetic priorities of some of those involved in video production. Film directors and producers who have been involved in the making of television commercials have included Terry Gilliam, Alan Parker, David Puttnam, Nicholas Roeg, Hugh Hudson, Ridley Scott, Tony Scott, Adrian Lyne, David Lynch, Tony Kaye, Andrew Niccol, Jonathan Glazer and Baz Luhrmann. Some have argued (typically as a criticism) that consequently ads have had a significant influence on film and video aesthetics.

Of the various media, viewers rate television as the most authoritative, influential and persuasive medium, so it is hardly surprising that advertisers make such heavy use of it (Arens, 2002, p. 510). However, a key problem for students and scholars in studying commercials is their lack of availability on DVDs in retail outlets. Such DVDs are largely confined to the industry either in the form of free promotional show-reels from particular agencies (which the characteristically invisible authorship of the genre makes difficult to trace) or as grossly overpriced collections of award-winning ads (a platform for directors to escape into more prestigious genres). Although commercials are now more easily (if illicitly) available via consumer-led initiatives such as YouTube, popular channels of distribution (including periodic television programmes featuring humorous and bizarre commercials) understandably over-represent ads which consumers find most entertaining. Since consumers are far less likely to record and retain commercials than programmes and films, another feature of the genre is its ephemerality.

The importance of commercials both economically and in the imagery of popular culture is belied by the lowly status and relative paucity of coverage devoted to advertising in the academic study of television. Since, as has frequently been observed, advertising is essential to commercial television (other than pay-per-view), it is a core function of television to deliver audiences to advertisers. Popular reactions mirror academic elitism – the emphasis given by many viewers to reporting their avoidance of commercials can be seen as echoing the guilt felt about 'wasting time' watching television at all. And yet the imagery deployed in advertisements generates a potent symbolic world reflecting dominant social values (Goffman, 1979), making them evocative sociocultural documents – as witness their prominence in the context of nostalgia. The ephemerality of commercials may indeed be a key reason why ads from one's earlier years can be so poignant.

Daniel Chandler

RECOMMENDED READING

Dickason, Renee (2000), *British Television Advertising*, Luton: Luton University Press.

Goldman, Robert (1992), *Reading Ads Socially*, London: Routledge.

Jhally, Sut (1987) *The Codes of Advertising: Fetishism and the Political Economy of Meaning in the Consumer Society*, New York: St Martin's Press.

Richards, Barry, MacRury, Iain and Botterill, Jackie (2000), *The Dynamics of Advertising*, Amsterdam: Harwood.

BIBLIOGRAPHY

Acuff, Dan (1997), *What Kids Buy and Why – The Psychology of Marketing to Kids,* New York: Free Press.

AEF (Advertising Education Forum) On-line database of articles pertaining to all aspects of children and advertising, available at URL <www.aeforum.org>, last accessed 2 March 2008.

Akass, Kim (2006), 'You Motherfucker: Al Swearengen's Oedipal Dilemma', in David Lavery (ed.), *Reading Deadwood: A Western to Swear By,* London and New York: I. B. Tauris.

Allen, Michael (2007), 'So Many Different Ways to Say it: Multi-Platform Storytelling in *CSI*' in Allen, Michael (ed.), *Reading CSI: Crime TV Under the Microscope,* London and New York: I. B. Tauris.

Allen, Robert C. (1985), *Speaking of Soap Operas,* Chapel Hill: University of North Carolina Press.

Allen, Robert C. (1989), 'Bursting Bubbles: "Soap Opera", Audiences, and the Limits of Genre', in Ellen Seiter et al. (eds), *Remote Control: Television, Audiences and Cultural Power,* London and New York: Routledge.

Allen, Robert C. (1995), *To be Continued … Soap Opera Around the World,* London: Routledge.

Allen-Mills, Tony (2007), 'Lost for words online as blog craze falters', *Times Online,* 25 March.

Alley, Robert S. (1985), 'Medical Melodrama', in B. G. Rose (ed.), *TV Genres: A Handbook and Reference Guide,* Westport: Greenwood.

Altman, Rick (1984), 'A Semantic/Syntactic Approach to Film Genre', *Cinema Journal,* vol. 23, no. 3.

Altman, Rick (1987), *The American Film Musical,* Bloomington: Indiana University Press.

Altman, Rick (1996), 'Cinema and Genre', in G. Nowell-Smith (ed.), *The Oxford History of World Cinema,* Oxford: Oxford University Press.

Altman, Rick (1999), *Film/Genre,* London: BFI.

Anderson, Christopher (1994), *Hollywood TV: The Studio System in the Fifties,* Austin: University of Texas Press.

Anderson, Kent (1978), *Television Fraud: The History and Implications of the Quiz Show Scandals,* Westport: Greenwood.

Andersen, Robin and Strate, Lance (eds) (2000), *Critical Studies in Media Commercialism,* Oxford: Oxford University Press.

Andrews, David (1998), 'Feminizing Olympic Reality', *International Review for the Sociology of Sport,* vol. 33, no. 1.

Ang, Ien (1985), *Watching* Dallas*: Soap Opera and the Melodramatic Imagination,* London: Routledge.

Ang, Ien (1991), *Desperately Seeking the Audience,* London and New York: Routledge.

Anthony, Andrew (2007), 'No Need to Pathologise', in Michael Allen (ed.), *Reading CSI: Crime TV Under the Microscope,* London and New York: I. B. Tauris.

Arens, William F. (2002), *Contemporary Advertising,* Boston, MA: McGraw-Hill.

Aristotle (trans. Ross, W. D., 1925), *Ethica Nicomachea,* London: Humphrey Milford.

Atkinson, Dave and Raboy, Marc (eds) (1998), *Public Service Broadcasting,* Paris: UNESCO.

Bailey, George and Lichty, Lawrence (1972), 'Rough Justice on a Saigon Street: A Gatekeeper Study of NC's Tet Execution Film', *Journalism Quarterly,* no. 49.

Bailey, Peter (ed.) (1986), *Music Hall: The Business of Pleasure,* Milton Keynes: Open University Press.

Banks, Jack (1996), *Monopoly Television: MTV's Quest to Control the Music,* Boulder: Westview.

Barnett, Steven (1990), *Games and Sets: The Changing Face of Sport on Television,* London: BFI.

Barnouw, Erik (1975), 'Television Theatre', in Eric Barnouw, *Tube of Plenty: The Evolution of American Television,* New York and Oxford: Oxford University Press.

Barr, Charles (1997), '"They Think It's All Over": The Dramatic Legacy of Live Television', in John Hill and Martin McLoone, (eds) *Big Picture, Small Screen: The Relations Between Film and Television,* Luton: University of Luton Press.

Barrett, Michèle and Barrett, Duncan (2001), Star Trek*: The Human Frontier,* Cambridge: Polity.

Barson, Michael (1985), 'The TV Western', in B. G. Rose (ed.), *TV Genres: A Handbook and Reference Guide,* Westport: Greenwood.

Baudrillard, J. (1983), 'The Ecstasy of Communication', in Hal Foster (ed.), *Postmodern Culture,* London: Pluto.

Baudrillard, Jean (1988), *Selected Writings* (ed. Mark Poster), Oxford: Polity.

Baxter, John (1970), *Science Fiction in the Cinema,* New York: Paperback Library.

Bazalgette, Cary and Buckingham, David (eds) (1995), *In Front of the Children: Screen Entertainment and Young Audiences,* London: BFI.

Bazalgette, Cary and Staples, Terry (1995), 'Unshrinking the Kids: Children's Cinema and the Family Film', in Cary

Bazalgette and David Buckingham (eds), *In Front of the Children: Screen Entertainment and Young Audiences*, London: BFI.

Bazalgette, Peter (2005), *Billion Dollar Game: How Three Men Risked it all and Changed the Face of Television*, London: Time Warner.

BBC Education (1994), *Middlemarch: A Viewer's Guide*, London: BBC Education.

BBC (1995), 'Pride and Prejudice': *From Page to Screen* (video-cassette), London: BBC Worldwide.

BBC (1996), *Producers' Guidelines*, London: BBC.

Bell, Allan (1991), *The Language of News Media*, Oxford and Cambridge, MA: Blackwell.

Bell, David and Hollows, Joanne (2005), *Ordinary Lifestyles: Popular Media, Consumption and Taste*, Maidenhead: Open University Press.

Bellah, Robert N., Madsen, Richard, Sullivan, William M., Swidler, Ann and Tipton, Steven M. (1992), *The Good Society*, New York: Knopf.

Benjamin, Walter (1977), 'The Author as Producer', in Walter Benjamin, *Understanding Brecht*, London: New Left.

Bennett, Tony et al. (eds) (1981), *Popular Television and Film*, London: BFI/Open University Press.

Bergson, H. (trans. Brereton, C. and Rothwell, R., 1911), *Laughter: An Essay on the Meaning of the Comic*, London: Macmillan.

Berkowitz, Dan (1997), *Social Meanings of News*, London: Sage.

Bernardi, Daniel Leonard (1998), 'Star Trek' *and History: Racing Toward a White Future*, Piscataway: Rutgers University Press.

Bianculli, D. (1992), *Teleliteracy*, New York: Simon & Schuster.

Bignell, Jonathan (2004), 'Sex and the City', in Jonathan Bignell, *An Introduction to Television Studies*, London and New York: Routledge.

Bignell, Jonathan (2005), *Big Brother: Reality TV in the Twenty-First Century*, Basingstoke: Palgrave Macmillan.

Billig, Michael (2005), *Laughter and Ridicule: Towards a Social Critique of Humour*, London, Thousand Oaks and New Delhi: Sage.

Biressi, Antia and Nunn, Heather (2004), *Reality TV: Realism and Revelations*, London: Wallflower Press.

Blaine, Allan (1994), 'Music Television', in Jeremy G. Butler, *Television: Critical Methods and Applications*, Belmont: Wadsworth.

Blakemore, Diane (1992), *Understanding Utterances: An Introduction to Pragmatics*, Oxford: Blackwell.

Billson, Anne (2005), Buffy the Vampire Slayer: *BFI Television Classic*, London: BFI.

Blood, Rebecca (2003), 'Weblogs and Journalism: do they connect?', *Nieman Reports*, Autumn, pp. 61–3.

Blumler, J. G. (1992), *The Future of Children's Television in Britain: an Enquiry for the Broadcasting Standards Council*, London: Broadcasting Standards Council.

Blumler, Jay and Gurevitch, Michael (1995), *The Crisis of Public Communication*, London: Routledge.

Blumler, J. G. (1998), *The Integrity and Erosion of Public Television for Children*, London: Broadcasting Standards Commission.

Boddy, William (1990), 'The Seven Dwarfs and the Money Grubbers: The Television Quiz Show Scandals Revisited', in Pat Mellencamp (ed.), *Logics of Television: Essays in Cultural Criticism*, Bloomington: University of Indiana Press.

Boddy, William (1992), *Fifties Television: The Industry and its Critics*, Urbana and Chicago: University of Illinois Press.

Boddy, William (1997), 'Senator Dodd Goes to Hollywood: Investigating Video Violence', in Lynn Spigel and Michael Curtin (eds), *The Revolution Wasn't Televised: Sixties Television and Social Transition*, New York: Routledge.

Boddy, William (1998), 'Sixty Million Viewers Can't Be Wrong: The Rise and Fall of the TV Western', in Ed Buscombe and Roberta Pearson (eds), *Back in the Saddle: New Approaches to the Western*, London: BFI.

Bondebjerg, Ib (1992), 'Intertextuality and Metafiction: Genre and Narrative in the Television Fiction of Dennis Potter', in M. Skormand and K. C. Schroder (eds), *Media Cultures: Reappraising Transnational Media*, London: Routledge.

Bonner, Frances (2003), *Ordinary Television: Analyzing Popular TV*, London: Sage.

Bourdieu, Pierre (1992), *Distinction* (1979, trans. R. Nice 1992), London: Routledge.

Bourdieu, Pierre (1998), *On Television* (trans. Priscilla Parkhurst Ferguson), New York: New Press.

Bowes, M. (1990), 'Only When I Laugh', in A. Goodwin and G. Whannel (eds), *Understanding Tele*vision, London and New York: Routledge.

Bowman, Shayne and Willis, Chris (2003), 'We Media: how audiences are shaping the future of news and information', *The Media Center at the American Press Institute*, available at: <http://www.hypergene.net/wemedia/>

Boyd-Barrett, Oliver and Newbold, Chris (1995), *Approaches to Media*, London: Arnold.

Boyd-Barrett, Oliver and Rantanen, Terhi (eds) (1998), *The Globalization of News*, London: Sage.

Boyd-Bowman, S. (1984), 'The Day After: Representations of the Nuclear Holocaust', *Screen*, vol. 25, no. 4–5.

Boyer, J. (1981), 'How Editors View Objectivity', *Journalism Quarterly*, no. 58.

Brandt, George (ed.) (1981), *British Television Drama*, Cambridge: Cambridge University Press.

Brandt, George (ed.) (1993), *British Television Drama in the 1980s*, Cambridge: Cambridge University Press.

Bratton, J. S. (ed.) (1986), *Music Hall: Performance and Style*, Milton Keynes: Open University Press.

Brecht, Bertolt (1964), *Brecht on Theatre: The Development of an Aesthetic*, ed./trans. by John Willett, London: Methuen.

Breed, Warren (1997), 'Social Control in the Newsroom: A Functional Analysis', in Dan Berkowitz (ed.), *Social Meanings of News*, London: Sage.

Britton, Andrew (1992), 'Invisible Eye', *Sight and Sound*, vol. 1, no. 10.

Broadcasting Act (1990), London: Stationery Office.

Broadcasting Act (1996), London: Stationery Office.

Brookes, Rod (2002), *Representing Sport*, London: Arnold.

Brookes, Rod (2004a), 'The Olympic Games' and 'The Superbowl', in Creeber, Glen (ed.), *50 Key Television Programmes*, London: Arnold.

Brookes, Rod (2004b), '24', in Creeber, Glen (ed.), *50 Key Television Programmes*, London: Arnold.

Brophy P. (ed.) (1994), *Kaboom!: Explosive Animation from Japan and America*, Sydney: Museum of Contemporary Art.

Brower, Sue (1997), 'Dallas', in Horace Newcomb (ed.), *Encyclopedia of Television*, Chicago and London: Fitzroy Dearborn.

Brown, Mary Ellen (1990), *Television and Women's Culture: The Politics of the Popular*, London: Sage.

Brown, Mary Ellen (1994), *Soap Opera and Women's Talk*, Thousand Oaks: Sage.

Brunsdon, Charlotte (1981), 'Crossroads: Notes on a Soap Opera', *Screen*, vol. 22, no. 4.

Brunsdon, Charlotte (1997), *Screen Tastes: Soap Opera to Satellite Dishes*, London: Routledge.

Brunsdon, Charlotte (1998), 'Structure of Anxiety: Recent British Television Crime Fiction', *Screen*, vol. 39, no. 3.

Brunsdon, Charlotte (2000), *The Feminist, the Housewife, and the Soap Opera*, Oxford: Oxford University Press.

Brunsdon, Charlotte (2003), 'Lifestyling Britain: The 8–9 Slot on British Television', *International Journal of Cultural Studies*, vol. 6, no. 5, pp. 5–23.

Brunsdon, Charlotte and Morley, David (1978), *Everyday Television: Nationwide*, London: BFI.

Brunsdon, Charlotte, D'Acci, Julie and Spigel, Lynn (eds) (1997), *Feminist Television Criticism: A Reader*, Oxford: Clarendon Press.

Brunsdon, Charlotte, Johnson, Catherine, Moseley, Rachel and Wheatley, Helen (2000), 'Factual Entertainment on British TV: The Midlands TV Research Group's 8–9 Project', *European Journal of Cultural Studies*, vol 4, no 1.

Bruzzi, Stella (2000), *New Documentary: A Critical Introduction*, London and New York: Routledge.

Buckingham, David (1987), *Public Secrets: 'EastEnders' and Its Audience*, London: BFI.

Buckingham, David (1995), 'On the Impossibility of Children's Television: The Case of Timmy Mallet', in Cary Bazalgette and David Buckingham (eds) *In Front of the Children: Screen Entertainment and Young Audiences*, London: BFI.

Buckingham, David (ed.) (2000), *Small Screens: Television for Children*, London: Continuum.

Buckingham, David, Davies, Hannah, Jones, Ken and Kelley, Peter (1999), *Children's Television in Britain*, London: BFI.

Butler, Jeremy G. (1994a), 'Narrative Structure: Television Stories', in Jeremy Butler (ed.), *Television: Critical Methods and Applications*, Belmont: Wadsworth.

Butler, Jeremy G. (1994b), *Television: Critical Methods and Applications*, Belmont: Wadsworth.

Butsch, Richard (2000), *The Making of American Audiences: From Stage to Television, 1750–1990*, Cambridge: Cambridge University Press.

Caldwell, John Thornton (1995), 'Excessive Discourse in the Mini-Series', in John Thornton Caldwell, *Televisuality: Style, Crisis, and Authority in American Television*, New Brunswick and New Jersey: Rutgers University Press.

Caldwell, John (2002), 'Prime-Time Fiction Theorizes the Docu-Real', in James Friedman (ed.), *Reality Squared: Televisual Discourse on the Real*, New Brunswick, New Jersey and London: Rutgers University Press.

Calvert, S. L., Huston, A. C., Watkins, B. A. and Wright, J. C. (1982), 'The effects of selective attention to television forms of children's comprehension of content', *Child Development*, vol. 53, pp. 601–10.

Canham-Clyne, J. (1996), 'When Both Sides Aren't Enough: The Restricted Debate over Health Care Reform', in J. Naureckas and J. Jackson (eds), *The FAIR Reader: An Extra Review of Press and Politics*, Boulder: Westview.

Cantor, Muriel G. and Pingree, Suzanne (1983), *The Soap Opera*, London: Sage.

Capsuto, Steven (2000), *Alternate Channels: the Uncensored Story of Gay and Lesbian Images on Radio and Television, 1930s to the Present*, New York: Ballantine.

Carpenter, Humphrey (1998), *Dennis Potter: The Authorized Biography*, London: Faber and Faber.

Carpenter, Humphrey (2000), *That Was Satire That Was: The Satire Boom of the 1960s*, London: Victor Gollancz.

Carpignano, P., Andersen, R., Aronowitz, S. and Difazio, W. (1990), 'Chatter in the Age of Electronic Reproduction: Talk Television and the "Public Mind"', *Sociotext*, no. 25/26.

Carson, Tom (1983), 'Homage to Catatonia', *Village Voice*, 19 April.

Carter, Cynthia, Branston, Gill and Allan, Stuart (eds) (1998), *News, Gender and Power*, London: Routledge.

Casey, Bernadette, Casey, Neil, Calvert, Ben, French, Liam and Lewis, Justin (2008), *Television Studies: the Key Concepts*, 2nd edn, London and New York: Routledge.

Cassidy, Jane and Taylor, Diane (1997), 'Doctor, doctor, where can I get an aspirin?', *Guardian*, 12 December.

Caughie, John (1991), 'Before the Golden Age: Early Television Drama', in John Corner (ed.), *Popular Television in Britain: Studies in Cultural History*, London: BFI.

Caughie, John (2000), *Television Drama: Realism, Modernism and British Culture*, London and New York: Oxford University Press.

Cawelti, John G. (1971), *The Six-Gun Mystique*, Bowling Green: Bowling Green University Press.

Cawelti, John (1976), *Adventure, Mystery and Romance*, Chicago: Chicago University Press.

Chamberlain, Daniel and Ruston, Scott (2007), '*24* and Twenty-First Century Quality Television' in Steven Peacock (ed.), *Reading 24: TV Against the Clock*, London and New York: I. B. Tauris.

Chambers, S., Karet, N. and Samson, N. (1998), *Cartoon Crazy?*, London: ITC.

Chandler, Daniel and Griffiths, Merris (2000), 'Gender-Differentiated Production Features in Toy Commercials', *Journal of Broadcasting and Electronic Media*, Summer, pp. 503–20, available at: <http://www.aber.ac.uk/media/Documents/short/toyads.html>, last accessed 2 March 2008.

Chapman, James (2006), *Inside the Tardis*, London and New York: I. B. Tauris.

Chion, Michel (1995), *David Lynch*, London: BFI.

Clark, Eric (1989), *The Want Makers*, New York: Viking.

Clarke, Alan (1986), '"This Is Not the Boy Scouts": Television Police Series and Definitions of Law and Order', in Tony Bennett, Colin Mercer and Janet Woollacott, *Popular Culture and Social Relations*, Milton Keynes: Open University Press.

Clarke, Alan (1992), '"You're Nicked!": Television Police Series and the Fictional Representation of Law and Order', in Dominic Strinati and Stephen Wagg (eds), *Come On Down? Popular Media Culture in Post-War Britain*, London: Routledge.

Clute, John and Nicholls, Peter (1999), *The Encyclopedia of Science Fiction*, London: Orbit.

Cohen, Ralph (1986), 'History and Genre', *New Literary History*, vol. 17, no. 2.

Cohen, S. (1972), *Folk Devils and Moral Panics*, London: MacGibbon & Kee.

Cohen, S. (1997), *Forbidden Animation*, Jefferson: McFarland.

Cohen, S. and Young, J. (1983), *The Manufacture of News*, London: Constable.

Collins, Jim (1992), 'Postmodernism and Television', in Robert C. Allen (ed.), *Channels of Discourse, Reassembled*, London and New York: Routledge.

Comolli, Jean-Luc (1980), 'Machines of the visible', in Teresa de Lauretis and Stephen Heath (eds), *The Cinematic Apparatus*, London: Macmillan.

Comolli, Jean-Luc and Narboni, Jean (1976), 'Cinema/Ideology/Criticism', in Bill Nichols (ed.), *Movies and Methods, I*, Berkeley: University of California Press.

Conboy, Martin (2004), *Journalism: A Critical History*, London: Sage.

Cook, Guy (1992), *The Discourse of Advertising*, London and New York: Routledge.

Cook Jim (ed.) (1982), *Television Sitcom*, BFI Dossier 17, London: BFI.

Cook, John R. (1995), *Dennis Potter: A Life on Screen*, Manchester and New York: Manchester University Press.

Copeland, Gary A. (2007), 'A History of Television Style', in Jeremy G. Butler (ed.) (2007), *Television: Critical Methods and Applications,* 3rd edn, Mahwah, New Jersey: Lawrence Erlbaum Associates.

Corner, John (1986), *Documentary and the Mass Media*, London: Arnold.

Corner, John (1992), 'Presumption as Theory: Realism in Television Studies', *Screen*, vol. 33, no. 1.

Corner, John (1995), *Television Form and Public Address*, London: Arnold.

Corner, John (1996), *The Art of Record*, Manchester: Manchester University Press.

Corner, John (2006), 'Analysing Factual TV: How to Study Television Documentary', in Glen Creeber (ed.), *Tele-Visions: An Introduction to Studying Television*, London: BFI.

Corrigan, Timothy (1991), 'Music from Heaven, Bodies in Hell: The Singing Detective', in Timothy Corrigan (ed.), *A Cinema Without Walls: Movies and Culture after Vietnam*, London: Routledge.

Coward, Rosalind (1987), 'Dennis Potter and the Question of the Television Author', *Critical Quarterly*, vol. 29, no. 4.

Creeber, Glen (1996), '"Banality with a Beat": Dennis Potter and the Paradox of Popular Music', *Media, Culture and Society*, vol. 18, no. 3.

Creeber, Glen (1998), *Dennis Potter: Between Two Worlds, A Critical Reassessment*, London and New York: Macmillan.

Creeber, Glen (2001a), '"Taking Our Personal Lives Seriously": Intimacy, Continuity and Memory in the Television Serial', *Media, Culture and Society*, vol. 23, no. 4.

Creeber, Glen (2001b), 'Cigarettes and Alcohol: Investigating Gender, Genre and Gratification in Prime Suspect', *Television and New Media*, vol. 2, May.

Creeber, Glen (2002), '"TV Ruined the Movies": Television, Tarantino and the Intimate World of *The Sopranos*' in David Lavery (ed.), *This Thing of Ours: Investigating* The Sopranos, New York: Columbia University Press.

Creeber, Glen (2004a), 'Who Wants to Be a Millionaire?', in Glen Creeber (ed.), *50 Key Television Programmes*, London: Arnold.

Creeber, Glen (2004b), *Serial Television: Big Drama on the Small Screen*, London: BFI.

Creeber, Glen (2007), The Singing Detective: *BFI Television Classic*, London: BFI.

Crowther, Bruce and Pinfold, Mike (1987), *Bring Me Laughter: Four Decades of TV* Comedy, London: Columbus.

Cumberbatch, Guy (1999), *Television: The Public's View*, London: ITC.

Curran, James and Park, Myung-Jin (eds) (1999), *De-Westernizing Media Studies*, London: Routledge.

Curran, J. and Seaton, J. (1991), *Power Without Responsibility*, London: Routledge,

Curti, Merle (1967), 'The Changing Concept of Human Nature in the Literature of American Advertising', *Business History Review*, no. 41.

D'Acci, Julie (1987), 'The Case of *Cagney and Lacey*', in Helen Baehr and Gillian Dyer (eds), *Boxed In: Women and Television*, London: Pandora.

D'Acci, Julie (1994), *Defining Women: Television and the Case of* Cagney and Lacey, Chapel Hill: University of North Carolina Press.

Dauncey, Hugh (1996), 'French Reality Television: More Than a Matter of Taste?', *European Journal of Communication*, vol. 11, no. 1.

Davis, Glynn and Dickinson, Kay (eds) (2004), *Teen TV: Genre, Consumption and Identity*, London: BFI.

Davis, Steven (1991), *Pragmatics: A Reader*, Oxford: Oxford University Press.

Dayan, David and Katz, Elihu (1992), *Media Events: The Live Broadcasting of History*, Cambridge, MA: Harvard University Press.

Day-Lewis, Sean (1998), *Talk of Drama: Views of the Television Dramatist Now and Then*, Luton: University of Luton Press.

Dean, Jodi (1997), 'The Truth is Out There: Aliens and the Fugitivity of Postmodern Truth', *Camera Obscura*, no. 40–1.

Delaney, Paul (1988), 'Potterland', *Dalhousie Review*, vol. 68, part 4.

Delaney, Sean, Forbes, Tess, Keramos, Anastasia, Laffey, Erinna and Ormsby, Andrew (1996), '*Mary Shelley's Frankenstein*;

Northern Exposure; *The Vicar of Dibley*: Information Source Pack', London: BFI Library and Information Services.

DeLong, Thomas (1991), *Quiz Craze: America's Infatuation with the Radio and Television Game Show*, Westport: Praeger.

Del Vecchio, Gene (1997), *Creating Ever-Cool – A Marketer's Guide to a Kid's Heart*, Gretna: Pelican.

De Moras, Lisa (1997), 'The Sound and the Fury', The Hollywood Reporter *1997–98 TV Preview*, September.

Derrida, Jacques (1990), 'The Law of Genre', in D. Attridge (ed.), *Acts of Literature* (trans. Avital Ronell), New York: Routledge.

Dholakia, Ruby Roy, Mundorf, Norbet and Dholakia, Nikhilesh (eds) (1996), *New Infotainment Technologies in the Home: Demand-Side Perspectives* (Lea's Communication Series), Boston, MA: Lawrence Erlbaum Associates.

Dichter, Ernest (1964), *Handbook of Consumer Motivations*, New York: McGraw-Hill.

Dickason, Renee (2000), *British Television Advertising*, Luton: Luton University Press.

Dickenson, Roger, Harindranath, Ramaswami and Linné, Olga (1998), *Approaches to Audiences: A Reader*, London: Arnold.

Donald, James (1985), 'Anxious Moments: *The Sweeney* in 1975', in Manuel Alvarado and John Stewart (eds), *Made for Television: Euston Films Limited*, London: BFI.

Donatelli, Cindy and Alward, Sharon (2002), '"I Dread You"?: Married to the Mob in *The Godfather, Goodfellas* and *The Sopranos*', in David Lavery (ed.), *This Thing of Ours: Investigating* The Sopranos, New York: Columbia University Press.

Donnelly, K. J. (2004), 'Walking with Dinosaurs', in Glen Creeber (ed.), *50 Key Television Programmes*, London: Arnold.

Doty, Alexander (1993), *Making Things Perfectly Queer: Interpreting Mass Culture*, Minneapolis: University of Minnesota Press.

Dovey, J. (2000), *Freakshow: First Person Media and Factual Television*, London: Pluto.

Drysdale, David (2006), '"Laws and Every Other Damn Thing": Authority, Bad Faith, and the Unlikely Success of *Deadwood*', in David Lavery (ed.), *Reading* Deadwood: *A Western to Swear By*, London and New York: I. B. Tauris.

Durkin, Kevin (1985), *Television, Sex-Roles and Children*. Milton Keynes and Philadelphia: Open University Press.

Durkin, Kevin (1995), *Developmental Social Psychology*, Oxford: Blackwell.

Dyer, Gillian (1982), *Advertising as Communication*, London and New York: Routledge.

Dyer, Richard (1986), *Heavenly Bodies: Film Stars and Society*, London: BFI/Macmillan.

Dyer, Richard (1992), *Only Entertainment*, London: Routledge.

Eaton, M. (1981), 'Television Situation Comedy', in Tony Bennett et al. (eds), *Popular Television and Film*, London: BFI/Open University Press.

Eaton, Mary (1995), 'A Fair Cop? Viewing the Effects of the Canteen Culture in Prime Suspect and Between the Lines', in David Kidd-Hewitt and Richard Osborne (eds), *Crime and the Media*, London: Pluto.

Eco, Umberto (1972), 'Towards a Semiotic Inquiry into the Television Message' (trans. Paola Splendore), *Working Papers in Cultural Studies*, no. 3.

Eco, Umberto (1987), *Travels in Hyperreality: Essays* (trans. William Weaver), London: Picador.

Edgerton, Gary (1985), 'The American Made-for-TV Movie', in B.G. Rose (ed.), *TV Genres: A Handbook and Reference Guide*, Westport: Greenwood.

Edgley, Charles (1988), 'Commercial Sex: Prostitution, Pornography and Advertising', in Kathleen McKinney and Sue Sprecher (eds), *The Social Context of Human Sexuality*, New York: Ablex.

Edelman, M. (1988), *Constructing the Political Spectacle*, Chicago: University of Chicago Press.

Eldridge, John (ed.) (1995), *Glasgow University Media Group Reader*, Volume 1, London: Routledge.

Ellis, John (1989, orig. pub. 1982), *Visible Fictions: Cinema, Television*, Video, London and New York: Routledge.

Emmanuel, Susan (1992), 'Ien Ang, Watching *Dallas*', in Martin Barker and Ann Beezer (eds), *Reading into Cultural Studies*, London and New York: Routledge.

Epstein, Edward Jay (2000), *News from Nowhere: Television and the News*, Chicago: Ivan R. Dee.

Epstein, Michael (1996), 'Spaced Out: The *Star Trek* Literary Phenomenon: Where no TV Series has Gone Before', *Television Quarterly*, vol. 28, no 1.

Erickson, Hal (1995), *Television Cartoon Shows: An Illustrated Encyclopedia, 1949–1993*, Jefferson: McFarland.

Esslin, Martin (1961), *The Theatre of the Absurd*, New York: Doubleday.

Evans, Jessica and Hesmondhalgh, David (2005), *Understanding Media: Inside Celebrity*, Maidenhead: Open University Press.

Fadul, A. (ed.) (1993), *Serial Fictions in TV: The Latin American Telenovelas*, São Paulo: ECA/USP.

Felperin, Leslie (1999), 'Genre: Teenpics', in P. Cook and M. Bernink (eds), *The Cinema Book*, 2nd edn, London: BFI.

Ferguson, Euan (2001), 'Why Chris Morris Had to Make *Brass Eye*', *Observer*, 5 August, p. 13.

Fetveit, A. (1999), 'Reality TV in the Digital Era: A Paradox in Visual Culture', *Media, Culture and Society*, vol. 21, no. 6.

Feuer, Jane (1983), 'The Concept of Live Television: Ontology as Ideology', in E. Ann Kaplan (ed.), *Regarding Television: Critical Approaches – an Anthology*, Frederick: University Publications of America/American Film Institute.

Feuer, Jane (1986), 'Narrative Form in American Network Television', in Colin MacCabe, (ed.), *High Theory/Low Culture*, Manchester: Manchester University Press.

Feuer, Jane (1992), 'Genre and Television', in R. Allen (ed.), *Channels of Discourse, Reassembled: Television and Contemporary Criticism*, London and New York: Routledge.

Feuer, Jane (1994), 'Melodrama, Serial Form, and Television Today', in Horace Newcombe (ed.), *Television: The Critical View*, New York: Oxford University Press.

Feuer, Jane (1995), 'Serial Form, Melodrama, and Reaganite Ideology in Eighties TV', in Jane Feuer, *Seeing Through the Eighties: Television and Reaganism*, London: BFI.

Fish, Stanley (1980), *Is There a Text in this Class?: The Authority of Interpretive Communites*, Cambridge, MA: Harvard University Press.

Fishbein, Leslie (1983), '*Roots*: Docudrama and the Interpretation of History', in Leslie Fishbein (ed.), *American History/American Television: Interpreting the Video Past*, New York: Frederick Ungar.

Fisher, David and Davies, Michael P. (eds) (1999), Who Wants to Be Millionaire?, New York: Hyperion.

Fishman, Mark (1997), 'News and Non-events: Making the Visible Invisible', in Dan Berkowitz (ed.), *Social Meanings of News*, London: Sage.

Fiske, John (1987a), 'Quizzical Pleasures', in John Fiske, *Television Culture*, New York and London: Routledge.

Fiske, John (1987b), *Television Culture*, New York and London: Routledge.

Fiske, John (1989), 'Moments of Television', in Ellen Seiter et al. (eds), *Remote Control: Television, Audiences, and Cultural Power*, London: Routledge.

Fitzpatrick, Michael (2000), *The Tyranny of Health: Doctors and the Regulation of Lifestyle*, London: Routledge.

Flitterman-Lewis, Sandy (1983), 'The Real Soap Operas: TV Commercials', in E. Ann Kaplan (ed.), *Regarding Television*, Frederick: University Publications of America.

Forrest, Emma (1998), 'Inside Story: The Future is Female', *Guardian*, 16 December.

Fowler, Roger (1992), *Language in the News*, London: Routledge.

Franklin, Franklin (1997), *Newszak and News Media*, London: Arnold.

Freadman, Ann (1988), 'Untitled: (On Genre)', *Cultural Studies*, vol. 2, no. 1.

Freud S. (trans. Strachey, J., 1976), *Jokes and their Relation to the Unconscious*, Harmondsworth: Penguin.

Frith, Simon (1996), *Performing Rites: On the Value of Popular Music*, Oxford: Oxford University Press.

Frow, John (2006), *Genre*, London and New York: Routledge.

Frye, Northrop (1957), *The Anatomy of Criticism: Four Essays*, Princeton: Princeton University Press.

Fuller, Graham (ed.) (1993), *Potter on Potter*, London: Faber and Faber.

Fuller, Graham (1996), 'Cautionary Tale', *Sight and Sound*, vol. 6, no. 3.

Fulton, Roger and Betancourt, John (2000), *Encyclopedia of TV Science Fiction*, London: Boxtree.

Fuqua, Joy V. (1995), 'There's a Queer in my Soap!', in Robert C. Allen (ed.), *To Be Continued . . . Soap Opera Around the World*, Chapel Hill: University of North Carolina Press.

Furniss, M. (1998), *Art in Motion: Animation Aesthetics*, Sydney: John Libbey.

Galtung, Johan and Ruge, Mari (1965), 'The Structure of Foreign News', *Journal of Peace Research*, no. 2.

Galtung, Johan and Ruge, Mari (1983), 'Structuring and Selecting News', in S. Cohen and J. Young (1983), *The Manufacture of News*, London: Constable.

Gans, H. (1979), *Deciding What's News*, New York: Vintage.

Gans, H. (1985), 'Are US Journalists Dangerously Liberal?', *Columbia Journalism Review*, November/December.

Gardner, Carl and Wyver, John (1983), 'The Single Play: From Reithian Reverence to Cost-accounting and Censorship', *Screen*, vol. 24, no. 4–5.

Garfinkel, Harold (1992), *Studies in Ethnomethodology*, Cambridge: Polity.

Geraghty, Christine (1987), 'The Continuous Serial – A Definition', in Richard Dyer, Christine Geraghty, Jordan Marion, Terry Lovell, Richard Paterson and John Stewart, *Coronation Street*, London: BFI.

Geraghty, Christine (1991), *Women and Soap Opera*, Cambridge: Polity.

Gibberman, Susan (1991), '*Star Trek*': *An Annotated Guide to Resources on the Development, the Phenomenon, the People, the Television Series, the Films, the Novels and the Recordings*, Jefferson: McFarland.

Gibbons, Tom (1998), *Regulating the Media*, London: Sweet & Maxwell.

Giddens, Anthony (1979), *Central Problems in Social Theory: Action, Structure and Contradiction*, London: Macmillan.

Giddings, Robert Selby (1990), *Screening the Novel*, London: Macmillan.

Gilbert, Stephen W. (1995), *Fight and Kick and Bite: The Life and Work of Dennis Potter*, London: Hodder & Stoughton.

Gillespie, Marie (1995), *Television, Ethnicity and Cultural Change*, London: Routledge.

Gitlin, Todd (1997), 'The Anti-Political Populism of Cultural Studies', in Marjorie Ferguson and Peter Golding (eds), *Cultural Studies in Question*, London: Sage.

Glasgow Media Group (1976), *Bad News*, London: Routledge & Kegan Paul.

Glasgow Media Group (1980), *More Bad News*, London: Routledge & Kegan Paul.

Glasgow Media Group (1982), *Really Bad News*, London: Writers and Readers.

Gledhill, Christine (1992), 'Speculations on the Relationship between Soap Opera and Melodrama', *Quarterly Review of Film Studies*, vol. 14, no. 1–2.

Goedkoop, Richard (1985), 'The Game Show', in B. G. Rose (ed.), *TV Genres: A Handbook and Reference Guide*, Westport: Greenwood.

Goffman, Erving (1979), *Gender Advertisements*. New York: Harper & Row.

Goldman, Robert (1992), *Reading Ads Socially*, London: Routledge.

Goodwin, Andrew (1992), *Dancing in the Distraction Factory: Music Television and Popular Culture*, Minneapolis: University of Minnesota Press.

Goodwin, A., Kerr, P. and Macdonald, I. (eds) (1983), *Drama-documentary*, BFI Dossier 19, London: BFI.

Gras, Vernon W. (2000), 'Dennis Potter's *The Singing Detective*: An Exemplum of Dialogic Ethics', in Vernon W. Gras and John R. Cook (eds), *The Passion of Dennis Potter*, New York: St Martin's Press.

Gray, Chris, Figueroa-Sarriera, Hiedi and Mentor, Steven (eds) (1995), *The Cyborg Handbook*, London: Routledge.

Greenwald, Jeff (1998), *Future Perfect: How 'Star Trek' Conquered Planet Earth*, Harmondsworth: Penguin.

Gregory, Chris (1997), *Be Seeing You: Decoding 'The Prisoner'*, Luton: University of London Press.

Gregory, Chris (2000), '*Star Trek*': *Parallel Narratives*, London: Macmillan.

Griffiths, Merris (2002), 'Blue Worlds and Pink Worlds – A Portrait of Intimate Polarity', in David Buckingham (ed.), (2002), *Small Screens*, London: Leicester University Press, pp. 159–84, available at <http://www. merrisgriffiths. co.uk/ bluepink.htm>, last accessed 2 March 2008.

Griffiths, Merris and O'Malley, Tom (2007), 'Media Literacy in Wales: A Critical Review of Industry and Education Policies', *Cyfrwng*, no. 4, pp. 7–23.

Gripsrud, J. (1995), *The 'Dynasty' Years: Hollywood Television and Critical Media Studies*, London: Routledge.

Gripsrud, J. (ed.) (1999), *Television and Common Knowledge*, London: Routledge.

Gruneau, Richard, (1989), 'Making Spectacle: A Case Study in Television Sports Production', in Lawrence Wenner (ed.), *Media, Sports and Society*, Newbury Park: Sage.

Gunter, Barrie and Furnham, Adrian (1998), *Children as Consumers: A Psychological Analysis of the Young People's Market*, London: Routledge.

Gunter, B. and McAleer, J. (1997), *Children and Television*, London and New York: Routledge.

Gunter, Barrie and Winstone, Paul (1992), *TV: The Public's View*, London: John Libbey.

Hackett, Pat (ed.) (1991), *The Andy Warhol Diaries*, New York: Warner.

Hall, Stuart (1973), 'Encoding and Decoding in Television Discourse', CCCS Stencilled Paper no. 7; also in Simon During (ed.) (1993), *The Cultural Studies Reader*, London and New York: Routledge.

Hall, S., Critcher, C., Jefferson, T., Clarke, J. and Roberts, B. (1978), *Policing the Crisis: Mugging, the State and Law and Order*, London: Macmillan.

Halliwell, Leslie (1987), *Double Take and Fade Away*, London: Grafton.

Hamamoto, Darrell (1991), *Nervous Laughter: Television Situation Comedy and Liberal Democratic Ideology*, New York: Praeger.

Hanely, Richard (1997), *The Metaphysics of 'Star Trek'*, New York: Basic Books.

Haralovich, Mary Beth (1992), 'Sitcoms and Suburbs', in Lynn Spigel and Denise Mann (eds), *Private Screenings: Television and the Female Consumer*, Minneapolis: University of Minnesota Press.

Harcup, Tony (2003), 'The Unspoken – Said', *Journalism*, vol. 4, no. 3, pp. 356–76.

Harper, Christopher (2000), *And That's the Way it Will Be: News and Information in a Digital World*, New York: New York University Press.

Harraway, Donna (1995), 'Cyborgs and Symbionts: Living Together in the New World Order', in Chris Gray, Heidi Figueroa-Sarriera and Steven Mentor (eds), *The Cyborg Handbook*, London: Routledge.

Harrington, C. Lee and Bielby, Denise D. (1995), *Soap Fans: Pursuing Pleasure and Making Meaning in Everyday Life*, Philadelphia: Temple University Press.

Harris, Geraldine (2006), *Beyond Representation: Television Drama and the Politics and Aesthetics of Identity*, Manchester: Manchester University Press.

Harrison, J. (2000), *Terrestrial Television News in Britain: The Culture of Production*, Manchester: Manchester University Press.

Harrison, Jackie (2005), *News*, London: Routledge Introductions to Media Communications.

Harrison, Taylor, Projansky, Sarah, Ono, Kent and Helford, Elyce (eds) (1996), *Enterprise Zones: Critical Positions on 'Star Trek'*, Oxford: Westview.

Hartley, John (1982), *Understanding News*, London: Routledge.

Hartley, John (1987), 'Invisible Fictions: Television Audiences, Paedocracy, Pleasure', *Textual Practice*, vol. 1, no. 2.

Hartley, John (1992a), *Tele-ology: Studies in Television*, London and New York: Routledge.

Hartley, John (1992b), *The Politics of Pictures: The Creation of the Public in the Age of Popular Media*, London and New York: Routledge.

Hartley, John (1996), *Popular Reality: Journalism, Modernity, Popular Culture*, London and New York: Arnold.

Hartley, John (1999), *Uses of Television*, London and New York: Routledge.

Hartley, John (2000), 'The Frequencies of Public Writing: Tomb, Tome and Time as Technologies of the Public', *Media in Transition Conference Articles*, available at <http://media-in-transition.mit.edu/articles/>, Cambridge, MA: Massachusetts Institute of Technology.

Hartley, John (2006), 'Television and Globalisation', in Glen Creeber (ed.), *Tele-Visions: An Introduction to Studying Television*, London: BFI.

Hartley, John and McKee, Alan (2000), *The Indigenous Public Sphere: The Reporting and Reception of Aboriginal Issues in the Australian Media*, Oxford: Oxford University Press.

Haug, Wolfgang Fritz (1986), *Critique of Commodity Aesthetics: Appearance, Sexuality, and Advertising in Capitalist Society*, Minneapolis: University of Minnesota Press.

Hayward, Jennifer Poole (1997), *Consuming Pleasures: Active Audiences and Serial Fictions from Dickens to Soap Opera*, Lexington: University Press of Kentucky.

Hayward, Phillip (1990), 'How ABC Capitalised on Cultural Logic – The "*Moonlighting*" Story', reprinted in Manuel Alvarado and John O. Thompson (eds), *The Media Reader*, London: BFI.

Heath, S. and Skirrow, G. (1977), 'Television: A World in Action', *Screen*, vol. 18, no. 2.

Hecker, Sidney and Stewart, David W. (1988), *Nonverbal Communication in Advertising*, Lexington, Toronto: D. C. Heath & Co.

Held, David (2000), *Globalizing World?*, London: Routledge.

Helter, Dana (ed.) (2007), *Makeover Television: Realities Remodelled*, London and New York: I. B. Tauris.

Hendershot, H. (ed.) (2004), *Nickelodeon Nation*, New York and London: New York University Press.

Henry, Astrid (2004), 'Orgasms and empowerment: *Sex and the City* and the third wave feminism', in Kim Ackass, Kim and Janet McCabe (eds) (2004), *Reading Sex and the City*, London and New York: I. B. Tauris.

Herbert, Daniel (2007), 'Days and Hours of the Apocalypse: *24* and the Nuclear Narrative', in Steven Peacock (ed.),

Reading 24: TV Against the Clock, London and New York: I. B. Tauris.

Herman, E. (1999), *The Myth of the Liberal Media*, New York: Peter Lang.

Herman, E. and Chomsky, N. (1988), *Manufacturing Consent: The Political Economy of the Mass Media*, New York: Pantheon.

Hermes, Joke (2005), *Re-Reading Popular Culture*, Malden, MA: Blackwell.

Herold, C. M. (1998), 'The "Brazilianisation" of Brazilian Television: A Critical Review', *Studies in Latin American Popular Culture*, vol. 7.

Herzog, Herta (1944), 'What Do We Really Know About Daytime Serial Listeners?', in Paul F. Lazarsfelf and Frank N. Stanton (eds), *Radio Research, 1942–3*, New York: Duell, Sloan and Pearce.

Hess Wright, Judith (1986), 'Genre Films and the Status Quo', in B. K. Grant (ed.), *Film Genre Reader*, Austin: University of Texas Press.

Hey, Kenneth (1983) '*Marty*: Aesthetics vs Medium in Early TV Drama', in Leslie Fishbein (ed.), *American History/American Television: Interpreting the Video Past*, New York: Frederick Ungar.

Hiddlestone, Janine (2006), 'All that Glitters: Coloring, Place and Identity in *CSI*', in Donn Cortez (ed.), *Investigating CSI: An Unauthorized Look Inside the Crime Labs of Las Vegas, Miami, and New York*, Dallas: Benbella.

Hilfer, Anthony (2000), 'Run Over by One's Own Story: Genre and Ethos in Dennis Potter's "*The Singing Detective*"', in Jonathan Bignell, Stephen Lacey and Madeleine MacMurraugh-Kavanagh (eds), *British Television Drama: Past, Present and Future*, London and New York: Palgrave.

Hill, Annette (1999), 'Crime and Crisis: British Reality TV in Action', in Ed Buscombe (ed.), *British Television: A Reader*, Oxford: Oxford University Press.

Hill, Annette (2005), *Reality TV: Audiences and Popular Factual Television*, London and New York: Routledge.

Hill, Annette (2007), *Restyling Factual TV: Audiences and News, Documentary and Reality Genres*, London: Routledge.

Hill, John (1991), 'Television and Pop: the Case of the 1950s', in John Corner (ed.), *Popular Television in Britain: Studies in Cultural History*, London: BFI.

Hiller, J. and Lovell, A. (1972), *Studies in Documentary*, London: Secker & Warburg.

Hills, Matt (2004), '*Doctor Who*', in Glen Creeber (ed.), *50 Key Television Programmes*, London: Arnold.

Hilmes, Michelle (1997*), Radio Voices: American Broadcasting, 1922–1952*, Minneapolis: University of Minnesota Press.

Hilton, Mary (ed.) (1996), *Potent Fictions: Children's Literacy and the Challenge of Popular Culture*, London: Routledge.

Himmelstein, Hal (1994), *Television Myth and the American Mind*, Westport: Praeger.

Hobbes, T. (1914), *Leviathan*, Letchworth: Aldine Press.

Hobson, A. Lowe and P. Willis (eds) (1980), *Culture, Media, Language*, London: Hutchinson.

Hobson, Dorothy (1982), '*Crossroads*': *The Drama of a Soap Opera*, London: Methuen.

Hobson, Dorothy (1989), 'Soap Operas at Work', in Ellen Seiter et al. (eds), *Remote Control: Television, Audiences, and Cultural Power*, London: Routledge.

Hockley, Luke (2000), 'Spectacle as Commodity: Special Effects in Feature Films', in Richard Wise and Jeanette Steemers (eds), *Multimedia: A Critical Introduction*, London: Routledge.

Hodge, B. and Tripp, D. (1986), *Children and Television*, Cambridge: Polity.

Hoffer, Thomas W., Musburger, Robert and Nelson, Richard Alan (1985), 'Docudrama', in B. G. Rose (ed.), *TV Genres: A Handbook and Reference Guide*, Westport: Greenwood.

Holland, Patricia (1997), 'Narrative Television', in Patricia Holland, *The Television Handbook*, London and New York: Routledge.

Hollingsworth, Mike and Norton-Taylor, Richard (1988), *Blacklist*, London: Macmillan.

Holmes, Su (2003), '"All You've Got to Worry About is the Task, Having a Cup of Tea, and Doing a Bit of Sunbathing": Approaching Celebrity in *Big Brother*', in Su Holmes and Deborah Jermyn (eds), *Understanding Reality Television*, London and New York: Routledge.

Holmes Su (2006), 'It's a Jungle Out There!: Playing the Game of Fame in Celebrity Reality TV', in Su Holmes and Sean Redmond (eds), *Framing Celebrity: New Directions in Celebrity Culture*, London and New York: Routledge.

Holmes, Su (2007), '"The Question Is – Is It All Worth Knowing?" The Cultural Circulation of the Early British Quiz Show', *Media Culture Society*, vol. 29, no. 1, pp. 53–74.

Holmes, Su, and Jermyn, Deborah (2003), *Understanding Reality Television*, London: Routledge.

Home, Anna (1993), *Into the Box of Delights*, London: BBC.

Hudson, R. (1972), 'Television in Britain: Description and Dissent', *Theatre Quarterly*, vol. 2, no. 6.

Hunningher, Joost (1993), '*The Singing Detective*: Who done it?', in George Brandt (ed.), *British Television Drama in the 1980s*, Cambridge and New York: Cambridge University Press.

Hurd, Geoffrey (1981), 'The Television Presentation of the Police', in Tony Bennett et al. (eds), *Popular Television and Film*, London: BFI/Open University Press.

Huston, Aletha C., Greer, D., Wright, John C., Welch, Renate and Ross, R. (1984), 'Children's Comprehension of Televised Formal Features with Masculine and Feminine

Connotations', *Developmental Psychology*, vol. 20, no. 4, pp. 707–16.

Hutcheon, Linda (1989), *The Politics of Postmodernism*, London: Routledge.

Iyengar, S. (1991), *Is Anyone Responsible?*, Chicago: University of Chicago Press.

Iyengar, S. and Kinder, D. (1987), *News That Matters*, Chicago: University of Chicago Press.

Iyengar, S., Peters, M. and Kinder, D. (1982) 'Demonstrations of the "Not-so-minimal" Consequences of Television News Programs', *American Political Science Review*, no. 81.

Jacobs, Jason (1998), 'No Respect: Shot and Scene in Early Television Drama', in Jeremy Ridgman (ed.), *Boxed Sets: Television Representations of Theatre*, Luton: University of Luton Press.

Jacobs, Jason (2000), *The Intimate Screen: Early British Television Drama*, New York and Oxford: Oxford University Press.

Jacobs, Jason (2003), *Body Trauma TV: The New Hospital Dramas*, London: BFI.

Jacobs, Jason (2004), '*Teletubbies*' in Glen Creeber (ed.), *50 Key Television Programmes*, London: Arnold.

Jacobs, Jason, (2006), 'Al Swearengen, Philosopher King', in David Lavery (ed.), *Reading* Deadwood: *A Western to Swear By*, London and New York: I. B. Tauris.

Jaglom, Leona M. and Gardner, Howard (1981), 'Decoding the worlds of television', *Studies in Visual Communication*, vol. 7, no. 1, pp. 33–47.

Jameson, Fredric (1993), *Postmodernism or the Cultural Logic of Late Capitalism*, London: Verso.

Jancovich, Mark (2001), 'Genre and Audience: Genre Classifications and Cultural Distinctions in the Mediation of Silence of the Lambs', in R. Maltby and R. Stokes (eds), *Hollywood Spectatorship*, London: BFI.

Jauss, Robert Hanns (1982), *Toward an Aesthetic of Reception* (trans. T. Bahti), Brighton: Harvester.

Jencks, Charles (1989), *What is Postmodernism?*, London: Academy Editions.

Jenkins, Henry (1992a), *What Made Pistachio Nuts? Early Sound Comedy and the Vaudeville Aesthetic*, New York: Columbia University Press.

Jenkins, Henry (1992b), *Textual Poachers: Television Fans and Participatory Culture*, New York: Routledge.

Jenkins, Steve (1984), '*Hill Street Blues*', in Jane Feuer, Paul Kerr and Tise Vahimagi (eds), *MTM – 'Quality Television'*, London: BFI.

Jensen, K. B. (1987), 'News as Ideology: Economic Statistics and Political Ritual in Television Network News', *Journal of Communication*, Winter.

Jermyn, Deborah (2007), 'Reasons to Split Up: Interactivity, Realism and the Multiple-Image Screens in *24*' in Steven Peacock (ed.), *Reading 24: TV Against the Clock*, London and New York: I. B. Tauris.

Jhally, Sut (1987), *The Codes of Advertising: Fetishism and the Political Economy of Meaning in the Consumer Society*, New York: St Martin's Press.

Johnson, Catherine (2005), *Telefantasy*, London: BFI.

Johnson, William (ed.) (1972), *Focus on the Science Fiction Film*, New York: Prentice-Hall.

Jordan, Marion (1981), 'Realism and Convention', in Richard Dyer, Christine Geraghty, Marion Jordan, Terry Lovell, Richard Paterson and John Stewart (eds), *Coronation Street*, London: BFI.

Jowell, Tessa (2004), Speech at Media Literacy Seminar, 27 January, available at: <http://www.culture.gov.uk/ Reference_library/Minister_Speeches/Ministers_Speech_ Archive/Tessa_Jowell/dcms_Jan_2004_BFI.htm>, last accessed 2 March 2008.

Kackman, Michael (2005), *Citizen Spy: Television, Espionage, and Cold War Culture, Commerce and Mass Culture Series*, Minneapolis: University of Minnesota Press.

Kaleta, Kenneth C. (1993), *David Lynch*, New York: Twayne.

Kant, I. (trans. Guyer P. and Matthews E., 2000), *Critique of the Power of Judgment*, Cambridge: Cambridge University Press.

Kapsis, Robert E. (1991), 'Hollywood Genres and the Production of Culture Perspective', in B. A. Austin (ed.), *Current Research in Film: Audiences, Economics and the Law*, Vol. 5, Norwood: Ablex.

Karpf, Anne (1988), *Doctoring the Media*, London: Routledge.

Katz, Elihu (1990), 'A propos des médias et de leurs effets', in L. Sfez and G. Coutlée (eds), *Technologies et symboliques de la communication*, Grenoble: Presses Universitaires de Grenoble.

Katz, Helen (1989), 'The Future of Public Broadcasting in the US', *Media, Culture and Society*, vol. 11.

Kavanagh, James H. (1990), 'Feminism, Humanism and Science in Alien', in Annette Kuhn (ed.), *Alien Zone: Cultural Theory and Contemporary Science Fiction Cinema*, London: Verso.

Kellner, Douglas (1990), *Television and the Crisis of Democracy*, Boulder: Westview.

Kellner, Douglas (1999), '*The X-Files* and the Aesthetics and Politics of Postmodern Pop', *Journal of Aesthetics and Art Criticism*, vol. 57, no. 2.

Kenway, Jane and Bullen, Elizabeth (2001), *Consuming Children: Education-Entertainment-Advertising*, Maidenhead: Open University Press.

Kerr, Paul (1984), 'Drama at MTM: *Lou Grant* and *Hill Street Blues*', in Jane Feuer, Paul Kerr and Tise Vahimagi (eds), *MTM – 'Quality Television'*, London: BFI.

Kilborn, Richard (1994), 'How Real Can You Get? Recent Developments in Reality Television', *European Journal of Communication*, vol. 9, no. 4.

Kilborn, Richard (2003), 'Performing the Real: The rise and fall of the docu-soap', in Richard Kilborn, *Staging the Real: Factual TV Programming in the Age of Big Brother*, Glasgow: Bell and Bain.

Kilborn, R. and Izod, J. (1997), *An Introduction to Television Documentary*, Manchester: Manchester University Press.

Kingsley, Hilary (1993), *Casualty: The Inside Story*, London: BBC.

Kirkham, Pat and Skeggs, Beverley (1998), 'Absolutely Fabulous: Absolutely Feminist?', in Christine Geraghty and David Lusted (eds), *The Television Studies Book*, London: Arnold.

Kisseloff, Jeff (1995), 'The Golden Age', in Jeff Kisseloff, *The Box: An Oral History of Television 1920–1961*, Harmondsworth: Penguin.

Klein, Amanda Ann (2006), '"The Horse Doesn't Get a Credit": The Foregrounding of Generic Syntax in *Deadwood*'s Opening Credits', in David Lavery (ed.), *Reading* Deadwood: *A Western to Swear By*, London and New York: I. B. Tauris.

Kline, Stephen (1993), *Out of the Garden: Toys and Children's Culture in an Age of TV Marketing*, London: Verso.

Knopf, Alfred A. (1992), *The Good Society*, New York: Tipton.

Kozloff, Sarah (1992), 'Narrative Theory and Television', in Robert C. Allen (ed.), *Channels of Discourse, Reassembled: Television and Contemporary Criticism*, London and New York: Routledge.

Krauss, Lawrence (1995), *The Physics of* 'Star Trek', London: HarperCollins.

Kubey, R. (ed.) (1997), *Media Literacy in the Information Age, Current Perspectives Information and Behavior*, vol. 6, New Brunswick: Transaction.

Kuhn, Annette (1978), 'The Camera I: Observations on Documentary', *Screen*, vol. 19, no 2.

Kuhn, Annette (ed.) (1990), *Alien Zone: Cultural Theory and Contemporary Science Fiction Cinema*, London: Verso.

Lacey, Nick (2000), *Narrative and Genre: Key Concepts in Media Studies*, London: Palgrave Macmillan.

Laing, Stuart (1991), 'Banging In Some Reality: The Original *Z Cars*', in John Corner (ed.), *Popular Television in Britain: Studies in Cultural History*, London: BFI.

Langford, Barry (2005), '"Our Usual Impasse": the Episodic Situation Comedy Revisited', in Jonathan Bignell and Stephen Lacey (eds), *Popular Television Drama: Critical Perspectives*, Manchester: Manchester University Press.

Lavery, David (ed.) (1995), *Full of Secrets: Critical Approaches to* 'Twin Peaks', Detroit: Wayne State University Press.

Lavery, David (2004), 'The Sopranos' on Glen Creeber (ed.), *50 Key Television Programmes*, London: Arnold.

Lavery, David (2006), '*Deadwood*, David Milch and Television Creativity' in Lavery, David (ed.), *Reading* Deadwood: *A Western to Swear By*, London and New York: I. B. Tauris.

Lavery, David, Hague, Angela and Cartwright, Marla (eds) (1996), *Deny All Knowledge: Reading* 'The X-Files', London: Faber and Faber.

Lee, M. and Solomon, N. (1990), *Unreliable Sources*, New York: Lyle Stuart.

Leets, Laura, de Becker, Gavin and Giles, Howard (1995), 'Fans: Exploring Expressed Motivations for Contacting Celebrities', *Journal of Language and Social Psychology*, vol. 14, no. 1–2.

Leiss, William, Kline, Stephen, SJhally, Sut and Botterill, Jacqueline (2005), *Social Communication in Advertising*. London: Routledge.

Leman, Joy (1991), 'Wise Scientists and Female Androids: Class and Gender in Science Fiction', in John Corner (ed.), *Popular Television in Britain: Studies in Cultural History*, London: BFI.

Lemish, Dafna (2007), *Children and Television – A Global Perspective*, Oxford: Blackwell

Lenburg, Jeff (1981), *The Encyclopedia of Animated Cartoons*, New York: Da Capo.

Leonard, Sean (2005), 'Progress against the Law: Anime and Fandom, with the Key to the Globalization of Culture', *International Journal of Cultural Studies*, vol. 8, no. 3, pp. 281–305.

Lewin, Kurt (1947), 'Frontiers in Group Dynamics, II. Channels of Group Life: Social Planning and Action Research', *Human Relations*, vol. 1, no. 2.

Lewis, Jon E. and Stempel, Penny (1999), *The Ultimate TV Guide*, London: Orion.

Lewis, Justin (1991), *The Ideological Octopus: An Exploration of Television and its Audience*, New York: Routledge.

Lewis, J. (2001), *Constructing Public Opinion*, New York: Columbia University Press.

Leyda, Jay (1996), 'Esther Shub and the Art of Compilation', in Kevin Macdonald and Mark Cousins (eds), *Imagining Reality: The Faber Book of Documentary*, Faber and Faber.

Leymore, Varda Langholz (1975), *Hidden Myth: Structure and Symbolism in Advertising*, New York: Basic.

Lichenstein, Therese (1990), 'Syncopated Thriller: Dennis Potter's "*The Singing Detective*"', *Artforum*, May.

Lichtenburg, Judith (1991), 'In Defence of Objectivity Revisited', in James Curran and Michael Gurevitch (eds), *Mass Media and Society*, London: Arnold.

Lindstrom, Martin (with Patricia B. Seybold) (2003), *BRANDchild*. London: Kogan Page.

Livingstone, Sonia and Bovill, Moira (1999), *Young People, New Media: Report of the Research Project: Children, Young People and the Changing Media Environment*, London: London School of Economics.

Livingstone, Sonia and Lunt, Peter (1994), *Talk on Television: Audience Participation and Public Debate*, London: Routledge.

Llewellyn-Jones, Margaret (ed.), *Frames and Fictions on Television: The Politics of Identity Within Drama*, Exeter: Intellect.

Lopate, Carol (1976), 'Daytime TV: You'll Never Want to Leave Home', *Radical America*, vol. 11, no. 1.

Lovell, Terry (1981), 'Ideology in *Coronation Street*' in Richard Dyer, Christine Geraghty, Marion Jordan, Terry Lovell, Richard Paterson and John Stewart (eds), Coronation Street, London: BFI.

Lovell, T. (1982), 'A Genre of Social Disruption?' in J. Cook (ed.), *Television Sitcom*, BFI Dossier 17, London: BFI.

Luckett, Moya (1999), 'A Moral Crisis in Prime Time: *Peyton Place* and the Rise of the Single Girl', in Mary Beth Haralovich and Lauren Rabinovitz (eds), *Television, History, and American Culture: Feminist Critical Essays*, Durham, NC: Duke University Press.

Lukow, Gregory and Ricci, Stephen (1984), 'The "Audience" Goes "Public": Inter-textuality, Genre, and the Responsibilities of Film Literacy', *On Film*, no. 12.

Lumby, Catharine (1997), *Bad Girls: The Media, Sex and Feminism in the 90s*, Sydney: Allen and Unwin.

Lumby, Catharine (1999), *Gotcha: Life in a Tabloid World*, Sydney: Allen and Unwin.

Lurie, Alison (1990), *Don't Tell the Grown-ups: Subversive Children's Fiction*, London: Bloomsbury.

Lury, Karen (2005), *Interpreting Television*, London and New York: Routledge.

Lyotard, Jean-Francois (1987), *The Postmodern Condition: a Report on Knowledge*, Manchester: Manchester University Press.

MacDonald, Fred J. (1987), *Who Shot the Sheriff? The Rise and Fall of the Television Western*, New York: Praeger.

Macdonald, Kevin and Cousins, Mark (eds) (1997), *Imagining Reality: The Faber Book of Documentary*, Faber and Faber.

MacMurraugh-Kavanagh, Madeleine K. (1997), 'The BBC and the Birth of "The Wednesday Play", 1962–66: Institutional Containment versus "Agitational contemporaneity"', *Historical Journal of Film and Television*, vol. 17, no. 3.

MacMurraugh-Kavanagh, Madeleine K. (2000), 'What's All This Then?: The Ideology of Identity in The Cops', in Bruce Carson and Margaret Llewellyn-Jones (eds), *Frames and Fictions on Television: The Politics of Identity Within Drama*, Exeter: Intellect.

MacNeill, Margaret (1996), 'Networks: Producing Olympic Ice hockey for a national Television audience', *Sociology of Sport Journal*, no. 13.

Mamber, Stephen (1972a), 'Cinéma Vérité in America', *Screen*, vol. 13, no. 2.

Mamber, Stephen (1972b), 'Cinéma Vérité in America, Part 2: Direct Cinema and the Crisis Structure', *Screen*, vol. 13, no. 3.

Marc, David (1989), *Comic Visions: Television Comedy and American Culture*, New York: Blackwell.

Marc, David and Thompson, Robert J. (1992), *Prime Time/Prime Movers: America's Greatest TV Shows and the People Who Created Them*, Boston, Toronto and London: Little, Brown.

Martin-Barbero, Jesus (1993), *From Media to Mediations*, Minneapolis: University of Minnesota Press.

Masciarotte, Gloria-Jean (1991), 'C'mon Girl: Oprah Winfrey and the Discourse of Feminine Talk', *Genders*, no. 11.

Mathijs, Ernest and Jones, Janet (eds) (2004), Big Brother *International: Format, Critics and Publics*, London: Wallflower Press.

Mattelart, Armand and Mattelart, Michèle (1998), *Theories of Communication: A Short Introduction* (trans. Susan Gruenheck Taponier and James A. Cohen), London: Sage.

Mattelart, Michèle (1986), 'Women and the Cultural Industries' (trans. Keith Reader), in Richard Collins (ed.), *Media, Culture and Society: A Critical Reader*, London: Sage.

Mattelart, M. and Mattelart, A. (1990), *The Carnival of Images: Brazilian Television Fiction*, New York: Bergin & Garvey.

Matthews, Peter (1996), 'Reviews: *Emma*', *Sight and Sound*, vol. 6, no. 9.

Maxwell, Richard (ed.) (2001), *Culture Works*, Minneapolis: University of Minnesota Press.

McCann, P. (1998), 'ITV Gives New Docusoap Prime Billing', *Independent*, 23 February.

McChesney, R. (1997), *Corporate Media and the Threat to Democracy*, New York: Seven Stories.

McCombs, M.E. and Shaw, D. (1972), 'The Agenda-setting Function of the Mass Media', *Public Opinion Quarterly*, no. 36.

McCabe, Janet (2007), 'Damsels in Distress: Female Narrative Authority and Knowledge in *24*', in Steven Peacock (ed.), *Reading 24: TV Against the Clock*, London and New York: I. B. Tauris.

McCabe, Janet and Akass, Kim (2007), *Quality TV: Contemporary American Television and Beyond*, London and New York: I. B. Tauris.

McHoul, Alec and O'Regan, Tom (1992), 'Towards a Paralogics of Textual Technologies: *Batman*, Glasnost and Relativism in Cultural Studies', *Southern Review*, vol. 25, no. 1.

McKinley, E. G. (1997), 'Beverley Hills 90210': *Television, Gender and Identity*, Philadephia: University of Pennsylvania Press.

McLaughlin, Lisa (1993), 'Chastity Criminals in the Age of Electronic Reproduction: Reviewing Talk Television and the Public Sphere', *Journal of Communication Inquiry*, vol. 17, no. 1.

McLean, Adrienne (1998), 'Media Effects: Marshall McLuhan, Television Culture, and *The X-Files*', *Film Quarterly*, vol. 5, no. 4.

McLuhan, Herbert Marshall (1962), *The Gutenberg Galaxy: The Making of Typographic Man*, 1st edn, Toronto: University of Toronto Press.

McNair, Brian (1995), *An Introduction to Political Communication*, London: Routledge.

McNair, Brian (1999), *News and Journalism in the UK*, London: Routledge.

McNair, Brian (2000), *Journalism and Democracy: An Evaluation of the Political Public Sphere*, London: Routledge.

McNeil, Alex (1996), *Total Television: A Comprehensive Guide to Programming from 1948 to the Present*, New York: Penguin Putnam.

McQuail, Denis (1992), *Media Performance*, London: Sage.

Medhurst, Andy and Tuck, Lucy (1982), 'The Gender Game', in J. Cook (ed.) *Television Sitcom*, BFI Dossier 17, London: BFI.

Medhurst, Andy and Tuck, Lucy (1996), 'Situation Comedy and Stereotyping', in John Corne and Sylvia Harvey (eds), *Television Times: A Reader*, London: Arnold.

Media Awareness Network, Advertising and Consumerism, Nueborne (2001), 'Advertising – It's Everywhere', available at <http://www.media-awareness.ca/english/parents/marketing/advertising_everywhere.cfm>, last accessed 2 March 2008.

Mellencamp, Patricia (1986), 'Situation Comedy, Feminism, and Freud: Discourses of Gracie and Lucy', reprinted in Charlotte Brunsdon, Julie D'Acci and Lynn Spigel (eds), *Feminist Television Criticism: A Reader*, Oxford: Oxford University Press.

Messenger-Davies, Máire (1997), *Fake, Fact and Fantasy: Children's Interpretations of Television Reality*, Mahwah: Lawrence Erlbaum Associates.

Messenger-Davies, Máire (2001), '*Dear BBC*': *Children, Television Storytelling and the Public Sphere*, Cambridge: Cambridge University Press.

Messenger-Davies, Máire and Corbett, Beth (1997), *The Provision of Children's Programming in the UK between 1992 and 1996*, London: Broadcasting Standards Commission.

Messenger-Davies, Máire and Machin, David (2000), 'Children's Demon TV – Reality, Freedom, Panic: Children's Discussions of *The Demon Headmaster*', *Journal of Media and Cultural Studies*, vol. 14, no. 1.

Meyer, Manfred (ed.) (1983), *Children and the Formal Features of Television – Approaches and findings in experimental and formative research*. New York, London and Paris: K. G. Saur.

Miles, Lawrence and Wood, Tat (2004), *About Time 4: 1975–1979* Mad Norwegian Press, Illinois.

Miller, Jeffrey S. (2000), *Something Completely Different: British Television and American Culture*, Minneapolis: University of Minnesota Press.

Miller, Toby (1997), The Avengers, London: BFI; Bloomington: Indiana University Press.

Miller, Toby, Lawrence, Geoffrey, McKay, Jim and Rowe, David (2001), *Globalization and Sport: Playing the World*, London: Sage.

Mills, Brett (2004a), 'Comedy Vérité: Contemporary Sitcom Form', *Screen*, vol. 45, no. 1, pp. 63–78.

Mills, Brett (2004b), '*To Death Us Do Part* and *All in the Family*' in Glen Creeber (ed.), *50 Key Television Programmes*, London: Arnold.

Mills, Brett (2004c), 'The Simpsons', in Glen Creeber (ed.), *50 Key Television Programmes*, London: Arnold.

Mills, Brett (2005), *Television Sitcom*, London: BFI.

Mills, Brett (2007), ' "Yes, it's war!": Chris Morris and comedy's representational strategies', in Laura Mulvey and Jamie Sexton (eds), *Experimental British Television*, Manchester: Manchester University Press.

Mittell, Jason (2004), *Genre and Television: From Cop Shows to Cartoons in American Culture*, London and New York: Routledge.

Modleski, Tania (1982), *Loving with a Vengence: Mass-Produced Fantasies for Women*, Hamden: Shoestring.

Mohammadi, Ali (ed.) (1997), *International Communication and Globalization: A Critical Introduction*, London: Sage.

Moir, Jan (1996), 'Oh, what a lovely ward!', *Observer*, 11 February.

Molotoch, Harvey and Lester, Marilyn (1977), 'News as Purposive Behaviour: On the Strategic Use of Routine Events, Accidents and Scandals', in Dan Berkowitz (ed.), *Social Meanings of News*, London: Sage.

Montgomerie, Margaret (1997), 'MiniSeries', in Horace Newcomb (ed.), *Encyclopedia of Television*, Chicago and London: Fitzroy Dearborn.

Moore, Suzanne (1988), 'Here's Looking at You, Kid!', in Lorraine Gamman and Margaret Marshment (eds), *The Female Gaze: Women as Viewers of Popular Culture*, London: Women's Press, pp. 44–59.

Moran, Albert (2005), 'Configurations of the New Television Landscape', in Wasko (ed.), *A Companion to Television*, Maldon, London and Victoria: Blackwell, pp. 291–307.

Moras, Lisa De (1997), 'The Sound and the Fury', The Hollywood Reporter *1997–98 TV Preview*, September.

Morley, David (1980), *The Nationwide Audience*, London: BFI.

Morley, David (1986), *Family Television: Cultural Power and Domestic Leisure*, London: Comedia.

Morley, David (1989), 'Changing Paradigms in Audience Studies', in Ellen Seiter et al. (eds), *Remote Control, Television, Audiences and Cultural Power*, London: Routledge.

Morley, David (1992), *Television Audiences and Cultural Studies*, London: Routledge.

Morreall J. (1983), *Taking Laughter Seriously*, Albany: State University of New York Press.

Morreall, J. (ed.) (1987), *The Philosophy of Laughter and Humor*, Albany: State University of New York Press.

Morris, Meaghan (1990), 'Banality in Cultural Studies', in Patricia Mellencamp (ed.), *Logics of Television: Essays in Cultural Criticism*, Bloomington: Indiana University Press; London: BFI.

Mort, Frank (1988), 'Boy's Own? Masculinity, Style and Popular Culture', in R. Chapman and J. Rutherford (eds), *Male Order: Unwrapping Masculinity*. London: Lawrence & Wishart, pp. 193–224.

Moseley, Rachel (2000), 'Makeover takeover on British television', *Screen*, vol. 41.

Mosley, Ivo (ed.) (2000), *Dumbing Down; Culture, Politics and the Mass Media*, London: Academic Press.

Mowlana, H., Gerbner, G. and Schiller, H. (1992), Triumph *of the Image: The Media's War in the Persian Gulf – A Global Perspective*, Boulder: Westview.

Mulvey, Laura (1975), 'Visual Pleasure and Narrative Cinema', in Laura Mulvey (1989), *Visual and Other Pleasures*, London: Macmillan, pp. 14–26.

Mumford, Laura Stempel (1995), *Love and Ideology in the Afternoon: Soap Opera, Women, and Television Genre*, Bloomington: Indiana University Press.

Munson, Wayne (1993), *All Talk: The Talk Show in Media Culture*, Philadephia: Temple University Press.

Murdock, G. and Golding P. (1973), 'For a Political Economy of Mass Communications', in R. Milliband and J. Saville (eds), *Socialist Register*, London: Merlin.

Murray, Susan, and Ouellette, Laurie (eds) (2004), *Reality TV: Remaking Television Culture*, New York: New York University Press.

Naureckas, J. and Jackson, J. (eds) (1996), *The FAIR Reader: An Extra Review of Press and Politics*, Boulder: Westview.

Neale, Steve (1980), *Genre*, London: BFI.

Neale, Steve (1990), 'Questions of Genre', *Screen*, vol. 31, no. 1.

Neale, Steve (2000), *Genre and Hollywood*, London: Routledge.

Neale, Steve and Krutnik, Frank (1990), *Popular Film and Television Comedy*, London: Routledge.

Neaverson, Bob (1997), *The Beatles Movies*, London: Cassell.

Nelson, Robin (1997a), *Television Drama in Transition: Forms, Values and Cultural Change*, London: Macmillan.

Nelson, Robin (1997b), 'Coda – Critical Postmodernism: Critical Realism', in Robin Nelson, *Television Drama in Transition: Forms, Values and Cultural Change*, London: Macmillan.

Nelson, Robin (2000), '"Flexi-Narrative" Form and a "New Affective Order"' (case study *Ally McBeal*), in Eckart Voights-Virchow (ed.), *Mediated Drama/Dramatized Media*, Frankfurt: Wissenschaftlicher Verlag Trier.

Nelson, Robin (2007), *State of Play: Contemporary 'High-end' TV Drama*, Manchester: Manchester University Press.

Newcomb, Horace (1974), *TV: The Most Popular Art*, New York: Doubleday.

Newcomb, Horace (ed.) (1976), *Television: The Critical View*, New York and Oxford: Oxford University Press.

Newman, Kim (2005), *BFI TV Classics:* Doctor Who, London: BFI.

Nichols, Bill (1985), 'The Voice of Documentary', in Bill Nichols (ed.), *Movies and Methods II*, Berkeley: University of California Press.

Nichols, Bill (1994), 'At the Limits of Reality (TV)', in Bill Nichols (ed.), *Blurred Boundaries*, Bloomington: Indiana University Press.

Nichols, W. (1976), 'Documentary Theory and Practice', *Screen*, vol. 17.

Nichols, W. (1991), *Representing Reality: Issues and Concepts in Documentary*, Bloomington: Indiana University Press.

Nicholson, Martha (1997), *David Lynch*, Austin: University of Texas Press.

Noble, Grant (1975), *Children in Front of the Small Screen*, London: Constable; California: Sage.

Nochlin, Linda (1971), *Realism*, Harmondsworth: Penguin.

Norden, Martin F. (1985), 'The Detective Show', in B. G. Rose (ed.), *TV Genres: A Handbook and Reference Guide*, Westport: Greenwood.

Nueborne, Ellen (2001), 'For Kids of the Web, It's an Ad, Ad, Ad, Ad World', *BusinessWeek Lifestyle*, available at: <http://www.businessweek.com/magazine/content/01_33/b3745121.htm>, last accessed 2 March 2008.

Ofcom (2004), 'Ofcom's Strategy and Priorities for the Promotion of Media Literacy – A Statement', available at: <http://www.ofcom.org.uk/consult/condocs/strategymedialit/ml_statement/>, last accessed 2 March 2008.

Okuda, Michael and Okuda, Denise (1999), *The 'Star Trek' Encyclopedia: A Reference Guide to the Future*, New York: Pocket.

Olson, R. Scott (1999), *Hollywood Planet: Global Media and the Competitive Advantage of Narrative Transparency*, New York: Lawrence Erlbaum Associates.

O'Shea, Alan (1989), 'Television as Culture: Not Just Texts and Readers', *Media, Culture and Society*, vol. 11, no. 3.

Ostgaard, Einar (1965), 'Factors Influencing the Flow of News', *Journal of Peace Research*, no. 2.

Owen, Susan A. (1999), 'Buffy the Vampire Slayer: Vampires, Postmodernity and Postfeminism', *Journal of Popular Film and Television*, vol. 27, no. 2.

Packard, Vance (1957/1962), *The Hidden Persuaders*, Harmondsworth: Penguin.

Page, Adrian (2000), *Cracking Morse Code: Semiotics and Television Drama*, Luton: University of Luton Press.

Paget, D. (1998), *No Other Way to Tell It: Dramadoc/ Docudrama on Television*, Manchester: Manchester University Press.

Palmer, Edward (1988), *Television and America's Children: A Crisis of Neglect*, Oxford: Oxford University Press.

Palmer, J. (1987), *The Logic of the Absurd: On Film and Television Comedy*, London: BFI.

Palmer, Sue (2006), *Toxic Childhood – How the modern world is damaging our children and what we can do about it*, London: Orion.

Parkin, Frank (1971), *Class Inequality and Political Order*, London: MacGibbon & Kee.

Paterson, Elaine (1989), 'Heller let loose', *Time Out*.

Paterson, Richard (1980), 'Planning the Family: The Art of the Television Schedule', *Screen Education*, no. 35, reprinted in M. Alvarado, Edward Buscombe and R. Collins (eds), *Screen Education Reader* (1993), London: Macmillan.

Patten, F. (2004), *Watching Anime, Reading Manga*, Berkeley, CA: Stone Bridge Press.

Pearson, Allison (1998), 'All the World's a Soap Set', *Daily Telegraph*, 28 May.

Pearson, Roberta and Uricchio, William (eds) (1991), *The Many Lives of the Batman: Critical Approaches to a Superhero and his Media*, London: Routledge.

Peary, D. and Peary, G. (eds) (1980), *The American Animated Cartoon*, New York: E. P. Dutton.

Peck, Janice (1994), 'Talk About Racism: Framing a Popular Discourse of Race on Oprah Winfrey', *Cultural Critique*, Spring.

Peck, Janice (1995), 'TV Talk Shows as Therapeutic Discourse: The Ideological Labor of the Televised Talking Cure', *Communication Theory*, vol. 5, no. 1.

Penley, Constance (1997), *Nasa/Trek: Popular Science and Sex in America*, London: Verso.

Perry, George (1983), *Life of Python*, London: Pavilion.

Peterson, Sophia (1979), 'Foreign News Gatekeepers and Criteria of Newsworthiness', *Journalism Quarterly*, no. 56.

Philo, G. (1990), *Seeing and Believing: The Influence of Television*, London: Routledge.

Pilling, Jayne (ed.) (1997), *A Reader in Animation Studies*, Sydney: John Libbey.

Pines, Jim (1995), 'Black Cops and Black Villains in Film and TV Crime Fiction', in David Kidd-Hewitt and Richard Osborne (eds), *Crime and the Media*, London: Pluto.

Plantinga, C. (1997), *Rhetoric and Representation in Non-Fiction Film*, Cambridge: Cambridge University Press.

Plato (trans. Gosling, J. C. B., 1975) *Philebus*, Oxford: Clarendon Press.

Plummer, Laura (1997), 'I'm Not Laura Palmer: David Lynch's Fractured Fairy Tale', *Literature/Film Quarterly*, vol. 25, no. 4.

Porter , Jennifer and McLaren, Darcee (eds) (1999), 'Star Trek' *and Sacred Ground: Explorations of* 'Star Trek', *Religion, and American Culture*, New York: Suny Press.

Postrel, Virginia (1999), 'The Pleasures of Persuasion', *Wall Street Journal*, 2 August.

Pratt, Mary Louise (1977), *Towards a Speech-Act Theory of Literary Discourse*, Bloomington: Indiana University Press.

Pratt, Mary Louise (1981), 'The Short Story: The Long and the Short of It', *Poetics*, no. 10.

Presnell, Don and McGee, Marty (1998), *A Critical History of Television's* 'The Twilight Zone', *1959–1964*, Jefferson: McFarland.

Prys, Catrin (2007), 'Don't Fence me in: *The Singing Detective* and the synchronicity of indeterminancy', in Laura Mulvey and Jamie Sexton (eds), *Experimental British Television*, Manchester: Manchester University Press.

Purser, Philip (1981), 'Dennis Potter', in George Brandt (ed.), *British Television Drama*, London: Cambridge University Press.

Putterman, Barry (1995), *On Television and Comedy: Essays on Style, Theme, Performer and Writer*, Jefferson: McFarland.

Quinn, Jane (1997), 'Getting Closer to Audiences: The BBC Experience', in Manfred Meyer (ed.), *Educational Television: What Do People Want?*, Luton: John Libbey Media/University of Luton Press.

Rabiger, M. (1998), *Directing the Documentary*, 2nd edn, London: Focal Press.

Radio Times (1996), 'Official Collector's Edition, *Star Trek* 30 Years', London: BBC.

Radway, Janice (1987), *Reading the Romance*, London: Verso.

Real, Michael (1975), 'The Super Bowl: mythic spectacle', *Journal of Communication*, vol. 25, no. 1.

Real, Michael (1989), 'Super Bowl Football versus World Cup Soccer: A Cultural–Structural Comparison', in Lawrence Wenner (ed.), *Media, Sports and Society*, Newbury Park: Sage.

Renov, M. (ed.) (1993), *Theorizing Documentary*, New York and London: Routledge.

Richards, Thomas (1997), *The Meaning of 'Star Trek'* (published in Britain as *'Star Trek' in Myth and Legend*), New York: Doubleday.

Richards, Barry, MacRury, Iain and Botterill, Jackie (2000), *The Dynamics of Advertising*, Amsterdam, Harwood.

Rimmer, Dave (1985), *Like Punk Never Happened: Culture Club and the New Pop*, London: Faber and Faber.

Ritchie, Jean (2000), *'Big Brother': The Unseen Story*, London: Channel 4.

Robards, Brook (1985), 'The Police Show', in B. G. Rose (ed.), *TV Genres: A Handbook and Reference Guide*, Westport: Greenwood.

Roberts, Graham (2006), 'BBC Worldwide' in Douglas Gomery and Luke Hockley (eds), *Television Industries*, London: BFI.

Roberts, Robin (1999), *Sexual Generations: 'Star Trek, The Next Generation' and Gender*, Urbana and Chicago: Illinois University Press.

Roberts, Thomas J. (1990), *An Aesthetics of Junk Fiction*, Athens, GA: University of Georgia Press.

Rock, Paul (1973), 'News as Eternal Recurrence', in Jock Curran and Stanley Young (eds), *The Manufacture of News*, London: Constable.

Rofel, Lisa (1995), *Other Modernities: Gendered Yearnings in China after Socialism*, Berkeley: University of California Press.

Roscoe, Jane (2004), 'The Jerry Springer Show', in Glen Creeber (ed.), *50 Key Television Programmes*, London: Arnold.

Roscoe, Jane and Hight, Craig (2001), *Faking It: Mock-Documentary and the Subversion of Factuality*, Manchester: Manchester University Press.

Rose, Brian G. (ed.) (1985a), *TV Genres: A Handbook and Reference Guide*, Westport: Greenwood.

Rose, Brian G. (1985b), 'Preface', B. G. Rose (ed.), *TV Genres: A Handbook and Reference Guide*, Westport: Greenwood.

Rose, Brian G. (1985c), 'The Talk Show', in B. G. Rose (ed.), *TV Genres: A Handbook and Reference Guide*, Westport: Greenwood.

Rosen, Jay (2003), 'Press Think', available at: <http://journalism.nyu.edu/pubzone/weblogs/pressthink/>, last accessed March 2008.

Rosenthal, A. (1988), *New Challenges for Documentary*, Berkeley: University of California Press.

Rosenthal, A. (ed.) (1999), *Why Docudrama?*, Carbondale and Edwardsville: Southern Illinois University Press.

Ross, Karen (1996), *Black and White in Media: Black Images in Popular Film and Television*, Oxford: Polity.

Rothenberg, Randall (1995), *Where the Suckers Moon: The Life and Death of an Advertising Campaign*, New York: Vintage.

Rowe, David (1999), *Sport, Culture and the Media*, Buckingham: Open University Press.

Rowe, Kathleen (1995), *The Unruly Woman: Gender and the Genres of Laughter*, Austin: University of Texas Press.

Ryall, Tom (1975/6), 'Teaching through Genre', *Screen Education*, no. 17.

Sande, Oystein (1971), 'The Perception of Foreign News', *Journal of Peace Research*, no. 8.

Sandler, K. (ed.) (1998), *Reading the Rabbit*, Piscataway: Rutgers University Press.

Sartre, Jean-Paul (1990), *What is Literature?*, London: Routledge.

Scannell, Paddy (1997), *Radio, TV and Modern Life*, Oxford and Cambridge, MA: WileyBlackwell.

Schatz, Thomas (1981), *Hollywood Genres: Formulas, Filmmaking, and the Studio System*, New York: Random House.

Scheurer, Timothy (1985), 'The Variety Show', in B. G. Rose (ed.), *TV Genres: A Handbook and Reference Guide*, Westport: Greenwood.

Schiller, Dan (1996), *Theorizing Communication: A History*, New York: Oxford University Press.

Schiller, Herbert I. (1989), *Culture Inc.: The Corporate Takeover of Public Expression*, Oxford: Oxford University Press.

Schiller, Herbert (1996), *Information Inequality: The Deepening Social Crisis in America*, London: Routledge.

Schlesinger, P. (1987), *Putting Reality Together*, London: Methuen.

Schlesinger, P. and Tumber, H. (1994), *Reporting Crime – Media Politics of Criminal Justice*, Oxford: Oxford University Press.

Schudson, Michael (1995), *The Power of News*, Cambridge, MA: Harvard University Press.

Schwartz, David, Ryan, Steve and Wostbrock, Fred (1999), *Encyclopedia of TV Game Shows*, New York: Checkmark.

Schwartz, Dona (1997), *Contesting the Super Bowl*, New York: Routledge.

Scounce, Jeffrey (1997), 'Science-Fiction Programs', in Horace Newcomb (ed.), *Encyclopedia of Television*, Chicago and London: Fitzroy Dearborn.

Seiter, Ellen (1995), 'Toy-based Video for Girls: My Little Pony', in Cary Bazalgette and David Buckingham (eds) (1995), *In Front of the Children: Screen Entertainment and Young Audiences*. London: BFI.

Seiter, Ellen (1999), *Television and New Media Audiences*, Oxford: Clarendon Press.

Seiter, Ellen, Borchers, Hans, Kreutzner, Gabriele and Warth, Eva-Marie (eds) (1989), *Remote Control: Television, Audiences and Cultural Power*, London: Routledge.

Selby, Keith and Cowdery, Ron (1995), *How to Study Television*, London: Macmillan.

Self, David (1984), *Television Drama: An Introduction*, London: Macmillan.

Shary, Timothy 92005), *Teen Movies – American Youth on Screen*, New York: Wallflower Press.

Shattuc, Jane M. (1997), *The Talking Cure: TV Talk Shows and Women*, London and New York: Routledge.

Shoemaker, Pamela (1991), *Gatekeeping*, San Mateo: Sage.

Shoemaker, Pamela (1996), *Mediating the Message: Theories of Influences on Mass Media Content*, New York: Addison Wesley Longman

Shubik, Irene (1975), *Play for Today: The Evolution of Television Drama*, London: Davis-Poynter.

Sigman, Aric (2005), *Remotely Controlled: How television is damaging our lives – and what we can do about it*, London: Vermillion.

Silver, Rachel (1988), *Casualty: Behind the Scenes*, London: BBC Worldwide.

Simpson, Mark (1994), *Male Impersonators: Men Performing Masculinity*. New York: Routledge.

Singer, Dorothy G. and Singer, Jerome L. (eds) (2001), *Handbook of Children and the Media*, London: Sage.

Skovmand, M. and Schroder, K. C. (eds) (1992), *Media Cultures*, London: Routledge.

Smythe, Dallas (1977), 'Communications: Blindspot of Western Marxism', *Canadian Journal of Political and Social Theory*, vol. 1, no. 3. Reprinted in Thomas Guback (ed.) (1990), *Counterclockwise: Perspectives on Communication*, San Francisco: Westview.

Smythe, Dallas (1978), 'Rejoinder to Graham Murdock', *Canadian Journal of Political and Social Theory*, vol. 2, no. 1–2.

Snider, Paul (1967), 'Mr Gates Revisited: A 1966 Version of the 1949 Case Study', *Journalism Quarterly*, no. 44.

Sobchack, Vivian (1987), *Screening Space: The American Science Fiction Film*, Piscataway: Rutgers University Press.

Sohn, Amy (2002), *Sex and the City: Kiss and Tell*, London: Macmillan.

Sontag, Susan (1991), *Illness as Metaphor and AIDS and its Metaphors*, Harmondsworth: Penguin.

Sparks, Richard (1993), 'Inspector Morse: The Last Enemy', in George Brandt (ed.), *British Television Drama in the 1980s*, Cambridge: Cambridge University Press.

Spigel, Lynn (1991), 'From Domestic Space to Outerspace: the 1960s' Fantastic Family Sit-com', in Constance Penley, Elisabeth Lyon and Lynn Spigel (eds), *Close Encounters: Film Feminism and Science Fiction*, Minnesota: University of Minnesota Press.

Spigel, Lynn (1992), *Make Room for TV: Television and the Family Ideal in Postwar America*, Chicago: Chicago University Press.

Spigel, Lynn (1996), 'From Theatre to Space Ship: Metaphors of Suburban Domesticity in Postwar America', in Roger Silverstone (ed.), *Visions of Suburbia: Symptoms and Metaphors of Modernity*, London and New York: Routledge.

Springhall, J. (1998), *Youth, Popular Culture and Moral Panics: Penny Gaffs to Gangsta Rap, 1830–1996*, New York: St Martin's Press.

Staab, Joachim Friedrich (1990), 'The Role of News Factors in News Selection: A Theoretical Reconsideration', *European Journal of Communication*, vol. 5, no. 4.

Stabile, C. and Harrison, M. (eds) (2003), *Prime Time Animation*, London and New York: Routledge.

Stamp, Shelley (2000), *Movie-Struck Girls: Women and Motion Picture Culture after the Nickelodeon*, Princeton: Princeton University Press.

Stark, Steven D. (1997), 'The Miniseries as History: Did *Roots* Change America?', in *Glued to the Set: The 60 Television Shows and Events that Made us Who we Are Today*, New York: Face Press.

Starker, S. (1991), *Evil Influences: Crusades against the Mass Media*, New Brunswick: Transaction.

Stead, Peter (1993), *Dennis Potter: Border Lines Series*, Bridgend: Seren.

Steeves, H. Peter (2005), '"It's Just a Bunch of Stuff that Happened": *The Simpsons* and the Possibility of Postmodern Comedy', in Mary M. Dalton and Laura R. Linder (eds), *The Sitcom Reader: America Viewed and Skewed*, Albany: State University of New York Press.

Stone, Joseph and Yahn, Tim (1992), *Prime Time and Misdemeanors: Investigating the 1950s TV Quiz Scandal – A DA's Account*, Piscataway: Rutgers University Press.

Stewart, Michael (1999), *Television Soap Opera, Block 3, Popular Genres, Popular Pleasures and Cultural Values*, Masters Programme, Milton Keynes: Open University Press.

Straubhaar, J. D. (1982), 'The Development of the Telenovela as the Pre-eminent Form of Popular Culture in Brazil', *Studies in Latin American Popular Culture*, no. 1.

Straubhaar, J. D. (1988), 'The Reflection of the Brazilian Political Opening in the Telenovela, 1974–1985', *Studies in Latin American Popular Culture*, no. 7.

Strinati, Dominic (1995), *An Introduction to Theories of Popular Culture*, London: Routledge.

Taylor, Don (1990), *Days of Vision, Working With David Mercer: Television Drama Then and Now*, Fulham, NH: Methuen.

Taylor, Ella (1989), *Prime-Time Families: Television Culture in Post-War America*, Berkeley: University of California Press.

Taylor, Joyce (1997), 'Success in Cable Networks: The Discovery Channel', in Manfred Meyer (ed.), *Educational Television: What Do People Want?*, Luton: John Libbey Media/Luton University Press.

Thomas, Howard (ed.) (1959), *The Armchair Theatre*, London: Weidenfeld & Nicolson.

Thomas, Lyn (1997), 'In Love With Inspector Morse', in Charlotte Brunsdon, Julie D'Acci, Lynn Spigel (eds), *Feminist Television Criticism: A Reader*, Oxford: Oxford University Press.

Thompson, Robert J. (1996), *Television's Second Golden Age: From 'Hill Street Blues' To 'ER'*, New York: Syracuse University Press.

Threadgold, Terry (1989), 'Talking about Genre: Ideologies and Incompatible Discourses', *Cultural Studies*, vol. 3, no. 1.

Todorov, Tzvetan (1975), *The Fantastic: A Structural Approach to a Literary Genre* (trans. Richard Howard), Ithaca: Cornell University Press.

Todorov, Tzevtan (1977), *The Poetics of Prose* (trans. Richard Howard), Ithaca: Cornell University Press.

Todorov, Tzvetan (1981), *Introduction to Poetics* (trans. Richard Howard), Brighton: Harvester Press.

Toll, Rober C. (1976), *On With the Show! The First Century of Show Business in America*, New York: Oxford University Press.

Toll, Robert C. (1982), *The Entertainment Machine: American Show Business in the Twentieth Century*, Oxford: Oxford University Press.

Tolson, Andrew (1996), *Mediations: Text and Discourse in Media Studies*, London: Arnold.

Took, Barry (1976), *Laughter in the Air*, London: Robson/BBC.

Tracey, Michael (1997), *Decline and Fall of Public Service Broadcasting*, Oxford: Clarendon Press.

Trinta, Aluizio R. (1997), 'News from Home: A Study of Realism and Melodrama in Brazilian Telenovelas', in Christine Geraghty and David Lusted (eds), *The Television Studies Book*, London, New York, Sydney, Auckland: Arnold.

Trujillo, Nick (1995), 'Machines, Missiles and Men: Images of the Male Body on ABC's Monday Night Football', *Sociology of Sport Journal*, no. 12.

Tuchman, Gaye (1978), *Making News*, New York: Free Press.

Tuchman, Gaye (1997), 'Making News by Doing Work: Routinizing the Unexpected', in Dan Berkowitz (ed.), *Social Meanings of News*, London: Sage.

Tuchman, Gaye (1999), 'Objectivity as Strategic Ritual: An Examination of Newsmen's Notions of Objectivity', in Howard Tumber (ed.), *News: A Reader*, Oxford: Oxford University Press.

Tudor, Andrew (1976), 'Genre and Critical Methodology', in Bill Nichols (ed.), *Movies and Methods: An Anthology*, Berkeley: University of California Press.

Tufte, Thomas (2000), *Living with the Rubbish Queen – Telenovelas, Culture and Modernity in Brazil*, Luton: University of Luton Press.

Tulloch, John (1976), 'Gradgrind's Heirs – the Quiz and the Presentation of "Knowledge" by British Television', *Screen Education*, no. 19.

Tulloch, John (1990), *Television Drama: Agency, Audience and Myth*, London and New York: Routledge.

Tulloch, John (1997), '*Doctor Who*', in Horace Newcomb (ed.), *Encyclopeadia of Television*, Chicago and London: Fitzroy Dearborn.

Tulloch, John (2000), *Watching Television Audiences: Cultural Theories and Methods*, London and New York: Arnold.

Tulloch, John and Alvarado, Manuel (1990a; orig. pub. 1983), *Doctor Who: The Unfolding Text*, London: Macmillan.

Tulloch, John and Alvarado, Manuel (1990b), 'Send-up: Authorship and Organization', in Tony Bennett (ed.), *Popular Fiction: Technology, Ideology, Production*, Reading, London and New York: Routledge.

Tulloch, John and Jenkins, Henry (1995), *Science Fiction Audiences: Watching 'Dr Who' and 'Star Trek'*, London: Routledge.

Tulloch, John and Moran, A. (1986), 'A Country Practice': *'Quality' Soap*, Sydney: Allen and Unwin.

Tunstall, Jeremy (1971), *Journalists at Work*, London: Constable.

Tunstall, Jeremy (1993), *Television Producers*, London and New York: Routledge.

Turnbull, Sue (2007), 'The Hook and the Look: *CSI* and the Aesthetics of the Television Crime Series', in Michael Allen (ed.), *Reading CSI: Crime TV Under the Microscope*, London and New York: I. B. Tauris.

Turner, Graeme (1989), 'Transgressive TV: From *In Melbourne Tonight* to *Perfect Match*', in John Tulloch and Graeme Turner (eds), *Australian Television: Programs, Pleasures and Politics*, Sydney: Allen and Unwin.

Turow, Joseph (1989), *Playing Doctor: Television, Storytelling and Medical Power*, Oxford: Oxford University Press.

Turow, Joseph (1997), *Breaking Up America*, Chicago: University of Chicago Press.

Vane, Edward T. and Gross, Lynne S. (1994), *Programming for TV, Radio and Cable*, Boston, MA and London: Focal Press.

Vaughan, D. (1983), *Portrait of an Invisible Man*, London: BFI.

Vervliet, Hendrik D. L. (ed.) (1972), *The Book Through 5000 Years*, London and New York: Phaidon. Originally published (1972) as *Liber Liborum – 5000 ans d'art du Livre*, Brussels: Éditions Arcade.

Wagg, Stephen (ed.) (1998), *Because I Tell a Joke or Two: Comedy, Politics and Social Difference*, London: Routledge.

Wagner, Jon and Lundeen, Jan (1998), *Deep Space and Sacred Time: 'Star Trek' in the American Myths*, Westport and London: Praeger.

Ward, Paul (2005), *Documentary: the Margins of Reality*, London and New York: Wallflower Press.

Wark, McKenzie (1994), *Virtual Geography: Living with Global Media Events*, Bloomington: Indiana University Press.

Waters, Ben (2005), The Office, London: BFI.

Waters, Malcolm (2000), *Globalization*, 2nd edn, New York: Routledge.

Waugh, Thomas (1985), 'Beyond Vérité: Emile de Antonio and the New Documentary of the 1970s', in Bill Nichols (ed.), *Movies and Methods II*, Berkeley: University of California Press.

Wayne, Mike (1998), 'Counter-Hegemonic Strategies in Between the Lines', in Mike Wayne (ed.), *Dissident Voices: The Politics of Television and Cultural Change*, London: Pluto.

Wells, Paul (1998), *Understanding Animation*, London and New York: Routledge.

Wells, Paul (2000), *Animation and America*, New Brunswick: Rutgers University Press.

Wenner, Lawrence (1989), 'The Super Bowl Pregame Show: Cultural Fantasies and Political Subtext', in Lawrence Wenner (ed.), *Media, Sports and Society*, Newbury Park: Sage.

Wertheim, Arthur Frank (1979), *Radio Comedy*, New York: Oxford University Press.

Whannel, Garry (1992), *Fields in Vision: Television Sport and Cultural Transformation*, London: Routledge.

Wheale, Nigel (1985) 'Recognising a "human-thing": Cyborgs, Robots and Replicants', in Nigel Wheale (ed.), *The Postmodern Arts: An Introductory Reader*, London: Routledge.

Wheen, Francis (1985), *Television: A History*, London: Century.

White, David Manning (1950), 'The Gatekeeper: A Case Study in the Selection of News', *Journalism Quarterly*, no. 27.

Wicke, Jennifer (1988), Advertising Fictions: Literature, Advertisement, and Social Reading, New York: Columbia University Press.

Williams, Alan (1984), 'Is a Radical Genre Criticism Possible?', *Quarterly Review of Film Studies*, vol. 9, no. 2.

Williams, Bruce and Delli Carpini, Michael X. (2000), 'Unchained Reaction: The Collapse of Media Gatekeeping and the Clinton–Lewinsky scandal', *Journalism*, vol. 1, no. 1.

Williams, Frances (1998), 'Suits and Sequins: Lesbian Comedians in Britain and the US in the 1990s', in Stephen Wagg (ed.), *Because I Tell a Joke or Two: Comedy, Politics and Social Difference*, London: Routledge.

Williams, K. (1998), *Get Me A Murder a Day! A History of Mass Communication in Britain*, London: Arnold.

Williams, Linda (1993), 'Mirrors without Memories: Truth, History and the New Documentary', *Film Quarterly*, vol. 46, no. 3.

Williams, Linda (1995), 'Film Bodies: Gender, Genre and Excess', in Barry Grant (ed.), *Film Genre Reader II*, Austin: University of Texas Press.

Williams, Sally (1997), 'When Children Rule, Ad Men Obey', *Industry Magazine*, 16 February.

Williamson, Judith (1978), *Decoding Advertisements: Ideology and Meaning in Advertising*, London: Marion Boyars.

Wilmut, Roger (1980), *From Fringe to Flying Circus: Celebrating a Unique Generation of Comedy, 1960–1980*, London: Methuen.

Wilmut, Roger (1985), *Kindly Leave the Stage! The Story of Variety, 1919–1960*, London: Methuen.

Wilmut, Roger and Rosengard, Peter (1989), '*Didn't You Kill My Mother-in-Law?': Alternative Comedy in Britain from the Comedy Store to Saturday Live*, London: Methuen.

Wilson, John (1996), *Understanding Journalism*, London: Routledge.

Winick, Charles, Williamson, Lorne G., Chuzmir, Stuart F. and Winick, Mariann Pezzella (1973), *Children's Television Commercials – A Content Analysis*, New York: Praeger

Winston, Brian (1993), 'The Documentary Film as Scientific Inscription', in Michael Renov (ed.), *Theorizing Documentary*, London: Routledge.

Winston, Brian (1995), *Claiming the Real: The Documentary Film Revisited*, London: BFI.

Winston, Brian (2000), *Lies, Damned Lies and Television*, London: BFI.

Wolff, Janet (1981), *The Social Production of Art*, London: Macmillan.

Woolery, George W. (1989), *Animated TV Specials: The Complete Directory to the First Twenty-Five Years, 1962–1987*, Metuchen: Scarecrow.

Worland, Rick (1998), 'Captain Kirk: Cold Warrior', *Journal of Popular Film and Television*, vol. 16.

Wright, Elizabeth (1989), *Postmodern Brecht: a Re-Presentation*, London: Routledge.

Wright, Peter (1999) 'The Shared World of *Doctor Who*', *Foundation – The International Review of Science Fiction*, no. 75, pp. 78–96.

Wright, Will (1975), *Sixguns and Society: A Structural Study of the Western*, Berkeley: University of California Press.

Young, Brian M. (1990), *Television Advertising and Children*, Oxford: Clarendon Press.

Index

Page numbers in **bold** indicate detailed treatment in a 'grey box' section; those in *italic* denote illustrations. TV programmes appearing in the Index are listed by title only unless there is risk of confusion with another work of similar title. Feature films are listed by title and date.

List of Illustrations

While considerable effort has been made to correctly identify the copyright holders, this has not been possible in all cases. We apologise for any apparent negligence and any omissions or corrections brought to our attention will be remedied in any future editions.

ER, Warner Bros. International Television; *Friends*, Warner Bros. International Television; *Lost*, Bad Robot; *Heartbeat*, Yorkshire Television; *Marty*, National Broadcasting Company; *Bonanza*, NBC TV; *Deadwood*, HBO Original Programming; *The Man from UNCLE*, Arena Productions; *The Avengers*, Canal+; *24*, Imagine Television; *Z Cars*, BBC; *Cagney and Lacey*, MGM Television Distribution; *CSI*, CBS Productions/Alliance Atlantis; *The Sopranos*, HBO; *Dr Who*, BBC; *Star Trek*, Norway Productions/Desilu; *The X-Files*, 20th Century-Fox International Television; *The Day After*, © American Broadcasting Company, Inc.; *Roots*, Wolper Productions; *The Singing Detective*, BBC/Australian Broadcasting Corporation; *Buffy the Vampire Slayer*, Warner Bros. International Television; *Twin Peaks*, Frost/Lynch Productions/ABC; *Ally McBeal*, David E. Kelley Productions; *Heroes*, Tailwind Productions; *Peyton Place*, ABC; *Coronation Street*, Granada Television; *Dallas*, Lorimar Productions; *A Country Practice*, JNP Films Pty Ltd; *Monty Python's Flying Circus*, BBC; *Absolutely Fabulous*, BBC; *Sex and the City*, HBO; *Ellen*, ABC; *The Office*, BBC; *Goodnight Mr Tom*, Carlton Television; *Play School*, BBC; *Sesame Street*, Sesame Workshop; *South Park*, Comedy Central; *Big Brother*, Bazal Productions; *The Family*, BBC; *Strictly Come Dancing*, BBC; 'Symphony Orchestra', Halas and Batchelor/BBC; *The Snowman*, Snowman Enterprises/Channel 4; *I Am Not An Animal*, BBC/Baby Cow Animation; *Akira*, Akira Committee; *The Simpsons*, Gracie Films/20th Century-Fox Television; *Beavis and Butthead*, MTV; *The Lucy Show*, Desilu Productions, Inc.; *Who Wants to Be a Millionaire?*, Celador Productions for Carlton Television; *The Tonight Show*, National Broadcasting Company; *The Oprah Winfrey Show*, King World International; *Ready, Steady, Go!*, Associated-Rediffusion Production; *Top of the Pops*, BBC; Levi's 'Laundrette' commercial, Bartle Bogle Hegarty/Levi Strauss & Co.